Making Diversity Work

NORMA CARR-RUFFINO, PH.D.
San Francisco State University

NETEFFECT SERIES

PEARSON
Prentice
Hall

Upper Saddle River, New Jersey

To Ava and Connor, a new generation of hope and light
And to Fredo, who is always there

Library of Congress Cataloging-in-Publication Data

Carr-Ruffino, Norma.
 Making diversity work / Norma Carr-Ruffino.
  p. cm. — (NetEffect series)
 Includes index.
 ISBN 0-13-048512-8
 1. Diversity in the workplace. 2. Multiculturalism. 3. Intercultural communication. 4.
Ethnic groups—Cross-cultural studies. I. Title. II. Series.
 HF5549.5.M5C3885 2005
 658.3'008—dc22

                                                    2004009529

Director of Production and Manufacturing: Bruce Johnson
Executive Editor: Elizabeth Sugg
Editorial Assistant: Cyrenne Boit de Freitas
Marketing Manager: Leigh Ann Sims
Managing Editor—Production: Mary Carnis
Manufacturing Buyer: Ilene Sanford
Production Liaison: Denise Brown
Full-Service Production: Holcomb Hathaway
Composition: Carlisle Communications, Ltd.
Director, Image Resource Center: Melinda Reo
Manager, Rights and Permissions: Zina Arabia
Interior Image Specialist: Beth Brenzel
Cover Image Specialist: Craig Jones
Design Director: Cheryl Asherman
Senior Design Coordinator/Cover Design: Christopher Weigand
Cover Printer: Phoenix Color
Printer/Binder: Phoenix Book Tech Park

Pearson Education Ltd.   Pearson Education Australia Pty. Limited
Pearson Education Singapore Pte. Ltd.   Pearson Education North Asia Ltd.
Pearson Education Canada, Ltd.   Pearson Educación de Mexico, S.A. de C.V.
Pearson Education—Japan   Pearson Education Malaysia Pte. Ltd.

10 9 8 7 6 5 4 3 2 1
ISBN 0-13-048512-8

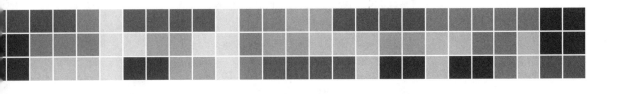

Contents

Understanding the Dominant Culture, Euro-Americans 179

Working With African Americans 215

8

Working With Arab Americans 261

9

Working With Latino Americans 303

10

Working With Asian Americans 345

Preface

How We Can Make Diversity Work

Diversity works when people are willing to focus their attention on proven concepts of diversity and then use them to develop essential skills.

DIVERSITY CONCEPTS

We make diversity work when we're willing to imagine how people from different backgrounds view the world and how these people are viewed by others around them. We make diversity work when we respect the rights, views, and values of "different others" just as we respect our own. Doing this opens us up to new concepts, such as:

- The substance of performance—such as goal achievement and relationship building—matters more than a person's style.
- Personal style reflects cultural norms as well as personal traits.
- For workers, managers, and professionals, many different personal styles can be successful.
- Different approaches to life and work may be valid and effective.
- There is no one best way to be successful in the workplace.

- The most innovative, profitable organizations are filled with people who express a wide variety of worldviews, values, customs, norms, and styles in an increasingly diverse and global marketplace.

Consider the following as background themes for building diversity skills:

- Always ask, "What's it like to be you?"
- Focus on substance, not style.
- Relate to the individual, not to a stereotype.

SCHOLARS AND ACTIVISTS WITHIN THE GROUP

In determining "what it's like to be you," we must look to leading scholars, researchers, experts, and activists from each of the diverse groups we are studying. We look to organizations of such scholars and activists to determine who are the leaders in expressing the group's cultural values and norms, positions on key issues, and visions of the future. We look for leaders who have devoted their careers to exploring the issues most important to their group. And we examine the research studies and surveys that these experts have conducted or have quoted in their published works.

In focusing on substance and not style, we use information about a person's cultural background to understand how it may influence personal style. Yet, we should remember that individual style always play a part and no one perfectly reflects her or his cultural heritage. We must guard against the tendency to categorize and to use new cultural information to establish new stereotypes. We must regularly remind ourselves to relate to the individual, not to a stereotype.

DIVERSITY SKILLS

Making Diversity Work provides in-depth information as well as activities to build such diversity skills as:

- Raising awareness to your cultural viewpoints and stereotypes.
- Recognizing typical values, habits, patterns, and concerns of each major cultural group: Euro-Americans, men and women raised in parallel gender cultures, African Americans, Arab Americans, Latino Americans, and Asian Americans.
- Recognizing the myths and stereotypes each group faces and how these myths evolved, the group's current demographic profile, and the cultural patterns and issues most important to group members.

- Meeting the leadership challenges and opportunities posed by the range of diverse employees in the workplace.
- Finding common ground on which multicultural employees can build productive, trusting relationships.
- Developing strategies to overcome barriers and enhance opportunities for members of each group to contribute to team and organizational excellence.
- Building productive relationships among team members, coworkers, customers, suppliers, and other business and personal contacts.
- Providing a work environment where all types of people can grow and thrive.
- Channeling diverse talents, viewpoints, and experiences toward building synergy, enhancing creativity, and developing innovative approaches and products.
- Functioning effectively in multicultural marketplaces in the United States and globally.

We enjoy deep rewards from doing this type of work. I believe that developing these diversity skills is essential to our ongoing growth—mental, psychological, and spiritual—not only as individuals, but also as a global village.

ACKNOWLEDGMENTS

Many thanks go to the expert reviewers who contributed to this book: Peter L. Banfe, Ohio Northern University; Gail F. Baker, University of Florida; and Ron Kapper, Corporate Trainer and Consultant.

Norma Carr-Ruffino, Ph.D.
Department of Management, College of Business
San Francisco State University

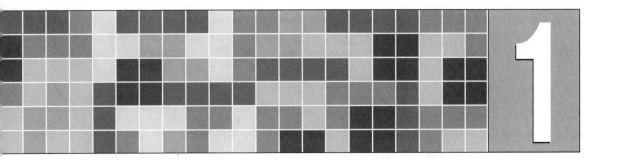

Introduction to Making Diversity Work

CHAPTER OBJECTIVES

- Identify the key factors that make up workplace diversity.
- Understand how the workplace is changing.
- Identify some workplace experiences of diverse employees.
- Describe key payoffs for effectively managing diversity.
- Identify the best approach to managing diversity.
- List the five-step process for becoming a diversity-savvy person.

Photo Researchers, Inc.

CHAPTER OVERVIEW

Are you building the people skills you need for success in a diverse workplace and marketplace? Diversity skills are a major factor in that marketable package of skills that you need because the ability to relate well to all types of people is an essential leadership skill these days—and it's becoming more important all the time. Diversity skills not only help you become more successful in your career, but also make you a more interesting, creative person. New and different people in your life bring new and different ideas and make you more interesting. Finally, your diversity skills can help your organization develop a more productive, innovative, and harmonious workforce.

Whether you are a brand-new hire, old hand, supervisor, or executive, you can be a leader in meeting job and organizational goals. As a leader in the fast-paced, ever-changing American workplace, what do you need to know about the diverse people you deal with? What people skills can you develop that will help you make powerful connections with these people? This chapter answers those questions and starts you on the road to acquiring these important skills.

The workplace is becoming more diverse. Not only have a record number of women moved into managerial, technical, and professional jobs, so have people from a diversity of cultural groups and lifestyles, people of all ages and abilities.

Effective management of diversity leads to success. When you manage the way you handle diversity, you begin to make the powerful people connections you need for career success. When your organization manages diversity effectively, it becomes more successful. This chapter describes specific steps to developing diversity skills that impact on-the-job success.

WHAT ARE THE KEY FACTORS THAT MAKE UP WORKPLACE DIVERSITY?

The workplace is changing dramatically, becoming more diverse in many ways. For example, minorities and women have been moving into all types of positions, including executive, managerial, technical, and professional jobs. In fact, about 85 percent of new employees are now women and minorities. However, 95 percent of top managers in major corporations are Euro-American men and on average, their income is higher. "Minorities" have gone a long way toward achieving equal opportunity, but they still have a way to go.

From Team Member to Global Customer

Business relationships are more diverse than ever, and diverse groups have diverse issues that are important to them. Suppliers and customers are increasingly international in scope, and they, along with global competition, are changing the way we do business. Self-managing work teams and more highly educated employees call for leaders and coworkers with diverse people skills.

You have great opportunities to build powerful, productive relationships with a wide range of people. In today's diverse workplace and global environment, cross-cultural skills are in great demand. You can also become a leader in helping to create the kind of workplace that attracts a wide range of talented people and keeps them coming back.

Workplace beliefs and environments are changing. We're moving from "We're all one big happy family" to "We're learning what it's like to walk in other people's shoes so we can fully appreciate what they need and what they can contribute." People who understand these trends are likely to become workplace leaders.

Our individual and cultural differences offer rich opportunities to move into new markets and to boost bottom-line profits. You can learn how to tap into these diversity opportunities. This book follows a five-step plan for developing diversity skills, which you'll learn about very soon.

How is this blossoming diversity affecting workplace relationships? Think of your own relationships. You probably relate best to people you feel comfortable with. And you probably feel most comfortable with people who are most like you. Encountering new and different people can be interesting, stimulating, even exciting. But it can also be stressful, confusing, and frustrating when you don't understand where they're coming from, what they're trying to communicate, and why they do what they do. It can also be uncomfortable when they harbor stereotypes about you—and you harbor stereotypes about them, especially when those stereotypes cause you, or them, to feel and act in prejudiced ways.

Stereotypical thinking, prejudiced feelings, and discriminatory actions are what kept the doors to opportunity closed for so long. Discrimination is a typical outcome of prejudiced thinking, and we all harbor prejudices. It's just the flavor and degree that vary because we are all products of our culture, and virtually all cultures are ethnocentric, believing "our way is the true way."

What do you need to know? As a leader in a diverse workplace, the most important knowledge you can gain is how to build multicultural skills. What skills do you need? You need those skills that provide the basis for building productive relationships with all types of people, skills for creating a work environment that provides challenge and support for people from all cultural backgrounds.

Achieving Unity and Respecting Diversity

Genetic experts verify that we are one species and one race—99.9 percent genetically alike and therefore, deeply connected.

Achieving the unity we need to achieve our goals, while respecting and valuing our diversity, is a major key to success. It may help to focus on the fact that every person in the world belongs to one species—the human species. Yet, each of us is as unique as a snowflake, and we each belong to a particular ethnic group that blends us all together into its own type of cultural "snow."

Diversity is more complex than sameness or simplicity. For example, humans are very complex living systems compared to one-celled amoebas. Humans have many parts and subsystems, such as the heart and the skin. Each is a unique system with its own function, but they work together as parts of the human body, forming a unity that supports the whole.

Unity is the glue that holds Americans together. We have a common core of human values, values of mind and heart, and we have common American values that tie us together.

The increasing diversity you encounter in your workplace will pose some challenges to your ability to do an excellent job, but that diversity can also be the source of amazing career success. You can learn some diversity success strategies that make all the difference. This book serves as an introduction to a book designed to increase your access to gaining diversity skills.

HOW IS THE WORKPLACE CHANGING?

The workplace is changing in most every way. The kinds of people we see in high-powered jobs are more diverse. The way people work together and the tasks they do are changing. And the way business is done throughout the world is changing by the day.

New Faces in New Jobs

People with university degrees and technical expertise come from all types of backgrounds these days. Since the 1960s, more and more African Americans, Latino Americans, Asian Americans, Arab Americans, and women have been entering college programs and technical areas that were formerly dominated by Euro-American men. As a result, these "minorities" have been moving into managerial, executive, technical, and professional careers formerly closed to them.

The workplace is becoming more diverse in other ways, too. For example, persons with disabilities have been finding ways to use the many abilities they do have to become productive employees. Many gay persons no longer try to hide their sexual orientation and want to be dealt with as employees who have rights equal to those of straight employees. Older employees now have the right to refuse mandatory retirement and can work as long as they are still productive. Obese persons are beginning to expect and gain some rights to be treated fairly and equally in the workplace. And people are becoming aware of the unfairness of "appearance bias" in general, especially when it's not essentially related to job productivity.

These dramatic changes in the workplace are producing some interesting challenges for everyone, from entry-level employees to top management. All must face the misunderstanding, communication breakdown, conflict, and even failure that can result when people from widely diverse backgrounds must pull together as a team or at least complete some sort of business transaction together. But these changes also offer bountiful opportunities for new levels of growth, innovation, expansion, and productivity. This book is about successfully meeting the challenges and prospering from the opportunities.

More Women and Immigrants

Since the 1960s, more and more women have started working outside the home for most of their adult lives. Some do this because they want careers, even though they may be wives and mothers; some because their family needs their income; and most for both reasons.

More and more ethnic minorities are in the workforce because immigration quotas were expanded in the 1960s, allowing more Latinos and

Asians to become citizens. In 1940, more than 85 percent of people who had come to the United States as immigrants were European, while in 1995, 75 percent were from non-European countries. Most are from Latin American (47 percent) and Asian (22 percent) countries. These immigrants tend to be younger on average and to have more children than the Euro-American population, further expanding their numbers.

According to the U.S. Department of Commerce, both minority population and purchasing power are going to grow at rates much higher than the population as a whole. From 2000 to 2045, minorities will account for 86 percent of the total U.S. population growth, increasing from 29 to 46 percent of the total population. The total minority population will surpass the non-minority population sometime between 2055 and 2060.

Even if current disparities in income persist, minority purchasing power will grow from 20 to 32 percent of total disposable income. Clearly, the ability to effectively market to ethnic groups will grow increasingly important. Companies that are unable to grab a share of the ethnic markets will find themselves catering to the fringes of the consumer population.

Snapshot 1.1 shows the ethnic makeup of the U.S. workforce in 2000, as well as the proportions of Euro-Americans and minorities in the better-paying middle- and top-level management jobs. Although Euro-American women and minorities made up 65 percent of the workforce in 2000, they held only 30 percent of middle-management jobs and 5 percent of top-management positions.

Income for these groups reflects the glass ceiling to higher-level jobs still in place in corporate America. Median incomes for full-time male and female workers, as well as household income by ethnic group, are shown in Snapshot 1.2 (U.S. Census Bureau 2003). Currently women working full-time make 74 percent as much as men who work fulltime.

Income is also affected by educational level and age. Snapshot 1.3 shows the percentage of persons age 25 and over in each major ethnic group that hold high school diplomas and bachelors degrees or higher. It also shows the median age of persons in each group.

The trend toward a more diverse population and workforce is expected to continue. Of the 26 million new workers coming into the workforce between 1990 and 2005, about 85 percent are expected to be women and minorities, as shown in Snapshot 1.4. A handy way to remember the proportions is to think in terms of sixths: Women will account for about four-sixths, minority men more than one-sixth, and Euro-American men one-sixth.

In the past, most American businesses functioned primarily within U.S. borders. Now even very small businesses may do much of their business in global markets. Corporate success now depends on building positive, productive relationships with people from many cultures around the planet. Corporate cultures that are open, flexible, appreciative, and savvy about cultural and lifestyle differences have a competitive edge. Having diverse employees at all

SNAPSHOT 1.1   Ethnic and gender segments of the U.S. workforce and of management, 2000.

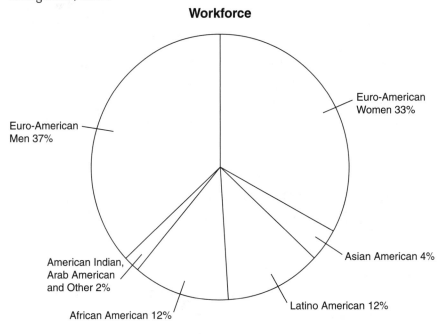

Workforce

Euro-American Women 33%

Euro-American Men 37%

American Indian, Arab American and Other 2%

African American 12%

Latino American 12%

Asian American 4%

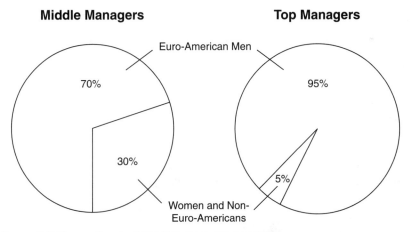

Middle Managers

Euro-American Men

70%

30%

Top Managers

Euro-American Men

95%

5%

Women and Non-Euro-Americans

Source: U.S. Census Bureau, 2000; U.S. Dept. of Labor, 2000.

SNAPSHOT 1.2 Income and poverty rates, 2000.

	Median Income			Poverty Rates
	Men (f.t.)*	Women (f.t.)*	Household	
Total	$39,100	$28,800	$42,200	12%
Male-Female Ratio	*100%*	*74%*		
Euro-American	42,200	30,800	46,300	8
African American	31,000	25,700	29,500	23
American Indian	28,900	22,800	32,100	26
Asian American	36,900	27,200	53,600	10
Latino American	25,000	21,000	33,600	22

Source: U.S. Bureau of Labor Statistics, 2001. *f.t. = fulltime

SNAPSHOT 1.3 Education and median age, 2002.

Ethnic Group	High School Diploma	Bachelors Degree Or Higher	Median Age
Total Population	84%	27%	36
Euro-American	89%	29%	39
African American	79%	17%	28
American Indian	n/a	n/a	30
Arab American	82%	36%	29
Asian American	87%	47%	32
Latino American	57%	11%	27

Source: U.S. Census Bureau, 2003.

levels in all functional areas enhances that edge—and is becoming ever more crucial for success and profitability as reliance on global transactions increases.

New Ways of Working Together

In the new technologically oriented companies, employees are more highly skilled and educated than ever. Old hierarchies and authoritarian bosses who dictated orders are fading into the archaic past. More common are

- self-managing work teams
- team leaders
- consultants and technical experts

SNAPSHOT 1.4   New workers entering the U.S. workforce, 1990–2005.

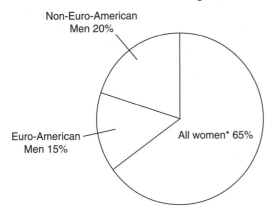

Non-Euro-American
Men 20%

Euro-American
Men 15%

All women* 65%

* 45% Euro-American Women
20% Non-Euro-American Women

Source: U.S. Bureau of Labor Statistics

Relationships with teammates, customers, and suppliers, and the information that flows between them, are the lifeblood of the organization. Corporations are increasingly built upon trust, collaboration, cooperation, and teamwork. In such organizations, it's more obvious than ever that people are the most valuable resource, that how we work together creates energy and innovation or decay and demoralization, and that our interactions spark the knowledge and information that fuel organizational growth and success.

Key trends that point to the need for multicultural leadership skills are:

- A shortage of qualified, educated workers means companies must be more responsive to workers' needs and expectations.
- The U. S. workforce is becoming dramatically more diverse at all levels. Workers expect more accommodation to their needs and identities than in the past.
- American corporations need higher-qualified employees in order to compete in the global marketplace.
- Companies need input from a workforce that "looks like America" to project a multicultural company image, contribute to marketing insights, and relate well to customers from all ethnic and lifestyle groups.
- Success in the global marketplace depends on building profitable relationships with people all over the world. Diverse people skills are as powerful in the global marketplace as they are in the American workplace.

New Approach = Substance vs. Style

Stereotypes about the ability of women and ethnic minorities to succeed in higher-level occupations and positions have been major barriers to their career advancement. Traditional business managers expected a work style and management style that looked like the Euro-American male's style. That's what became the standard in the American workplace. And certain stereotypes didn't fit, such as certain groups being too emotional, too passive, too excitable, too "technical," too low-key, too high-key, and so on. These stereotypes never applied to everyone in these groups and at best focused on style rather than substance.

What matters are the answers to key performance questions, such as:

- Does the employee's decision meet the criteria we set?
- Has the employee achieved the goals we set?
- Has the employee maintained the quality standards we set?
- Are the bottom-line results good?

In other words, it's possible that an employee may get just as good results—or even better results—by going about the job in a different way. There is rarely just one good way to get results. In fact, diverse ways of approaching problems and tasks can result in innovative solutions and actions. Savvy leaders have learned to be open to many styles. They can see through the style to the substance—of an idea, a potential skill, or performance results.

New Terms That We Use for People

People are very sensitive about the labels others attach to them. Most prefer no labels at all. Yet, how do we discuss the issues of cultures and subcultures, of diverse groups in a pluralistic society, of prejudice and discrimination based on group stereotypes? Obviously, verbal communication requires the use of descriptive terms. Such terms tend to change over time in response to social and cultural changes and interactions.

When group labels are continually used in a limiting, demeaning, scornful, or hostile way, they eventually are resented by the people they refer to. Therefore, if we want to show respect and appreciation for others, we want to use the terms they prefer. This can be difficult since members of a particular group rarely have unanimous opinions about preferred terms.

The terms used here are terms adopted by a multicultural task force at a large university that met weekly for many months to work out terminology and basic policy concerning diverse groups:

- African Americans
- Arab Americans
- Asian Americans (e.g., Chinese Americans, Asian-Indian Americans)
- Euro-Americans
- Jewish Americans

- Latino Americans (e.g., Mexican Americans, Puerto Rican Americans)
- American Indians

The theme is equality based on the fact that we're all Americans, and most of us are native Americans. If we go back far enough, all of us have ancestors who came from somewhere else, and the newest citizen is just as much an American as the one whose ancestors came centuries ago.

If your ancestors were immigrants from Europe, you're a Euro-American, often called *white*, and you're a member of the dominant majority in American culture. Most Asian Americans don't think of themselves as Asian Americans so much as *Chinese Americans* or *Filipino Americans* or one of the many Asian subcultural groups. The same is true for Latino Americans.

Some people are considered members of a "diverse" group for reasons other than ethnicity. These groups include:

- Persons with disabilities
- Gay, lesbian, and bisexual persons
- Older persons
- Obese persons

When you're relating one-to-one with people from any of these groups, you rarely need to refer to the group or groups they identify with. You're dealing with the individual. However, when you deal with groups or need to discuss groups with an individual, consider beginning with questions about how the person feels about the various names for the groups. It's best to reach some agreement about appropriate terms.

SELF-TEST

Indicate the best answers to the following 10 multiple-choice questions.

1. During the coming decade, the proportion of new employees coming into the workplace that are women and minorities is expected to be roughly

    A. one-sixth

    B. two-sixths

    C. three-sixths

    D. five-sixths

2. Asian Americans make up what proportion of the U.S. population?

    A. 10%

    B. 20%

    C. 1%

    D. 4%

3. Euro-American men make up what proportion of the workforce?

   A. 65%

   B. 35%

   C. 75%

   D. 50%

4. Euro-American men make up approximately what proportion of top managers?

   A. 50%

   B. 35%

   C. 95%

   D. 75%

5. African Americans make up what proportion of the workforce?

   A. 12%

   B. 25%

   C. 2%

   D. 5%

6. Which diversity-group term is not used in this book?

   A. American Indians

   B. Asian Indian Americans

   C. Asian Americans

   D. Native Americans

7. Which diversity-group term is used in this book?

   A. physically challenged

   B. handicapped

   C. persons with disabilities

   D. crippled persons

8. Which term is used in this book?

   A. African Americans

   B. Black Americans

   C. colored persons

   D. Afro-Americans

9. Which term is used in this book?

   A. White persons

   B. Anglo-Saxons

   C. Caucasians

   D. Euro-Americans

10. Which term is used in this book?

   A. gay person

   B. homosexual

C. queer

D. same-sex orientation

SELF-TEST FEEDBACK

Each correct answer is worth 10 points. If you score less than 70 points, you should review the materials and re-take the Self-Test.

1. During the coming decade, the proportion of new employees coming into the workplace that are women and minorities is expected to be roughly

   A. No, not one-sixth

   B. No, not two-sixths

   C. No, not three-sixths

   D. Yes, five-sixths

2. Asian Americans make up what proportion of the U.S. population?

   A. No, not 10%

   B. No, not 20%

   C. No, not 1%

   D. Yes, 4%

3. Euro-American men make up approximately what proportion of the workforce?

   A. No, not 65%

   B. Yes, 35%

   C. No, not 75%

   D. No, not 50%

4. Euro-American men make up what proportion of top managers?

   A. No, not 50%

   B. No, not 35%

   C. Yes, 95%

   D. No, not 75%

5. African Americans make up what proportion of the workforce?

   A. Yes, 12%

   B. No, not 25%

   C. No, not 2%

   D. No, not 5%

6. Which diversity-group term is not used in this book?

   A. No, American Indians is used

   B. No, Asian Indian Americans is used

C. No, Asian Americans is used

D. Yes, the term not used is Native Americans

7. Which diversity-group term is used in this book?

A. No, physically challenged is considered a euphemism

B. No, handicapped has a demeaning connotation

C. Yes, persons with disabilities is the preferred term

D. No, crippled persons is demeaning

8. Which term is used in this book?

A. Yes, African Americans is the preferred term these days

B. No, black Americans is not bad but has problems

C. No, colored persons is outdated although People of Color is acceptable when referring to a broad range of "nonwhite" groups

D. No, Afro-Americans was used for a while in the 1960s and 1970s, but is no longer preferred

9. Which term is used in this book?

A. No, white persons are not actually "white" and the term is vague

B. No, Anglo-Saxons is a vague term

C. No, Caucasians is a vague term

D. Yes, Euro-Americans is the preferred term

10. Which term is used in this book?

A. Yes, gay person is the term preferred in the gay community

B. No, homosexual is clinical and old-fashioned

C. No, queer is sometimes used in the community, but is not the preferred term for others to use

D. No, same-sex orientation is not the preferred term

WHAT ARE SOME TYPICAL WORKPLACE EXPERIENCES OF DIVERSE EMPLOYEES?

A key to gaining diverse people skills is being able to mentally slip inside other persons' skins for a time and see the world through their eyes. You'll gain great power in understanding their thinking and feeling and the issues most important to them. Here are some examples.

Career women often find themselves in catch-22 situations. For example, people expect women to be emotional, indecisive, and vulnerable. But business leaders are expected to be in control of their emotions, decisive, and able to roll with the punches. If women project the typical image, they're not seen as potential leaders. But if they project the "business leader" image, they're often seen as too hard and masculine, even abnormal.

Men are expected to be aggressive, ambitious, and proud. But many corporate cultures are changing in ways that call for leaders who are cooperative and who focus more on challenging and supporting others than on personal achievement. Many men are confused about what companies expect of them, just as they're confused about what the women in their lives expect. The dramatic changes in women's roles have had a major impact on men's lives.

African Americans who have a problem with a "brother or sister" typically take the bull by the horns and confront the issue directly. They go straight to the person, "tell it like it is," and try to work it out immediately. To them, this approach is real and honest. But to most other people in a workplace, it may be threatening and may imply anger that might erupt into violence. When Euro-American, Asian American, and Latino American coworkers feel threatened by African Americans' "confrontation, rage, or violence," it's usually because they misinterpret their cultural behavior patterns.

Asian Americans are taught that one of the highest values is to control one's reactions and to become mature enough to put relationships before personal concerns. As a result, they may be very indirect about expressing criticism or disagreeing. Often, they don't show or express strong emotion, especially outside the family circle. When Euro-American, Latino American, and African American coworkers conclude that Asian Americans are closed, secretive, inscrutable, and even cold, it's usually because they're unaware of Asian cultural values.

Arab Americans have increasingly been profiled as possible terrorists, who may be members of some violent fundamentalist Muslim sect, and who may represent great danger in our midst. Actually, about three-fourths of Arab Americans are Christians and U.S. citizens. They are devoted to the United States and more concerned than the average American about recent hostilities. Many of them have made and are making significant contributions to the arts, business, and politics.

Latino Americans are often stereotyped by Euro-Americans as having a "mañana" (literally, "tomorrow") attitude. This stereotype implies that they're not ambitious, productive go-getters, as Americans tend to be. Actually, most Latino Americans are hard workers, but they tend to wait for orders from the boss. Their cultural beliefs include greater respect for authority than most Euro-Americans hold—and greater acceptance of themselves as subordinates to a powerful boss. Also, Latinos tend to be more accepting than Euro-Americans of undesirable circumstances, often seeing such situations as God's will. When Euro-Americans judge Latino Americans as lacking initiative, it's usually because they don't understand these aspects of their cultural background.

Gay persons are sometimes avoided by coworkers on the assumption that gays don't have "normal" relationships. Coworkers have made such comments as "I just don't feel comfortable socializing with Joe (a gay man). Maybe he'll come on to me sexually," or "Maybe he'll get jealous of my friendship with a guy he's attracted to, when to me we're just hanging out." Joe would probably say, "Hey, I'm *me* first and foremost, just a person. My sexual orientation is just one slice of the whole pie that's me. What's more, I'm very sensitive to the discomforts and fears of straight guys." Studies indicate that people in the gay community have a whole range of relationships, as people in any community do, and that overall they're as likely to have "normal relationships" as people from any cultural group.

Persons with disabilities are thought to be a small minority by most people and are often seen as distinctly "different," even abnormal. Actually, most people have some type of disability, usually fairly minor. Persons classified as "disabled" simply have a disability that affects their ability to perform one or more major life functions, such as walking, reading, or hearing. They're not really "different" from the person who limps around occasionally with back trouble, the person who wears contacts, or the person who doesn't hear too well out of one ear. It's just a matter of degree. Even persons with a severe disability, such as paralysis from the neck down, may learn to live and work independently and often to make significant contributions through their careers.

Persons who are obese often are as healthy as most other adults, depending upon the extent of their obesity and their age. Many cruel myths and stereotypes surround obesity in our culture. The type of discrimination obese employees experience has an element of appearance bias and is related to skin-color discrimination, which is also a form of appearance bias. Obese persons also experience discrimination based on assumptions about what they cannot do, similar to that experienced by persons with a disability. Recent court rulings that support the employment rights of obese persons are based on their rights to "reasonable accommodation" under laws that protect the disabled.

Older persons are often assumed to be rigid, dogmatic, and forgetful. Their younger coworkers may avoid them and may wonder why these "old folks" haven't retired or when they're going to retire. Research indicates that aging itself does not cause any significant loss of intelligence, memory, or learning capacity. However, with age, one's habits tend to come home to roost. People who abuse or neglect their bodies start paying the price in their later years, while people with good eating and exercise habits tend to remain healthy and vibrant. People who habitually spend much of their time in negative thinking tend to become even more negative with age, while those who work on a positive outlook and self-growth become more delightful to be around.

Other groups that have distinct issues include American Indians, Jewish Americans, and bi-ethnic persons (those whose parents are from two distinctly different cultural backgrounds). For example, the person whose mother is Euro-American and whose father is African American tends to experience a unique type of cultural conflict while growing up. Because of the limitations of time and space, these other groups are not included in this book, even though they are valuable and important groups.

Every cultural subgroup has its own unique set of values, habits, customs, life circumstances, and issues to resolve. Understanding the key cultural themes and issues of each group can give you great insight and power for building good work relationships and helping other team members do the same.

WHAT ARE SOME KEY PAYOFFS FOR EFFECTIVELY MANAGING DIVERSITY?

You want to be the type of business leader who uses an active, change-oriented, multicultural approach. Such leaders are discovering a surprising wealth of payoffs for their organizations. Benefits accrue at all levels: personal, interpersonal, and organizational. They include:

1. attracting and retaining the best available human talent
2. increasing organizational flexibility
3. gaining and keeping greater market share, locally and globally
4. reducing costs
5. improving the quality of management
6. creating and innovating more powerfully
7. solving problems more effectively
8. increasing productivity
9. contributing to social responsibility
10. bottom line: increased profits

We'll explore briefly why and how each of these payoffs is important.

Payoff #1: Attracting and Retaining the Best People

Attracting and retaining the best people as employees requires that organizations meet potential employees' needs, show respect for them as individuals, and use multicultural skills when working with them.

Attracting Qualified People

As qualified employees become scarcer, employers must become more flexible. They can no longer afford to convey the implicit message "This is what we offer and how we do things. Fit in or leave." Now, they must adapt to potential employees who say, "These are my needs and goals; they must be met if I am to stay."

Retaining High-Potential Employees

To retain good employees, firms must be truly committed to treating all employees fairly and valuing diversity. Employers who appear to favor some personal orientations and stifle others risk paying the price of low productivity due to a restricted pool of applicants, employee dissatisfaction, lack of commitment, turnover, and even sabotage. University of Alabama Professor John Sheridan's research indicates that professionals (both strong and weak performers) stay an average of 14 months longer in firms whose main focus is "interpersonal orientation" values than in firms whose focus is "work task" values. Sheridan estimates that the work task–value firms incurred opportunity losses of $6 to $9 million more, over the six-year period studied, than the interpersonal-value firms. Sheridan concludes that it makes more sense to foster an interpersonal orientation culture rather than to try to find individuals who will fit into a work task culture.

Payoff #2: Increasing Organizational Flexibility

Companies are teaming up, forming alliances to pool their resources and tighten relationships with suppliers and customers. An alliance may require that two teams or units from two different companies blend together to act as a link between the firms involved. The most frequently cited source of problems with alliances is "different corporate cultures," according to a *Harvard Business Review* survey. Multicultural skills can be applied to working in various corporate cultures as well as working with individuals from various ethnic cultures.

Payoff #3: Gaining Greater Market Share

Companies that manage diversity effectively are better able to expand their share of markets—locally and globally—and to keep it. For example, the spending power of African Americans, Latino Americans, and Asian Americans was estimated at $650 billion in 2000. In California, these three groups make up nearly 50 percent of the population. About half of all business travelers are women. Diverse employees can help to attract and retain these types of customers. Their experiences and perspectives can certainly be valuable in building sales.

Teams That Look Like the Customer Base

Such diversity is the best way to be sure the organization remains flexible enough to capture diverse markets and provide adequate customer service. Studies by Taylor Cox and others indicate that diverse teams are less likely to get trapped in groupthink and are more likely to achieve enhanced critical thinking. They are more likely to produce products and services better tailored to diverse customers.

African American employees motivated Avon to develop products for women of color.

Also, customers tend to perceive that someone of their own ethnicity or sex is better able to serve their needs, and this can influence them in choosing one service or product over another. Using diversity to improve marketing skills within ethnically diverse domestic markets can help a company to market more effectively internationally, too.

Learning how to be responsive to local markets and to project the right image to them will help the company sharpen its skills for the international marketplace.

Teams That Prevent Blunders

Diverse employees can prevent many awkward public relations problems. They can also help in those one-on-one provider–customer interactions that are becoming increasingly common as companies focus on providing services, information, and custom products to customers. It makes sense for a company to employ a workforce that mirrors its customer base. Having African Americans, Latino Americans, and women on decision-making teams can help prevent these kinds of problems:

- An advertisement for a major telephone company featured a drawing of animals making telephone calls from various continents. A gorilla was making the call from Africa. Many African Americans were incensed.
- General Motors launched a major marketing campaign in Mexico to sell its Chevrolet Nova. In Spanish "no va" means "doesn't go." Almost no one went to buy them.
- A major bank instructed its tellers, all women, to wear straw hats with a band reading "Free and Easy Banking." The word "Banking" was hidden under the turned-up brims. When the women realized why customers were snickering, they were upset.

Payoff #4: Reducing Costs

A multicultural approach saves money in the long run and often even in the short run. Diversity efforts reduce the high turnover rate of nontraditional employees and the costs that go with it. Around 1990, the cost of turnover per person was estimated at $5,000 to $10,000 for hourly workers and from $75,000 to $200,000 for an executive at the $100,000 salary level. It's even greater now.

On the other hand, when a nontraditional manager is included in a development program or gets a promotion, other nontraditional employees at lower levels notice and feel more hopeful and committed to the company. Such companies are more likely to be sought out by nontraditional recruits, which reduces the costs of recruiting. They also may save money defending against grievances, complaints, and lawsuits regarding discrimination, sexual harassment, and similar problems. In addition to lost time and legal fees for dealing with such problems, other costs are job-related stress, lower morale, lower productivity, and greater absenteeism and turnover.

> *Euro-American men who graduate from universities where African American students comprise 8 to 17 percent of the student body earn roughly 15 percent higher wages than those who graduate from "lily white" schools, according to Jonathan Marshall's research.*

Payoff #5: Improving the Quality of Management

Diversity can prod managers to learn fresh approaches to business problems, to see issues from new perspectives, and to add new contacts to their business networks. Exposure to diverse colleagues can help managers develop breadth and openness.

Also, much of what an organization learns in trying out a special training program for diversity purposes may later be broadly applied to all employees. For example, we all like to be appreciated for our uniqueness and to be treated with respect.

Payoff #6: Creating and Innovating More Powerfully

Traditional assembly-line industrial organizations required creative thinking from only a few, but post-industrial organizations with their self-managing work teams require it of many. If people from diverse backgrounds are truly respected, supported, and appreciated, they'll be willing to contribute their ideas to group sessions. This in turn gives the group a broader range of diverse ideas to choose from, increases group synergy, and prevents groupthink.

Numerous researchers reached the conclusion that creativity is fostered by diversity; this is supported by research showing that the tolerance of diversity, defined as judging relatively few behaviors as deviant from norms, is a defining characteristic of innovative organizations. Diverse teams and organizations typically generate more options, especially more creative options and higher-quality ideas—because opposing viewpoints are introduced and resolved. Groupthink is less probable.

On the other hand, when organizations expect minorities to adapt to a Euro-Americans corporate culture, they fail to capitalize on the innovative and creative outcomes of a diverse workforce. A multicultural approach, where both the corporation and diverse employees make adaptations, enhances innovative outcomes.

For best results, relationships among team members must be predominantly positive. However, a certain amount of conflict is natural and inevitable, and if it is managed well, it can be constructive. Excessive group conflict interferes with productivity, closes down communication, wastes energy, and even causes people to leave. But too little conflict may signal complacency, repression, or old approaches to addressing new problems, according to Susan Jackson's research. The challenge is to stir innovation, manage conflict, and prevent breakdown.

Payoff #7: Solving Problems More Effectively

Culturally diverse workforces have the potential to solve problems better because of several factors: a greater variety of perspectives brought to bear on the issue, a higher level of critical analysis of alternatives, and a lower probability of groupthink that creates a higher probability of generating many alternate solutions.

Payoff #8: Increasing Productivity

All of the benefits mentioned so far work together to generally increase organizational productivity. Specifically, an effective approach to managing diversity helps diverse teams and individuals to be more productive. Important questions to ask each employee include:

- What's most important to you?
- What do you expect from this project, from your job?
- What are your goals for this task, for your job?

Learning about each employee's unique values, expectations, and goals is essential to effectively working with diverse team members on team projects. It's also essential for leaders in helping others with job objectives, job performance, and career plans.

Job performance, dedication, and attendance are boosted when employees perceive they are valued and cared for by their organization. Employees are more productive when they enjoy coming to work, feel happy to be working where they're seen as worthy and competent, and can relax into being themselves. In addition, such employees are more innovative, even without any direct reward or personal recognition. Groups that are diverse in terms of ethnicity, age, values, background, and training are more productive and innovative than homogeneous groups, according to studies by R. Eisenberger.

The Center for Creative Leadership identified 12 companies that showed exceptional leadership in encouraging diversity. All of the companies were in the top half of *Fortune* magazine's "most admired" corporations, and 80 percent were in the top 20 percent. Also, over a 20-year period, companies with a reputation for progressive human resource practices had more profitability and financial growth than their competitors, according to Harvard's Rosabeth Kanter.

Payoff #9: Contributing to Social Responsibility

The organization can become an agent for change to make the world a better place. If one organization can thrive by creating an environment where diverse people can work effectively together, this serves as a model for the entire world. A Los Angeles executive said, "In this area, the situation is so desperate and so in need of role models, that if we in corporations can't advance minorities so they can turn around and do what needs to be done in their communities, I don't see any of us surviving. The bigger picture we have to deal with is the minority situation in this country."

Payoff #10: Bottom Line: Increased Profits

Global competition is an established fact of life now. The re-engineering, restructuring, and downsizing of the 1990s reflect the reality that U.S. business can no longer afford bureaucratic, hierarchical structures with a homogeneous group running the show. We can no longer afford the luxury of paying big salaries to layer upon layer of managers to carry information back forth between workers, managers, and staff experts, information that all can now access through their computers. We're realizing the potential power of setting up informational networks where many workers can instantly interact.

We can no longer afford to pay tiers of high-salaried managers to set goals and make plans for workers and then try to motivate them and keep them productive. We're realizing that work teams and individual workers should be setting their own goals and making their own plans. When they do, they're likely to be self-motivated and work out their own productivity issues.

We can no longer afford to exclude people with the talents and skills we so desperately need for business success. All of the benefits they bring to the workplace add up to increased career success and company profits—provided we learn to build productive working relationships with each other.

WHAT IS THE BEST APPROACH TO MANAGING DIVERSITY?

Traditionally, business has handled diversity by adopting the "Melting Pot Myth," but people of color and women never "melted in" because they don't look or act like the dominant majority, Euro-American men. In recent decades, legal action has opened many doors of opportunity, but it has not necessarily changed the beliefs and attitudes, nor the thoughts and feelings, that led to discrimination in the first place.

Savvy leaders in forward-thinking companies value diverse employees for the unique contributions they make to the company's success. They are crafting an inclusive multicultural approach to managing diversity, an approach that welcomes all types of employees—and then appreciates and nurtures

SNAPSHOT 1.5   Evolution of managing diversity.

Approach: assimilation → legal   → valuing diversity   → multicultural
Basis: melting pot myth → EEO/AA → differences as assets → inclusive corporate cultures

them. This approach goes straight to the root of the corporate culture—its basic values, strategies, and ways of doing things. It expands the culture to reflect and include all of the major employee groups within the company—so that everyone feels at home and included in the inner circle.

Snapshot 1.5 is a summary of how corporations have managed diversity through the years.

WHAT IS THE FIVE-STEP PROCESS FOR BECOMING A DIVERSITY-SAVVY PERSON?

Building diversity skills can be easy if you take it step by step, using this five-step process.

Step 1   *Become aware of culture*—its elements, pervasiveness, and impact, as well as similarities and differences between major cultural groups.

Step 2   *Learn about your own culture*—recognize that the beliefs and customs that you may accept as reality are only one way of viewing the world, the way of your culture.

Step 3   *Recognize your own biases,* the ways in which you stereotype, assume, judge, and discriminate, so you can own them and move beyond them.

Step 4   *Learn about other cultures,* the environments of people you encounter in the workplace, so you can recognize when cultural differences may be at the root of problems and so you can appreciate the contributions people from diverse cultures make to the work situation.

Step 5   *Build interaction skills* and practice new behaviors through self-analysis activities, skill builder case studies, interviews, and applying your new understandings to actual people situations at work, school, anywhere you encounter diverse groups.

Lay the Foundation

The first four chapters of this book take you through Steps 1, 2, and 3. The Bridging Cultural Differences for Job Success chapter makes you aware of culture's pervasive influence, and you learn some key cultural patterns that will help you recognize cultural similarities and differences. The Beyond Stereotypes to Powerful Connections chapter helps you to recognize your own biases and learn about the nature of stereotyping, prejudice, and discrimination—and the type of contact that leads to collaboration. The Creating an Inclusive Multicultural Workplace chapter gives you a thorough grounding on what works and what doesn't work for establishing an organizational climate where diverse people can thrive and contribute.

Understand Each Culture: What's It Like to Be You?

The remaining chapters in this book provide the materials you need to work through Steps 4 and 5. You'll focus on learning about other cultures, building interaction skills, and practicing new skills. The process of learning to see the world through another's eyes is based on asking the right questions, and these chapters are structured to give you some answers, as shown in Snapshot 1.6.

You get to learn about the cultures of others, ranging from the parallel cultural worlds of men and women to various African American, Arab American, Asian American, and Latino American subcultures.

Make Your Skills Count

But what can one person do about managing diversity? Regardless of your position, your skills can make a difference. You can take whatever leadership role your situation allows. To begin with, you can notice the contributions of employees from groups that seem to be excluded in some way, and you can talk up their positive qualities. You can tell the stories of those who suc-

SNAPSHOT 1.6   Process for learning about cultures.

Key Questions	Chapter Structure
What are the key barriers to career success for this group?	Stereotypes and myths versus reality
How did it get that way?	Connections to the past
What's going on now?	Current profile
What really makes these people tick?	Cultural worldviews, values, customs
How can I build productive relationships with them?	Leadership challenges and opportunities
How can I apply my new knowledge and practice multicultural skills?	Cases, other skill builders

ceed, helping to make them stars in the company grapevine of myths and legends. You can visibly support them in any way that seems right. You can unfailingly respect their dignity and speak out against disrespect in the form of wisecracks, jokes, put-downs, exclusion, and similar behavior. If you have the power, you can provide information and training for other employees to help them understand and appreciate people from excluded groups.

FINAL SELF-TEST
Indicate the best answers to the following 10 multiple-choice questions.

1. Managing diversity effectively reduces costs in the long run because
    A. the turnover rate of nontraditional employees is greatly reduced
    B. recruiting costs are reduced when minorities seek out such companies
    C. culturally diverse workforces collaborate to solve problems more effectively
    D. all of the above

2. The most immediate business advantage of managing diversity effectively is
    A. achieving a more homogeneous workforce
    B. entering new global markets
    C. attracting and retaining the best available human talent
    D. all of the above

3. Culturally diverse workforces that collaborate can solve problems better because
    A. a diverse group brings many diverse viewpoints to the situation
    B. there is a higher probability of groupthink
    C. there is a lower probability of brainstorming
    D. all of the above

4. Companies should manage diversity primarily because
    A. they can't get enough qualified minorities
    B. they should hire the best persons for jobs
    C. it pays off to meet the needs of today's diverse workforce
    D. a focus on diversity is divisive

5. Companies that effectively manage diversity tend to be
    A. small- to medium-size companies
    B. in the top half of the *Fortune* most admired corporations
    C. slower growth but better reputations than competitors
    D. struggling for recognition

6. The foundation for developing diversity skills includes
    A. learning about other cultures
    B. learning about other lifestyles
    C. recognizing your own cultural biases
    D. building your interaction skills

7. The first step in the five-step process of building diversity skills is
    A. learn about your own culture's values and ways
    B. become aware of culture's impact
    C. learn about other cultures
    D. build interaction skills

8. The last step in the five-step process of building diversity skills is
    A. learn about other cultures
    B. learn about your own cultural biases
    C. build interaction skills
    D. become aware of culture's impact

9. The best way to learn about key barriers to career success of diverse groups is to
    A. examine their current profile
    B. study their cultural worldviews
    C. study the stereotypes and myths about them
    D. examine specific case studies

10. The best way to see the world through the eyes of someone from another group is to
    A. examine their current profile
    B. study their cultural worldviews, values, customs, issues
    C. study the stereotypes and myths about them
    D. examine specific case studies

FINAL SELF-TEST FEEDBACK

Each correct answer is worth 10 points. If you score less than 70 points, you should review the materials and re-take the Final Self-Test.

1. Managing diversity effectively reduces costs in the long run because
    A. No, although the turnover rate of nontraditional employees is greatly reduced, there are other results too
    B. No, although recruiting costs are reduced, there are other results
    C. No, although culturally diverse workforces collaborate to solve problems more effectively, there are other results

D. Yes, all of the above is the best response

2. The most immediate business advantage of managing diversity effectively is

   A. No, achieving a more homogeneous workforce is an advantage but not the most immediate

   B. No, although entering new global markets is an advantage, it's not the most immediate

   C. Yes, attracting and retaining the best available human talent is the most immediate advantage

   D. No, all of the above are true but this response does not address the most immediate advantage

3. Culturally diverse workforces that collaborate can solve problems better because

   A. Yes, a diverse group brings many diverse viewpoints to the situation

   B. No, there is not a higher probability of groupthink

   C. No, there is not a lower probability of brainstorming

   D. No, all of the above are not true

4. Companies should manage diversity primarily because

   A. No, although they can't get enough qualified minorities, this is not the primary reason they should manage diversity

   B. No, although they should hire the best persons for jobs, this does not address the diversity issue

   C. Yes, it pays off to meet the needs of today's diverse workforce. This is the best response because if you meet needs, then you will attract and retain the best persons, including qualified minorities

   D. No, a focus on diversity never needs to be divisive

5. Companies that effectively manage diversity tend to be

   A. No, small- to medium-size companies may mange diversity well, but they have not been the ones cited as most effective

   B. Yes, firms in the top half of the *Fortune* most admired corporations are cited as managing diversity most effectively

   C. No, firms with slower growth but better reputations than competitors are not the ones cited in studies

   D. No, firms struggling for recognition are not the ones cited in studies

6. The foundation for developing diversity skills includes

   A. No, learning about other cultures comes after the foundation material

   B. No, learning about other lifestyles comes after the foundation material

C. Yes, recognizing your own cultural biases is one of the foundation areas

D. No, building your interaction skills comes after the foundation material

7. The first step in the five-step process of building diversity skills is

A. No, learning about your own culture's values and ways is a later step

B. Yes, becoming aware of culture's impact is the first step

C. No, learning about other cultures is a later step

D. No, building interaction skills is a later step

8. The last step in the five-step process of building diversity skills is

A. No, learning about other cultures is an earlier step

B. No, learning about your own cultural biases is an earlier step

C. Yes, building interaction skills is the last step

D. No, becoming aware of culture's impact is an earlier step

9. The best way to learn about key barriers to career success of diverse groups is to

A. No, examining their current profile is desirable, but not as closely connected to barriers as other aspects are

B. No studying their cultural worldviews is desirable, but not as closely connected to barriers as other aspects are

C. Yes, studying the stereotypes and myths about them is most closely related to the barrier they face

D. No, examining specific case studies is desirable, but not as closely connected to barriers as other aspects are

10. The best way to see the world through the eyes of someone from another group is to

A. No, examining their current profile is desirable, but not as closely connected to seeing through their eyes as other aspects are

B. Yes, studying their cultural worldviews, values, customs, and issues is the best way

C. No, studying the stereotypes and myths about them is desirable, but not as closely connected to seeing through their eyes as other aspects are

D. No, examining specific case studies is desirable, but not as closely connected to seeing through their eyes as other aspects are

THE BOTTOM LINE

Managing diversity is the challenge of the new millennium—for our communities and our planet as well as for our workplaces. Do we want join a world of prejudice, bigotry, hatred, rage, riots, terrorism, and war? Or do we want to join in our common humanity and work through our differences so we can achieve great things together in peace and harmony? If we want harmony, then common sense tells us that workplace and community discrimination against whole groups of people must come to an end.

Managing diversity is also the opportunity of the new millennium. It offers opportunities to grow personally and collectively, to learn new ways of collaborating, to create a synergy that sparks innovation and accelerates human knowledge and achievement.

Chapter Review

1. The key factors that make up workplace diversity are:
   - minorities and women moving into different types of positions—executive, managerial, technical, and professional
   - global business markets—suppliers and customers are international in scope
   - respecting diversity in the workplace—recognizing what makes us the same and respecting what makes us different

2. The workplace is changing in the following ways:
   - Since the 1960s, more "minorities," immigrants, and women have gained advanced degrees and technical expertise and are entering the workforce at all levels.
   - Increasing numbers of people with disabilities, gays, older employees, and those with weight challenges expect to be treated fairly in the workplace.
   - Many large and small businesses are functioning in the global marketplace.
   - Old business hierarchies are changing with the use of self-managing work teams with team leaders, as well as hiring outside consultants and technical experts.
   - Key future trends point to the need for multicultural leadership skills

3. Diverse employees can have negative experiences, such as career women being perceived as too aggressive, African Americans as too confrontational, Asian Americans as aloof and cool, Latino Americans as lacking iniative, older persons as being "forgetful," and so forth.

4. The key payoffs for managing diversity are:
   - attracting and retaining the best talent
   - increasing organizational flexibility
   - gaining greater market share
   - reducing costs
   - improving the quality of management
   - sparking innovation
   - sharing more effective problem solving
   - increasing productivity
   - boosting social responsibility
   - gaining increased profits
5. Effective managers are moving beyond the "melting pot" and legal approaches to a multiculture management approach.
6. The five-step process for building diversity skills is:
   - become aware of the impact of culture and cultural differences
   - learn about your own culture
   - recognize your biases
   - learn about other cultures—what it's like to be someone from each culture
   - build interaction skills

Bridging Cultural Differences for Job Success

CHAPTER OBJECTIVES

- Understand what culture is and how to recognize the key elements of culture.
- Recognize the nine basic ways that cultures differ.
- Identify the connection between our values and how we earn a living.

CHAPTER OVERVIEW

Culture is the collective programming of individuals' minds that determines how a group of individuals perceives reality. In fact, the people in a culture collectively agree on what reality is. We agree on the beliefs that form the foundation of the culture, the beliefs that are most important, and what the culture values the most. We agree on the norms, the do's and don'ts, the rules by which people will live and be judged. And these basic agreements differ from culture to culture.

If you want to deal effectively with workers who come from various "realities," you must understand their cultures and your own. Cultural understanding gives you some clues about why people from various cultures and subcultures think and act as they do. It will also help you maintain your balance and poise when culture clash occurs—and help others to maintain theirs.

Culture clash occurs when a person's sense of rightness is challenged by conflicting beliefs and values held by someone from another culture. The person may respond with several emotions, such as confusion, frustration, disgust, and anger, which tend to block the resolution of the conflict. Typical outcomes are communication breakdown and poor working relationships. Being able to recognize cultural patterns and differences can help you handle such cultural conflict, and the accompanying emotions, with greater ease.

Coming out of your "cultural cave," taking off your cultural blinders, and enjoying a more universal view of the workplace is the first step in gaining multicultural skills. This experience and knowledge in turn will help you recognize typical problems and opportunities that stem from cultural differences. Understanding when to ask key questions is critical to uncovering hidden problems or opportunities.

WHAT IS A CULTURE?

Culture is the environment in which you live. Because it's like the air you breathe, you're probably unaware of most of its content. You learned it from your parents, teachers, the media, everyone and everything you knew as you grow up. Culture is what a particular group agrees is reality. It becomes the backdrop for the ways people think, feel, speak, and act. For every aspect of culture that we're aware of, there are about 1,000 aspects that we're unaware of. Anthropologists such as Ashley Montagu agree on three characteristics of culture.

- Culture is learned, not innate.
- The various facets of culture are interrelated. If you touch a culture in one place, everything else is affected.
- Culture is shared, and it defines the boundaries of different groups.

Culture is far more than mere custom that can be easily changed from the outside, even though it's always changing and evolving naturally from the inside. Surface aspects may change rapidly, but core aspects tend to be very resistant to change.

Cultural Elements

As a cultural group, people decide what to believe about the world, which beliefs are most important (values), who their heroes and heroines are, what stories or myths are important to express their values, how to do things—the rituals by which they act out their values, the networks of people connections,

---

CULTURAL LEVELS

Cultural groups are found at many levels of society:

- World culture = humanity; common values and customs found in all cultures
- Major culture = a regional or national group that represents a common culture
- Subculture = a cultural group within a major culture
- Corporate culture = an organization within a major culture

and which symbols will serve as shortcuts to remind people of these cultural bonds. All of these elements of culture underlie how the people in a major culture decide to handle their families, schools, churches, government, housing, business, and science. They're expressed in a culture's art forms, food, dress, play, and every other aspect of life.

A value is an enduring belief that one way of acting or being is preferable to another. A value system is an organization of such beliefs along a continuum of relative importance, a prioritizing of beliefs into a set or cluster. Norms are cultural do's and don'ts about how to act. Some values and their related norms may be talked about but most are just understood.

Heroes, heroines, and role models may also be called champions, stars, or big wheels. They're often seen as fearless leaders or courageous adventurers. They personify the core values and the strength of the organization or group. They become symbolic figures whose deeds are out of the ordinary—but not so far out that people can't identify with them. People like to think "Maybe I can do that too." Such leaders become great motivators, the people everyone will count on for inspiration when things get tough. They tend to be intuitive, to envision the future, to experiment, and to appreciate the value of celebrations and ceremonies.

A myth is a story or saying whose function is to bind together the thoughts of a group and promote coordinated social action. It may be a legend that symbolizes a central belief of the culture. It's often more symbolic than factual, but may be either. Some myths are based on powerful truths; some on manipulative, hurtful lies; still others on harmless little white lies.

Rituals are the "way we do things around here." They include the customary day-to-day actions people take, their expected actions and responses. Core values have no impact without ritual and ceremony. The unwritten rules of personal communication, the rituals of social interaction, govern relationships between bosses and workers, professionals and support staff, men and women, old and young, insiders and outsiders.

Work rituals spell out standards of acceptable behavior and how such procedures as strategic planning, budgeting, or report writing should be carried out. Recognition rituals, such as awards, are more formal. They acknowledge achievements that are valued and signal that the person belongs to the culture. Rituals meet people's need to belong. They help establish and maintain some common values and goals that connect people in the group. A true ritual is always connected to a myth that represents some basic group value. Otherwise, it's just a habit that does nothing but give people a false sense of security.

Networks of relationships, such as the grapevines, are the primary means of communication within an organization. They tie together all parts of the company without respect to the organization chart. They not only transmit information, they also interpret its significance. In most organizations, only about 10 percent of its business takes place in formal meetings and events. The real process of making decisions, gathering support, and developing opinions, happens before or after the meeting. Of course, formal networks are important too. They include the formal organization chart, task forces, work teams, professional and trade associations, and similar groupings.

Symbols are shortcuts that remind people of those cultural elements that bind them together. A song, banner, flag, logo, picture, motto, or brand name may bring up corporate values. A nickname or motto may recall a heroine or star. A figure of speech may recall a key myth or ritual. A good symbol can serve to trigger communal thoughts and feelings about a common cause or goal.

Self-Analysis 2.1 will help you learn more about your cultural heritage and identity by creating a cultural profile. In Self-Analysis 2.2 you will identify hidden aspects of your own and other cultural groups.

Self-Analysis 2.1 Your Cultural Profile

Purpose: To identify key aspects of your cultural heritage and identity.

Step 1   Complete the following statements.

Step 2   Determine the importance of each specific category for you (e.g., is being a college graduate a major or minor part of your identity?). Place a number, from 1 to 5, beside each category you've listed according to its importance, using 5 for essential aspects of your identity and 1 for the least influential aspects.

My **gender** is: _____

My **sexual orientation** is (heterosexual, homosexual, bisexual): _____

My **ethnic group** is (ancestors' country of origin): _____

The **nation** where I was born is: _____

The **part of the country** I grew up in is: _____

The **occupation** I'm in or want is: _____

The **company** I work for is: _____

My **religion** or philosophy is: _____

My **socioeconomic** class is (middle, lower, upper): _____

My **educational** level is: _____

My **parents' educational** level is: _____

Other groups or aspects that have influenced my identity are: _____

Step 3   Write a few words about your cultural profile. Include any thoughts, feelings, surprises, or insights.

Self-Analysis 2.2 Cultures You've Known

Purpose: To recognize the hidden aspects of your own and other cultural groups.

Instructions: *Respond to the questions about five cultural elements in your national culture (Step 1). Then, pick one or more other areas (Step 2) and respond to the same questions about the five cultural elements.*

Step 1   *National Culture*

- *Rituals:* What rites and rituals gave you a feeling of national unity—an overall community with common purpose? For example, saying the Pledge of Allegiance.

- *Heroes:* What heroes personified key national values? For example, George Washington.

- *Myths:* What stories or legends are known by most everyone? For example, how George Washington cut down the cherry tree and then could not lie about it.

- *Symbols:* What symbols served to unify, to express values? For example, the flag.

- *Values:* What values are expressed by the previous cultural elements? For example, patriotism, courage, persistence, and honesty.

Step 2   *Other Cultures.* Pick at least one other area of your life—such as your workplace, school, family, religious community, or social organization—and give examples of important rituals, heroes, myths, symbols, and values that are elements of that culture.

SELF-TEST
Indicate the best answers to the following 6 multiple-choice questions.

1. Culture is
   A. innate
   B. learned
   C. unchanging
   D. obvious to everyone

2. For every conscious cultural factor, there are how many hidden factors?

    A. 10 or more

    B. 1,000 or more

    C. 100 or more

    D. a million or more

3. A value is

    A. something you want

    B. an enduring belief that one way of acting/being is preferable to another

    C. a cultural role model

    D. a way of doing things

4. Rituals are primarily

    A. religious ceremonies

    B. "the way we do things around here" in all types of organizations

    C. ways of telling stories

    D. ways people communicate within an organization

5. Symbols are primarily

    A. shortcuts for other cultural elements

    B. any item that brings up cultural values

    C. items that can trigger communal thoughts and feelings

    D. all of the above

6. A myth is primarily

    A. a role model that personifies core values

    B. a story or saying that binds together the thoughts of a group

    C. a shortcut that reminds people of the ties that bind

    D. "the way we do things around here"

SELF-TEST FEEDBACK

Each correct answer is worth 17 points. If you score less than 68 points, you should review the materials and re-take the Self-Test.

1. Culture is

    A. No, we are not born with culture.

    B. Yes, culture is learned

   C. No, it's not unchanging although core aspects tend to change
      very slowly

   D. No, most cultural aspects are not obvious at all to members of
      the culture

2. For every conscious cultural factor, there are about how many hidden
   factors?

   A. No, not 10 or more

   B. Yes, 1,000 or more

   C. No, not 100 or more

   D. No, not a million or more

3. A value is

   A. No, it's not something you want—that's a goal

   B. Yes, it's an enduring belief that one way of acting/being is
      preferable to another

   C. No, it's not a cultural role model—that's a hero or heroine

   D. No, it's not a way of doing things—that's a custom or ritual

4. Rituals are primarily

   A. No, although rituals are used in religious ceremonies

   B. Yes, they are "the way we do things around here" in all types of
      organizations

   C. No, they are not the ways of telling stories, although such ways
      may become rituals

   D. No, they're the way people communicate within an organization—
      that's networks or the grapevine—but ways of communicating can
      become rituals

5. Symbols are primarily

   A. No, although they can be shortcuts for other cultural elements

   B. No, although they can be any item that brings up cultural values

   C. No, although they can be items that can trigger communal
      thoughts and feelings

   D. Yes, they are all of the above

6. A myth is primarily

   A. No, not a role model that personifies core values; that's a hero
      or heroine

   B. Yes, a story or saying that binds together the thoughts of a group

   C. No, not a shortcut that reminds people of the ties that bind;
      that's a symbol

   D. No, not "the way we do things around here"; that's a ritual

HOW DO CULTURES DIFFER?

Cultures differ in thousands of ways, and categorizing the major differences into nine areas gives us a practical basis for comparison. These categories, based primarily on the work of anthropologists and sociologists such as E. T. Hall and Geert Hofslede, deal with the ways people view themselves in relation to others and to the world and how they act out those viewpoints. Taken together, these differences reflect one of three underlying themes—dependence, independence, or interdependence—that are connected to whether a culture's economy is mainly agricultural, industrial, or information/service-based. First, work through Self-Analysis 2.3. Then after you've read about the

Self-Analysis 2.3	Your Cultural Beliefs and Values

Purpose: To determine your personal beliefs and values and how they relate to the nine major differences between cultures.

Instructions: For each of the following numbered pairs of statements, circle A or B according to which statement best reflects your orientation.

1. A. I create my life by what I do and by what I allow.
   B. I'm just a cog in the wheel of life. Most of what happens to me is outside my control.

2. A. My top priority is to achieve my personal goals.
   B. My top priority is to be a good son/daughter, wife/husband, boss/worker, mother/daughter; that is, to fulfill those roles expected of me.

3. A. I'm happiest when I'm ahead or winning.
   B. I'm happiest when I'm working or playing with friends, family, or coworkers.

4. A. My top priority at work is getting the job done.
   B. My top priority at work is maintaining good relationships with people.

5. A. If a top manager asked me to discuss my ideas, I'd be comfortable.
   B. If a top manager asked me to discuss my ideas, I'd be nervous and uncomfortable.

6. A. People who have talent and work hard can become very successful.
   B. People need the right family background and connections to become very successful.

7. A. My motto is "Nothing risked, nothing gained."
   B. My motto is "Stick with the tried and true."

8. A. I believe that "the exception makes the rule."
   B. I believe that we must stick to the rules of the game or we'll have chaos.

Self-Analysis 2.3 | Your Cultural Beliefs and Values *continued*

Feedback

1. A. internal source of control, individualism, independent
   B. external source of control, collectivism, dependent
2. A. me-first, individualism
   B. us-first, collectivism
3. A. achievement first, competitive, individualism
   B. relationships first, cooperative, collectivism
4. A. achievements and tasks first, linear-time orientation
   B. relationships first, circular-time orientation
5. A. focus on equality, democratic orientation, direct communication
   B. focus on class differences: status, rank, deference to authority, indirect communication
6. A. risk-taking orientation, focus on future change, independence, individualism
   B. security-seeking orientation, focus on tradition, hierarchy and the status quo, dependence, collectivism
7. A. equality, risk-taking orientation
   B. security-seeking, avoid-uncertainty orientation
8. A. risk-taking, equality
   B. security-seeking, deference to authority

nine major types of cultural differences, review your responses to learn how your beliefs and values fit into the picture.

Cultural Difference #1: I'm Controlled or I Control?

The most basic beliefs we have are about who or what creates our environment and causes the events within that environment. How much is caused by our own attitudes and actions? How much by a Supreme Being? How much is just chance or coincidence? Beliefs about the cause of life events dramatically affect every other aspect of culture.

I'm Controlled

People from I'm-controlled cultures might say, "Things happen to me and I have little control over my life. It depends on my boss, my customer, fate, luck, God's will." Most cultures fall into this camp, including most African,

Asian, Arab, and Latino cultures. Women in all cultures are more likely than men to hold this viewpoint.

I Control

People from I-control cultures might say, "What happens to me is up to me. It depends on what I do or don't do. God helps those who help themselves." Most Western cultures, especially Euro-American, and especially men, hold this viewpoint.

Cultural Difference #2: Us-First or Me-First?

This is the most important cultural difference for understanding how people interact with others. Cultures that focus on us-first are called collectivist cultures because individuals are seen first as members of a family or cohesive group. Cultures that focus on me-first are called individualist cultures because they believe that each individual must first take responsibility for her or his own life and should have the freedom to succeed or fail.

It's similar to looking at a bouquet. Do you focus first on the whole bouquet with the attitude that one flower alone might be out of context and lost? Or do you focus first on each individual flower and then notice how the group forms a bouquet?

Us-First

"I should first integrate my goals, thoughts, and actions with those of my group. Working within what the group wants and needs, I can try to get what I want and need. People should always stay close to their parents and relatives and never stray far." Hofstede's research indicates that most cultures fall into this camp, including most African, Asian, Arab, and Latino cultures. Certain families, religious groups, and subcultures within individualist cultures have collectivist values. Women in all cultures are likely to hold collectivist viewpoints.

Me-First

"I must first focus on my personal goals. I work toward better things for my family and work team and community, but my personal goals must come first. I'll stay with a group as long as it doesn't block my efforts to meet my own wants and needs.

When people grow up, they have to cut the apron strings and make their own way in the world. European cultures fall into this camp, with Euro-Americans being the most individualistic.

Cultural Difference #3: Tight Ties or Loose Ties?

Cultures vary by how much alike people are, how homogeneous or diverse. This in turn helps determine whether people feel bound together by many ties or only loosely connected with few ties.

Many Ties That Bind = Us-First

"I see people first as part of a particular family or organization or community and they see me that way. If I fail, the others in my group will 'lose face' and feel shame, so I should try to cover up my failure. If I succeed, the glory goes to my group, not to me." This mindset predominates in Eastern cultures and is held by a majority of the world's people.

"As I grew up, I thought of myself as part of 'we' rather than 'I.' It's important to me to protect my family and close friends and to be loyal to them. I expect them to protect and be loyal to me. Who I am is a member of my family, work group, and community. The ideal way to live is in close relationship with them. I belong to several groups and organizations. I depend on those relationships. We make decisions together, and I believe in those decisions. Who my friends are depends a great deal on the groups I belong to."

"My status and prestige comes from these relationships. The groups I belong to provide what I need—expertise, order, duty, and security. I'm loyal first to my parents and immediate family, then my relatives, and then the clan or nearby community. Success and satisfaction in life come from living up to those loyalties. If I gain material success, I'll share it with my family and close friends."

"When I was a university student, I studied hard to pass exams in order to acquire the status of a degree. Now, I seek the satisfaction of a job well recognized. It's very important for me to preserve face, or respect, from my family and friends and to avoid shaming them through my failure. My job life and private life are inseparable. It's okay if my boss inquires about my private life, and I expect the boss to help out with family or personal problems. On the job, relationships are even more important to me than getting tasks done. I must develop a relationship with the people I work with and become adopted into the work group before I can do a good job on my tasks."

Loose Ties = Me-First

"I am unique, one of a kind. Growing up means becoming my own person. If I fail in life, it's strictly my fault, and I would probably feel guilty and want to be by myself till I got over it. What I value most are autonomy, self-reliance, self-identity, emotional independence, and individual initiative."

"When I was a university student, I worked hard in order to master the subject matter for my major. It's important to me to maintain my self-respect and avoid guilt. On the job, I value challenges, individual achievement, and personal ambition. I want the satisfaction of a job well done, especially by my own standards. I keep my job life and private life separated. Getting tasks done is more important than spending time on work relationships."

These are typical views of people from Western cultures. The United States is one of the most loosely knit cultures of modern times.

Cultural Difference #4: Achievement-First or People-First?

Most cultures place greater value on building and maintaining strong interpersonal relationships than on getting things done. Others value most highly a person's (or group's) achievements. People-first values are found most often in us-first cultures, while achievement-first predominates in me-first cultures. A people-first orientation reflects feminine values, while an achievement orientation reflects masculine values. However, in both types of cultures, men dominate the political and workplace arenas, as research indicates that no country or culture is dominated by women in these areas.

People-First = Connecting, Cooperating = Feminine Aspect

"I focus on building and maintaining positive, personal relationships. The type of life I build is more important than the things I accumulate. I value my hunches and intuition. What motivates me is contributing to my family, workplace, and community. I work in order to live rather than live in order to work."

The Scandinavian cultures are the most people-focused. The roles and viewpoints of men and women are not as separate as in most cultures. Neither men nor women need be to ambitious, competitive, or focused on material success. Men and women may respect whatever is small, weak, and slow. Values within political and work organizations center around interpersonal relationships and concern for the weak.

Achievement-First = Focus on Competition, "Things" = Masculine Aspect

"I am very ambitious, and I believe I'm here to work. Hard work will bring me independence. Men should be assertive, ambitious, and competitive. They should work for material success, and respect whatever is big, strong, and fast. Women should serve and care for the intangible qualities of life, for the children, and for the weak."

The most masculine culture by far is Japan's, while U.S. culture is moderately masculine. Such cultures define very different social roles for men and women, with a focus on clear gender roles. They tend to be patriarchal, materialistic, performance-oriented, and factual. Political and corporate values stress material success and assertiveness. While Euro-Americans, especially men, tend to be highly competitive in social interaction and in task performance, Latino Americans, African Americans, and Asian Americans favor a more cooperative approach.

Cultural Difference #5: Equality or Not?

Some cultures, primarily Western ones, are based on the ideal that all persons have equal value and status as human beings. People are therefore entitled to equal opportunity to achieve and advance in the society. Other cultures accept the idea that some people are naturally more powerful, affluent, and privileged than others. They therefore accept the inequality of rank and status in a hierarchical or stratified society. In these cultures, people from different levels feel a greater sense of "power distance" than do people who live in more egalitarian cultures.

Inequality = Rank/Status Cultures

"My company's organization chart looks like a pyramid, with a few autocratic leaders at the top and many ordinary workers at the bottom. If my country had an organizational chart, it would look that way too. Our leaders are very strong and powerful. We depend on them to make the right decisions. We expect them to control things. If they asked us what to do, we would assume they were weak and should step down. The leaders we admire are good people, similar to good fathers who take care of things. Of course, they live well, with people to take care of menial tasks for them. Such leaders should have the trappings of wealth that go with the territory. I expect my boss to make the decisions, give me clear orders, and to take a personal interest in me and my family. I do not speak up to my boss unless he tells me to. I would never contradict my boss, either at work or elsewhere. My status depends on the status of my boss and my company."

Nearly all so-called under-developed and developing countries have such vertical societies. When people from these cultures move to Western countries to work, they often initially feel lost because their leaders are not so authoritarian and patriarchal. For example, people from Latino and Asian cultures pay more homage to the boss than do people from Western cultures. They may be appalled at the idea of arguing a point with the boss or seeing the boss pitch in to help out in a pinch. They are much less likely to point out potential problems with their manager's decisions and may have difficulty speaking up when team decisions need to be made. To them, bosses do the bossing and employees do the work, and deviations from that norm imply that one or the other can't do their jobs properly.

Equality = Democratic Cultures

"My company's organization chart looks sort of like a low box. The organizational chart of my daughter's company looks like a web within a circle with the executive team at the center. I believe that my boss has power because he's worked his way up to boss, not because he's better than me. I appreciate it when my boss consults me about decisions that affect me and my job. I like it even more when he lets me or the team make the decisions. I like being independent, but I don't mind choosing to be interdependent with my work team."

In moderately egalitarian cultures—such as the United States, Japan, and most European countries—consultation is usually appreciated but not necessarily expected. Participative environments are initiated by the participative leader, not by subordinates. Ideal leaders are pragmatically democratic. Moderate status differences and privileges for leaders are acceptable. Rules and laws are expected to apply to superiors and subordinates alike. Change normally starts with the top leaders, but key people throughout the organization must buy into the change if it is to be effective and lasting.

In very egalitarian cultures—such as the Scandinavian countries, Israel, and Austria—subjecting yourself to the power of others is seen as undesirable. Everyone should have a say in everything that concerns them. Status differences are suspect. Ideal leaders are democratic and loyally carry out the will of their groups. Change comes about through group consensus. Leaders must persuade and influence the group. Former leaders are usually comfortable with accepting new, less powerful roles, for the power differential is in the roles, not the people who fill them. In general, women are more likely than men to value equality in relationships and to manage in a democratic way.

Cultural Difference #6: Take Risks or Play It Safe?

In cultures that value playing it safe, people like to avoid risks and uncertainty. People are not comfortable with unstructured, unclear, or unpredictable situations, so they adopt strict codes of behavior and a belief in absolute truths in order to avoid such uncertainty.

Play It Safe

"We keep things under control in my culture. We do it by:

- making sure that everyone knows the rules and not allowing people to break the rules without punishment.
- making sure that people know what's expected by designating precise relationships, assignments, and schedules.
- arranging life so that everyone knows what to expect."

"Since change creates many unknowns and uncertainties, we don't like change and try to prevent it by sticking with tradition."

People in play-it-safe cultures are also generally more active, aggressive, emotional, security-seeking, and intolerant. Greece is the most certainty-oriented culture, followed by Japan. Most European and Latino cultures fall into this pattern.

Take Risks

"'Nothing ventured, nothing gained' is my motto. Rules have their place, but there are exceptions to every rule. I like change and new adventure. I like investing in the future and looking forward to possible payoffs. For a business to be successful, people must come up with new ways of doing things, new products and services, and new technology."

People in risk-taking cultures tend to be more contemplative and tolerant, and less aggressive and emotional than those in play-it-safe cultures. The United States has a moderately risk-taking culture, and Singapore is by far the most risk-taking culture researchers have studied.

Cultural Difference #7: Time—Step-by-Step or Dive-Right-In?

Some cultures see time as a series of points along a line and people doing one task at a time. Others see time as a circle into which they jump, doing many tasks at one time.

Dive-Right-In Time

"Time is like a circle, and I use points of time within the circle. Several things may be happening at once in this circle because several people may need my attention at any one time. After all, it's more important to maintain good relationships with others and to complete transactions with others than to do one thing at a time on a preset schedule. Each point in time is sacred but only because I give myself fully to the moment, to the relationships, events, or activities of the moment. An activity simply takes as much time as is needed for its completion, so if the activity is important, the time it takes is irrelevant."

Circular-time cultures include Latino, Middle Eastern, and some Asian and African cultures. In the U.S. workplace, it is likely that many African Americans, Asian Americans, and Latino Americans are circular-time people. While they may necessarily adapt to the Euro-American time orientation when they work in U.S. organizations, they tend to return to their own time orientation for social and family events.

Euro-Americans sometimes feel they don't really have the full attention of a busy circular-time person. They worry that the person may never get around to the most important business at hand. Some feel that nothing seems solid or firm with circular-time people, particularly regarding the future. Often, there are changes in the most important plans, right up to the very last minute. In circular-time organizations, systems need a much greater centralization of control because the top person deals continually with many people.

In some cultures, time is determined by repeated cycles of activities, such as the agricultural cycles of planting, cultivating, and harvesting. People in such cultures do not see time as stretching into the future, but focus on the past and present. This orientation is dominant in Cuban, Mexican, and many African tribal cultures.

Step-By-Step Time

"Time is made up of the past, the present, and an infinite future. I pay most attention to the future. Time can be separated into units or steps with fixed beginnings and endings for events. I measure my time and budget it as I schedule appointments, decide on the starting and ending times for events, get to things on time, meet my deadlines, and plan ahead. The best way to use my time is to focus on one task, appointment, or event at a time." This view is prevalent in Western countries, especially the United States.

Cultural Difference #8: Space—Come Close or Back Off?

Cultures differ in how much personal space individuals expect to occupy, how close they stand or sit to one another, and how much physical contact they have. In the workplace, this translates into different perceptions about comfortable office sizes and layout and requirements for privacy in workstations.

Come-Close Space

"I'm from the Middle East. When I talk with business associates and friends, we stand close enough to be able to feel each other's breath on our face and catch each other's scent. We touch each other a great deal as we interact. My male business associates often embrace instead of shaking hands."

People in Latino cultures prefer slightly more distance than those in Middle Eastern cultures, but they like to stand closer and touch more than do people in Western cultures. Asian cultures like the most space and least public touching of all.

Back-Off Space

"I'm a Euro-American. When I talk with business associates and social acquaintances, it's usually at arm's length, about two or three feet away. Of course, I'm closer to my lover as well as family members and close friends.

I notice that I stand farther away when I want to protect myself or stay un-involved. If someone moves too close into my space, I usually feel uncom-fortable and back up till I feel comfortable. It really bugs me if a person keeps moving in even after I back off."

Western cultures are basically non-contact societies. In most Asian cul-tures, perhaps because of dense populations, people maintain an even greater distance for all but family and close friends.

Cultural Difference #9: Communicating Directly or Indirectly?

While there are many variations in communication style, two that stem directly from the key cultural patterns we've discussed are directness and indirectness.

Using Go-Betweens and Implied Messages

"I try to maintain harmony and get along with people, so I never say things that would offend them. Saying no directly would be offensive, so I try to gently let them know that I'm not terribly enthusiastic about something. To make an initial overture or bring up a sensitive topic, I usually ask someone close to the other person to feel them out first."

People in most cultures use an indirect style of communication, espe-cially in those cultures identified as us-first, people-first, rank/status, and play-it-safe. In us-first cultures with many close ties, many messages can be im-plied because people have been socialized alike and are on "the same wave-length." And in many cultures, go-betweens are used to broach sensitive topics. In all cultures, women are likely to use an indirect style, such as hint-ing, implying, keeping quiet in order to keep peace, and mentioning prob-lems or desires to associates of the decision maker in the hope that they'll "put in a good word."

Going to the Person; Getting to the Point

"I try to build trusting relationships based on honesty and sincerity. It's im-portant to be upfront and genuine in my dealings with people. If I have a problem with a person, or a proposal, I go directly to that person first and try to work it out."

The direct style is typical in Western cultures, especially those that fo-cus on I-control, me-first, achievement-first, equality, and risk taking. Within those cultures, men are more likely than women to use a direct communi-cation style.

WHAT IS THE CONNECTION BETWEEN OUR VALUES AND HOW WE EARN A LIVING?

Cultural values and customs are greatly affected by a group's dominant way of making a living, whether it's primarily agricultural (the economically underdeveloped countries of the world), industrial (the developing countries), or post-industrial (the developed countries).

Agricultural Economy = Dependent Worldview

In many countries that are primarily dependent upon an agricultural economy, the value system of the masses in the peasant class is quite different from that of the elite ruling class. The masses are quite dependent on the extended family and village groups. They are likely to believe they're controlled, put the group first and have many close ties, focus on cooperative relationships, accept status differences, avoid change and risk, view time as circular, like physical closeness at least with family, and use an indirect communication style. All this adds up to a worldview that's primarily dependent on external forces, the family, and village groups.

The dependent pattern is traditionally typical of most women in all cultures and of men and women in most Asian, Latino, and African cultures, in fact of most of the world's peoples.

Industrial Economy = Independent Worldview

As a culture moves into a manufacturing-based economy, values shift to a more independent focus that's needed for success in the workplace. People are likely to believe they're in control, put their own goals first, have looser ties with others, focus on competitive achievement, demand equality, take calculated risks to bring needed change, view time as points on a line, keep most people at arm's length, and use a direct communication style. An independent worldview is traditionally typical of men in Western cultures.

Post-Industrial Economy = Interdependent Worldview

As a culture moves to an information- and service-based economy, it begins to shift to an interdependent focus. Some values and customs seem similar to dependence on the surface, but a major difference is that people are aware of their individuality and independence. Instead of feeling dependent upon local groups for survival, they choose to join workplace groups that may be local or global. The purpose is a higher level of achievement through working together. One key difference, then, is that group members bring to the group the strength of their individuality and independence. A related difference is that group members choose to be interdependent—it's a preference rather than a need.

People in post-industrial economies are likely to believe they're in control. They may embrace elements of both the me-first and us-first orientations—as autonomous people, they choose to put the work team first in order to achieve greater things together. They focus on cooperative relationships in order to achieve greater success. They're also likely to demand equality, take calculated risks, be flexible in how they use time and physical closeness, and use a direct communication style.

FINAL SELF-TEST

Indicate the best answers to the following 10 multiple-choice questions.

1. People from I'm-Controlled cultures are likely to say
   - A. what happens to me is up to me
   - B. God helps those who help themselves
   - C. it depends on God's will
   - D. plan your work and work your plan

2. In Us-First cultures
   - A. job and private life are inseparable
   - B. "we" is more important than "I"
   - C. preserving face and avoiding shame are very important
   - D. all of the above

3. People in Me-First cultures are likely to say
   - A. I should integrate my goals with those of the group
   - B. I will always stay close to my parents and relatives
   - C. my personal goals must come first
   - D. team loyalty is of highest importance to me

4. In cultures with tight ties, people are likely to say
   - A. I think of myself as part of "we"
   - B. I'm unique, one of a kind
   - C. if I fail, it's my own fault
   - D. growing up means becoming my own person

5. People in Achievement-First cultures might say
   A. I focus on building positive relationships
   B. I value my hunches and intuition
   C. hard work will bring me independence
   D. I work in order to make a living

6. People in Rank/Status cultures might say
   A. my company's organizational chart looks like a low box
   B. my boss has power because he's worked his way up
   C. I like it when my boss consults me
   D. my company's organizational chart looks like a pyramid

7. People in Play-It-Safe cultures might say
   A. we keep things under control
   B. nothing ventured, nothing gained
   C. there are exceptions to every rule
   D. I like investing in the future

8. Cultures that have an independent focus tend to highly value the characteristic of
   A. tight-knit collectivism
   B. hierarchical focus
   C. equality
   D. indirect communication

9. Cultures with an interdependent worldview are likely to have what type of economic system?
   A. agricultural
   B. industrial
   C. post-industrial
   D. semi-agricultural

10. People in cultures with loose ties are likely to say
   A. I seek the satisfaction of a job well recognized.
   B. on the job, I value challenges, individual achievement, and personal ambition
   C. it's most important for me to protect my family and be loyal to them
   D. I want to succeed primarily to make my family and my group look good

FINAL SELF-TEST FEEDBACK

Each correct answer is worth 10 points. If you score less than 70 points, you should review the materials and re-take the Final Self-Test.

1. People from I'm-Controlled cultures are likely to say
    A. No, *what happens to me is up to me* is an I-Control view
    B. No, *God helps those who help themselves* is an I-Control view
    C. Yes, *it depends on God's will* indicates a lack of personal control
    D. No, *plan your work and work your plan* is an I-Control view

2. In Us-First cultures
    A. No, although job and private life are inseparable
    B. No, although "we" is more important than "I" is a part of it
    C. No, although preserving face and avoiding shame are very important
    D. Yes, all of the above are key aspects

3. People in Me-First cultures are likely to say
    A. No, *I should integrate my goals with those of the group* is an Us-First view
    B. No, *I will always stay close to my parents and relatives* is an Us-First view
    C. Yes, *my personal goals must come first* is the best answer
    D. No, *team loyalty is of highest importance to me* is an Us-First view

4. In cultures with tight ties, people are likely to say
    A. Yes, *I think of myself as part of "we"* is the best answer
    B. No, *I'm unique, one of a kind* is a loose-ties view
    C. No, *if I fail, it's my own fault* is a loose-ties view
    D. No, *growing up means becoming my own person* is a loose-ties view

5. People in Achievement-First cultures might say
    A. No, *I focus on building positive relationships* is a people-first view
    B. No, *I value my hunches and intuition* may be a factor, but is not complete
    C. Yes, *hard work will bring me independence* is the best answer
    D. No, *I work in order to make a living* may be a factor, but is not complete

6. People in Rank/Status cultures might say
    A. No, *my company's organizational chart looks like a low box* is an aspect of equality
    B. No, *my boss has power because he's worked his way up* is an equality view

    C. No, *I like it when my boss consults me* happens in equality cultures

    D. Yes, *my company's organizational chart looks like a pyramid* is the best answer

7. People in Play-It-Safe cultures might say

    A. Yes, *we keep things under control* is the best answer

    B. No, *nothing ventured, nothing gained* is a take-risks view

    C. No, *there are exceptions to every rule* is a take-risks view

    D. No, *I like investing in the future* is a take-risks view

8. Cultures that have an independent focus tend to highly value the characteristic of

    A. No, tight-knit collectivism is typical of dependent cultures

    B. No, hierarchical focus is typical of dependent cultures

    C. Yes, equality is the best answer

    D. No, indirect communication is typical of dependent cultures

9. Cultures with an interdependent worldview are likely to have what type of economic system?

    A. No, agricultural systems are linked to dependent worldview

    B. No, industrial systems are linked to independent worldview

    C. Yes, post-industrial is the best answer

    D. No, semi-agricultural is not a type mentioned in this discussion

10. People in cultures with loose ties are likely to say

    A. No, *I seek the satisfaction of a job well recognized* is a tight-ties view

    B. Yes, *on the job, I value challenges, individual achievement, and personal ambition* is the best answer

    C. No, *it's most important for me to protect my family and be loyal to them* is a tight-ties view

    D. No, *I want to succeed primarily to make my family and my group look good* is a tight-ties view

THE BOTTOM LINE

This is just the beginning of your exploration into the fascinating world of cultures, how they are alike, and how they differ. You'll start to notice how people's viewpoints, values, and customary actions reflect their cultural background. You can build your skills by observing, listening, and caring. You're laying the foundation of powerful people connections.

Chapter Review

1. Culture is the environment in which you live, and the key elements are values, heros or heroines (role models), myths, rituals, networks, and symbols.

2. Cultures differ in nine major categories of beliefs and practice:
   - I-control or I'm controlled
   - us-first or me-first
   - tight ties vs. loose ties
   - achievement-first or people-first
   - equality or rank–status
   - take risks or play it safe
   - step-by-step or dive-right-in time
   - come-close or back-off space
   - communicating directly or indirectly

3. Cultural values and customs are greatly affected by a group's dominant way of earning a living. Agricultural economies tend to foster a dependent worldview; industrial, independent; and post-industrial, interdependent.

Beyond Stereotypes to Powerful Connections

CHAPTER OBJECTIVES

- Understand the nature of exclusion and how it is related to stereotyping, prejudice, and discrimination.
- Recognize why people form stereotypes.
- Understand how and why people become prejudiced.
- Recognize discriminatory behaviors.
- Identify ways in which exclusion affects employees.
- Establish powerful contacts that heal prejudice.
- Apply seven strategies that build powerful connections.

PhotoEdit

CHAPTER OVERVIEW

Overcoming stereotyping, prejudice, and discrimination frees people to establish the collaborative, cooperative relationships that are so essential and valuable in today's workplace. Learning how to make that type of person-to-person contact builds powerful relationships.

Insights into the nature of exclusion and how to move beyond stereotypes, prejudice, and discrimination to workplace collaboration boosts innovation, motivation, productivity, career success, and company profits.

WHAT IS THE NATURE OF EXCLUSION IN THE WORKPLACE?

All Americans have inherited a culture rich in diversity, with a history of important contributions made by individuals from all walks of life. The concept of equality is precious to most Americans, and increasingly, all qualified people are finding opportunity in the workplace. Unfortunately, Americans have also inherited a legacy of prejudice, where even today certain individuals are sometimes excluded just because they belong to a disparaged group. This legacy means that few Americans grow up without developing some degree of stereotyping and prejudice. These mindsets are woven into the very tapestry of our culture, springing up from the grass roots of family; filtering down from the top levels of government, business, and society; and feeding back on themselves at all levels in between.

Leading-edge businesses know they need all kinds of Americans as customers and as talented employees. To be valuable employees, people must move beyond the stereotypes and prejudices that exclude whole groups of people. They must learn how to break down the walls of prejudice—and to help others do so. This can bring huge rewards—both individually and collectively.

Exclusion results from forming ingroups and outgroups. Companies and individuals may avoid or exclude someone because of a belief that people from that group are inferior in some way. When people do this, they make judgments about an individual based on group affiliation without ever getting to know the person. These judgments turn into actions if companies or employees do not give that person a fair chance on the job, or if the workplace is set up in a way that automatically ignores or denies access to such people. Three terms are often used to describe these varying levels of exclusion.

Stereotyping refers to labeling and categorizing things or people, which can be necessary and useful in making sense of complex reality, but harmful when "people categories" become too rigid to allow for individual differences. In each of the following examples, the first statement is a simple stereotype, while the second statement reflects a rigid category.

> Example #1: "Juanita is Latino American, you know—they're very devoted to their families." Or, "they all have language problems."

> Example #2: "Jake is gay, and gays tend to be very outgoing." Or, "we know gays are not very stable people."

Prejudice refers to the systematic tendency to pre-judge people who are different as somehow deficient or to view a whole category of people as better or worse than another.

> Example #1: "I avoid immigrants like Juanita. I just don't like trying to cope with people I can't understand and who don't know what I'm talking about."

> Example #2: "I don't want to be in a position of depending on Jake—he may be here today and gone tomorrow if his lover dumps him."

Discrimination refers to actions or practices that result in members of a less-powerful group being treated differently in ways that disadvantage them.

> Example #1: "I vote against hiring Juanita. We need someone like Jane who can deal with all the communication issues and understands the system."

> Example #2: "We shouldn't give this long-term project to Jake because he may not be around to see it through to completion."

Attitudes and practices like these create barriers to personal and company success. People who stereotype, prejudge, or discriminate fail to recognize the full potential of all the members of a diverse work team and diminish the potential power of the group. But groups are made up of individuals, and change begins with one person and expands person by person. *You can play an important role in changing attitudes like these in your company.*

WHY DO PEOPLE STEREOTYPE?

People stereotype in order to manage complex realities by using categories to store new information, quickly identify things, handle multisensory experiences, and make sense of things. People may attach strong emotion to their stereotypes, even when they're false, and often use stereotypes to justify their dislike of someone.

Aspects of Stereotyping

The practice of stereotyping is rooted in the basic human need to categorize the billions of bits of data that constantly bombard us.

Making Complex Reality Manageable

When people stereotype, they form large classes and clusters for guiding their daily adjustments to life. They must deal with too much complexity in the environment to be completely open-minded. They don't have time to learn everything about every new object, person, or situation they encounter. Of necessity, people associate each new item with an old category in their mind in order to make some sense of the world.

Short-Cutting with Big Categories

People tend to place as much as they can into each class and cluster. The mind wants to clump events in the *grossest* way that will help its owner do what he needs to do. People like to solve problems as easily as possible, so they try to fit new problems quickly into a satisfactory category. Then, they can deal with a new problem the same way they dealt with other problems from that category.

Quickly Identifying New Things

A stereotype enables people to readily identify a new object or person by relating it to something they already know. Stereotypes have a close and immediate tie with what people see, how they judge, and what actions they take. In fact, their whole purpose is to help people make responses and adjustments to life in a speedy, smooth, consistent way.

Incorporating Multisensory Experiences

For each mental category, people have a thinking and feeling tone or flavor. Everything in that category takes on that flavor. For example, Joe not only knows what the term *Southern belle* means, he also has a feeling tone of favor or disfavor that goes along with that concept. When Joe meets a woman that he decides is a Southern belle, that feeling tone determines whether he likes her more or less than he would if he got to know her on her own merits.

Being Rational—Or Not

Stereotypes may be more or less rational. A rational stereotype starts to grow from a kernel of truth and enlarges and solidifies with each new relevant experience. A rational stereotype can give a person information that can help predict how someone will behave or what might happen in a situation. An irrational stereotype is one that's formed without adequate evidence.

Adding the Emotional Whammy

People's minds are able to form irrational stereotypes as easily as rational ones, and to link intense emotions to them. An irrational idea that is engulfed by an overpowering emotion is more likely to conform to the emotion than to objective evidence. Therefore, once a person develops an irrational stereotype that she feels strongly about, it's difficult for her to change that stereotype based on facts alone. She must deal with the emotion and its ties to her deepest fears.

Justifying Dislike

Sometimes, people form stereotypes linked to emotions—such as hostility, suspicion, dislike, disgust—and set up the framework for prejudice toward an entire group of people based on their experience with one or a few. When people become prejudiced toward a group, they need to justify their dislike, and any justification that fits the immediate conversational situation will do.

So, stereotyping is part of the human need to categorize the massive amounts of information we encounter every day. Categorizing and labeling are ways of making sense of the world and managing the stuff we must do. Stereotyping, when used in this technical sense, is a rational thing to do. The problems arise when we make our categories too fixed and our labels too permanent—and what most people call *stereotyping* refers to this fixed, permanent aspect. Rigid stereotyping of groups of people often leads to prejudice and discrimination.

WHAT DO I NEED TO KNOW ABOUT PREJUDICE?

Virtually everyone harbors some prejudices according to most researchers. Some prejudice is a matter of blind conformity to prevailing cultural beliefs and customs. However, in most cases, prejudice seems to fulfill a specific irrational function for people, such as making them feel superior to others or using others as scapegoats for the prejudiced person's own resentment or guilt. Prejudice usually is tied to a person's deepest fears, although the connection is normally subconscious and therefore hidden from awareness. Prejudice can be played out in the workplace toward anyone who is considered "different" because of gender, ethnicity, sexual orientation, physical ability, age, socioeconomic class, or any other difference that bothers the beholder. Prejudice may be expressed by denying it, rationalizing it, acting it out, discriminating against others, or using them as scapegoats.

ABOUT PREJUDICE

Researchers have uncovered these interesting facts about prejudice:

- Prejudice is found in all types of people and in every ethnic group.
- Prejudice occurs in the mind but can be acted out in ways that exclude others.
- Prejudiced acts can be performed by nonprejudiced as well as prejudiced people.

The best way to decide if an action is prejudiced is how it affects another person. You can't prove someone is prejudiced, but you may prove that their acts exclude and disadvantage another person.

Some Types of Prejudice

Surveys by the National Opinion Research Center indicate that stereotypes are still prevalent. Many of the Euro-American men holding leadership positions in the workplace believe that other ethnic groups are less intelligent, less hard working, less likely to be self-supporting, more violence prone, and less patriotic than they.

People typically talk about prejudice in terms of workplace prejudice, sexism, racism, ethnic prejudice, and other ism's.

Workplace prejudice is still active in American culture. Each of the following organizations has stated in their research reports that prejudice is the biggest advancement barrier that diverse employees face today: Catalyst, Executive Leadership, and the U.S. Glass Ceiling Commission.

Sexism is prejudice based on gender and is said by some to be the root of all prejudice and discrimination. While women are roughly half the world's population, they are a minority in economic and political arenas and have fewer rights and privileges than men.

Racism is prejudice based on racial group and is typically a problem in societies where there is a predominant majority group and one or more cultural subgroups. However, telling who belongs to what race is often impossible. And when anthropologists are asked about this, one expert may say there are only three races in the world, while another may say there are 300—or anywhere in between. Yet, much of the discrimination in society takes place in the name of race.

Anthropologist Ashley Montagu discusses this puzzle at length in his book *Man's Most Dangerous Myth*. He concludes that there is no such thing as "race" as we know it, and our belief in the racial myth is extremely dangerous to the survival of people on this planet. That's because people typically believe that racial traits are inborn, so a person cannot change her inherited racial qualities.

Montagu says a more realistic and humane concept is that of cultural ethnicity. Clearly, there are distinct ethnic differences and similarities among the world's cultures. Ethnic traits are learned from the culture and are not permanently fixed in the genes, so a person can change his ethnic characteristics.

> *Genetic code mapping reveals that in all humans, our genetic heritage is 99.99 percent identical.*

Ethnic Prejudice is based on a person's membership in an ethnic subculture, which is a segment of a larger culture or society. Members of the subculture participate in shared activities in which the common origin and culture are significant ingredients. A subculture is unique because of its particular beliefs and values and customs, heroes and heroines, myths and stories, and social networks.

Other ism's include ageism, classism or class snobbery, and homophobia, or antigay prejudice. Besides ethnic minorities and women, groups that experience discrimination in the workplace include persons with disabilities, gay persons, older employees, and obese persons. To a lesser extent, persons from lower socioeconomic groups may be targets of prejudice, as symbolized by such derogatory terms as *trailer trash* and *poor white trash*.

Some Expressions of Prejudice

People may express prejudice by subtly discriminating, by denying or rationalizing it, by acting it out, or by using outgroup members as scapegoats.

Subtly discriminating. Expressing stereotypes or prejudices is not considered appropriate in most social circles today and can be illegal in the workplace. When prejudiced persons discriminate in a subtle way, rather than blatantly, it helps them hide their beliefs, even from their own awareness, so they can see themselves as fair and democratic. Denial and rationalization are ways of subtly discriminating.

Denying.   People may repress the inner conflict their prejudice creates by denying it. If they admit prejudice, they admit to being both irrational and unethical. For this reason, it is not unusual to hear someone we perceive as being quite prejudiced saying, "I'm not prejudiced, but . . . "

Rationalizing.   People may justify their prejudice by offering "rational" defenses of it. For example, they gather evidence in favor of their prejudiced beliefs by using such tactics as:

- Noticing only those traits, actions, and events that confirm a decision they have already made and failing to notice those that do not. "See that Platian loafing over there? Typical!" Meanwhile, they don't notice the Platian who is busy and productive.
- Saying it must be true because other people think so too. "Everybody thinks those people are sneaky" (or dirty, stupid, rude, etc.), claiming truth by consensus.
- Blaming the target or shifting the blame back onto those who accuse them of prejudice. "It's their own fault they don't get ahead" (that others shun them, etc.) or "They're just as prejudiced as we are." (So that makes it okay.)
- Defending prejudicial thinking or actions by saying they are exceptions to a usual pattern. "Some of my best friends are Platians, but . . . "

Acting out.   People may act out their prejudice with varying degrees of hostile energy. Talking against "others" requires relatively little energy, actively avoiding them takes more. Stepping up the energy level, people may also discriminate against the "others," physically attack them, or, as in Nazi Germany, even participate in exterminating them. While some people would never move to a more intense degree of action, for others, activity on one level makes it easier to move to a more intense level.

Scapegoating. Most societies encourage, officially or unofficially, the open expression of hostility toward certain groups that serve as scapegoats, or safety valves, for guilt, anger, and aggression. Scapegoating is a form of group projection that helps people feel superior by projecting their own shortcomings and failures on other people and blaming them for the society's problems.

Self-Analysis 3.1 | **How Privileged Are You?**

1. What are some privileges that you enjoy in life? List a few.

2. How do the privileges affect your life? Do they affect your personal power? Ability to achieve your goals? Your success?

3. Which of these (or other) privileges are unavailable to some people because of the group they belong to? Beside each unavailable privilege, write the name of the group.

4. What are some privileges that are unavailable to you that people from certain other groups enjoy? List each privilege and beside it, the group(s) that has access to it.

5. How does this lack of privilege affect your life? Your personal power? Your ability to achieve your goals? Your success?

WHAT DO I NEED TO KNOW ABOUT DISCRIMINATION?

While a "minority" person can discriminate against a "majority" person (I refuse to cooperate with you because you're "white."), large-scale ongoing discrimination by one group against another can only occur when the group doing the discriminating has greater power. A group that has greater power inevitably enjoys more privileges.

A power imbalance is essential to perpetuate discrimination. For example, an African American clerk may dislike a Euro-American executive and never try to get to know him as a person. Her actions are not discriminatory because she does not have the power to take actions that exclude him in ways that disadvantage his career. On the other hand, the executive does have the power to discriminate against her.

A privilege imbalance goes hand in hand with a power imbalance, meaning that a group with power also benefits from distinct privileges that other groups do not have. Self-Analysis 3.1 will help you identify how privileged you are. The President's Race Advisory Board reported in 1998 that Euro-American "privilege is built into the daily indignities that minorities endure and whites generally do not." The report gave these examples:

- Euro-Americans aren't followed by store detectives who see the word "shoplifter" in the color of their skin.
- Euro-Americans don't find themselves paying more for a car than the average African American customer.
- Euro-Americans don't find themselves waiting for service or being refused it altogether, as minorities, too often, still do.

Self-Analysis 3.2 | Examine Your Viewpoints

Instructions: *Mark each item as true or false.*

1. I have little or no difficulty deciding what is right and what is wrong. □ T □ F

2. I thrive on variety and change. □ T □ F

3. I like my routines. □ T □ F

4. I often enjoy being with people who some would call strange or weird. □ T □ F

5. I know how I feel about most situations and don't need to keep thinking about them.
   □ T □ F

6. I often ask myself why I did certain things or why I think or feel as I do. □ T □ F

7. I need to know exactly where I am going and when. □ T □ F

8. I do not always agree with people from other groups, but I usually understand why they
   might think and feel as they do. □ T □ F

9. I hate it when people change my plans. □ T □ F

10. Few actions are totally right or wrong. Most actions stem from complex situations and
    have varying effects. □ T □ F

11. There is only one right way to do most things. □ T □ F

12. I can feel comfortable with most situations, even if I'm not sure what's going on.
    □ T □ F

13. I prefer to focus on a few simple things rather than a wide variety. □ T □ F

14. People basically create the life they have and the sooner they take responsibility for it,
    the better it will be. □ T □ F

15. Most actions can be classified as either proper or improper. □ T □ F

16. I think I know my own strengths and shortcomings pretty well. □ T □ F

17. I don't start a job until I know exactly how to do it. □ T □ F

18. People have different ideas about what's proper and improper; that's fine with me.
    □ T □ F

19. I need to know what's going on and what to expect at all times. □ T □ F

20. I'm comfortable *feeling my way* through a task if necessary. □ T □ F

FEEDBACK

Odd-numbered statements represent rigid, authoritarian tendencies, and even-numbered statements represent open, flexible tendencies.

Step 1   Add up the odd-numbered statements you marked as *true*. That's your *rigidity* score.

Step 2   Add up the even-numbered statements you marked as *true*. That's your *openness* score.

Step 3   Analyze your scores. Since 10 is the maximum score in each category, this gives you a preliminary reading of your tendencies on a scale of 1 to 10. For example, if your rigidity score is 3 and your openness score is 7, your level of openness is about 70 percent and rigidity is about 30 percent. This is only a ballpark figure, of course.

Step 4   Read on. After computing your score, go to the section titled "The Authoritarian Link to Prejudice" to learn more about rigid, authoritarian tendencies.

What Is a Prejudice-Prone Personality?

While everyone is prejudiced to some extent, the degree of prejudice varies greatly and a large body of psychological research explains why. The original work on the authoritarian personality was done in 1950 by Harvard Professor G.W. Allport. Since then, more than 1,200 well-accepted scientific studies have been conducted on this topic—far more than for any other personality aspect.

> *Many studies indicate that people who score high on an authoritarianism scale also show a consistently high degree of prejudice against all other cultural groups.*

Thinking Processes

The thinking processes of highly prejudiced people are in general different from those of less prejudiced people. Their prejudice is not likely to be merely a specific attitude toward a specific group—though they may rationalize it that way. More likely, it's a reflection of their whole way of thinking about the world they live in. The process is likely to include either-or-thinking, such as:

- Whenever they think of nature, of law, of morals, of men and women, they think in terms of good/bad, right/wrong, black/white, maleness/femaleness, and so on. There's little gray in their thinking.
- They tend to be uncomfortable with categories that encompass variety, and are more comfortable if categories are limited to similar things.
- Their habits of thought are rigid and they don't change their mental set easily, but persist in their "tried-and-true" ways of reasoning.
- They have a real need for things to be definite and do not cope well with uncertainty in their plans.
- They tend to agree with such statements as "There are only two kinds of people" and "There is only one right way to do something."

- They divide the world into proper and improper.
- They need precise, orderly, clear-cut instructions before proceeding with a task.

Self-Analysis 3.2 will help you learn more about your viewpoints and thinking processes.

Typical Traits

Prejudice-prone people tend to have what's known as an *authoritarian personality*, which includes these typical traits:

- rigid beliefs
- intolerance of weakness in themselves and others
- aggressive, punishing
- suspicious, cynical
- extreme respect of authority; a strong commitment to conform to the prevailing authority structure
- politically conservative

The Authoritarian Link to Prejudice

This set of characteristics usually produces an adult who is extremely angry and has a habit of repressing that anger. When anger is not expressed, it can take the form of displaced aggression against powerless groups. This stance directly contradicts the outward respect for law and order maintained by most authoritarian individuals. Almost invariably, when the parents of such people have been studied, they are also highly prejudiced against other cultural groups.

Prejudice is clearly more than an occasional lapse in judgment for people with rigid, authoritarian personality traits. It is embedded in every facet of their personalities. For these individuals, changing their prejudiced viewpoints means changing their whole life pattern. Complete Self-Analysis 3.3 to find and change your own judgmental beliefs.

The Less-Prejudiced Personality

Tolerant people have adopted thinking processes that tend to be relatively open and flexible. They

- rarely see things in terms of black or white, but instead see many shades of gray
- are usually comfortable differentiating among the variety within a category
- can be comfortable with new people and uncertain situations
- often empathize with those who are different—and are sensitive to others' ways of seeing and feeling

- are self-aware and assess the quality and meaning of their thoughts, feelings, and actions
- tend to take responsibility for what happens to them in life and for the life they create
- know their own strengths and shortcomings
- have a great deal of inner security, can handle threats to their self-esteem, and can be at ease with all sorts of people
- handle moral conflict pretty well and can be fairly flexible and tolerant
- deal fairly well with situations that are marked by uncertainty
- can feel safe saying "I don't know"
- can feel their way through a task

Self-Analysis 3.4 will prepare you to open up to new experiences and people.

Self-Analysis 3.3 Changing Judgmental Beliefs

Purpose: Finding and changing judgmental beliefs that create conflict.

Step 1   **Describe a problem situation.** Write a few words about a relationship situation you would like to improve, one that may involve your own stereotyping or prejudice.

Step 2   **List your beliefs about the situation.** Write a few words about (a) the beliefs you think promote harmony in the situation and (b) the beliefs you think undermine harmony or promote conflict in the situation.

Step 3   **List your beliefs about the other person(s).** Write a few words about (a) the beliefs you think support the other person(s) involved in the situation and (b) the beliefs you think undermine the other person(s).

Step 4   **List your beliefs about yourself.** Write a few words about (a) the beliefs you think are self-empowering in the situation and (b) the beliefs that you think undermine you.

Step 5   **Examine the beliefs carefully.** Focusing on the non-supportive beliefs, consider the idea that all the things you dislike or despise in others, you also dislike or despise in yourself. If you despise cruelty in others, you despise it in yourself, either because you are sometimes cruel with others or because you are sometimes cruel with yourself, or both. Look for patterns and insights about who you are and how you judge yourself. See if you recognize your self-judgments being reflected in your judgments of others. Write a few words about (a) things you dislike in others and (b) patterns and insights you see emerging from this self-awareness process.

(continued)

Self-Analysis 3.3   Changing Judgmental Beliefs   *continued*

Step 6   **Ask yourself,** "Do these beliefs still help me? Am I ready to change them?"

Step 7   **Use the change process:**

Take responsibility for having created the beliefs that support conflict.

Accept and acknowledge that these beliefs are judgmental, but that it is perfectly human to have these judgmental beliefs. Embrace them with love and compassion, without judging them.

Feel the feelings. Get out of your head and into your body where you sense some feeling. Let feelings of love and compassion rise up into your heart area, up through the top of your head. Then, let them surround and permeate your entire body with joy and peace.

Step 8   **Focus on new, positive beliefs**. Ask yourself:

- "What beliefs can I adopt that reflect goodwill and trust to replace the old fear-based ones?" Write a few words about them.

- "What other positive beliefs would facilitate and support harmony in this situation?" Write a few words about them.

Step 9   **Embrace these new beliefs and** make them a part of who you are.

Self-Analysis 3.4   Opening Up to New Experiences

Purpose: This exercise is designed to help you open up to different types of people. It is especially helpful for people who score above average on the authoritarian personality scale.

Step 1   Examine the motivators and barriers to getting to know new types of people. Motivators cause us to reach out to others and often involve curiosity, courage, and a sense of adventure. Barriers cause us to mentally separate ourselves from others.

Barriers	Motivators
I don't know what to expect.	It may be fun.
I don't feel comfortable.	It may be interesting.
Maybe they won't like me.	They may like me.
Maybe I won't like them.	I may like them.
Maybe they won't treat me well.	I may learn something.
I may end up looking foolish.	I may end up feeling better about myself.

Self-Analysis 3.4 **Opening Up to New Experiences** *continued*

I don't know what to say.	I may gain experience, perspective, understanding, empathy, compassion.
I don't know how to act.	
Others:	Others:

Step 2   Think of a time when you did **not** say yes to an opportunity to experience a new situation with someone you did not know well. What were some of the barriers that held you back? Check off the barriers that apply in the list shown here. Add others that you experienced.

Step 3   Think of a time when you **did** say yes to such an opportunity. What motivated you? Check off the motivators that apply in the list shown here. Add others that you experienced.

Step 4   In the second situation, what happened after you said yes? Was the experience more positive or negative? If it was more negative, what lessons can you draw from this experience?

Step 5   In the first situation, what **might** have happened if you had said yes? What experiences, opportunities, advantages, and lessons might you have had? What lessons can you learn from this now?

SELF-TEST

Indicate the best answers to the following 10 multiple-choice questions.

1. Stereotyping is
   A. treating people from less-powerful groups in ways that disadvantage them
   B. pre-judging people who are different as somehow deficient
   C. labeling or categorizing people
   D. distorting a person's traits in order to exclude them

2. Discrimination is
   A. treating people from less-powerful groups in ways that disadvantage them
   B. pre-judging people who are different as somehow deficient
   C. labeling or categorizing people
   D. distorting a person's traits in order to exclude them

3. Prejudice is
   A. treating people from less-powerful groups in ways that disadvantage them
   B. pre-judging people who are different as somehow deficient
   C. labeling or categorizing people
   D. distorting a person's traits in order to exclude them

4. The reason we stereotype people is
   A. to make complex reality more manageable
   B. to quickly identify new people
   C. to justify our dislike for an entire group of people
   D. all of the above

5. Prejudice is found
   A. throughout the Western world
   B. in countries where there are many minority groups
   C. in all types of people and in every ethnic group
   D. in countries with large economic gaps between rich and poor

6. Experts say there are how many races?
   A. 3
   B. 30
   C. 300
   D. experts do not agree

7. *Man's Most Dangerous Myth* by Ashley Montagu refers to the myth of
   A. race
   B. ethnicity
   C. sexism
   D. classism

8. People engage in subtle discrimination by
   A. expressing stereotypes
   B. expressing prejudice
   C. denying and rationalizing their discrimination
   D. objecting to equal opportunity measures

9. The prejudiced-prone personality tends to
   A. see many shades of gray in situations
   B. know his or her own strengths and shortcomings pretty well
   C. can tolerate ambiguity
   D. divide the world into proper and improper

10. The less-prejudiced personality tends to
    A. see many shades of gray in situations
    B. have rigid beliefs
    C. be intolerant of weakness in themselves and others
    D. be aggressive and punishing

SELF-TEST FEEDBACK

Each correct answer is worth 10 points. If you score less than 70 points, you should review the materials and re-take the Self-Test.

1. Stereotyping is
    A. No, although treating people from less-powerful groups in ways that disadvantage them is related to stereotyping
    B. No, although pre-judging people who are different as somehow deficient is related to stereotyping
    C. Yes, labeling or categorizing people is the best answer
    D. No, although distorting a person's traits in order to exclude them is an aspect of stereotyping

2. Discrimination is
    A. Yes, treating people from less-powerful groups in ways that disadvantage them is the best answer
    B. No, although pre-judging people who are different as somehow deficient is related to discrimination
    C. No, although labeling or categorizing people is related to discrimination
    D. No, although distorting a person's traits in order to exclude them is related to discrimination

3. Prejudice is
    A. No, although treating people from less-powerful groups in ways that disadvantage them stems from prejudice
    B. Yes, pre-judging people who are different as somehow deficient is the best answer
    C. No, although labeling or categorizing people is related to prejudice
    D. No, although distorting a person's traits in order to exclude them is related

4. The reason we stereotype people is
   - A. No, although to make complex reality more manageable is an aspect
   - B. No, although to quickly identify new people is an aspect
   - C. No, although to justify our dislike for an entire group of people is an aspect
   - D. Yes, all of the above is the best answer

5. Prejudice is found
   - A. No, although it is in fact found throughout the Western world
   - B. No, although it is in fact found in countries where there are many minority groups
   - C. Yes, in all types of people and in every ethnic group is the best answer
   - D. No, although it is in fact found in countries with large economic gaps between rich and poor

6. Experts say there are how many races?
   - A. No, not 3
   - B. No, not 30
   - C. No, not 300
   - D. Yes, *experts do not agree on race* is the best answer; most experts now think race is not a useful or valid concept

7. *Man's Most Dangerous Myth* by Ashley Montagu refers to the myth of
   - A. Yes, race is the answer
   - B. No, ethnicity refers to cultural differences
   - C. No, sexism refers to bias based on gender
   - D. No, classism refers to bias based on socioeconomic status

8. People engage in subtle discrimination by
   - A. No, although they may express stereotypes
   - B. No, although they may express prejudice
   - C. Yes, denying and rationalizing their discrimination is the best answer
   - D. No, such people usually say they support equal opportunity measures

9. The prejudiced-prone personality tends to
   - A. No, they usually don't see many shades of gray in situations
   - B. No, they usually do not know their own strengths and shortcomings pretty well
   - C. No, they usually don't tolerate ambiguity well
   - D. Yes, *divide the world into proper and improper* is the best answer

10. The less-prejudiced personality tends to
    - A. Yes, *see many shades of gray in situations* is the best answer
    - B. No, they tend not to have rigid beliefs

C. No, they tend to be tolerant of weakness in themselves and others

D. No, they are usually not aggressive and punishing

WHAT ARE THE EFFECTS OF EXCLUSION?

The general effects of being excluded normally include stressful emotions that may be turned inward or outward, but may also be worked through in a personal growth process. People who do the excluding are also affected, and long-run results include cutting off opportunities for diverse relationships and greater joy. The workplace effects of exclusion cover every career aspect, from being recruited to being promoted. For employees on the job, exclusion undermines their levels of trust, motivation, and productivity.

General Effects of Being Excluded

Most people who are excluded experience difficulty in coping with feelings of rejection and inferiority. No one can hear the message that they are inferior every day without it affecting how they feel about themselves.

Some people from "disadvantaged" groups seem to handle their status easily and show little evidence that it bothers them—in fact, it may aid their personal growth and maturity. Others become so rebellious that they develop defenses that continually provoke the very snubs they resent. Most people fall somewhere between these two extremes, showing a mixture of both acceptance and resistance to their status.

It is human nature to develop ego defenses against repeated devaluation or exclusion. Some turn their defensiveness inward on themselves or their ingroup. Others turn it outward toward the dominant group or toward other excluded groups. Typical responses are shown in Snapshot 3.1.

Notice that some responses, such as "feeling sympathy for all victims" can be a step in personal growth. Similar growth outcomes include:

- seeing the world from a larger perspective
- accepting the reality of exclusion
- finding ways to overcome barriers to achieving personal goals
- identifying or creating new doors of opportunity

General Effects of Rejecting Others

When people stereotype and reject others, the immediate payoff is feeling "better than." This may give them a momentary morale boost, but it's a short-lived cheap thrill. The long-run effects include feeling guilty and depriving themselves of learning from a diverse range of people. Also, in a world of "bet-

SNAPSHOT 3.1   Ego defenses in response to discrimination.

Turning Outward	Turning Inward
Obsessive concern and suspicion	Self-dislike
Slyness and cunning	Denial of own group
Clannishness, clustering with own group	Withdrawal, passivity
Prejudice against other groups	Attacking members of own group
Aggression, rebellion	Striving for symbolic status
Competitiveness	Clowning, playing the fool
Trying harder	Sympathy with all victims

ter thans," everyone is bound to come out "worse than" sometimes. The more time people spend immersed in stereotyped, prejudiced, and discriminatory thoughts, the more time they spend in a critical, blaming, judging state of mind.

Research studies indicate that highly prejudiced people experience less zest for life, less joy, than more tolerant people. This is understandable when you stop to think that the more prejudiced a person is, the more she views life through a negative lens. When she thinks of those "lesser others," her thoughts may focus on distaste, resentment, revulsion, anger, and similar unpleasant, even stressful, emotions. And she's likely to experience some anxiety and fear that she too will be excluded—rejection is a large part of her mindset. Prejudice therefore negatively affects the personalities of the prejudiced person and her target.

Specific Workplace Effects of Being Excluded

Prejudice against certain groups of employees affects every aspect of their careers.

Recruitment practices.   Some companies recruit for higher-paying jobs by contacting placement firms, publications, and organizations rarely accessed by diverse persons. Contacts in diverse communities are primarily used to recruit people for lower-level jobs.

Screening practices.   Aptitude and intelligence tests may measure the Euro-American way of seeing and doing things, but may not be accurate for assessing diverse individuals' aptitude for job success. Also, some firms require diplomas, degrees, and experience that are not necessarily good predictors of job success. Diverse candidates are more likely to lack these credentials, but might have the necessary skills for job success. Some companies require diverse persons to have experience in areas where they previously had been effectively blocked.

Compensation practices. On average, women and men from ethnic subgroups earn about 70 percent of Euro-American male salaries, even at the vice-presidential level. Above the worker level, they also receive fewer benefits.

Tracking and job segregation. Placing women in clerical work and not including them in training and development for other better-paying jobs is one example of tracking. To some extent, discrimination in every job phase from recruitment to promotion results in a dual labor market in which diverse employees work disproportionately in occupations and industries with lower prestige, status, and compensation. Within organizations, they typically work in jobs and departments that are less influential and have lower status than those held by Euro-American men.

Promotion practices. In many companies, promotion practices are secretive and very difficult for outsiders to understand. Unwritten, informal rules or expectations usually have a much greater impact than written procedures.

For example, many studies indicate that Euro-American male executives and managers continue to harbor stereotyped views of diverse employees, views that shape the promotion decisions. For example, a woman is disadvantaged if she is married—"We didn't promote her because she has children and her family responsibilities will interfere." She is also disadvantaged if she is single—"We didn't promote her because she's likely to get married and have children and quit."

Layoff, discharge, and seniority practices. Seniority practices can work against diverse employees because they tend to have been employed by companies for less time than their Euro-American counterparts. Because many women and people of color were barred from certain occupations in the past, they have not had the time to accrue the seniority of other workers.

Career alternatives. Discrimination can make it more difficult for diverse employees to choose career alternatives when they hit the glass ceiling. Because they are usually paid less and thus have fewer assets, they find it more difficult to get loans to start their own businesses.

Effects of Exclusion on Employee Performance

Exclusion has a great impact on employee performance. It undermines employee trust, motivation, and productivity.

Effects on trust.   Prejudice and discrimination sabotage trust. Given the history of inter-group prejudice, trust is more difficult to build across cultural groups than it is within them. Diverse employees tend to feel less free to spontaneously express their opinions and ideas in the workplace. They tend to engage in much more internal prescreening or self-censorship in order to fit into the work group.

Effects on motivation.   A lack of acceptance and opportunities can have a detrimental effect on motivation. Because of their experiences, diverse employees often must ask, "Was this event caused by discrimination or by other factors?" "Is my boss criticizing me because my work is not up to standards or because I'm African American?" This can present major problems when attempting to process feedback and stay motivated.

Expectancy theory holds that the motivation to perform on a job depends on answers to these questions:

- If I put forth enough effort, will it produce the performance level the boss wants?
- If I achieve the performance level the boss wants, will I get what I want (praise, raise, promotion)?
- Is it worth it to me?

Effects on productivity.   Jane Elliott, an elementary school teacher, experimented with the effects of prejudice on productivity with her class. Her results are described in the documentary film *A Class Divided.* Elliott separated students into blue-eyed and brown-eyed groups. On the first day, she told the class that the brown-eyed group was inferior and made them wear collars for clear identification of their status. She reinforced this difference in various ways, such as giving certain privileges to the "superior" group. On the second day, the roles were reversed. On both days, the superior group discriminated against the "inferiors," calling them names and otherwise ostracizing them.

The work performance of the inferior group declined significantly after just a few hours of the discriminatory treatment. The test scores of the students went up on the day they were in the advantaged group and down on the day they were in the disadvantaged group. The change in the behavior of the teacher and fellow students had an immediate impact on the performance of the students.

LEADER EXPECTATIONS

Leader expectations are communicated to employees in several ways, and these kinds of questions can identify them:

- What amount of output does the leader ask for?
- Are the goals challenging and desirable?
- To what extent does the leader believe the employee can achieve high goals?
- How supportive is the leader?
- What overall climate (favorable tone, positive responses) does the leader set?
- What amount of input (information relevant to getting the job done) does the leader give employees?
- What amount of feedback (information about how well the employee is doing) does the leader give?

You can help set an inclusive tone in your work groups. Remember, if the team and the company wants top performance, there must be no outgroups. Everyone must be a member of the ingroup.

WHAT TYPE OF CONTACT HEALS PREJUDICE?

The type of contact that heals prejudice contains three parts:

1. It is between people who consider themselves basically equal human beings.
2. It goes deeper than superficial conversation—to really getting to know people.
3. All parties need each other, need to work together in order to achieve a goal that is meaningful and important to all.

Types of contact can include the superficial, true acquaintance, conflict, and collaboration.

Superficial contact. Where segregation is the custom, contacts tend to be superficial, either because they are very casual or because they are firmly fixed into superior–subordinate relationships. Superficial contact is more likely to increase, rather than decrease, prejudice because we tend to selectively notice behavior that confirms our stereotypes.

True acquaintance.   Contacts that go beyond the superficial to form true acquaintances can lead to acceptance. A true acquaintance can serve to change beliefs about diverse groups and bridge the walls of prejudice.

Conflict.   Clashes of interests and values do occur between groups, and these conflicts are not necessarily an expression of prejudice. Some conflicts grow out of economic competition that is not necessarily rooted in prejudice, but tends to aggravate any prejudice that exists.

Collaboration.   Research indicates that Euro-Americans who live side by side in public housing projects with African Americans of the same general economic class tend to be more friendly, less fearful, and have less stereotyped views than those who live in segregated arrangements. Merely living together is not enough, however. It is only when people become jointly active in the community that their views change. The resulting communication is the decisive factor in the quality of the relationships that develop.

> The key to moving beyond prejudice is working together
>
> toward common goals that are highly valued, in situations
>
> where people need each other to achieve their goals.

The workplace offers innumerable opportunities to work together toward common goals. The trend toward working in teams—project teams, self-managing teams, entrepreneurial teams, customer teams, supplier teams—offers an ideal laboratory for healing prejudice.

Vignette   Contact That Counts

A public housing project in Los Angeles was converted to private condominiums that low-income families were able to purchase. Owners established a homeowners association that met regularly for the purpose of making the neighborhood as livable and vital as possible. During the Los Angeles riots of 1992, homeowners took a united stand against any invasion of their neighborhood, and it was spared from vandalism. Residents who were interviewed by the *Los Angeles Times* credited the friendships built by people from various subcultures for the solidarity they displayed during the crisis.

WHAT ARE THE SEVEN STRATEGIES FOR MOVING BEYOND STEREOTYPING TO POWERFUL CONNECTIONS?

You have begun the process of moving beyond stereotypes, prejudice, discrimination, exclusion, and even intolerance to appreciation, inclusion, and collaboration with others. You are ready to continue the process and become a role model and coach for others who are willing to move beyond. Keep these seven strategies in mind.

Strategy #1: Get in Touch with Stereotypes and Prejudices

Our mass media generally supports cultural stereotypes, continually reviving and reinforcing them. Therefore, it's important that intelligent people move beyond shallow, limiting, and harmful stereotypes of diverse groups.

You stand to benefit greatly from moving beyond stereotypes and prejudice, as does your career, your organization, and the planet for that matter. And staying stuck in prejudice, no matter how hidden or subtle, has great costs.

It's not nearly as satisfying to dislike people and look down on them as it is to appreciate them, collaborate with them, and have fun together. Further, prejudice sets in motion a negative cycle of action and reaction that divides and separates and throws up barriers to building trust. It prevents people from having the productive and harmonious workplace and society that would benefit us all. So, how do you break the habit?

The most important step is merely wanting to know about your own stereotypes and prejudices so you can open up to more accurate information. People often hide their prejudiced beliefs, so uncovering them can be challenging, but it's a challenge worth pursuing. Then you can begin to notice thoughts that occur when you see certain people, judgmental thoughts that lead to feelings of aversion, dislike, suspicion, and similar feelings that prevent good interaction and block collaborative relationships.

Strategy #2: Open Your Mind to Other Viewpoints and Listen

Open up to new ideas so you can replace irrational, rigid stereotypes with some rational, flexible categories, perhaps better defined as background information. Remember, even valid background information you gather and store away about various groups of people is not set in concrete. Think of each category of background information as flexible and open to change. It's there to help you understand where a person might be coming from and provide clues about what questions to ask. This frees you up so you can get to know people on their own merits, as unique individuals,

SNAPSHOT 3.2 Focus on the individual against a culture background.

Diverse Society

Employee's
Background

Woman

Catholic

Latino American

**Individual
Employee**

Older

Married

Two grown children

to empathize with them, and to build honest, trusting relationships. Snapshot 3.2 illustrates how to focus on the individual against a cultural background.

Accepting. Respect their right to have different beliefs and viewpoints, lifestyles and business images, work styles, and job behaviors. You do not need to adopt a belief or custom yourself in order to respect another's right to do so. Be willing to listen and learn about diverse people and groups, and to examine your own ego needs, beliefs, and viewpoints that block your ability to respect and appreciate others. Be willing to change false beliefs.

Listening. Good listeners are rare. Most of us take turns talking instead of listening to get another's ideas that we might incorporate into our own. Be willing to listen with an open mind to other viewpoints and to new information that might change a biased belief.

Opening. Open-minded persons look beyond labels, categories, and sweeping statements. They insist on knowing the evidence for broad generalizations before accepting them as true. They're open to new evidence that might lead them to modify a category.

Strategy #3: Learn about Other Groups

Educate yourself and others about the key differences among diverse groups. Appreciate those differences—see them as individual, colorful facets of the kaleidoscope of humanity.

Once you begin to understand the typical stereotypes, biases, and barriers that members of a particular group must cope with every day, you have a better chance of anticipating how your own actions may be perceived. When you become familiar with a group's values and customs and how they view certain issues, you can better interpret their actions and words. The goal of cultural understanding is to be able to walk in another person's shoes for a while, to see the world as that person sees it, and feel what he or she feels.

Strategy #4: Express Respect and Appreciation

Once you've opened your mind and replaced stereotyped beliefs, the next step is to become comfortable and imaginative in expressing respect and appreciation, primarily through your actions but also through your conversations. Every time you choose to focus on goodwill and trust instead of focusing on fear and mistrust, you automatically move to respecting and appreciating instead of judging and belittling. It can be become a healing and profitable habit.

To experience respect and appreciation for others, you need to open up to your intuition and empathy—practice putting yourself in the other person's shoes. If you are unable to empathize with "minorities," you may feel forced to be on guard, put strangers into categories, and react to them as a group rather than as individuals.

If you're unwilling to learn about the background as well as the uniqueness of people you encounter, you're likely to resort to stereotyping. Clearly, the willingness to feel empathy for others—to see the world as they see it and to feel what they're feeling—can help you to move beyond prejudice.

Strategy #5: Build Trust

Building trust can be a difficult challenge given the history of stereotyping, prejudice, and betrayal among diverse groups. You build trust by building authentic relationships, in which you respect and appreciate others and show it through words and actions. When you are consistent, keep your commitments, and show respect time after time, then people begin to trust you.

Where there is a long legacy of mistrust, it may take a long time to build trust. It can be destroyed in a moment of perceived betrayal, and the healing process may be difficult or impossible. The best preventive is to consistently choose an attitude of friendship and trust toward other people and to act in ways that respect and preserve those relationships. Before you act, ask yourself, "Will this harm or help the relationship?"

Strategy #6: Work with Diverse People Toward Common Goals

You have learned that superficial contact alone does not help people to overcome stereotypes and prejudices toward a group. What does work is teaming up with others on projects that help you achieve important common goals.

Strategy #7: Go for Creativity and Innovation

The great power of working with a diverse team is the greater range of creativity it opens up for you and your company. Diverse people produce diverse ideas and ways of doing things. Diverse idea pools, like diverse gene pools, provide us with more variety and options. This means more and better innovation, crucial in today's fast-moving, globally competitive marketplace. To maximize the creative opportunities, you must seek collaboration, work toward putting it all together, and use the synergy—the team advantage—that's generated.

Seek collaboration.   Continually seek opportunities to collaborate one-on-one and in teams in order to bridge cultural gaps. Self-managing work teams can be especially effective because members must take so much responsibility for setting the goals, figuring out how to achieve them, and actually doing it. The success of such teams depends on building trust and working closely together.

Ask, "How can I create teams of 'minorities' to work toward common goals?" Value unity, which is not uniformity, but the integration of the goals and efforts of many individuals. See that in unity there can be great diversity. Understand that each part is vital to the success of an emerging whole.

Work toward synthesis.   Share a vision of people gathering together the separate elements that form the whole project and work team. See them bringing the whole into active expression. Envision them acting as one to create a new reality—including new projects, processes, products, relationships, and corporate culture. Understand that synthesis is *not* the same as melting-pot assimilation.

Use the synergy.   Recognize that extra creative spark, that increment of information, knowledge, friendship, or other benefit that is the by-product of people getting together and working together. Use it to carry the team and the organization to new heights of excellence and innovation. Celebrate that added gift, the whole creative package that is more than the sum of what each person brings to the table.

FINAL SELF-TEST

Indicate the best answers to the following 10 multiple-choice questions.

1. How are persons who experience significant exclusion from the dominant group affected by the exclusion?
   A. most naturally find their own sources of self-esteem
   B. most continually provoke the snubs they resent through their rebellious attitudes and behaviors
   C. most show some mixture of acceptance and resentment
   D. most develop self-hate, turning their resentment inward

2. Excluded persons who turn their ego defenses outward react by
   A. denying they are members of their own group
   B. slyness and cunning
   C. attacking members of their own group
   D. clowning, playing the fool

3. Excluded persons who turn their ego defenses inward react by
   A. obsessive concern and suspicion
   B. slyness and cunning
   C. attacking members of their own group
   D. prejudice against other groups

4. How are persons who are highly prejudiced affected by their prejudice?
   A. their world becomes more hierarchical, with everyone categorized as better or worse
   B. their range of contacts is narrow and they are relatively isolated
   C. they're more likely to fear being despised by others
   D. all of the above

5. Effects of exclusion on employee performance include
   A. trust is sabotaged
   B. motivation is undermined
   C. productivity declines significantly
   D. all of the above

6. The type of contact that heals prejudice
   A. is casual and superficial
   B. goes beyond the superficial to form true acquaintance
   C. occurs when people need each other to achieve common goals
   D. all of the above

7. The most important step in overcoming stereotypes and prejudice is
   A. visiting the homes of people from that group
   B. joining organizations where that group is predominant
   C. wanting to know about your prejudice so you can open up to better information about the stereotyped group
   D. spending more time with people from the stereotyped group

8. During the coming decade, the proportion of new employees coming into the workplace that are women and minorities is
   A. one-sixth
   B. two-sixths
   C. three-sixths
   D. five-sixths

9. A multicultural approach reduces costs in the long run because
   A. the turnover rate of nontraditional employees is greatly reduced
   B. recruiting costs are reduced when minorities seek out such companies
   C. culturally diverse workforces that collaborate solve problems more effectively
   D. all of the above

10. Culturally diverse workforces that collaborate can solve problems better because
    A. a diverse group brings many diverse viewpoints to the situation
    B. there is a lower probability of groupthink
    C. there is a higher probability of generating creative solutions
    D. all of the above

FINAL SELF-TEST FEEDBACK

Each correct answer is worth 10 points. If you score less than 70 points, you should review the materials and re-take the Final Self-Test.

1. How are persons who experience significant exclusion from the dominant group affected by the exclusion?
   A. No, most don't naturally find their own sources of self-esteem
   B. No, most don't continually provoke the snubs they resent through their rebellious attitudes and behaviors
   C. Yes, most show some mixture of acceptance and resentment
   D. No, most don't develop self-hate, turning their resentment inward

2. Excluded persons who turn their ego defenses outward react by
    A. No, denying they are members of their own group is an inward focus
    B. Yes, slyness and cunning is the best answer because such action is focused outside self and own group
    C. No, attacking members of their own group is an inward focus
    D. No, clowning, playing the fool is an inward focus

3. Excluded persons who turn their ego defenses inward react by
    A. No, obsessive concern and suspicion are not focused inward
    B. No, slyness and cunning are not focused inward
    C. Yes, attacking members of their own group is the best answer because it is turning inward
    D. No, prejudice against other groups is not turning inward

4. How are persons who are highly prejudiced affected by their prejudice?
    A. No, although their world becomes more hierarchical, with everyone categorized as better or worse, there is more
    B. No, although their range of contacts is narrow and they are relatively isolated, there is more
    C. No, although they're more likely to fear being despised by others, there is more
    D. Yes, all of the above is the best answer

5. Effects of exclusion on employee performance include
    A. No, although an effect is that trust is sabotaged
    B. No, although an effect is that motivation is undermined
    C. No, although an effect is that productivity declines significantly
    D. Yes, all of the above

6. The type of contact that heals prejudice
    A. No, it is not casual and superficial
    B. No, although it does go beyond the superficial to form true acquaintance
    C. Yes, it occurs when people need each other to achieve common goals is the best answer
    D. No, it's not all of the above

7. The most important step in overcoming stereotypes and prejudice is
    A. No, visiting the homes of people from that group is nice, but not enough
    B. No, joining organizations where that group is predominant is good, but insufficient

    C. Yes, wanting to know about your prejudice so you can open up to better information about the stereotyped group is the best answer

    D. No, spending more time with people from the stereotyped group is good, but insufficient

8. During the coming decade, the proportion of new employees coming into the workplace that are women and minorities is

    A. No, not one-sixth

    B. No, not two-sixths

    C. No, not three-sixths

    D. Yes, roughly five-sixths

9. *A multicultural approach reduces costs in the long run because*

    A. No, although the turnover rate of nontraditional employees is greatly reduced

    B. No, although recruiting costs are reduced when minorities seek out such companies

    C. No, although culturally diverse workforces that collaborate solve problems more effectively

    D. Yes, all of the above is the best answer

10. Culturally diverse workforces that collaborate can solve problems better because

    A. No, although a diverse group brings many diverse viewpoints to the situation

    B. No, although there is a lower probability of groupthink

    C. No, although there is a higher probability of generating creative solutions

    D. Yes, all of the above is the best answer

THE BOTTOM LINE

Acquiring the foundation for assessing statements you hear about people from various cultural backgrounds is a major step toward expanding your worldview. By observing, listening, and caring, you can develop more powerful people connections.

Chapter Review

1. Exclusion relates to forming ingroups and outgroups and leads to stereotyping, prejudice, and discrimination. When this happens, judgments are made about individuals based on group affiliation.

2. Stereotyping enables people to make reality manageable, create short cuts, and quickly identify (or misidentify) new things. We incorporate multisensory experiences into our stereotyped categories, which may be rational or irrational and often carry an emotional charge. We use irrational, emotional stereotypes to justify dislike.

3. People become prejudiced for a variety of reasons (e.g., to feel superior or because of fear).

4. The authoritarian personality exhibits rigid beliefs, intolerance of weaknesses, aggression, suspicion, extreme respect of authority, and political conservativeness.

5. Exclusion affects employees' outward and inward behavior. Outward behavior can include concern and suspicion, slyness and cunning, clannishness, prejudice against other groups, aggression or rebellion, competitiveness, and trying harder. Inward behavior can include self-dislike, denial of own group, withdrawal and passivity, attacking members of own group, striving for symbolic status, clowning, and sympathy with all victims.

6. Contact that heals prejudice takes place between those who consider each other equal, at levels deeper than superficial conversation, and between those who need each other to work together toward a meaningful goal.

7. Seven strategies for moving beyond stereotyping to powerful connections:
   - get in touch with stereotypes and prejudices
   - open your mind to others
   - learn about other groups
   - express respect and appreciation
   - build trust
   - work with diverse people toward common goals
   - go for innovation

Creating an Inclusive Multicultural Workplace

4

CHAPTER OBJECTIVES

- Understand the great melting pot and other diversity myths
- Identify legal approaches to managing diversity
- Know the Valuing Diversity Approach
- Understand the basis for an inclusive, multicultural approach
- Understand how to implement an inclusive multicultural approach

CHAPTER OVERVIEW

American culture, diverse subcultures, and corporate culture each play important roles in the ability of your company to hire and retain the diverse talent it needs because people must fit in and feel appreciated if they are to stay and contribute. You, and each employee, play an important role in making your corporate culture the type that welcomes all types of people and includes them in the "inner circle." Your ability to bridge cultural differences and build profitable workplace relationships determines your job success.

Until the 1960s, most companies adhered to the melting-pot approach to deal with workplace diversity. Because this didn't work for women and ethnic minorities, the Civil Rights laws of the 1960s ushered in the legal approach to managing discrimination. Now savvy companies are going beyond old approaches. Their focus is on valuing diverse employees for the unique contributions they can make to the company's success. They are crafting a multicultural approach to managing diversity—and a corporate culture that welcomes all types of employees to its doors and then appreciates and nurtures them. The first step in bridging the cultural gap is to understand the four major historical phases of dealing with cultural diversity in the American workplace.

WHAT ABOUT THE GREAT MELTING POT?

"America has always handled its diversity so well," some say. "Why, we're the Great Melting Pot." But the melting pot has been a cruel myth for aspiring career women and for non-European minorities. Who has it worked for? In society in general, it has worked for all immigrants from European countries. In the workplace, it has worked for male immigrants from those countries.

European immigrants were expected to learn the American ways so they could be assimilated and absorbed. The goal was to create a seamless American culture and workplace. This worked fairly well for European men because Western cultures have much in common and people from those cultures look much alike. Although the Jewish, Irish, Italian, and Eastern European immigrants experienced some distinct prejudice and discrimination, within a generation or two they blended in.

On the other hand, people of color actually lived in segmented and segregated subcultures and women grew up alongside men in parallel but different worlds. People of color and women simply don't look like Euro-American men, the dominant culture of the workplace, and they were never truly assimilated.

MOVE BEYOND DIVERSITY MYTHS

People tend to avoid discussions of workplace discrimination. Many avoid even thinking about it. It should come as no surprise, therefore, that myths about this topic are more prevalent than the realities.

Myth #1: The American Workplace Is a Melting Pot

Traditionally, business has handled diversity by adopting the melting-pot myth, but people of color and women never "melted in" because they don't look or act like the dominant majority, Euro-American men.

Myth #2: The Equal Pay and Equal Opportunity Laws Have Eliminated Workplace Inequities

In the 1960s, Civil Rights laws began to open many doors of opportunity. However, the laws did not necessarily change the beliefs and attitudes, the thoughts and feelings that led to discrimination in the first place. Many of the people with the authority to make changes found ways around these laws. And most employees who are discriminated against are unlikely to report their employers to a government agency.

Myth #3: If We Ever Needed Affirmative Action, We No Longer Need it Now

Very few women or minorities have made it to the top of middle- to large-sized corporations—even after 30 years of affirmative action programs. About 95 percent of top managers in these companies are still Euro-American men. On the other hand, large numbers of "minorities" have moved part way up the ladder, and experts say that affirmative action is the most powerful career boost for them. Until women and minorities are adequately represented at all levels, corporate management still needs the guidance and motivation that affirmative action law provides.

Myth #4: Affirmative Action Imposes Hiring and Promotion Quotas on Companies

It's against the law for the federal government to set affirmative action (AA) quotas for corporations, and it's against the spirit of the law to hire or promote unqualified people.

Myth #5: Affirmative Action Is Really Reverse Discrimination

AA opponents often focus on the reverse discrimination myth. They say that because AA requires companies to fill quotas, they're forced to hire and promote women and minorities who are often less qualified than the white men who are being discriminated against.

Supporters of AA say it's ludicrous to believe that AA has the long-term general effect of discriminating against the most powerful, dominant group in the workplace. Supporters point out that Euro-American males have always had their own brand of AA—the old school ties, the old boys' network, and other ingroup privileges that few notice.

Myth #6: We Can't Afford to Spend Much Time or Money on Diversity Initiatives

We must focus on bottom-line profits. Actually, companies that succeed in New Economy markets do it through talented employees. Inclusive, savvy corporate cultures are attracting and retaining the best talent—which translates into greater success and profits.

How the Melting-Pot Myth Affects People of Color and Women

In the past, newcomers usually bought into the melting-pot belief system, which led them to new beliefs, such as:

- I must become just like the dominant group.
- My native country is inferior; America is better.
- I must fit in, no matter what I have to do.
- I won't teach my children about the old country;
  let them be Americans.

Children of immigrants picked up on this attitude and many grew up to be ashamed of their parents' "old country" ways.

Whether assimilation was a conscious or unconscious goal in dealing with diversity, the ideal was to ignore differences and treat everyone the same. The biblical Golden Rule was the ideal:

Do unto others as you would have them do unto you.

This rule usually works in a homogeneous culture, but in a multicultural workplace, life is not so simple. A more appropriate Golden Rule might be:

*Do unto others as **they** would have you do unto them.*

People may prefer to be treated in ways you haven't even thought of because they may have quite different values and habits than you. You must treat people differently when they are different if you want to be fair. This is a much more complex and difficult task than treating everyone alike.

Other Problems with the Melting-Pot Myth

You can see that the melting-pot ideal has never been ideal for all. Here are some additional problems with this approach:

- Those who don't look the part can't blend in.
- Forcing everyone to take a similar approach leaves untapped potential that could blossom from different approaches.
- In a competitive environment, assimilation is stifling and deadly.
- When diverse newcomers are expected to fit in, they focus on doing the expected or accommodating the norm, on playing it safe, instead of making innovative suggestions.
- Newcomers avoid doing or saying things that might label them as "different."
- The more energy newcomers must expend on adapting, the less they have for developing innovative ideas and personal strengths.

Talented newcomers tend to go (and grow) where they're appreciated for who they are—to companies with a more supportive multicultural approach.

Obviously, the more diverse the workforce becomes, the more important it becomes for organizations to solve the problems presented by the melting-pot approach, to dismantle the traditional barriers to full productivity and contribution, and to develop an approach that's more inclusive. The major barrier to the upward mobility of minorities and women is the glass ceiling to middle and top-level positions, as determined by the government's Glass Ceiling Commission. Inclusive, multicultural corporate environments will overcome that barrier.

Cultural Glue: The American Dream

What about American unity? What glue holds Americans together as a nation? Certainly, two primary values that have pulled immigrants to these shores and kept them here are freedom and opportunity—the freedom to pursue one's own lifestyle and religion and the opportunity to make a decent living. A whole set of values formed around the American Dream, shaped the society, and is remarkably strong in holding it together. Americans have rallied around a common consumer market and media. Their political system lets them participate and have influence, and their political–legal system effectively sets the rules of the making-money game and referees conflicts. Their many interest groups get to have their say through members' votes and whatever influence they can wield within the system.

GROWING UP AMONG MANY "POTS"

A group of friends who grew up in a North Texas city during the 1940s was reminiscing about their "all-WASP" childhood. Ralph said, "You know, I never knew a Mexican American when I was growing up; never talked to one except for the man who sold tamales from a cart on the street. But I know there had to be a Mexican American community somewhere." Others agreed that this was a common experience. Andrea said, "I never had any African American friends either. Of course, that's easier to understand, with the severe segregation and all. The only African Americans I knew were the cleaning women who came to our home sometimes."

WHAT ABOUT EQUAL OPPORTUNITY LAWS?

Because the melting-pot approach did not provide equal opportunities for people of color and women, the legal approach was introduced by government in the late 1960s. First came the Civil Rights Act that established Equal Employment Opportunity (EEO). Later came an executive order establishing AA. EEO strengthens the individual employee's *rights* to equal opportunity and better jobs, but the employee must take action to complain about unfairness. AA requires employers to take action to bring in under-represented groups of people into better jobs. This increases the chances for a minority employee to *actually get* one of those jobs—without having to file a complaint.

Where people of color and women formerly faced brick walls, doors to opportunity appeared, so this legal approach has been more effective for their upward mobility than the melting-pot approach. Although most business leaders agree that the equal opportunity approach has been generally beneficial, most people don't understand it well. Euro-American men tend to resent it, and many minorities and women don't know why they need it. How did it all come about and what does it mean?

Equal Employment Opportunity: Good But Not Enough

Businesses with more than 15 employees are subject to EEO laws. EEO was an important step forward for people of color and women, because people who are discriminated against can complain to their employers, based on EEOC guidelines. If an employer doesn't satisfy a complaint, the employee can go directly to a regional EEOC office and file a complaint there. If the employee can get other employees to join the complaint, it may become a class action. And if the EEOC cannot get the employer to resolve the discriminatory issue, the employees may be able to file a class action lawsuit. The courts then decide the matter.

> *In 1964, Title VII of the Civil Rights Act established the Equal Employment Opportunity Commission (EEOC) to define and enforce acceptable employment policies and practices, especially as they affect minorities and women.*

The advantage of EEO law is that it gives an employee a direct way to deal with job discrimination. The disadvantage is that it is extremely difficult for an individual to prove discrimination. Those who go outside the company to complain are usually branded as troublemakers and blackballed throughout the industry. Although such retaliation is illegal, it is almost impossible to prove when it's handled by word of mouth and never put in writing. Individuals who pursue this route usually find their career progress put on hold for years. Often they must change occupations or industries and start over.

In 1991, an amendment to the Civil Rights Act increased the money damages that employees can receive if they prove discrimination occurred. Before, they could only recover lost back pay with interest. Now, they can receive money for compensatory and punitive damages—if they can prove that they were subjected to malicious, illegal behavior that resulted in undue stress. Still, the problem is in the proving.

Affirmative Action: A Major Impact

AA is a legal attempt to open up equal opportunity for three categories of women and minorities:

1. **Students** trying to get into public colleges and universities
2. **Contractors** trying to win bids from government agencies
3. **Employees** trying to get hired and promoted by corporations

We'll focus on AA for corporate employees.

Because EEO alone does not have a significant impact on the upward mobility of minorities and women, AA was enacted. AA law is not so obvious as EEO to individual employees.

The average employee will never meet with an AA official and never file an AA complaint. That's because AA works in the background, normally with a human resources administrator, and at times with the top management team, developing an AA program that's approved by an officer from the Labor Department's Office of Federal Contract Compliance Programs (OFCCP). The compliance officer may periodically review the company's progress toward the diversity goals it has set in its AA program.

That's why individual employees usually don't know that the higher-level job opportunities they found were open to them only because of the company's AA plans and goals.

But what exactly is AA and how does it work? Beginning in 1967, a series of executive orders signed by then-President Johnson empowered AA by

- requiring AA plans from firms doing business with the federal government
- randomly and periodically monitoring such firms for compliance with plans
- cutting off the federal contracts for firms that don't comply

Specifically, all federal government contracts include provisions that prohibit employment discrimination because of race, color, religion, national origin, or sex. Any business that enters into federal contracts of more than $50,000 per year must develop an AA plan for hiring and promoting "under-utilized" minorities, setting goals and time targets, and periodically filing progress reports.

Adequate representation of minorities and women at all job levels usually relates to their proportions in the available workforce. This focus on overall numbers, proportions, and representations takes the pressure off the individual minority person who is striving for an opportunity.

The individual does not have to prove discrimination. Instead, discriminatory results are implied when, for example, 40 percent of the available workforce of actual employees are women, but only 5 percent are managers. The employer is then expected to set reasonable short- and long-term goals, over a period of several years, to increase the proportion of women in the better-paying managerial, professional, and technical jobs.

AFFIRMATIVE ACTION PRINCIPLES

The bipartisan government body, Commission on Civil Rights, issued the updated statement of principles, "Affirmative Action in the 1980s," which defines six principles.

Principle #1: The AA Problem–Remedy Approach Is Necessary

The first AA principle is that discrimination is an entrenched problem that won't be resolved without the AA remedy. It is such a problem that prior to AA few women or persons of color pursued education and training for higher-level occupations because they could see their investment would not pay off. There would be no jobs open to them, even if they became well qualified.

Principle #2: Colorblind Remedies Don't Work

The second principle is that discrimination is a self-perpetuating process that colorblind laws have not been able to change. Discrimination will never end without AA to break the cycle and create new, more equitable processes when these factors are present:

- a history of widespread prejudice
- conditions of inequality with Euro-American males
- resulting barriers that have *not* been removed by measures that are colorblind and gender-neutral—that is, by measures that ignore ethnicity and gender

The main point is that under such conditions as we still have in the United States, remedies for discrimination that insist on *colorblindness* or *gender neutrality* are not sufficient. The only effective remedy to the problem is a type of AA that responds to discrimination as a self-sustaining process and sets specific hiring and promotion goals for dismantling it. The commission went on to respond to the major criticisms of AA concerning hiring quotas, lower standards, the stigma of AA hiring, and claims of reverse discrimination.

Principle #3: Hiring Quotas Are Illegal

Quotas cannot be imposed on an employer by normal AA law. It is illegal for the government to demand hiring quotas of any private employer. This means that companies set their own numerical goals, which are then approved by a federal contract compliance officer. The goals are not quotas because they are flexible and approximate. If a company doesn't meet its diversity goals, it's not penalized as long as management can show they're making a good-faith effort to create a diverse workforce. AA programs and goals will end when all groups are reasonably represented at all levels of the company.

Why do most people believe that AA imposes quotas? First, people who politically oppose AA love to refer to quotas because most people consider them unfair. Quotas imply a company must hire anyone from a minority group, even the unqualified—obviously a poor practice and unfair. Second, some companies *do* impose their own quotas because they've neglected their AA program and face a sudden urgency to make up for lost time. This is poor diversity management in the extreme.

Finally, in extremely rare cases of deeply entrenched discrimination that's completely impervious to change—such as the Birmingham Fire Department—minority employees may sue. A judge *may* rule that the nature and extent of the discriminatory problem is so entrenched that the court must set quotas in order to bring about change. This occurs through the court system, not the OFCCP, and is not how the normal AA process works.

Principle #4: Affirmative Action Never Dictates Lower Standards

Nothing in the law calls for lowering valid standards. Companies that don't use long-range planning for recruiting, hiring, and training minorities may find themselves making little progress toward a diversified workforce. Sometimes, when a federal review is looming, such companies voluntarily set their own quotas and then lower their hiring or promotion standards in order to meet their own quotas. But the government does not require this sort of crisis management and does not condone it.

On the other hand, AA plans often require companies to examine their standards, and if standards cannot be shown to be related to successful performance, they must be discarded. Certain tests or requirements may be irrelevant to job success. They may simply measure the Euro-American males' way of thinking and performing. They may not even do that, but are simply some sort of screening device with little job relevance.

The use of such invalid tests and standards may deny opportunities to some people for reasons unrelated to merit. In situations where the use of valid standards serves to exclude women and minorities, civil rights law does *not* require the selection of unqualified minorities and women. It does, however, encourage the following:

- restructuring of jobs
- development of new standards that are equally related to successful performance but do not exclude
- development of training programs that prepare the excluded to meet valid standards

Within a few years of the passage of the EEO and AA laws, there was a significant increase in the enrollment of women and persons of color in college, university, and advanced vocational programs that would qualify them for the higher-level jobs that companies were now willing to offer them. Sometimes, it took class action suits to get companies to open up their own advanced training programs, but gradually most large companies made some progress.

Principle #5: "Affirmative Action Stigma" Is Manageable

The Civil Rights Commission addressed the charge that AA further stigmatizes minorities and women when, for example, people adopt the attitude that an African American gained her position because of AA rather than because of merit. Such a woman has difficulty gaining respect and credibility. Often, the problem is actually the faulty implementation of AA plans. For example, a woman may be placed as a "token" in a situation where she faces open hostility or lack of basic support. When the resulting isolation or failure causes her to quit or be removed, the employer may cite this as the reason for not promoting other women.

Company leaders set the tone by their attitudes toward diverse employees. When they signal respect, trust, and support, others are unlikely to devalue minority capabilities. Even when leadership support is grudging, many minorities and women say that an opportunity with stigma is better than no opportunity at all, which is what they had before AA. To them, throwing out AA means throwing out opportunity. They say that until some proven alternative to AA comes along, the stigmatization argument is invalid.

Principle #6: Affirmative Action Is Not Reverse Discrimination

The remedial use of goals, timetables, and setting aside a certain percentage of government contracts to go to minorities and women in order to bring about workplace equity for all ethnic groups has become part of international law. In 1969, the United Nations treaty called *Declaration of All Forms of Racial Discrimination* became international law. The treaty is clear about measures designed to bring ethnic groups into the mainstream. It says that *AA measures shall not be considered discrimination or reverse discrimination.*

The only qualification regarding such measures is that they be removed as soon as they are no longer required. By 1984, 107 nations had ratified it—more than for any other treaty that has emerged from the U.N., but the United States Senate has never seriously debated nor ratified it.

A similar U.N. treaty calling for the same rights for women was passed in 1979—the *Convention on the Elimination of All Forms of Discrimination Against Women.* It calls for nations to "embody the principle of equality of men and women in their national constitution or other appropriate legislation." Because Congress also refuses to act on this U.N. treaty, the United States is the only industrialized democracy that has not ratified it.

Strong Affirmative Action Programs

The major problems of AA, such as the glass ceiling, backlash, and stigma, have already been mentioned, but the bottom line is: AA has been the most powerful tool society has ever used to open doors of opportunity where formerly there were brick walls blocking the entry of people of color and women into upwardly mobile career paths. Because of it, the United States has more women managers than any country in the world—and people no longer believe that an African American man or a Latino American woman could not possibly succeed as a manager in a Fortune 500 company.

Yet by 2004, only a handful of women and minorities had worked their way up to CEO of such a company. About 95 percent of top managers are still Euro-American men and they're paid 25 percent more than minorities and women at every level, including vice presidents.

That means we still need strong AA programs in corporations. If we as a culture want to complete our path toward equal opportunity for all, we must retain the best of AA and build on it by creating multicultural company climates that are welcoming to minorities and women.

SELF-TEST

Indicate the best answers to the following 6 multiple-choice questions.

1. A key aspect of traditional melting-pot assimilation is:
    A. valuing diversity
    B. eliminating cultural differences through assimilation and absorption into the mainstream culture
    C. empowering all groups
    D. adaptation as a two-way shared street

2. The best way for an organization to meet a diverse employee's needs is to:
    A. create an inclusive corporate culture
    B. assimilate all new employees
    C. treat employees as one big happy family
    D. hold special "cultural recognition days"

3. The major barrier facing the upward mobility of minorities in today's corporations is:
    A. the glass ceiling
    B. discriminatory hiring procedures
    C. closed recruiting practices
    D. language differences

4. AA is legally empowered through:
    A. requiring AA plans from firms doing business with the federal government
    B. monitoring such firms for compliance with plans
    C. cutting off the federal contracts for firms that don't comply
    D. all of the above

5. Who develops AA plans?
    A. the company
    B. the OFCCP

    C. federal reviewers

    D. the company in conjunction with local minority groups

6. The major problem of AA is:

    A. companies are not really required to observe it

    B. it has generated widespread resentment and backlash

    C. it has never opened many doors for minorities

    D. it changes the corporate culture

SELF-TEST FEEDBACK

Each correct answer is worth 15 points. If you score less than 70 points, you should review the materials and re-take the Self-Test.

1. A key aspect of traditional melting-pot assimilation is:

    A. No, valuing diversity is a recent approach

    B. Yes, eliminating cultural differences through assimilation and absorption into the mainstream culture is the best answer

    C. No, empowering all groups is not an aspect

    D. No, adaptation as a two-way shared street is not an aspect

2. The best way for an organization to meet a diverse employee's needs is to:

    A. Yes, create an inclusive corporate culture is the best answer

    B. No, assimilating all new employees is a melting-pot approach

    C. No, treating employees as one big happy family is a melting-pot slogan

    D. No, holding special "cultural recognition days" is great, but superficial

3. The major barrier facing the upward mobility of minorities in today's corporations is:

    A. Yes, the glass ceiling

    B. No, although a factor is discriminatory hiring procedures

    C. No, although a factor is closed recruiting practices

    D. No, although a factor can be language differences

4. AA is legally empowered through:

    A. No, although requiring AA plans from firms doing business with the federal government is a factor

    B. No, although monitoring such firms for compliance to plans is a factor

    C. No, although firms that don't comply can lose their federal contracts

    D. Yes, all of the above is the best answer

5. Who develops AA plans?

   A. Yes, the company is the answer

   B. No, the OFCCP only approves and monitor

   C. No. federal reviewers only monitor

   D. No, the company does not have to bring in local minority groups to develop the plan, although they can consult them

6. The major problem of AA is:

   A. No, companies are required to observe it

   B. Yes, the best answer is it has generated widespread resentment and backlash

   C. No, in fact it has opened many doors for minorities

   D. No, change in the corporate culture is a by-product of AA but not a major problem

WHAT IS THE VALUING DIVERSITY APPROACH?

During the 1970s, when companies were opening new doors to diverse persons in order to meet EEO/AA requirements, most of them were still using the melting-pot approach, expecting everyone to adapt to their Euro-American male corporate cultures. Minorities and women had difficulty fitting in. Even those who seemed to fit in didn't like the price it exacted; that is, giving up important aspects of their own culture and personality. Company leaders, human resource executives, and corporate consultants looked for ways to encourage productive work relationships and to stem turnover rates of diverse employees. Meeting these needs led to the valuing diversity approach.

Valuing diversity is based on moving beyond a tolerance of diverse others to an appreciation of what they have to offer. It involves seeing a diverse workforce as a treasure trove of valuable opportunities for innovation, networking, marketing savvy, and similar assets. The approach primarily involves a shift in beliefs and attitudes away from "we're all alike (or should be)" to "we're each unique and that's the source of our greatness."

The valuing diversity approach focuses primarily on educating people through experiential and informational seminars to make appropriate attitude shifts. It emerged in the 1980s and is still a part of managing diversity.

Self-Analysis 4.1	Being Tolerated and Being Appreciated

Purpose: To experience the difference between tolerance and appreciation.

Step 1   Being tolerated

    A. Think of a time when you felt tolerated. Write a few words about it.

    B. How did it feel to be merely tolerated? Write a few words about your feelings.

    C. How did feeling tolerated affect your relationship with the tolerant person(s)?

Step 2   Being appreciated

    A. Think of a time when you felt appreciated. Write a few words about it.

    B. How did it feel to be truly appreciated? Did you feel respected? Write a few words about your feelings.

    C. How did feeling appreciated affect your relationship with the appreciative person(s)?

WHAT IS THE INCLUSIVE, MULTICULTURAL APPROACH?

Beyond the melting-pot myth, the legal approach, and even the valuing diversity approach is a more action-oriented approach that is called the inclusive, multicultural approach. It is based on valuing diversity and goes farther to find ways to shift the corporate culture itself, to make it more inclusive and therefore multicultural. The goal is to create a corporate culture that supports and nurtures all types of employees. Snapshot 4.1 is a summary of how corporations have managed diversity through the years.

The inclusive approach is a diversity-within-unity approach. Unity is provided through a strong corporate culture that focuses on the best niche for the organization to fill and on the purpose of the organization, as well as on valuing diversity (see Snapshot 4.2). And diversity is provided for through a strong emphasis on appreciating each individual—respecting the uniqueness of every employee, including her or his values, lifestyle, and cultural heritage. Above all, the multicultural approach is an inclusive approach. No one is excluded simply because he or she was not born a member of the in-group—or has changed physically in ways that don't affect basic job performance.

SNAPSHOT 4.1   Evolution of managing diversity.

Approach: assimilation →legal   →valuing diversity   →multicultural

Basis: melting-pot myth→EEO/AA→differences as assets→inclusive corporate cultures

SNAPSHOT 4.2   Inclusive strategies that overcome barriers to inclusion.

Inclusive Strategies	Barriers to Inclusion
Personal Level	
Become aware of prejudice and other barriers to valuing diversity	Stereotypes, prejudices
Learn about other cultures and groups	Past experiences and influences
Serve as an example, walk the talk	Stereotyped expectations and perceptions
Participate in managing diversity	Feelings that tend to separate, divide
Interpersonal Level	
Facilitate communication and interactions in ways that value diversity	Cultural differences
Encourage participation	Group differences
Share your perspective	Myths
Facilitate unique contributions	Relationship patterns based on exclusion
Resolve conflicts in ways that value diversity	
Accept responsibility for developing common ground	
Organizational Level	
All employees have access to networks and focus groups	Individuals who get away with discriminating and excluding
All employees take a proactive role in managing diversity and creating a more diverse workplace culture	A culture that values or allows exclusion
All employees are included in the inner circle that contributes to the bottom-line success of the company	Work structures, policies, and practices that discriminate and exclude
All employees give feedback to teams and management	
All employees are encouraged to contribute to change	

Leaders encourage the organization to adapt in ways that support all types of employees, and they help all employees become oriented to the organization, a two-way street. Corporate leaders make certain the organization's values and norms accommodate a wide range of workers. They make sure that everyone has a chance to build multicultural skills and to update and refine them continually.

This inclusive approach aims to support and empower all employees in learning, stretching, and moving up because leaders pay attention to this issue at the individual, interpersonal, and organizational levels. Leaders develop strategies to bring all employees into the "inner circle" and remove barriers to inclusion. The multicultural approach is also about making sure that the systems and practices of the organization support employee empowerment through natural evolvement, so that stop-and-go types of AA programs are unnecessary. It's a comprehensive managerial process for developing an environment that works for all employees. Empowering the total workforce is achieved through such strategies as pushing decision making down to lower levels, organizing self-managing work teams, providing adequate education, and supporting career development.

The inclusive, multicultural approach to diversity management is not about Euro-American males managing women and minorities, nor is it about focusing on women and minorities to the exclusion of Euro-American men. It's about all managers empowering whoever is in their workforce.

- This inclusive approach focuses on understanding individuals and valuing the cultural background they came from.
- It's about respecting that heritage without assuming that a particular individual adheres to all aspects of the heritage.
- It's about asking questions in a sensitive, respectful manner based on your expanded knowledge and awareness of cultural differences.

This approach views diverse employees as persons who can enrich the work team or organization, who can interact with others to create innovative sparks, entrepreneurial genius, and total-quality performance.

Key Aspects of a Multicultural Approach

The most important activities for building a multicultural approach are:

- Modify the corporate culture toward a multiculture that incorporates the values and customs of all of the subcultures—essential foundation for all other changes.
- Include all employees in bottom-line efforts.
- Build on equal opportunity and AA principles.
- Adapt corporate systems and practices that respect members of all subcultures.
- Build consensus for changing to an inclusive culture.

Elements of an Inclusive Corporate Culture

Changing the corporate culture is most effective when top management makes a commitment to shifting the culture in ways that accommodate, motivate, and empower all employees. The ultimate goal is for everyone to grow and develop, to be effective and productive, to interact to create a synergy that sparks innovation and commitment. But any person anywhere in the organization can have an influence on change. Wherever you are on your career path, you can accept a leadership role in this kind of change.

The most powerful change starts in the basic cultural elements:

- *values* that build respect for all kinds of persons and that build trust—a high value for diversity
- *heroines and heroes*, role models of success from all the diverse groups
- *stories*, myths, and legends about diverse heroes and heroines and new ways of succeeding in an inclusive organization
- *rituals*, ways of doing things and ways of interacting with each other, that expand to include the ways typical of all groups
- *ceremonies* that are meaningful to people of all groups, that incorporate the customs of all groups, that recognize people from all groups
- *symbols* and slogans that touch people from all groups and communicate an inclusive worldview

Culture change is the basis for all other organizational change. Lasting change must come from inside the organization—and from the foundation of core beliefs and values. Role modeling and persuasion are the best methods of leading change, while coercion doesn't really work at all. When key leaders in all areas and at all levels become committed to change, this critical mass will bring along most other employees in its wake.

The Freedom to Be Authentic

Every person and every human culture needs to express who they are. The strong desire of many former communist countries and ethnic groups to claim a separate culture reflects this universal need. When groups unite to achieve certain common purposes, they can greatly increase their power. But when they can't find ways to accommodate cultural differences and blend them into a group strength, they lose their joint power. At the corporate level, such groups may simply lose the opportunity to achieve greater goals, but at the societal level, they may deteriorate into anarchy and bloodshed, as happened during the Los Angeles riots and in Bosnia.

Whether in a national culture or a corporate culture, people are more productive and enthusiastic when have the freedom to express their own values and determine their own lifestyle. The most effective organizations learn how to combine and balance the drive for individual freedom and achievement with the drive for belongingness and group affiliation. And they focus on building and maintaining trust, an essential ingredient.

Free Choice and Cultural Enrichment

A key American strength is our willingness to recognize that diverse members have a desire and a right to self-development, acculturation or integration at their own chosen rate. Diverse groups have a right to an integrated or independent economic base, to social, religious and political institutions, and to political recognition as part of a united country. This has been the American genius for embracing diversity within a common unity.

Asian Americans and Latino Americans still embrace certain basic cultural values and customs—even after three or more generations in the United States.

Creating an inclusive corporate culture means dealing with these cultural realities. The least effective policy an organization can pursue is to insist that members of any group give up cherished beliefs and practices. People always resist such pressure—usually by going underground and engaging in passive-aggressive behavior. Of course, hidden behavior is much more difficult to deal with than open, direct behavior.

Because cultural accommodation is a two-way street, the process is subtle and complex, and trying to force it on any of the parties may create as many problems as it solves. The best approach is to allow people the freedom to assimilate into the mainstream culture and the corporate culture to the extent they desire and to retain their cultural heritage as they see fit. This approach must rest on appreciating differences and respecting each person's cultural heritage and their decisions about what to retain. Cultural change takes time, and a relaxed, accepting attitude allows the shifts to occur with minimal friction.

When ethnic groups retain those distinctive and colorful ways that they treasure, the organization is enriched. All individuals decide those aspects of their ethnic cuisine, art, philosophical and spiritual beliefs, myths, and stories that they want to hold dear and to express. When people are allowed and encouraged to preserve these treasures, they become more interesting and valuable to the whole organization and to the nation. They "prevent drab standardization in a culture dominated by advertising, brand names, malls, and sedative television," to quote Dr. Taylor Cox.

Diversity Training for All

The inclusive, multicultural approach is a relatively new concept for many employees. Training is normally needed at all levels of the organization for positive change to occur. Training usually begins at the top because top management must thoroughly understand the concept and apply it consistently in their own thinking and acting.

Training sessions tend to focus on the ways that people are both alike and different in values, attitudes, behavior styles, ways of thinking, and cultural background. Common goals of the educational programs are for participants to:

- expand their awareness and acceptance of cultural and individual commonalities and differences
- understand the nature and dynamics of cultural and individual differences
- explore their own feelings and attitudes about people they view as "different"
- identify ways that differences might be tapped as workplace assets
- build better work relations with people from all societal groups

This approach leads people to appreciate the value, richness, and creativity that can flow from a diverse workforce. It focuses on helping everyone better understand some key commonalities and differences among employees from various groups and how differences can be valuable to the organization. It exhibits real concern and commitment to providing a corporate culture where people from all groups can thrive. When employees thrive, the company tends to thrive.

Self-Analysis 4.2   A Question of Change

Purpose: To stimulate thinking about ways to make your workplace more supportive of all employees.

Record your responses and any additional insights, including further questions, that could lead to creative solutions for your particular organization, perhaps for all organizations.

Step 1   **Consider the viewpoints of all stakeholders.** Who are the stakeholders that have widely varying viewpoints in your organization? Examples might be sales employees, women in the accounting department, African American employees, Euro-American managers.

   A. List the stakeholders, each on a separate page.

Self-Analysis 4.2 A Question of Change *continued*

       B. Under each stakeholder, write a one-line statement that you think represents that group's general viewpoint.

       C. Under each one-liner, list the major corporate changes you think people in that group might want.

Step 2   **Develop a concept of culture.** Imagine that everyone in the organization agreed that the underlying problem of prejudice and inequity is rooted in the current corporate culture. What effect might this have?

Step 3   **Identify barriers to mutual respect and trust.** If you and other key people conducted a long, hard, critical examination of "why we haven't been able or willing to value and appreciate our diversity," what barriers do you think you would find?

Step 4   **Take responsibility for personal growth.** Imagine that most of the employees worked deeply with their beliefs and feelings about prejudice and diversity? Would this eliminate most of the barriers noted in Step 3? What barriers would remain?

Step 5   **Influence culture change.**

- Would this process be enough to begin some positive change in corporate values, norms, structures, and power? What specific changes might occur? What else would be needed?

- Is there any evidence of overt or subtle paternalism, threats, or punishment in the organization? Be specific.

- Would this process be enough to begin shifting this pattern? How might this evolve? What else would be needed?

- Could this process lead to collaboration based on mutual trust, as peers committed to solving a common problem within a common framework? How might this evolve? What else would be needed?

Self-Analysis 4.3 Beliefs about What Needs Changing

Purpose: To become aware of the role and power of individuals changing their beliefs.

Step 1   How can we become conscious of what needs changing? We might start by examining some core beliefs, attitudes, thoughts, feelings, decisions, and day-to-day action choices. Examine this core belief:

(continued)

Self-Analysis 4.3   **Beliefs about What Needs Changing**   *continued*

Belief #1: America is the great melting pot. If African Americans can't succeed in business, it's not because Euro-American managers and coworkers don't welcome them. It's because they don't have what it takes to succeed.

Based on this belief, what needs to be done in the workplace? In society in general? What ideas come to mind? Write about them here.

Step 2   Now think about this alternate core belief:

Belief #2: American culture, systems, institutions, and beliefs are what block African Americans from succeeding in business. The stereotypes, prejudice, institutionalized discrimination, and personal discrimination by Euro-Americans create the problem.

Based on this alternate belief, what needs to be done in the workplace? In society in general? What ideas come to mind? Record them.

Step 3   Record your insights regarding the difference a belief makes.

WHAT CAN I DO TO IMPLEMENT THE MULTICULTURAL APPROACH?

Your role in implementing a multicultural approach is to develop some key leadership traits, get to know people as individuals, include everyone in the inner circle, give feedback sensitively, and set the stage for the creativity the diversity can trigger.

Strategy #1: Develop Key Leadership Traits

Unlike people who stereotype, leaders who value differences tend to:

- study reliable sources of information about the characteristics of various cultural groups—and base their beliefs on valid data
- acknowledge that people within an ethnic group vary and that they have many voices and many individual styles and patterns
- resist the tendency to evaluate differences
- avoid negative connotations

A multicultural approach enhances acceptance, tolerance, and understanding of differences.

Strategy #2: Learn the Unique Needs and Talents of Each Person

Take time to get to know each employee as well as his or her cultural group. The more you learn about each person, the better you will be able to collaborate with that person as an individual and as part of a work team. What you don't know may keep you from doing your own job effectively. Here are some suggestions that may help.

Avoid appearance stereotypes.   Don't assume race or ethnicity from appearance alone. Many Latinos have Asian features, and many Blacks have Latino, Jamaican, or other origins and strongly distinguish themselves from African Americans. Bi-ethnic persons' cultural backgrounds are not easy to determine from appearance only.

Avoid ethnic stereotypes.   Don't assume that all foreign or minority workers are impoverished or deprived. Get to know the background of each one.

Put emotions in perspective.   Don't take emotional outbursts personally. Ask, are emotional outbursts a normal way of responding to the situation in that person's culture? Remember, also, that newcomers often experience a time of frustration and anger during the adaptation phase.

Discover other people's values.   Watch how they behave. When someone behaves consistently in similar circumstances, it suggests a value at work.

Clarify which values apply in each situation.   Identify precisely which value or values are at play in a given situation. It is one thing to know that a person values family ties more than you do. It is more difficult to recognize that the family ties value is at stake when that person is absent from work for what would seem like a trivial family matter to you. Your tendency may be to judge by your standards for consistent attendance at work rather than by his standards of family loyalty.

Apply employee values to work enhancement.   Look for the positive side of the other person's values—not only how that value is positive in the other's culture, but also how that same value could be applied in ways that are consistent with organization values and objectives. Apply the value to the job at hand. How can you bring the person's value into play so that it helps achieve job objectives? For example, when you need teamwork to accomplish something previously done by individuals, the person from a tightly woven culture is likely to rise to the occasion.

Apply relevant training.   Determine each new employee's knowledge of the system and train each one accordingly. Has this employee faced the complexities of the U.S. corporate system before? You may need to train some employees in very basic ways.

Determine each employee's primary thinking pattern.   If you see that abstract and hypothetical thinking is not familiar to them, try using examples, stories, and hands-on experience.

Determine each employee's primary learning pattern.   Be patient while employees are in the process of gaining necessary knowledge and experience. You may have to answer more questions, even very basic ones, than you would with Euro-American male employees.

Reinforce successful new behavior.   Choose reinforcers, recognition, and rewards that the recipients value as such. Give them in a way that is in line with that person's values.

Understand cultural style differences.   For example, learn to accept compliments gracefully and without suspicion; take them in stride. Some cultures use compliments and flattery as a normal, polite way of interacting.

Strategy #3: Include Everyone in the Inner Circle

You must bring all of the employees you can into the inner circle and its key learning loops if you want the inclusive, multicultural approach to succeed. Ask, who is a part of the inner circle and who is left out? If bottom-line success is your most important priority, it makes sense to get all of the employees working toward it. Learning how to do this is a key managing-diversity skill. Here are some suggestions:

- Specify the skills and capabilities that are required to work in the inner circle and to contribute to the company's bottom line.
- Get to know all of the employees, their weaknesses and strengths.
- Develop strategies to overcome the obstacles that stand in the way, to bridge the gaps between necessary skills and capabilities and those the employee now has.
- Provide them with required knowledge and skills.

Give all employees quality treatment. Savvy leaders understand how to give all employees quality treatment, another key managing-diversity principle. Quality treatment differs somewhat for each employee. Base your treatment on a connection with each person's humanity and individuality—and on your understanding of the requirements of the work.

Here are some general actions and attitudes that constitute quality treatment:

- believe in each employee and communicate that belief
- explicitly communicate high standards and high expectations
- promote a respect for diversity
- show each person that he or she is important to you and the organization
- provide support to *all* employees
- value people through your procedures and practices
- teach people the basis of success in the organization, including the unwritten rules; be an effective mentor
- lead people to engage in learning loops of continuous learning for improvement—and bring them into that inner circle that is continuously learning to contribute more to the bottom line

Strategy #4: Give Feedback Sensitively

People from tightly woven cultures often have some difficulty giving and getting feedback in the direct style used in most organizations and by most U.S. managers and workers. Many Asians and Middle Easterners have been taught never to confront others directly. And other European groups, such as the British, tend to be subtler when communicating about performance.

In the United States, feedback is a standard part of performance assessment and an integral part of management and creative collaboration. Your style can either respect or violate the values of harmony and consensus as practiced in some other cultures. Here are some suggestions for giving feedback sensitively.

Choose the right time and place.   What is culturally appropriate for giving feedback to this employee? Shall it be in a formal or informal session? Directly or using a third party? In private or in a group? Oral or written or both?

Clarify your commitment.   Stress the results you are working toward and the importance of the process of asking for feedback, giving feedback in the spirit of improvement, and receiving it as needed information.

Specifically describe behavior.   Tell the other person what you have seen or understand them to have said or done. Keep in mind possible cultural differences that may affect behavior.

Give positive acknowledgment.   Describe what stands out for you or excites you about what the other person did or said.

Give supporting information.   Share information, data, or facts that you have that pertain to what the other person has done.

Give an I-message.   Openly and frankly share your opinions and preferences as your own. Avoid talking in terms of absolute rights and wrongs.

Open up possibilities.   Share ideas and suggestions you have for the other's work or performance.

Share your experience.   Explain your experiences with activities or work similar to the recipient's, barriers or problems you encountered, and ways to solve them. Avoid a know-it-all or self-righteous attitude.

Offer clear expectations.   Be clear about what you mutually agreed upon in the past or are now asking the other person to do.

Use creative questioning.   Raise questions that clarify the content or direction of the recipient's performance. Questioning can bring out cultural differences.

Give support.   Offer support, resources, and information to enable the other person to fulfill her or his agreements and meet your expectations.

Summarize.   Recognize what each of you has contributed during and after this feedback session.

Ask for feedback.   Get feedback on how the other person has received your feedback. Listen for clues about cultural or individual differences that may affect the situation.

Giving feedback about job performance is crucial to employees' success and can help to build trust or destroy it. Therefore, becoming aware of cultural differences concerning evaluation, appraisal, and criticism is crucial to your success as a leader.

Strategy #5: Set the Stage for Creativity

A more diverse workforce is a more innovative workforce. The idea pool is naturally more varied and therefore larger. To tap this potential, leaders must set the stage for creativity to occur.

Research indicates that the following actions foster creativity in diverse groups:

- Create a nonjudgmental environment that encourages people to risk exploration without having to produce a "winner" every time.
- Avoid judgmental words such as good, bad, better, best, mistake—words that kill creativity.
- Cultivate an appreciation of bizarre questions and ideas without negatively labeling them as weird or crazy.
- Produce a noncompetitive atmosphere that focuses on performance and end results, rather than on the how-tos of creative discovery.
- Foster a cooperative spirit that encourages people to learn from each other and delight in each others' success.
- Provide reasonable, organic structure and discipline to bring out creativity.
- Have fun and encourage people to get carried away by the sheer fun of creating something.
- Support employees in ways that allow them to release their anxieties about whether their creation is good enough.

Self-Analysis 4.4 | Who's in the Inner Circle?

Purpose: To get a clear picture of insiders and outsiders in your organization.

Step 1 Think of the organization where you work. Think about which employees are involved in continuous improvement and continuous learning—in learning loops that directly affect the success of the organization, its bottom-line results. In other words, think about which employees are included in the inner circle.

Step 2 Place symbols, such as triangles or circles, inside the inner circle that represent employees you know. You might use a different symbol, incorporating colored ink or pencil, for each employee—or a different symbol for each work team, unit, or department that's in the inner circle.

Step 3 Which employees are not included in the inner circle? They may be in learning loops, but not those that make a real difference. Draw symbols for those employees in the area outside the inner circle.

Step 4 What does this picture say to you about your organization?
  - About its effectiveness in managing diversity?
  - About its effectiveness in utilizing all its human resources?
  - About its effectiveness in developing all of its employees' potential for contribution?

FINAL SELF-TEST

Indicate the best answers to the following 6 multiple-choice questions.

1. A major business advantage of the multicultural approach is:

   A. to attract and retain the best available human talent

   B. to achieve higher creativity and innovation

   C. to gain and keep minority market share

   D. all of the above

2. A key aspect of the multicultural approach is:

   A. focusing on women and minorities

   B. valuing diversity and acculturation

   C. getting serious about AA

   D. all of the above

3. A key aspect of the inclusive approach is to:

   A. set hiring quotas for minorities

   B. adapt corporate systems and practices to reflect a valuing-diversity culture

   C. show all new people the company way of doing things

   D. phase out the AA program

4. Training programs in inclusive corporations ideally focus on:

   A. training Euro-American males to adopt a multicultural approach

   B. ongoing diversity training for all employees

   C. success and skills training for minorities and women

   D. a diversity training retreat for all employees

5. The most basic change that must take place for a traditional organization to accommodate diverse employees is in:

   A. its culture

   B. its hiring practices

   C. its systems and practices

   D. its training program

6. In order to value diversity, companies must focus on:

   A. the ideals of tolerance for fellow workers

   B. building mutual respect and appreciation

   C. building on the melting pot ideal

   D. holding onto traditional corporate values

FINAL SELF-TEST FEEDBACK

Each correct answer is worth 15 points. If you score less than 70 points, you should review the materials and re-take the Final Self-Test.

1. A major business advantage of the multicultural approach is:

   A. No, although an advantage is to attract and retain the best available human talent

   B. No, although an advantage is to achieve higher creativity and innovation

   C. No, although an advantage is to gain and keep minority market share

   D. Yes, all of the above is the best answer

2. A key aspect of the multicultural approach is:

   A. No, the focus is not just on women and minorities

   B. Yes, valuing diversity and acculturation is the best answer

   C. No, getting serious about AA is not a key aspect, although building on the current AA program is part of it

   D. No, all of the above is not the best answer

3. A key aspect of the inclusive approach is to:

   A. No, setting hiring quotas for minorities is nearly always bad policy

   B. Yes, adapting corporate systems and practices to reflect a valuing-diversity culture is the best answer

   C. No, showing all new people the company way of doing things is a melting-pot approach

   D. No, phasing out the AA program is premature and illegal

4. Training programs in inclusive corporations ideally focus on:

   A. No, although a factor is training Euro-American males to adopt a multicultural approach

   B. Yes, ongoing diversity training for all employees

   C. No, although a factor is success and skills training for minorities and women

   D. No, although a part of it could be a diversity training retreat for all employees

5. The most basic change that must take place for a traditional organization to accommodate diverse employees is in:

   A. Yes, its culture is the best answer because culture is the root of all permanent ongoing change

   B. No, although its hiring practices are a factor

   C. No, although its systems and practices are factors

   D. No, although its training program is a factor

6. In order to value diversity, companies must focus on:

   A. No, tolerance for fellow workers is insufficient

   B. Yes, building mutual respect and appreciation is the best answer

   C. No, forget the melting pot, which never was ideal

   D. No, holding onto traditional corporate values means continuing to exclude people from many groups

THE BOTTOM LINE

Managing diversity presents some interesting challenges. More importantly, managing diversity offers opportunities for all of us to grow, personally and collectively, to learn how to connect with each other in powerful new ways, and to create a synergy that sparks innovation and accelerates human knowledge and achievement.

Chapter Review

1. The Great Melting Pot works fine for Euro-American men but women and people of color never "melted in." They were marginalized.

2. The 1964 Civil Rights Act created the EEOC, but we needed Affirmative Action requiring businesses to set goals for hiring and promoting minorities. Six AA principles refute the Melting Pot myth and the backlash against AA:

   ■ The AA problem–remedy approach is essential to equal opportunity.

   ■ Colorblind remedies don't promote equal opportunity. We must notice gender and ethnicity in order to overcome discriminatory practices.

   ■ Hiring quotas are illegal; companies set long-term goals and target dates.

   ■ AA never dictates lower standards for hiring and promoting minorities.

   ■ The stigma of being an "AA hire" is regrettable but better than not being hired or promoted at all.

   ■ AA is not reverse discrimination; it is a mild attempt to bring more balance to a workplace of inequitable power and privilege.

3. The valuing diversity approach goes beyond tolerance of diverse others to an appreciation of what they have to offer.

4. The goal of the inclusive, multicultural approach is to create a corporate culture that supports and nurtures all types of employees.

5. Strategies to implement a multicultural approach include:

   ■ develop key leadership traits

   ■ learn the unique needs and talents of each person

   ■ include everyone in the inner circle

   ■ give feedback sensitively

   ■ set the stage for creativity

Men and Women Working Together

5

CHAPTER OBJECTIVES

- Identify male–female myths and stereotypes.

- Understand how men and women grow up with different worldviews and communication styles.

- Describe cultural stereotypes that affect gender roles and expectations, how these are dramatically changing, and men's reactions to the changes.

- Recognize women's cultural barriers to workplace success.

- Know how to recognize, handle, and prevent sexual harassment.

- Identify strategies for overcoming gender barriers.

CHAPTER OVERVIEW

About half of the people you work with are likely to be of the opposite gender. After all, men make up about 55 percent of the U.S. workplace, while women are 45 percent. Yet, we know from research that men and women face quite different expectations and experiences when they enter the workplace. This is because society views men and women as having quite different traits and roles. That means that boys and girls grow up in different worlds—parallel but different. We raise boys and girls differently, so they naturally develop different ways of viewing the world and different methods of communicating about their worlds. You want to build powerful relationships at work—and today that means learning to bridge this gender gap.

On the other hand, no man or woman buys into the total "average package" of beliefs and behaviors typical of his or her gender. Every person has a masculine and a feminine side, and of course, no one person expresses all of the values and patterns discussed here. If you are tempted to use this gender information to form new stereotypes, stop yourself. Remember to stay open and flexible as you interact with each person. Deal with the unique individual, bringing into play your understanding of his or her background.

After reading this chapter, you will have many insights into typical differences in the ways people view men and women. You will know what it is like to be a man or a woman in the American culture and workplace—from the stereotypes they encounter, to the past events most important to their current situation, to the values, customs, and issues most important to them. You will be able to form powerful working relationships with both men and women.

WHAT ARE MAJOR MYTHS AND STEREOTYPES ABOUT MEN AND WOMEN?

Most of the myths and stereotypes about men and women are either false or distorted, partial truths. In fact, most stem from the patriarchal culture typical of most of the world's societies.

Myth #1: The Typical American Family Consists of a Husband with a Career and a Wife Who Stays Home and Takes Care of the Two Children

This myth reflects traditional male–female roles. The woman belongs at home doing housework and raising children, and the man belongs in the workplace earning a living for the family. This pattern was typical from about 1900 to 1960. Now, only about 15 percent of U.S. families fit that description—and even then only temporarily while the children are very young—making the roles more myth than reality.

Myth #2: There Are Only Two Types of Women: Good and Bad

In the past, "good women" were placed on a pedestal, called ladies and treated like little madonnas or dolls, while "bad women" were called sluts or whores. There was not much gray area in between. Women who had reputedly ever had sex outside marriage were bad and the others were good.

This myth, and resulting stereotypes, tend to define women primarily by their sexual relationship to men. It was not until the women's movement of the late 1960s that such stereotypes, along with the resulting double standard for sexual behavior and the accompanying language such as "ladies," were challenged by a widespread group of people. The stereotype is now more subtle and less predominant in the United States than in the past, but it's more pronounced in Latino cultures than the mainstream American culture.

Myth #3: Women's Status in Society Is Equal to Men's

The myth is that since women legally earned voting rights, equal opportunity, and affirmative action, they've gained equal status. However, we know that only 5 percent of top managers in the Fortune 1000 and 11 percent of Congress are women. And women at all corporate levels average 25 percent less pay than men. This tells us that although women have come a long way toward economic and political equality, they still have a long way to go. The types of special efforts that triggered women's progress must continue for women to eventually achieve equal status.

Myth #4: Real Men Are in Control of the Situation

In patriarchal cultures (meaning virtually all of the world's modern cultures), being in control has high value. Men have traditionally been given these types of messages by men in authority: "You're letting things get out of control," "Control your wife," and "You've got to take charge."

This myth implies that men are superior. At home, they should be master of the house; in the workplace, they should be the managers. But more and more American women are expecting to have equal relationships at home and in the workplace. Relationship styles and management styles are changing. The trend is that people are expected to control themselves and take control of their own lives, then come together as basic equals to collaborate on joint projects. Trying to control others is becoming frustrating and counterproductive for men.

Myth #5: Real Men Don't Cry

People in our culture typically tell little boys that "big boys don't cry." Neither are they afraid. They are brave and confident. They may get angry and fight back, but they don't whimper or snivel. In hundreds of little ways, men get the message that they should not be emotional or show their feelings. Most boys learn to hide their feelings. By the time they grow up, many have denied their feelings for so long that they're numb to them, out of touch with them.

Once they're men, it's generally all right to show anger in certain situations, such as to get things done or to defend one's honor. And it's acceptable to show some feelings with one's mate in romantic settings. Otherwise, feelings are to be buttoned up, locked in, and kept contained. And that's the major problem with this stereotype. Unacknowledged and unexpressed feelings don't go away. They build and fester, contributing to stress and its related illnesses.

Myth #6: Women Are Too Emotional and Soft to Be Real Leaders

This is actually a role stereotype based on a false belief. The belief that women are too emotional and soft led to most of the other stereotypes that block women's careers. According to the 1995 Glass Ceiling Commission, these are the beliefs that create the greatest barriers:

- Women are too emotional.
- Women are too passive, too aggressive, not aggressive enough.
- Women aren't tough enough to fill some positions.
- Women can't or won't work long or unusual hours—or relocate.
- Women can't or won't make tough decisions.
- Women can't crunch numbers.
- Women don't want to work.
- Women aren't as committed to careers as men.

Some women do have these traits. However, such traits are primarily learned, they are a matter of style rather than substance, and they can be managed and used to advantage in the workplace.

DO MEN AND WOMEN REALLY GROW UP WITH TWO DIFFERENT WORLDVIEWS?

Women and men are much more alike than not. Most differences are probably more cultural than physical, and individual men and women vary greatly as to their degree of typically masculine or feminine traits. Still, even though girls and boys grow up side by side, they increasingly live in two different worlds. Because we as a culture and as individuals treat boys and girls, men and women, so differently, their experiences and worldviews are dramatically different.

Cultural Socialization of Girls and Boys

We raise boys and girls differently in our culture. They play differently as children. They have different values and experiences as teenagers. Since we are a patriarchal culture, boys gain more respect as they grow into men. As girls grow into women, they have more difficulty being perceived as competent leaders.

Some differences in the ways boys and girls are socialized in the American culture are described next. Read the table in Snapshot 5.1 from the top down, by column, since each column represents a socialization process by gender, not a comparison of types of experiences.

SNAPSHOT 5.1   Process of growing up by gender.

Girls and Women	Boys and Men
Girls experience a less active childhood than boys.	Boys lead a more active childhood, controlling their world with physical actions.
Girls are taught to be reactive more often than proactive.	Boys are taught to be self-sufficient, autonomous, a closed system.
Girls learn to experience lines of power going from women to men; power is gained through men.	Boys learn to ignore their need to be dependent.
Girls learn to think ahead about how people might respond, to "psych out" situations, to be "schemers."	Eventually, males begin to deny they even have dependency needs.
Girls are encouraged to believe that a man's approval is more valuable than a woman's.	Males lose touch with the feelings that accompany dependency needs, then with other feelings.
Teenage girls begin competing with each other for male attention.	Boys and men become task-oriented, compartmentalized, mechanical, and highly rational.
Girls and women learn they're expected to be selfless helpers, not have needs for great space, territorial or psychological.	As a result, men become quite dependent on women as the emotional, nurturant "translators" or bridges between men and family members, men and others.
Women learn to live for and through others, to define themselves in terms of their relationships with others.	

TEENAGE DIFFERENCES

Many of the old stereotypes and socialization patterns are still in place for teenagers today. Peggy Orenstein's research indicates that girls routinely report feeling:

- resignation about the greater power that society grants boys
- resignation about society's acceptance of boys' greater assertiveness and power to disrupt
- pressure to emphasize appearance and minimize brains to win favor
- pressure to acquiesce in second-rate status
- a fear of failure in science and math

Boys and Men: More Respect

As boys grow into men, their time and activities gain respect and tend to be viewed as important, while girls' time and activities are seen as less important. This tendency is tied to the fact that beginning with the Industrial Revolution, men went off to work they got paid for, while women stayed home and did not get paid. In our society, income is seen as an indicator of a person's importance and value. Women are expected to be respectful of men's more important responsibilities. As little boys become adults, they take on the parent role with women, serving as their protectors. Men are thus seen as competent and tend to indulge women. On the other hand, as little girls become women, they retain much of the child role, needing to be protected and indulged, and thus they are seen as less competent than men.

Girls and Women: Lower Status

Many studies have shown that males are considered more competent than females, at least outside the home. Researcher A. Kohn in 1988 asked people to evaluate an article, some copies with a woman's byline and identical copies with a man's byline. The article with the male byline was rated as better by 98 percent of the evaluators.

In his book *Powertalk!* Jerry Eisen describes a study of mixed-group conversations, where 97 percent of interruptions were made by men. There were fewer interruptions when women were speaking with women or when men were speaking with men. In mixed-group studies of who does most of the talking, men talk from 58 percent to 92 percent of the time. Most women are unaware of this type of domination, perceiving that they did a fair share of the talking in 75 percent of the situations.

Men are allowed to take the lead and dominate in many subtle ways, as Deborah Tannen's research confirmed. For example, both men and women tend to regard topics introduced by women as tentative, whereas topics introduced by men are treated as material to be pursued. Men use humor to take the lead. They tend to remember and repeat jokes, using the opportunity to take center stage and gain control. Most women tend to forget jokes, rarely try to repeat them, and serve as a supportive audience, laughing at the jokes men tell.

HOW DO DIFFERENT WORLDVIEWS AFFECT MALE AND FEMALE COMMUNICATION STYLES?

As a result of their different socialization patterns, men and women interpret and relate to their environments differently. Men tend to take more initiative, which results in their being more self-protective and assertive. They

SNAPSHOT 5.2   Gender difference in worldview focus.

Women's Focus	Men's Focus
Connection	Status
Establish rapport	Report information
Cooperate	Compete
Play down expertise	Display expertise

tend to be more focused, future-oriented, and objective, with a greater urge to master. Other major differences in viewpoint and focus, according to Deborah Tannen's ground-breaking research, are shown in Snapshot 5.2.

An awareness of these tendencies can help us understand why men and women often see things so differently. Awareness also helps us foresee possible misunderstandings and communication breakdowns and, in turn, helps us improve male–female relationships and communicate more effectively. Let's explore Tannen's findings in more detail.

Connection or Status?

Women live in a world of intimacy and men in a world of status concerns. Women, in their world, focus on connecting with others via networks of supportive friends. Much of their communication is aimed at minimizing differences and building on commonalties and agreements. The ultimate goal is to attain maximum consensus and to function in relationships where people are interdependent. Men certainly have their old-boy networks, but their world of status places higher priority on independence where the purpose of much communication is on giving or taking orders. The ultimate goal is to attain more personal freedom.

Rapport Talk or Report Talk?

Women like "rapport talk" because it establishes or maintains connections with others. The focus is on feelings and includes personal thoughts, reactions to the day's events, and the details of life. Men prefer "report talk," because it provides factual information that the listener needs to know about what's going on in the world. Women's major aim in listening is to communicate interest and caring; men's major interest is to get information. Women will frequently reveal their weaknesses, especially when the other person is feeling discouraged. The rationale: Sharing such personal information will make the other feel equal, and thus closer. Men nearly always feel that revealing a weakness would just lower their status in the other person's eyes.

Cooperative or Competitive?

Women's words and actions often revolve around giving understanding, while men's are more likely to revolve around giving advice. These tendencies are probably based on the different ways men and women measure power. Women view helping, nurturing, and supporting as measures of their power. The activities they engage in include giving praise, speaking one-on-one, and private conversations. The main arenas for these activities are the telephone, social situations, and the home. Men perceive different measures of their power, such as having information, expertise, and skills. The activities they engage in include giving information, speaking more and longer, and speaking to groups. The main arenas for these activities are the workplace and public places.

In the work arena, women tend to approach decision making in a participative way: "I cannot and should not act alone when it comes to important decisions." Men tend to feel they must act alone and must find their way without help. Women focus on mastering their jobs and increasing their skills, consulting and involving others in the process, and developing positive relationships with their peers. Men tend to focus on competition and power, hierarchy and status. Women may not stand up for their rights because they want to avoid conflict. Men are less likely to be afraid of conflict and are more willing to confront issues in order to clear the air. Men are more likely to be intimidating to others, while women are more often perceived as approachable.

Women are more likely to be uncomfortable taking the initiative. Because women tend to be more accommodating and self-sacrificing, they are also more likely to allow frustration to build. To overcome problems arising from these tendencies, women can develop assertiveness skills and habits. Men need clear facts in the communication process. They experience more difficulty coping with unclear situations and expressing mixed feelings. To overcome these difficulties, they can get in touch with their emotions and intuitive side.

Expertise: Play It Up or Down?

A major source of power for managers, professionals, and other leaders is their expertise. Women tend to downplay their expertise, act as if they know less than they really do, and operate as one of the group or audience. Men are more apt to display their expertise and act as if they know more about their area than others in the group know. They're more likely to be comfortable taking center stage.

The male expert's main goal is to persuade, and he often firmly states his opinions as facts. In contrast, when female experts speak with males, their approach tends to be assenting, supporting, agreeing, listening, and going along. They want to emphasize similarities between themselves and listeners and to avoid showing off. Their concerns: "Have I been helpful? Do you like me?" The male experts' approach tends to be dominating, talking more, interrupting, and controlling the topic, whether they are speaking with males or females. They want to emphasize their superiority and display their expertise. Their concerns: "Have I won? Do you respect me?"

Male listeners usually don't understand that the female expert's main concern is to not offend, so the males often conclude that she is either indecisive, incompetent, insecure, or all of the above. They respond by offering their own opinions and information and by setting the agenda themselves; that is, they incorrectly perceive a power vacuum and try to take over.

Support By Agreeing or Disagreeing?

Women tend to show support by agreeing with others, while men help out by disagreeing to reveal problems and provide alternatives. Women's feedback style tends to be more positive and plentiful. They keep a running feedback loop going with such responses as "mmmm, uh huh, yes, yeah." They ask questions, take turns, and give and want full attention. They usually agree, and they laugh at humorous comments. They focus on the meta-message even more than the literal message. Men give fewer listener responses. They are more silent and listen less. They are more likely to challenge statements and focus on the literal message.

Because women listen so attentively, they may think a man's silence implies concentration on their meta-message, when in fact he may not be listening. Later she says, "But I told you all about that yesterday!"

Most men challenge any statement they disagree with, so men tend to interpret a woman's silence as consent or agreement. Later, when her actions are incompatible with her "agreement," they conclude that she is insincere or changeable: "Women!" As we begin to understand the different worlds that men and women live in, we can begin to find ways to bridge such communication gaps.

Communication Style: Tentative or Assertive?

With their focus on rapport, connection, intimacy, and playing down their expertise, women's communication styles tend to be more tentative than men's. Because the business world is accustomed to an assertive male approach to communication, women's credibility is undermined by a tentative, overly polite, uncertain, or indecisive approach. Several studies indicate that women perpetuate the lower-credibility stereotype with the following types of behavior:

- **Women ask more questions**, about three times as many as men on average.

- **Women make more statements in a questioning tone**, with a rising inflection at the end of a statement.

- **Women use more tag questions**; that is, brief questions added at the end of a sentence: " . . . don't you think?" " . . . okay?" " . . . you know?"

- **Women lead off with a question more frequently**. "You know what?" "Would you believe this?"

- **Women use more qualifiers and intensifiers**. Qualifiers or "hedges" include *kind of, sort of, a little bit, maybe, could be, if*. Such qualifiers soften an assertive statement, but also undermine its assertiveness. Intensifiers include *really, very, incredible, fantastic, amazing*, especially when those words are emphasized. The meta-message is: "Because what I say, by itself, is not likely to convince you, I must use double force to make sure you see what I mean."

Researchers have noted striking similarities between the conversations of women with men and the conversations of children with adults. They conclude that women tend to express their thoughts more tentatively and work harder to get someone's attention, which may in turn reflect basic power differences.

On the other hand, it's not unusual for men to carry assertiveness too far and to be perceived as overbearing or authoritarian. The most effective conversational approach for leaders is usually one that conveys *both* their sensitivity as well as commitment to their beliefs and statements. Both women and men become more effective when they communicate assertively, expressing their thoughts and feelings clearly but with respect for the thoughts, feelings, and rights of others.

HOW DO CULTURAL STEREOTYPES ABOUT MALE AND FEMALE TRAITS AFFECT GENDER ROLES AND EXPECTATIONS?

While some traits may have a genetic component, we know that culture plays a large role. In patriarchal cultures, men and women have a different status and different roles. Different traits provide a rationale for this and so are emphasized.

Stereotyped Traits

Almost from the moment we're born, we begin learning gender stereotypes and myths. Most of us also begin learning about inequality in relationships from the patriarchal system of family, church, and culture. Although the patriarchal system is beginning to change in the United States, boys and girls are still socialized in very different ways. And boys and girls still grow up in two worlds, overlapping but different.

Self-Analysis 5.1   Traits of Men and Women

Purpose: To become aware of your beliefs about gender traits and roles.

1. What are the traits or qualities that you like to see in men, traits and actions that you admire or feel comfortable with? List them.
2. What are the traits or qualities that you like to see in women, traits and actions that you admire or feel comfortable with? List them.
3. Keep them in mind as you work through this course, looking for how they affect your beliefs and actions when dealing with men and women.

People generally expect men and women to express different traits, and the traits they admire in men are often traits they don't admire in women and don't expect women to express. Men's traits—such as aggressive, strong, and independent—are those traditionally expected of business leaders. That's why business women report they must walk a fine line between being considered too feminine and too masculine. The traits they need for business success are *not* the traits people expect or perceive in women, as Snapshot 5.3 indicates.

This "traits disadvantage" that businesswomen have dealt with is beginning to recede as companies recognize the increasing importance of some of women's typical traits—such as a focus on personal connections, interpersonal relationships, and nurturing leadership—in managing today's participative workplace, which is increasingly peopled by well-educated employees working in self-managing teams. Men who are very

SNAPSHOT 5.3   Typical perceived male and female traits.

Feminine Traits	Masculine Traits
emotional	aggressive
talkative	strong
sensitive	proud
affectionate	confident
moody	independent
patient	courageous
romantic	disorganized
cautious	ambitious
thrifty	
(Men also said *manipulative*.	
Women said *creative*.)	

aggressive and ambitious may need to develop more sensitivity and patience. All of us can benefit by becoming more well rounded and balanced, allowing the best of our personalities to emerge from both sides, the feminine and the masculine.

Developing this balance is becoming important for effective modern marriages, too. In the old survival times, men and women needed each other for a balance. Today's power couples, where both partners balance important careers with a fruitful family life, tend to develop themselves as whole persons first, then form partnerships from preference rather than need.

Traits and Power Differentials

Not only are traits learned, they are affected by the power the culture accords to each group. When we are socialized at home in ways that establish and reinforce a power differential between men and women, male–female interactions in the workplace reflect interactions between the more powerful and the less powerful. For example, why do some women use tears to influence men, while men tend to use logical arguments to influence both men and women? Yes, through socialization, women have been allowed to express emotions and men have not. But also, men usually have more power in male–female relationships and therefore have the upper hand. It may be that women's logic would be ignored and they feel they must resort to tears in order to have an effect. Researchers make two major conclusions about gender and power tactics: (1) gender affects power tactics but (2) that's because men are accorded more power than women.

Gender Affects Power Tactics

Women are more likely to withdraw or express negative emotions, while men are more likely to use bargaining or reasoning. However, in a partnership between gay men, if one partner perceives himself as less powerful, he is likely to use withdrawal or expressions of negative emotions, and the more powerful partner is likely to use bargaining or reasoning. The same dynamics were found between two women in a lesbian partnership.

Power, Not Gender, Is the Issue

Regardless of gender or sexual orientation, people who see themselves as relatively more powerful in a relationship tend to use persuasion and bargaining, while those who feel they are lower in power tend to use withdrawal and emotion.

Regardless of sexual orientation, a partner with relatively less power tends to use "weak" strategies, such as manipulation and pleading. Those in more powerful positions

> As Rosabeth Kanter found in her studies of men and women in organizations, behaviors believed to be typical of women are actually behaviors that are typical of the powerless.

are more likely to use autocratic and bullying tactics. Signs of conversational dominance, such as interrupting, were also linked to the balance of power. Interruption is not so much a male behavior as a tactic of the powerful.

Gender Differences as a Prototype of Group Differences

All cultures differentiate between male and female behavior, and usually when a given behavior pattern becomes associated with one sex, it will be dropped by the other. Recently, many sociologists and anthropologists have started to see gender differences primarily as cultural differences and have started applying cross-cultural techniques to solve gender problems. Some experts say that gender is not just one of many cultural differences, but is *the* most important cultural difference, the root paradigm of difference, just as the inequality of patriarchy is the paradigm of all inequality among groups.

Instead of seeing women's culture as a subculture within each ethnic culture, they declare that the two most basic cultural groups are women and men. Between these two groups, we find the prototypical cultural distinctions, after which all other cultural distinctions are modeled. If organizations can learn to accept and deal with gender differences, all other differences can be handled in due course. On the other hand, a great deal of diversity work remains superficial when gender issues are not first recognized and managed. This is because beliefs about gender influence us in the most fundamental ways about how to be with others and make choices in life.

To reach your full potential, you need to develop both your masculine and feminine qualities. The balance varies for each person, depending on genes, the environment, and the decisions and choices you make in life. When humans were in a primitive survival mode, it worked out well to differentiate gender traits according to gender roles. In today's new economy, it seems to work best when we balance the masculine with the feminine—within ourselves as individuals as well as in our homes, organizations, and our society. Where we've done this, we've discovered that we're more well rounded, we come closer to realizing our full potential, and we tap into more of our innate power at all levels, individual to global.

HOW HAVE GENDER ROLES EVOLVED? WHAT ARE THE NEW TRENDS?

Women in Western cultures have traditionally been viewed as a wholly different species from men, invariably an inferior species. Those primary and secondary sex differences that exist are greatly exaggerated and are inflated into imaginary distinctions that justify discrimination. In the past, most men felt an in-group solidarity with half of the humans on earth, other men, and with the other half, an irreconcilable conflict.

SNAPSHOT 5.4   Masculine and feminine strengths.

Typical Masculine Strengths Women Can Develop	Typical Feminine Strengths Men Can Develop
Being powerful and forthright.	Recognizing, accepting, and expressing feelings.
Becoming entrepreneurial.	
Making a direct, visible impact on others rather than just functioning behind the scenes.	Respecting feelings as an essential part of life, as guides to authenticity and effectiveness, rather than as barriers to achievement.
Stating your own needs and refusing to back down, even if the immediate response is not acceptance.	Working for self-fulfillment as well as for money.
Focusing on a task and regarding it as at least as important as the relationships with the people doing the task.	Valuing nonwork roles as well as work identity.
Building support systems with other women and sharing competence with them, rather than competing with them.	Being able to fail at a task without feeling failure as a person.
	Expressing the need to be nurtured at times.
Helping other women succeed; networking.	Touching and being close to both men and women without sexual connotations.
Intellectualizing and generalizing from experience.	Listening empathetically, actively experiencing another's reality without feeling responsible for solving others' problems.
Behaving *impersonally* sometimes.	
Not turning anger, blame, and pain inward.	Sharing feelings as the most meaningful part of one's contact with others, accepting the risk and vulnerability such sharing implies.
Moving beyond feelings of suffering and victimization by taking responsibility.	
Being invulnerable to destructive feedback.	
Responding to resentments and anger directly rather than with passive resistance, nagging.	Building support systems with men and women, sharing competencies without competition, and sharing feelings and needs with sincerity.
Responding directly with *I* statements, rather than with blaming *you* ones.	Relating to experiences and people on a personal level rather than assuming that the only valid approach to life and interpersonal contact is an abstract, rational, or strictly objective one.
Becoming an effective problem solver by being analytical, systematic, and direct.	
Becoming a risk taker (calculating probabilities and making appropriate tradeoffs).	Accepting the emotional, spontaneous, and irrational parts of the self.

Self-Analysis 5.2 | Balancing the Masculine–Feminine Within

Purpose: To gradually balance your masculine and feminine sides.

Step 1.   If you're a man, review the feminine strengths shown in Snapshot 5.4. If you're a woman, review the masculine strengths. Check off the opposite-gender strengths you feel you adequately express. Are there ways you can express them more appropriately to achieve your personal and career goals?

Step 2.   Select a typical opposite-gender strength that you want to develop more fully. List some ways you can become more aware of this trait, build it, and express it. Write down how it will balance some complementary same-gender trait you often express. Work on this new trait for a week or more; select a time frame that seems practical.

Step 3.   During and after the time frame, jot down notes about how you expressed the trait, thoughts and feelings that came up, people's reactions, and any insights. How can developing this trait make you a stronger person or help you understand and relate better to others? How can it help you achieve career and personal goals? Get in touch with any resistance you felt about integrating this trait. Did you uncover any hidden beliefs during this process? Remember, even if you simply become more aware of the trait, that is progress!

Step 4.   Pick another strength to work on, and repeat Steps 2 and 3. Keep working on strengths until you're satisfied with your own feminine–masculine balance.

The Patriarchal System

Patriarchy refers to the rule of a family or tribe by men, and a social system in which descent and succession are traced through the male line. It began by brute force and muscle power. Once established, men's superiority and advantage were institutionalized into every sphere of life. It's being undermined because brain power and relationship power are becoming true power. As men's superiority is undermined, some are resorting to extreme measures to hold onto it, even to physical abuse and rape, according to Robert Bly, Sam Keen, and other men's movement leaders.

Men's movement author Walter Farrell defines a patriarchy as the male areas of dominance, responsibility, and subservience in a culture, reinforced by both genders for the purpose of serving survival needs of both. Patriarchy has given men the authority, privilege, and responsibility that come with being in charge. Women's privileges involved being provided for and protected, if they picked the right man and all went well. Both men and women have been rewarded with "identity" when they followed the rules and punished with invisibility when they failed—or sometimes even death if they rebelled against the rules. Leaders were picked from the men who best followed the rules.

Feminist Movements

Women's groups have arisen from time to time to protest the limitations and unfairness to women and men that patriarchy imposes. The most recent feminist movement began in the 1960s and has made significantly more progress than any previous movement. Perhaps gender equality is an ideal whose time has come.

> *Feminists come in many political shades and stripes, but most agree with this simple definition according to feminist leader Gloria Steinem: A feminist is someone who believes in equal rights for women.*

Most feminists believe that the inequality inherent in patriarchy does not serve women's best interest and that equality in the workplace will lead to equality in the family. They focus on eliminating all discriminatory barriers to women's moving up in the work world as the key to the overall liberation of women. They believe that changes in the labor market conditions that women face will force changes in family dynamics. Economic power is a prerequisite to a balance of power in family relationships.

From Patriarchy to Equality

As we've moved from an agricultural economy through an industrial to a post-industrial economy, cultural values have shifted dramatically. The women's movement is a reflection of that basic shift. Marriage relationships are the most influential in a society, because children learn about life and relationships by observing their parents. Leaders of both the men's and women's movements propose that we move beyond patriarchy or matriarchy—beyond hierarchy—to a system that relies on leadership that arises spontaneously from those who are willing and able to lead in particular situations. Snapshot 5.5 explains changing relationships.

Megatrends That Opened Doors

Beginning in the 1960s, John Naisbett's research organization identified a series of megatrends that combined to accelerate the pace at which women moved into managerial, professional, technical, and leadership roles that had been almost exclusively Euro-American male territory.

Social Change

The 1960s brought major social upheavals. Those that most affected gender issues were greater acceptance of divorce, greater sexual freedom, and greater acceptance of equal opportunity for women and minorities. Such social changes

SNAPSHOT 5.5   Traditional and new male–female relationships.

	Traditional Marriage Relationships	New Relationships
Major goal:	Survival	Fulfillment
Relationship focus:	Role mates, to create a whole	Soul mates, whole persons, to create synergy
Effect on roles:	Segregated roles	Common roles
Family obligations:	Must have children	Children are a choice
	Woman raises children, man makes money; woman risks life in childbirth, man risks life in war	Both raise children and both make money Childbirth relatively risk-free; ideally no more war
Partner choice:	Parental influence primary; women try to marry "up"	Parental influence secondary; both marry for love
The contract:	Lifetime; no divorce Neither party can end contract	As long as both parties want to stay together Either party can end contract
Status of parties:	Woman is property of man; man expected to provide and protect	Each equally responsible for self and other
	Both are subservient to needs of family	Both balance needs of family with needs of self
Emotional expectation:	Love emerges from mutual dependence	Love is based on choice
	I'll stay no matter what	I'll stay unless you abuse me or we grow in different directions

allowed women more freedom of choice. During the 1970s, women began moving into many fields of study and occupations formerly closed to them.

Economic Change

As blue-collar jobs moved offshore, a growing number of husbands no longer earned an income that would support a family, and their wives went to work. As divorce became more economically feasible for women, an increasing percentage of women became heads of households. For all of these reasons, middle-class working mothers, once a sign of liberation, became an economic necessity during the 1980s. As the average worker's take-home pay went down, family income grew an average of less than 1 percent per year, even with many wives working. Buying a home became more expensive and took a larger share of family income, and renters found it more difficult to save up a down payment. An ever-greater proportion of women will continue to enter the workforce and stay there, even when they have small children. This means that working mothers will be the largest potential source of qualified workers for the next decade.

Emphasis on Ethical Values

The excesses of the 1980s—from the spending of a Donald Trump to the grand larceny of Wall Street dealers and savings and loan officers—brought a new respect for ethical principles. Also, biotechnology is poised to solve many of our health and poverty problems. But people are also realizing a corresponding need to define ethical values to regulate the industry. Several recent surveys indicate that people believe women can bring special talents to dealing with and cleaning up ethical issues, and that people tend to trust women's ethical standards and level of honesty. This applies to both the business and political worlds. Women represent a "fresh face" without the backroom connections and long years of deal making.

Management Style Change

In *Megatrends* 2000 Naisbett said that the underlying theme of all of the megatrends is the individual. While people are working together in more dynamic ways than ever, the trend is for power in work groups to stem from the power of the individuals within the groups. Leaders who know how to empower others have an edge.

Women's Management Style Fit

This megatrend makes the natural management style of most women a plus because women are generally more comfortable with empowering others than wielding power over them. Differences between men's and women's management styles according to studies by John Naisbett, Judith Rosener, and others:

- Women are usually socialized to win commitment from people rather than to give orders and apply controls.
- Women tend to adapt more naturally to the role of teacher/facilitator/coach than they do to the role of director/overseer.
- Women have historically been trained to focus on helping others achieve success, usually husbands and children.
- Most women believe in allowing everyone to contribute and feel powerful and important because this is good for employees and the organization.

- Women are more likely to share power and information.
- Women are more democratic, participative, and consultative.
- Women place more emphasis on collaborative decision making.
- Women are likely to decentralize decision making and responsibility, moving these functions down to worker levels.
- Women show greater concern with process and fairness.
- Women are more concerned with the quality of outcomes, while retaining a pragmatic concern for the numbers.
- Women lead with a less autocratic, less domineering, less ego-involved style.
- Women are less concerned with titles and formal authority and more concerned with responsibility and responsiveness.
- Women are less concerned with empire building, power, and domination and less conscious of their "turf."

Current Socioeconomic Profile

Some of the most dramatic changes in gender dynamics center around new roles for women, higher educational achievement, women as heads of households, and a continuing but slowly shrinking pay gap.

Occupations

Women are 52 percent of the U.S. population and 46 percent of the workforce, but only 40 percent of all managers and less than 5 percent of top managers. While most managers, precision production workers, machine operators, and laborers are men, most clerical and service workers are women. Professionals, which include teachers and nurses as well as doctors, lawyers, and accountants, are nearly half and half as are technical and sales workers.

Euro-American men are 35 percent of the population and 39 percent of the workforce; yet they are:

- 92 percent of senior managers in mid- to large-sized corporations (5 percent are women; 3 percent are men of all other ethnic groups)
- 82.5 percent of the Forbes 400 persons worth at least 265 million dollars
- 80 percent of Congress (12 percent were women and 8 percent male "minorities" in 2004)
- 84 percent of state governors
- 70 percent of tenured college faculty
- 90 percent of daily newspaper editors
- 77 percent of TV news directors

According to the 1995 Glass Ceiling Commission, Euro-American men "dominate just about everything but NOW and the NAACP." It is clear that they hold the most powerful positions in the economic and political arenas.

Nearly 60 percent of wives are in the workforce, raising family income by one-third on average. Women with dependent children are more likely to work than women with adult children. And women are increasingly likely to delay marriage and children in order to finish college and establish themselves in a career.

Education

Although there has traditionally been a male–female education gap, with more men getting degrees, the gap had closed for 2000 graduates, with women slightly outnumbering men. The fields where women graduates increased most dramatically are business—taking 47 percent of the degrees, compared to 9 percent in 1970—and science—taking 51 percent, compared to 13 percent earlier.

The Pay Gap

In 2000, women's median weekly earnings were 75 percent of men's. The pay gap was more or less 60 to 65 percent from the 1950s to 1980. The 10 percent improvement since 1980 probably reflects men's lower pay, women's higher educational achievement, women's choice of formerly male-dominated fields that pay more, and the tendency to delay having children and take fewer years off from careers once children arrive.

The pay gap is especially tough for single mothers. On average, these women must survive on about one-third the median income of married-couple families. Therefore, they are nearly six times as likely to live in poverty. In fact, at all ages, more women than men live in poverty. For example, women over 65 are twice as likely as older men to live in poverty. And they live longer—by about seven years on average.

SELF-TEST #1

Indicate the best answers to the following 10 multiple-choice questions.

1. The stereotyped belief that creates the greatest barrier for career women is:

    A. women can't communicate effectively

    B. women are too emotional

    C. women talk too much

    D. women are too self-centered

2. The gender gap between status and connection means that:
   A. women live in the world of intimacy and men in the world of hierarchy
   B. men focus on connections in the old-boys' network and women focus on gaining status in the corporate world
   C. women have fewer connections and lower status than men
   D. women have more connections within organizations, but men have higher status

3. A gender gap between men and women exists because:
   A. women focus on reporting information and men focus on networking
   B. women focus on establishing expertise and men focus on teamwork
   C. women focus on connection and men focus on status
   D. women focus on competition and men focus on displaying expertise

4. The gender gap between rapport talk and report talk means that women focus on talk that expresses:
   A. feelings
   B. personal thoughts
   C. reactions to the day's events
   D. all of the above

5. A typical female tendency is to:
   A. challenge
   B. confront
   C. agree
   D. seek the spotlight

6. The gender gap between cooperation and competition means that:
   A. women confront conflict to clear the air
   B. men focus on mastering the job and increasing their skills
   C. women measure power by how much support they're able to give others
   D. women measure power by the information, expertise, and skill they can offer

7. One of the traits most admired in men is:
   A. patient
   B. thrifty

C. cautious

D. aggressive

8. One of the traits most admired in women is:

   A. proud

   B. confident

   C. does not use harsh language

   D. independent

9. Patriarchy refers to:

   A. rule of a family or tribe by men

   B. a social system in which descent and succession are traced through the male line

   C. father rule, a set of social relations that enable men to benefit materially and ideologically from women's work

   D. all of the above

10. In traditional marriage relationships:

    A. the major goal is fulfillment

    B. roles tend to be segregated

    C. roles tend to be common

    D. parental influence in partner choice is secondary

SELF-TEST #1 FEEDBACK

Each correct answer is worth 10 points. If you score less than 70 points, you should review the materials and re-take the Self-Test.

1. The stereotyped belief that creates the greatest barrier for career women is:

   A. No, it's believed that women can communicate effectively

   B. Yes, women are too emotional is the best answer

   C. No, although some say women talk too much, that's not the greatest barrier

   D. No, *women are too self-centered* is not a stereotyped belief

2. The gender gap between status and connection means that:

   A. Yes, women live in the world of intimacy and men in the world of hierarchy is the best answer

    B. No, in fact, the reverse is true, with men focusing on status and women on connections

    C. No, although women may have lower status, they likely have more connections

    D. No, although men do have higher status in organizations, they also have the most important connections there

3. A gender gap between men and women exists because:

    A. No, the reverse is true; women focus on networking and men on status

    B. No, women tend to play down expertise and men focus on displaying it

    C. Yes, women focus on connection and men focus on status is the best answer

    D. No, women don't focus on competition, although men do focus on displaying expertise

4. The gender gap between rapport talk and report talk means that women focus on talk that expresses:

    A. No, although feelings are a factor

    B. No, although personal thoughts are a factor

    C. No, although reactions to the day's events are a factor

    D. Yes, all of the above is the best answer

5. A typical female tendency is to:

    A. No, challenge is typical of males

    B. No, confrontation is typical of males

    C. Yes, agree is the best answer

    D. No, seeking the spotlight is typical of males

6. The gender gap between cooperation and competition means that:

    A. No, although men are likely to confront conflict to clear the air

    B. No, both men and women often focus on mastering the job and increasing their skills

    C. Yes, the best answer is, women measure power by how much support they're able to give others

    D. No, in fact men measure power by the information, expertise, and skill they can offer

7. One of the traits most admired in men is:

    A. No, patient is mentioned as a female trait

    B. No, thrifty is mentioned as a female trait

C. No, cautious is mentioned as a female trait

D. Yes, the best answer is aggressive

8. One of the traits most admired in women is:

   A. No, proud is listed as a male trait

   B. No, confident is listed as a male trait

   C. Yes, the best answer is does not use harsh language

   D. No, independent is listed as a male trait

9. Patriarchy refers to:

   A. No, although an aspect is rule of a family or tribe by men

   B. No, although an aspect is a social system in which descent and succession are traced through the male line

   C. No, although an aspect is father rule, a set of social relations that enable men to benefit materially and ideologically from women's work

   D. Yes, the best answer is all of the above

10. In traditional marriage relationships:

   A. No, the major goal is not fulfillment

   B. Yes, the best answer is roles tend to be segregated

   C. No, roles don't tend to be common

   D. No, parental influence in partner choice is in fact primary

---

WHAT ARE THE CULTURAL BARRIERS TO WOMEN'S CAREER SUCCESS?

Most career women must overcome both internal barriers and external barriers to workplace success that are rooted in the American culture. Internal barriers include self-limiting beliefs about women's abilities and roles. External barriers include the glass ceiling, inflexible work arrangements, and pay disparity.

Self-Limiting Beliefs

Traditions from the past affect today's career woman in two basic ways: (1) how she pictures herself and, therefore, the roles and behaviors she's comfortable with, and (2) what others expect of her—their preconceived notions of her abilities, traits, strengths, and weaknesses and their resulting beliefs about proper roles and behaviors. These traditional beliefs and expectations often lead to problems with self-limiting and conflicting beliefs. Leaders who understand how such beliefs create internal barriers are in a better position to help women overcome them. Self-limiting beliefs many women still hold include:

- I should not be ambitious.
- I should wait to be asked.
- I should never parade my achievements and expertise or "toot my own horn."
- I am not supposed to be good in math, finance, computer, mechanical, technical, engineering, decision making, and other male fields.
- I should stay out of office politics.
- I don't need to learn about the inner workings of the company (the hierarchy, chain of command, sources of power, career paths).
- I should just let others have their way rather than cause a scene.
- I need to steer clear of risky ventures.
- Criticism of my work or ideas is criticism of me.
- All I need to get ahead is to improve myself and work hard.
- If I do good work, my boss will notice and promote me.

Some women have beliefs that cause them to personalize events, criticism, and messages of others, to react emotionally, and to act out such emotions. These are beliefs typical of the powerless, regardless of gender, and usually are learned from the women in the family and community.

Some women have difficulty understanding how upward mobility works. If they've rarely worked on teams, they may have beliefs about self-development that prevent them from recognizing the necessity of networking and teamwork. They may neglect developing a power base, and they may not see how they can meet personal goals through helping the team achieve organizational goals.

Conflicting Beliefs

Certain conflicting beliefs that can lead to fear of success tend to be unique to women and may include:

- I want a successful career, *BUT* men don't want relationships with strong, achieving career women.
- I want a successful career, *BUT* Prince Charming may come along, sweep me off my feet, and carry me away to live happily ever after.
- I want a successful career, *BUT* good wives and mothers stay home and take care of the home and kids.

The beliefs that limit women and cause conflict all stem from cultural beliefs, values, and stereotypes about women. Therefore, even when women move beyond such beliefs, they must cope daily with people who still hold similar beliefs. Building a network of supportive friends and coworkers can help career women retain a sense of balance and self-confidence as they juggle career demands with home demands. An understanding, supportive manager can make all the difference. Sometimes, the manager can take the lead in helping a woman employee recognize the beliefs that may be holding her back.

Pay Inequity

Although the United States leads the world in the proportion of women managers, we are not as advanced in providing pay equity. Median income for full-time women workers is only about 75 percent of male workers' income. Some argue that women generally have less training, experience, and job commitment than men and that this accounts for the pay gap. However, the 75 percent figure represents every management level.

> Women vice presidents earn only 75 percent of male vice presidents' income.

It's virtually certain that women who have made it to the vice presidential level have better training, experience, performance, and job commitment than their male peers. Yet they earn 25 percent less on average.

Some analysts believe that, in general, women are less committed to careers than men because women take primary responsibility for raising children, which requires them to interrupt their careers. But a Census Bureau study indicates that the earnings are the same for women with no work interruption as for those who had at least one work interruption of six months or more since age twenty-one. The Census Bureau concludes that structural factors and discrimination, rather than discontinuous employment, explain the earnings gap. And much of the female "gain" reported in some studies actually reflects declining median male wages since the 1970s.

The Glass Ceiling

Fortune magazine's recent survey found only 19 women among 4,012 directors and highest-paid executives, 0.5 percent, not much better than in 1978 (0.16 percent). Although the United States leads the world in percentage of women managers, the 40 percent figure can be very deceptive for the following reasons:

- 33 percent of managers are women in the 38,000 companies reporting to the EEOC.
- 25 percent of managers were women in the 200 largest companies.
- 5 percent of vice presidents are women.
- 7.5 percent of all women employees work as managers, compared to 15 percent of all male employees.

- Women managers still tend to be clustered in the lower-paying, entry levels of management, such as working supervisor and first-line supervisor.

- Women managers' pay lags behind men's at every level, averaging about 75 percent.

- When women move into an occupation in significant numbers, the occupation goes down in status and pay, and men tend to move out of it. Conversely, if an occupation loses status and pay for other reasons, women are more likely to be hired into it.

- Women are likely to hit a glass ceiling to top-level, and even middle-level, positions. Therefore, few women are making it beyond lower-level management and may have little hope of doing so in the near future. The women who make up the "5 percent of top managers" include women who started their own firms.

> In the 1990s Norma Carr-Ruffino conducted a survey of women managers that revealed 90 percent think the glass ceiling is the most important issue facing women managers.

The Carr-Ruffino survey of women managers identified the following barriers as the most difficult to overcome:

- Top management harbors stereotypes about women, especially regarding women's ability to gain acceptance in a top role, women's level of career commitment, and women's decision-making ability.

- Women are often excluded from key informal gatherings where information and opinions are exchanged, deals are made, and so forth.

- Women's contributions and abilities are not taken as seriously as men's.

- Women have more difficulty finding mentors.

- Women don't get equal opportunities to serve on important committees and project teams.

Leaders who want to attract and retain the best-qualified women must eliminate the stereotypes, attitudes, and practices that create a glass ceiling. Even those women who don't aspire to the top prefer to stay in companies that have opened all of the doors to qualified women and have helped them move up.

Two recent surveys of male and female managers of large American companies found that although women expressed a much higher probability of leaving their current employer than men, and had higher actual turnover rates, their major reason for leaving was lack of career growth opportunity or dissatisfaction with the rate of progress. Effective leaders are sensitive to career women's needs and are open to helping them meet those needs.

Inflexible Working Arrangements

Women become frustrated when the demands of work and demand for blind corporate loyalty conflict with other valuable parts of their lives and prevent their full participation in the organization. Some corporate systems and practices are designed for those men whose wives handle most family responsibilities. Some are designed by men who are workaholics and expect others to be. Such expectations are unreasonable for women who can't ignore family responsibilities but are committed career professionals.

> *Women who take maternity leave are 10 times more likely to lose their jobs than employees on other kinds of medical leave.*

Good employees can be retained through the child-bearing years if leaders are flexible, accepting, and supportive of family needs. Asking for flexible alternatives or family benefits should not be the kiss of death to career ambitions, but it is in many companies.

Pregnant women are often transferred, demoted, harassed, or fired. "Mommy-track" or part-time work is usually the boring, low-level grunt work that blocks chances of gaining the skills required to advance professionally. These practices and attitudes must be changed if a firm wants to attract and retain career women who also become mothers.

If women are to have ongoing careers, rather than just jobs, they need:

- adequate maternity and family medical leave, usually much more than the three months required by law
- help in obtaining affordable, quality child care and elder care
- flexible job structures and benefits, such as flextime, job sharing, part-time arrangements, contract work, and home offices

Rather than lose competent women who go through a phase of needing more time for their small children, some companies are giving them whatever they need to do part or all of their work in a home office—fax machines, computers, and cell phones. Some can pack the work into three or four days instead of five. Some need to come into the office once or twice a week for meetings. Some women hire a sitter to help out while they work at home. The major advantages: they're near their children, they can handle crises and illnesses themselves, and they don't spend time and energy commuting every day.

SELF-TEST #2

Indicate the best answers to the following 10 multiple-choice questions.

1. The best definition of a feminist is:
    A. one who believes in the superiority of women
    B. a lesbian who is politically active
    C. one who believe in equal rights for women
    D. a member of the National Organization for Women

2. Euro-American men make up what percent of top corporate positions?
    A. 39%
    B. 77%
    C. 95%
    D. 65%

3. A focus of women's natural leadership style is:
    A. more emphasis on executive decision making
    B. more concern with structure and lines of authority
    C. more emphasis on collaborative decision making
    D. more centralization

4. Being a woman is becoming a workplace advantage because:
    A. women's fresh perspective is needed to stabilize traditional organizations
    B. women's supportive ways of leading are needed in participative corporate cultures with well-educated employees
    C. women's viewpoints are needed to deal with Japanese and German business leaders
    D. women's high-tech savvy is needed

5. Women's leadership profile includes:
    A. using leadership power based on charisma, work record, and contacts
    B. using power to coerce others
    C. identifying themselves with jobs
    D. working at an unrelenting pace

6. A typical belief that limits women's career success is:
    A. I should showcase my skills and abilities
    B. office politics is fun

C. I should not be ambitious

D. taking calculated risks is a good way to get ahead

7. A typical conflicting belief that sabotages women's career success is:

A. I should not be ambitious but I need to toot my own horn

B. I should wait to be asked but I must take initiative

C. I want a successful career but men don't want relationships with strong, achieving career women

D. I'm good in math and finance but women aren't supposed to be good in math and finance

8. Women's pay, as compared with men's pay, is:

A. worse now than in the 1970s

B. almost equal

C. about 75 percent

D. about 60 percent

9. The glass ceiling for women refers to the fact that:

A. few women and minorities are making it beyond lower-level management

B. companies make it clear that women won't make it to the top

C. not enough women have gained the experience for top jobs

D. all of the above

10. Which is the #1 barrier to the top, as reported by women managers?

A. exclusion from key informal gatherings where information is shared

B. women's contributions and abilities are not taken as seriously as men's

C. women have more difficulty finding mentors

D. top management harbors stereotypes about women's leadership ability

SELF-TEST #2 FEEDBACK

Each correct answer is worth 10 points. If you score less than 70 points, you should review the materials and re-take the Self-Test.

1. The best definition of a feminist is:

A. No, it's not one who believes in the superiority of women

B. No, it's not a lesbian who is politically active

C. Yes, the best answer is one who believe in equal rights for women

D. No, it's not a member of the National Organization for Women

2. Euro-American men make up what percent of top corporate positions?

   A. No, not 39%

   B. No, not 77%

   C. Yes, 95%

   D. No, not 65%

3. A focus of women's natural leadership style is:

   A. No, it's not more emphasis on executive decision making

   B. No, it's not more concern with structure and lines of authority

   C. Yes, the best answer is more emphasis on collaborative decision making

   D. No, it's not more centralization

4. Being a woman is becoming a workplace advantage because:

   A. No, it's not about stabilizing traditional organizations

   B. Yes, the best answer is women's supportive ways of leading are needed in participative corporate cultures with well-educated employees

   C. No, it's not about dealing with Japanese and German business leaders

   D. No, everyone's high-tech savvy is needed; men are generally known more for this aspect and women for the people skills

5. Women's leadership profile includes:

   A. Yes, the best answer is using leadership power based on charisma, work record, and contacts

   B. No, using power to coerce others is not part of the profile

   C. No, identifying themselves with jobs may be a problem but is not a leadership trait

   D. No, working at an unrelenting pace is not part of the profile

6. A typical belief that limits women's career success is:

   A. No, *I should showcase my skills and abilities* is not a self-limiting belief

   B. No, *office politics is fun* is not a typical belief

   C. Yes, the best answer is *I should not be ambitious*

   D. No, *taking calculated risks is a good way to get ahead* is not a self-limiting belief

7. A typical conflicting belief that sabotages women's career success is:

   A. No, *I should not be ambitious but I need to toot my own horn* is not typical

   B. No, *I should wait to be asked but I must take initiative* is not typical

C. Yes, the best answer is *I want a successful career but men don't want relationships with strong, achieving career women*

D. No, *I'm good in math and finance but women aren't supposed to be good in math and finance* is not typical

8. Women's pay, as compared with men's pay, is:

A. No, it's not worse now than in the 1970s

B. No, not almost equal

C. Yes, it's about 75 percent

D. No, not about 60 percent

9. The glass ceiling for women refers to the fact that:

A. Yes, the best answer is few women and minorities are making it beyond lower-level management

B. No, in fact companies don't make it clear that women won't make it to the top

C. No, in fact enough women have gained the experience for top jobs

D. No, all of the above is not correct

10. Which is the #1 barrier to the top, as reported by women managers?

A. No, although a factor is exclusion from key informal gatherings where information is shared

B. No, although a factor is women's contributions and abilities are not taken as seriously as men's

C. No, although a factor is women have more difficulty finding mentors

D. Yes, the best answer is top management harbors stereotypes about women's leadership ability

SKILL BUILDER 5.1   The Case of New Mother Jessica

Jessica is the mother of an 18-month-old child. She is a loan officer with Trust Bank. Jessica resigned from her previous job because the maternity leave was inadequate for her to make the adjustment to a new baby. When she went to work for Trust Bank, it was with the understanding that it would not be a high-pressure position—no expectation that she would work overtime or make business trips. However, Jessica is beginning to feel pressure to do just that. Jessica approaches you, her manager, to tell you that she has decided she must resign in order to find a part-time job, about three days a week. She says, "My son needs more of my time and attention just now. I need to work, and I want to work, but I have decided to give his needs top priority for the next year or two."

As Jessica's manager, what should you do?

   A. Respect Jessica's wishes to leave?

   B. Tell Jessica that you will lighten her workload?

   C. Tell Jessica that there will be no more pressure to work overtime or travel?

   D. Ask Jessica how you can help her meet her family needs and still retain her job?

Feedback

   A. No, allowing her to leave without exploring of the issue is not a good choice. If Jessica is a valuable employee, this option means giving up.

   B. No, lightening her load is good, but you'll probably need to do more than this.

   C. No, easing up on the pressure is good, but you'll probably need to do more.

   D. Yes, asking what she needs is best. Work with her to provide what she needs to manage both work and family obligations.

What Actually Happened

Jessica's manager, a career woman herself, knows that Jessica is highly effective at bringing in new customers and keeping them satisfied. She also knows that Jessica only occasionally needs to meet face-to-face with customers.

They devised a plan for Jessica to work three to four days a week, most of those days in a home office. One day a week, Jessica comes into the bank for staff meetings. The bank provides a personal computer, fax, and cell phone for Jessica. In turn, Jessica pays a sitter to watch her child while she's working at home.

This arrangement frees Jessica to do her work at home and allows her to be available when her child needs her. It eliminates most of the costly commute time, and the cell phone allows her to be available to customers throughout the business day, even when she's doing household errands.

Five years later, Jessica is still with the company, and each year she's one of the top producers. In fact, last year she won an award for being her company's top-producing loan officer nationwide. She told her manager, "Because you did so much to accommodate me, I was motivated to really do the best job possible for you, the company—and of course, for me and family."

HOW ARE MEN RESPONDING TO WOMEN'S NEW ROLES AND EXPECTATIONS?

About half of Euro-American men think they're losing influence and job advantage, while only a third of other respondents think that, according to recent surveys by *Harvard Business Review*.

Losing Power: Personal vs. Collective

Recent surveys indicate that the major dilemma men are wrestling with is the power problem—the profound difference between personal and collective power. Most men do not feel very powerful; they report that they are:

- having a harder time making a living than their fathers did
- dealing with a boss telling them what to do
- trying to figure out how to be what woman want: sensitive as well as strong; soft and cuddly as well as firm and "manly."

As a result, many men feel they've failed in their gender role. Men's movement leaders say the women's movement has triggered changes for men in every life area, and most haven't adjusted to it yet. Men look around them and see that they're in danger because men are 83 percent of the homeless, 90 percent of AIDS deaths, and 94 percent of prison inmates. They're three times as likely as women to be murdered, likely to live seven years less than women, and much more likely to die of alcoholism, heart attack, or suicide.

In fact, men live in a more violent world than women. The more violent the crime, the more likely the victim is a man. Yet, men aren't allowed to see themselves as victims. After all, collectively they hold the power in the United States. And if a man is Euro-American, his complicity in maintaining the patriarchy is even greater for the simple reason that Euro-American men continue to dominate in business, government, and the professions.

Yet, because so many men feel personally powerless, some are threatened by feminism and resist changes designed to give women more collective power. Men also live with the knowledge that women are afraid of men. Decent, protective men still know that it's men who make it dangerous for women to walk city streets alone at night, men who rape and assault and beat them so that they are forever frightened. These are some of the contradictions that men must live with; there are many others.

Feeling Pressure to Perform and Pressure to Change

When men were asked, "What are the biggest pressures on men today?" answers indicated that men are feeling much pressure these days, and it's coming at them from all directions. Traditional pressures remain: to succeed in careers, to provide for families, to be strong and courageous and protective. Men also seem to feel a great deal of pressure from women to change their ways, their very natures, and they don't fully understand what's expected of them. Many don't know how to be sensitive or vulnerable and still be the strong protector, the man in control. Adding to these pressures is their sense that it's becoming harder to make a good living, the planet is being destroyed, and politics is a mess.

When males were asked, "Have men been helped or hurt by feminism?" the researchers got emphatic responses from both sides. The majority felt that feminism has generally helped both sexes by allowing them to see beyond traditional roles and stereotypes. About 25 percent were vehemently anti-feminist, blaming the movement for promoting anti-male and anti-family attitudes. Still others held that change is always a double-edged sword, and the full impact of feminism is yet to be felt.

When the researchers asked men, "What are the best and worst things about women?" their replies focused on empathy, support, warmth, and nice bodies. But many revealed a deep hurt and resentment for the changing roles women have assumed. And for some, women's emotionalism is a drawback.

Unemployed men commit suicide at twice the rate of employed men. Among women, suicide has no correlation to employment status. Men's self-worth is more tied to their jobs. They often feel humiliated, violated, helpless, angry, and guilty over job loss. At all ages, men's higher suicide rates are likely to be tied to a lack of emotional support systems. Men often bond by giving each other criticism, women by giving each other support.

Being Groomed for Violence

Men are more likely to be subjected to violence throughout their lives. In fact, they're trained from childhood to endure and aspire to situations that include violence.

CULTURAL VIOLENCE

Men's advocates such as Walter Farrell suggest some ways in which we subject men to violence and reward them for being violent:

- unnecessary circumcision (without anesthesia) of baby boys
- violent sports (for school boys) such as football, hockey, and boxing
- approval by girls and parents when boys excel at violent sports
- government money to schools to support violent sports and military ROTC

CULTURAL VIOLENCE   *continued*

- the draft of young men into military service
- entertainment dollars to adult males for violent activities such as rodeos, car racing, football, boxing, ice hockey, and violent films and television programs
- media glorification of men who use guns and the easy access to guns in society

Historically, the "killer male" was essential to survival, marriage, and the family. In the future, the communicative male will be essential. Men's movement author Walter Farrell says, "For the first time in human history, what it takes to survive as a species is compatible with what it takes to love." Some men's movement leaders say it's time for us to ask, "How do we want our future to be and how do we adapt?" All of us have the potential for killer-protector and for nurturer-connector. What will encourage males to develop the nurturer-connector within them? A good start is for each of us to notice when men and boys express nurturing-connecting attitudes, to openly appreciate men and boys who act in nurturing-connecting ways, and to reward them appropriately.

Experiencing Barren Father–Son Relationships

More and more men are becoming aware that the way they were raised affects their leadership style and therefore their careers, as well as every other aspect of their lives. For example, some men are beginning to talk about the lack of loving, touching, even liking in their experiences with their fathers.

Some express a very deep sadness and quite a bit of anger that their fathers had never told them that they loved them, were rarely around, and never hugged or kissed them, even when they were little kids. Along with feelings of emptiness and inadequacy because fathers didn't think their sons were "good enough" to justify their love, there was also a loss of role models: "These men just didn't know what men do. Sometimes they learned the most exaggerated male tendencies, such as adopting strict macho behavior. But they certainly didn't learn about father–child tenderness and love," says men's movement leader Bernie Zilbergeld.

The upside? These men want to avoid the same mistakes with their sons. They are trying to learn comfortable ways to express love to their own children. And they're becoming more appreciative of women's style of relating to others and its empowering aspects. They are also seeing that equal sharing of the money-making and child-rearing roles will allow them the time and space for more intimate relationships with their children.

Not Asking for Emotional Support

Father–son arm's-length relationships are just one aspect of the lack of emotional support men typically give and get from one another. Most lack the powerful tool most women use to heal women friends—emotional support for one another. For men, stress often builds, sometimes leading to depression and even suicide.

> In 1970, young men aged 25 to 34 committed suicide at twice the rate of young women. In 1990, it was four times the rate. Young men's suicide rate increased 26 percent, while women's decreased 33 percent.

From adolescence to old age, men are more likely than women to commit suicide. During adolescence, boys' suicide rates go from slightly less than girls' to four times as great. Psychologists speculate that during puberty boys begin to feel intense pressure to perform, pursue, and pay—to be daring and take risks. Boys also sense it isn't acceptable to discuss fears, anxieties, and self-doubt.

Men older than 65 are 14.5 times more likely to commit suicide. They're also more likely to skip needed medication and get inadequate nutrition and thus die through self-neglect. A husband whose wife dies is about 10 times more likely to commit suicide than a wife whose husband dies. Men tend to have fewer intimate friends and family than women, so for men, the loss of love is more devastating.

An Emerging Men's Movement

Many men are confused about what's expected of them now, where the boundary lines are drawn, and how they want to be in this new era. Strong women won't put up with a dominating, dictatorial, or brutal man—but they don't want a weak man either. Men's movement leaders are filling the void with ideas about what men need and with meetings to explore the meaning of being a man today. Most participants are heterosexual, middle-class, midlife Euro-American men.

The men's movement is helping some men move into equitable male–female relationships by giving them permission to be vulnerable and intimate. Men who never learned to share their fear are allowed to do so. Talking about feelings is healing, and when the talk is heard compassionately, even more healing takes place. When men have their men's movement weekends to get in touch with the wild man and warrior parts of themselves, they acknowledge the patriarchy of the past with its structure, discipline, and ritual that helped men overcome obstacles, protected women, and sustained human survival. The men's movement also helps men move on to the modern age. It encourages men to give themselves permission to ask, "Who do I really want to become? How do I want to get there?" By doing this, they can reach a deeper level of personal power.

HOW ARE MEN RESPONDING SPECIFICALLY TO CHANGES IN THE WORKPLACE?

In the past, it was extremely unlikely that a man would ever work for a woman manager or be expected to take equal responsibility with his wife for housework or child care—as many do today. On the other hand, men say they were and are expected to do the most dangerous jobs of the society.

Dealing with Women Managers

Recent surveys by *Working Woman* magazine have asked men what they thought of women managers. Here are some typical comments:

- They obsess on getting one small thing right, and it's blown out of proportion.
- Some are detail-oriented, not conceptual—no sense of corporate mission, the big picture.
- They're too sensitive and take things too personally.
- Some don't get down to business fast enough. First, you have to spend time with them on a personal level.
- They're harder on other women. There's more pettiness or jealousy.
- When two women are at each other's throats, it ruins team spirit.
- When women bond together against men, it's demoralizing.
- Unmarried women bosses make men nervous, especially if their work is their life and they work 14-hour days because they have no home life.
- They don't conceal anger or bitterness as well as men.
- We'd rather work for men. Getting a performance review from a woman is like being lectured by mother; it's very castrating.

Studies by *The Wall Street Journal* indicate that men in predominantly male workplaces are more loyal to their companies than men who work with lots of women. It's largely a matter of comfort. Men think they can be themselves around other men, so it's easier to bond. It's also a matter of status because men attach less prestige to professions that attract a large number of women. Men in traditionally male work environments, such as manufacturing plants, are more upset at the prospect of women invading their turf than are men in hospitals, where women have long been a presence.

Meeting Career Demands

A major source of male frustration, and for some resentment and envy, is that they are trapped in the provider role. A married woman with an employed husband has some choice about work—when, whether, and how much to work. If she has children, the family may need or want the money she can earn, but her decision to stay home with the children or to work part time will normally be admired by friends and neighbors. It will almost never be considered lazy, selfish, or inappropriate. Men say they don't have that luxury.

When men are asked if they would like to take a six-month paternity leave to be with their newborn child, nearly 80 percent say yes, if it wouldn't hurt the family economically and if their wife approved.

Men are more likely than women workers to agree to relocate to undesirable locations and to work less desirable hours. Full-time working men work nine hours per week more in the workplace than full-time working women. However, the women work about 17 hours per week more in the home. Therefore, women typically work eight hours more per week than men.

Doing the "Worst" Jobs

Of the 25 jobs rated the worst in *The American Almanac of Jobs and Salaries,* 24 are 95 to 100 percent male occupied. Ratings are based on a combination of salary, stress, work environment, outlook, security, and physical demands. Worst jobs include truck driver, sheet-metal worker, roofer, boilermaker, lumberjack, carpenter, construction worker, football player, welder, coal miner, and ironworker. Men are expected to brave the hazards and do the dangerous, tough jobs.

- 94 percent of workers who die on the job are men.
- There is one job safety inspector for every six fish and game inspectors.
- Every workday hour a construction worker in the United States loses his life.
- Only men are subject to military draft and combat requirements.

Holding the "Protector" Jobs

Men protect the innocent and helpless, women and children, and the ability to protect generates respect. But men must cope with the dark side of the world in order to protect, and the price is a loss of innocence.

Men suffer the price of war more than women. The aftermath of war is devastating. After World War I, it was called shell shock; after Vietnam, post-traumatic stress disorder. There's also the chemical warfare aftermath, such as Agent Orange and the Gulf War Syndrome. Other results cited by men's movement author Walter Farrell are:

- More Vietnam veterans have committed suicide since the war ended than were killed in the Vietnam War itself.
- About 20 percent of all Vietnam veterans, and 60 percent of combat veterans, were psychiatric casualties.
- In 1978, more than 400,000 Vietnam veterans were either in prison, on parole, on probation, or awaiting trial.
- In 1990, more than 20,000 Vietnam veterans were homeless in Los Angeles alone.

In cultures where men must be protectors, weakness is ridiculed. Young boys search out those with weaknesses, taunting and picking on them. Valuing men as protectors gives us police brutality, the military mentality, and gangs.

> *The National Cancer Society finds that cancer is six times more likely to occur among people who repress their feelings than among cigarette smokers.*

Needing Career–Family Balance

Most men feel a rising pressure to share housework and spend time with their children, since most mothers work outside the home. In 1998, nearly two-thirds of men surveyed said they want the freedom to join women in balancing work–family conflicts during the child-raising years. Men who were surveyed in 1990 reported twice as many work–family conflicts as in 1985. Conflicts include an inability to find child care during overtime hours. But few men felt they could be honest with bosses about family demands and often made up excuses such as "other meetings to attend." The message such men want is that they won't be taken off the fast track or considered marginal just because they express work–family concerns and accept family-oriented benefits.

Men need flexibility about relocating, just as women do. The days may be over when companies can insist that moving up the ladder means moving around the country. In 1994, surveyed companies reported that 45 percent of employees turned down requests to relocate, citing family ties or spouse's employment as key reasons, up from 30 percent in 1986. Companies who are retaining good employees are adapting to their needs.

HOW DO I RECOGNIZE, HANDLE, AND PREVENT SEXUAL HARASSMENT?

Wherever men and women work, there is a certain amount of sexual interaction on the job. When does it become harassment? When the behavior is unwanted, unsolicited, and nonreciprocal; when it asserts a person's sex role over her or his function as a worker; or when it creates an environment that seems hostile to the employee. Sexual harassment can be about anyone of any gender or sexual orientation harassing an employee. Sexual harassment is about misuse of power, not attraction and flattery.

The Equal Employment Opportunities Commission has identified two types of sexual harassment:

1. **Quid prod quo**—"I'll give you job favors for sexual favors" or "I'll take away job favors unless you give me sexual favors."
2. **Hostile environment**—sexuality is discussed, displayed, or used in a way that poisons the workplace for you—this can include workplace porn or a boss who has consensual sex with your coworker, causing an unfair situation for you.

During the 1990s, about 75 percent of court cases on sexual harassment were based on the hostile environment form alone, with only about 6 percent based on quid pro quo alone, and 19 percent based on both forms.

Courts have ruled that the standards of a reasonable woman (instead of the traditional "reasonable man") must be used to determine sexually offensive conduct in organizations when the plaintiff is a woman. The Civil Rights Act of 1991 gives employees the right to jury trials and to limited punitive damages for sexual harassment—in addition to the reinstatement and back pay formerly provided.

WHAT IS SEXUAL HARASSMENT?

Examples of sexual harassment from court cases include:

- physical contact such as patting, stroking, hugging, kissing
- comments on a woman's clothing, body, or appearance
- swearing or "dirty" jokes, pinups, pictures, graffiti, and other visual depictions that are embarrassing or degrading to most women
- indirect harassment caused by being subjected to an environment where sexual harassment occurs even though you are not a target
- favoritism that constitutes a hostile environment; for example, when one employee submits to sexual favors and is rewarded while others who refuse are denied promotions or benefits

What Do We Need to Know about Sexual Harassment?

Sexual harassment is pervasive in the workplace. Most surveys indicate that more that half of women employees have experienced it. Sexual harassment is more about power, domination, and hostility than flirting or sexual attraction. A person who is attracted to you in a positive, respectful sense does not harass you.

Men and women view harassment differently. Men have traditionally thought that women who complain of men's sexual advances have somehow asked for it. They have attempted to label such women as a seductress, trouble-maker, bimbo, fantasizer, frustrated wallflower, voluntary martyr, or nut case. Most women have some sense of the wide disparity between how men and women view sexual harassment and the stereotypical labels that may be pinned on them if they file a complaint. Understandably, most women have refused to file claims, believing that doing so would only make a bad situation worse.

> *About 90 percent of sexual harassment complaints are filed by women, and in most cases, the male harasser has power over the female harassee. About 99 percent of cases are proved valid.*

WHY DOES SEXUAL HARASSMENT OCCUR?

The most common causes of sexual harassment stem from people who:

- abuse power in trying to obtain sexual favors
- try to use sex to gain power
- use power to decrease the power of a victim by reference to her or his sexuality and gender identity
- are reacting to a personal crisis
- won't accept that an affair is over
- have a psychological or substance abuse disorder
- are confused about dealing with new gender roles in the workplace

How Do Men Feel about Sexual Harassment?

Most men feel confusion and concern over sexual harassment. They also object when they think women get away with flirting and men get punished for responding.

Confusion and Concern

Most men are confused about just where the behavioral boundaries are drawn now and at a deeper level, there is an anxiety about changing norms. Some men's movement leaders say the workplace is an easy extension of male adolescence, where boys win attention and other rewards for performing and pursuing. Many men are confused by the sudden switch in rules, and some are concerned about the possibility of a woman with some ulterior motive falsely accusing them of sexual harassment.

Many men don't understand how their girlie calendars and pinups in the office constitute harassment. Some assume they merely make women feel inferior by comparison and that's why they object to them. Women's advocates disagree, saying that pinups signal that sexiness is what counts in the workplace and everywhere else. Such symbols imply that women coworkers are viewed primarily as sex objects rather than fellow human beings and professionals.

The major concern men have is that women can now threaten men with a sexual harassment charge and could theoretically victimize men with false accusations of harassment. Companies can certainly set up procedures for investigating and handling sexual harassment complaints that would make it very difficult for men to be victimized and still provide protection and fairness for women. Conservatives advocate throwing out sexual harassment laws. Liberals say that would be throwing out the baby (women's legitimate problems with men's sexual dominance) with the bath water (women's potential misuse of the laws).

Objections

Men's specific objections to sexual harassment policies include:

- Women still play their old sexual games without being penalized.
- Women still buy the romance formula of the man pursuing and persisting, and the women attracting and resisting until the man overcomes her resistance.
- Women still send mixed messages, saying "no, no" when they mean "yes, yes" or "maybe."
- Women still dress and behave seductively in the office. Miniskirts, slit skirts, thin blouses, plunging necklines, heavy perfume, and flirting are all provocative. These traditional indirect female initiatives are signals to most men to take direct initiative.
- Sexual harassment laws often create a hostile environment for men where the females are like children who must be protected by law.

Some men say that if women would communicate honestly and directly, there wouldn't be a problem. One said, "If a woman tells a man directly, with no mixed messages, that she thinks he's sexually harassing her, at least 99 percent of men will stop in that case." Actually, this is difficult for many women because they consider it direct confrontation, which they take great pains to avoid.

Men's advocates say that sexual harassment education needs to focus on the fact that for men to pursue and persist has been functional throughout history. Today, when we are struggling toward equality, it's no longer functional, at least in the workplace. Women need to understand that to attract and resist is natural because it's also been functional throughout history, but it is no longer functional in the workplace.

What Can Men Do to Avoid Problems?

Let's assume men are the ones who worry about being the harasser, although in a small percentage of cases women are the harassers. If you're a man, you can avoid being accused of sexual harassment by using these strategies:

- **Raise your awareness.** Sexual harassment is a rather complex issue, but you can learn enough to stay out of trouble.
- **Respect the word "no."** When you're at work, it's best to forget the old idea that a woman's "no" may not really mean "no" or that it merely makes the conquest more challenging and exciting.
- **Align your attitude.** Are you still harboring the belief that women are inferior? That men should be in control? If so, work on shifting your beliefs to align with current reality.
- **Support clear policies** and training that spell out what harassment is and how the organization will handle it. If you understand sexual harassment and your company has clear policies about its definition and consequences, you can relax and be yourself (assuming your attitude is in line).
- **Be a role model.** Now that you're savvy about sexual harassment, help other men get it by treating coworkers with respect. For example, refer to women as women, not as "girls," "chicks," "ladies," or similar names. Don't participate in story telling and jokes that demean women as a group. Let others know you don't want to hear or see women being referred to as sex objects.

What Can Women Do to Avoid Problems?

Women can help ease the situation by becoming aware of men's confusion and complaints and, through a greater awareness, sending clear, straight messages. Some specific recommendations for women are:

- **Avoid the sexual stereotype trap.** Women don't need to automatically and unthinkingly fall into others' expectations about their role. *Sex object* is one of the age-old stereotypes that women can avoid by dressing and acting in a businesslike, professional way. Check flirtatious or femme fatale tendencies at the office door.
- **Avoid sexual liaisons at work.** The objective of the office sex game is to increase the man's status with other men. This is one of the ways a man becomes "one of the boys" who make decisions about

promotions and salaries. A woman may therefore increase the status of any man she has sex with and at the same time decrease her own status.

- **Say no tactfully but clearly.** Women can let men know if they don't like being called "honey," "babe," and similar names. Women can send I-messages when they say no to requests for a drink, lunch, dinner, or a date: "I like you, but I don't go out socially with business friends," "I like you, but I never go out with married men," "I value our relationship, but my husband would be hurt if he couldn't share the occasion," "I like you, but I'm not comfortable with going beyond a business relationship." The underlying message is you're not interested in sexual involvement and will always say no to such overtures.

What Can Organizations and Leaders Do?

As a leader, you can use your influence to ask that the organization's policies be designed to prevent most sexual harassment and effectively handle cases that do occur. Leaders must be sure that cases are handled professionally so that everyone's rights are protected. Preventive actions include:

- Management establishes and publicizes a strong policy that specifically describes the kinds of actions that constitute sexual harassment and sets out the consequences for offenders.
- Management suggests that if a manager–subordinate relationship becomes "serious," one party should change jobs out of fairness to other subordinates.
- Management regularly signals that it is committed to fighting harassment.
- The firm provides training seminars designed to sensitize employees.
- The firm sets up complaint procedures and mechanisms that encourage private complaints of harassment and bypass immediate supervisors who are often the source of the problem.

A 1998 survey of 900 companies indicated that complaints have dropped significantly in those companies that take these actions.

What Should a Harassed Employee Do?

Let's pretend the recipient of the harassment is a woman, since that's the typical pattern. A woman in business cannot afford to allow any man to persist in actions that constitute sexual harassment. To do so signals to other men that such behavior may be condoned and sets a poor example for the entire work team. A woman need not accept such a victim role. Here are some specific steps to take.

Be clear.   Say no to overtures, tactfully but clearly. Mean it; give no mixed messages. Object to any sexually inappropriate behavior, communication, or symbolism—again tactfully but clearly and directly.

Confront.   If objectionable behavior continues, tell your harasser that this behavior must stop immediately. Follow up with a memo documenting what you said and hand it to him in the presence of a witness.

Document.   Keep notes of what happened, when, and where. Note who, if anyone, witnessed it. Discuss the incident with any witnesses to nail it down in their minds. Ask them to make a note about it with a date.

Confide.   If you wish to keep the matter officially confidential while you try to put a stop to the behavior, tell only trusted work associates. Ask them to keep brief notes. These people can later testify on your behalf.

Look for a pattern.   Chances are very good that he has harassed other women. Seek out women who have worked with him. Engage in discreet, probing conversations to learn if they have been harassed. If you can establish that he has a pattern of harassment, your case is greatly strengthened.

Report.   If the harassment continues, find out who you should report it to, often someone in the human resources department. If you need further emotional support and advice, look for a local women's organization that provides such services.

Consider alternative steps.   If you don't like the way your organization handles your complaint, you can carry it further—to the EEOC or to court. Consider consulting an attorney who specializes in such cases. Local women's organizations and bar associations may recommend someone. Some courts have recently allowed class action suits where sexual harassment is common in an organization. Carefully weigh the pros and cons.

Be timely.   Determine the statute of limitations for reporting sexual harassment in your state. In most states, you must file a claim within six months of the last occurrence.

How Should Complaints Be Resolved?

Guidelines for resolving sexual harassment complaints include:

■ Take sexual harassment complaints as seriously as other grievances; investigate them as thoroughly.

- Keep such matters entirely confidential.
- Find out what the complainant wants and try to accommodate her.
- Carefully investigate. Appoint an investigative team: one man and one woman who are objective outsiders. Look for documentation, witnesses, confidants, and observers.

If the team cannot substantiate that sexual harassment has occurred (she says it did; he says it didn't), tell the complainant why the firm cannot take definitive action and ask her to report any further occurrences or any instances of retaliation. Tell the accused: The organization had a duty to investigate; he is cleared, but if another complaint is filed, it will have more serious implications.

If the team substantiates that sexual harassment has occurred, use disciplinary procedures that are similar to those used in cases of nonperformance of job duties. Normally, the first offense calls for a warning and some sensitivity training. The second offense calls for some form of punishment: no bonus, no promotion, a demotion, docked pay, or temporary suspension. The third offense calls for dismissal. Ensure that no one retaliates against the complainant, no matter what the outcome.

SELF-TEST #3

In each of the 4 cases, do you think the actions constitute sexual harassment?

1. A male supervisor occasionally compliments his young assistant with remarks such as "You ought to wear short skirts more often" and "Sit and talk to me a little longer; I'm enjoying the view." Is this sexual harassment?

   A. Yes

   B. No

2. A female doctor is discharged from a medical residency program. She tries to understand what went wrong. She remembers that she did not react favorably to a supervising professor's invitation to go out for drinks, compliments about her hair and legs, and questions about her romantic life. He made comments that seemed to imply that he'd like to help her get through the program, but she sensed that going out with him would be part of the relationship. At first, she tried to smile her way through these incidents. Later, she gave disapproving looks or turned away. When he kept on, she finally told him one day that she was busy and abruptly walked away. Is this sexual harassment?

   A. Yes

   B. No

3. A male journalist willingly enters into a love affair with his female supervising editor. She has always rated his work performance as excellent. After a few months, he breaks off the affair. At his next performance review, the journalist receives a less-than-satisfactory rating from her. Is this sexual harassment?

   A. Yes

   B. No

4. Rosita, an advertising copywriter, has been passed over for promotion. A colleague, Hazel, got the job. Rosita is sure Hazel is having an affair with the boss. Several times in the past year, the boss has gone on business trips that called for a copywriter to go along. Each time, he took Hazel instead of Rosita, even though in at least one instance Rosita was the one who had done most of the work on the account he was calling on. Rosita has heard talk from other employees. Rumor has it this is not the first affair the boss has had, nor the first time he has promoted a girlfriend. Is this sexual harassment?

   A. Yes

   B. No

SELF-TEST #3 FEEDBACK

Check your responses to the minicases. Each correct answer is worth 25 points. If you scored less than 75 points, you should review the sexual harassment materials and re-take the Self-Test.

   A. A male supervisor—A. Yes. If these comments create discomfort for the assistant, they could be viewed as creating a hostile environment for her. If the assistant cannot bring herself to confront her supervisor about the issue, she should talk with a mediator, such as a human resource representative. The supervisor should be informed about the effects of his behavior and told to stop.

   B. A female doctor—A. Yes. What actually happened: The female doctor filed sexual harassment charges, and a highly publicized and controversial court case ensued. While the university did not admit that a hostile environment for women existed, they readmitted the female doctor and made other concessions in a settlement. Insiders speculated that the supervising professor was informally reprimanded and sexual harassment training was given to all persons involved in the residency program.

C. A male journalist—A. Yes. When a supervisor enters into a sexual relationship with an employee, a hostile environment is created for all of the employee's coworkers. In this case, the male journalist had an unfair advantage over his coworkers. Because humans are emotional beings, it's quite possible that the performance review was not as objective as it should have been. Since the male journalist entered into the sexual relationship willingly, he cannot claim sexual harassment. He can claim that the performance review was not objective, but his involvement in the affair puts him in a weak position. One of them should have changed jobs.

D. Rosita—A. Yes. If the boss is having an affair with one of his employees, he's creating a hostile environment for the other employees. Rosita may be able to make a case of discrimination based on sexual harassment. The boss is in a weak position if it can be shown that he is having an affair with Hazel. His position is even weaker if it can be shown that he's had affairs with other employees and has shown favoritism toward them. One of them should have changed jobs.

HOW CAN I BREAK THROUGH GENDER BARRIERS?

Barriers to career success are rooted in gender inequality and a failure to value the unique traits and talents that women, as well as men, bring to the workplace. The first step in creating win–win successes is to accept and promote gender equity in the corporate culture and consciously value what women and men can contribute.

Upon this foundation of basic equity and valuing of many talents and ways of expressing them, you can build bridges over such typical barriers as lack of career planning, pay inequity, the glass ceiling, lack of proper training, communication blocks, sexual harassment, and career–family conflicts.

You can personally help to overcome these barriers by being aware, becoming a role model, and helping coworkers to become aware. In the process, you and your coworkers will be changing the corporate culture.

Strategy #1: Value Equality in Relationships

You can help people understand the dramatic shifts in male–female relationships at work and at home. Help them to see the advantages of equality in relationships; for example:

- ***Shared responsibility***, resulting in less stress for men because they now have help making the decisions, earning the family income, and fulfilling other responsibilities that can become burdensome and stressful.

- **More authentic communication** is a natural result of equality in relationships, as research on assertiveness training indicates.
- **Better relationships with women** can be built as aggressive tactics are replaced with assertive ones, since women are less likely to resort to passive-aggressive responses.
- **More freedom** to develop and express all facets of the self grows when people go beyond the limited confines of stereotyped gender traits and roles.

Strategy #2: Promote Gender Equity in the Corporate Culture

The differences in worldviews of men and women suggest some possible difficulties for women in most organizations. They are likely to feel pressured to change their work style and leadership style and experience conflict between leadership and gender roles. If they do become more directive, they are more likely than men to receive negative reactions. Actually, a variety of styles can be effective if the corporate culture values and embraces gender differences.

You can recognize ways in which the corporate culture fails to reflect women's values as well as men's. Help to resolve the conflicts and disadvantages this poses for women and start changing the culture accordingly.

Strategy #3: Value Gender Differences

For many years, women minimized their differences from men and stressed equality in order to show that they could work as effectively as men and deserve equal treatment and rewards. The men who supported them tried not to notice this most noticeable of differences. Admitting one's differences in the American workplace has traditionally meant accepting inferiority. That's because we tend to jump to the conclusion that differences are either good or bad, rather than a source of interesting possibilities. Those who are different are commonly relegated to the edge of a work group. They may be devalued personally and their contributions ignored.

Diverse skills.   Today's organizations, and those of the future, need a different mix of skills, not only because women are present in larger numbers, but because of the ways work itself is changing in the age of the smart machine. Jobs require less muscle and motor skills and more information and people skills. While women continue to acquire many traditional male workplace skills, men must also now master things women have been taught to do well. What these are becomes clearer when we look at organizations run largely by women.

Diverse beliefs and customs.   When women create their own corporate cultures by starting their own companies, the style that emerges is more democratic and less hierarchical, reflecting these beliefs and customs:

- that allowing everyone to contribute and feel powerful and important is good for employees and the organization
- the tendency to share power and information
- more emphasis on collaborative decision making
- more democratic, participative, consultative management
- more decentralization of decision making and responsibility
- greater concern with process and fairness
- more concern with quality of outcomes, while retaining a pragmatic concern for quantitative outcomes
- less autocratic, domineering, ego-involved management
- less concern with titles and formal authority, more concern with responsibility and responsiveness
- less concern for empire building, power and domination, and consciousness about one's turf

Diverse leadership styles.   Typical male leadership styles have stressed tasks and achievements first. Women's leadership style focuses on people first, tasks second and so is more indirect. Studies show that women leaders achieve higher quality and productivity through these strategies:

- greater responsiveness and concern for individual feelings, ideas, opinions, ambitions, and on- and off-the-job satisfactions
- skill at enhancing other people's self-worth
- desire to get others excited about their work
- emphasis on skills as a listener and conversationalist
- high value placed on loyalty, longevity, and interpersonal skills

This represents a balance of masculine and feminine strengths, which would work nicely in today's workplace.

Strategy #4: Communicate Across the Gender Gap

Recognize the different ways women and men view the world and communicate about it. Use your knowledge to bridge the gaps. Recognize when a misunderstanding or a miscommunication is rooted in an assertiveness problem. Help others understand and resolve such problems. Relate to others in an assertive manner and teach this approach to others.

Strategy #5: Support Career Planning

Support women and men in developing and implementing their career plans by treating them all as valued individuals. Don't assume women are not as career committed as men. Encourage people to answer these questions:

- What do you want from your career?
- What goals do you want to set?
- What contributions do you want to make?
- What events might limit your career efforts in the foreseeable future?
- What sort of work life–personal life balance do you want?
- What can the company do to help?

Career planning may be blocked by self-limiting beliefs. Encourage people, especially women, to overcome self-limiting cultural beliefs. Suggest alternative self-empowering beliefs.

Strategy #6: Help to End Pay Inequity and the Glass Ceiling

Pay inequity is endemic in our workforce, a huge problem that no leader could solve alone. However, you can become aware of the ways women have been discriminated against when it comes to pay. You can analyze the compensation packages of all of the employees under your influence. And you can use your influence to eliminate inequities and make sure that women and men receive fair compensation.

Do your share to end or overcome all of the ways—including those many small, hidden, or subtle ways—that the company discriminates against women.

Strategy #7: Give Needed Training

Women need training geared to their particular needs. They may need encouragement to acquire math, computer, technological, and other typically male skills the firm needs. Some women need some all-women classes. Studies indicate that women achieve higher levels of mastery when they take such classes without men around. Women often don't get equal opportunities to attend higher-level management training programs that prepare managers for promotion.

Strategy #8: Resolve Conflicts in Career and Family Demands

The core gender issues, both social and professional, can only be addressed when women and men explore and create equal partnerships. Professional and social relationships must be managed out of respect for individual talents and needs. Relationships must be aligned with a common vision that includes more than profit making. Such a partnership balances care-taking and bread-winning and views social, emotional, and spiritual needs on a par with economic responsibility. Key areas that we can bring into balance in organizations include:

- having the freedom to strike a balance between work and home
- moving beyond woman as sex object and man as success object
- accepting men and women taking paternity leaves and maternity leaves without the company stigmatizing them
- providing flexible systems and benefits for both men and women without stigmatizing those who take advantage of them

Successful companies are providing the type of flexibility dual-career families need. In the 1990s, only 10 percent of firms with 10 or more employees provided such direct benefits as day care or financial assistance with child care, but their numbers are growing.

Strategy #9: End Gender Stereotypes and Sexual Harassment

Many men feel a loss of power, are concerned about reverse discrimination, and express difficulties accepting a woman as their manager. Women may still be sending mixed messages about their sexual interests. Help men and women drop the old role stereotypes about the men's place and the women's place. Take the lead in raising awareness of how such stereotypes limit men and unfairly block women. Speak up when you see people acting out the old myths and assumptions about men's and women's traits, their "place," and their limitations.

Support clear, effective company policies regarding sexual harassment. Make sure that everyone on your team understands the issues and the policies. Be a role model in the way you treat people. If complaints occur, resolve them fairly and firmly.

Women and men need to work in holistic, balanced organizations that reflect the values and customs of both genders. Such organizations allow and encourage people to develop more of their talents and potentials and use those talents to achieve personal and team goals.

FINAL SELF-TEST

Indicate the best answers to the following 10 multiple-choice questions

1. The main issue for career women during child-bearing years is:
   A. flexible office space
   B. adequate maternity leave, child care, and flexible job arrangements
   C. adequate and equal pay
   D. job stability with little or no travel or need to change locale

2. Surveys indicate that the major dilemma men are wrestling with is:
   A. getting or keeping a job
   B. relating well to women
   C. power—the profound difference between personal and collective power
   D. expressing feelings

3. Men are more likely than women to experience personal problems from:
   A. being groomed for violence by society
   B. experiencing barren father–son relationships
   C. feeling unable to ask for emotional support
   D. all of the above

4. Men are more likely than women to experience problems from:
   A. working for women managers
   B. taking the greater share of household responsibilities
   C. holding the "worst" jobs that are the most dangerous, physically difficult, and "dirty"
   D. all of the above

5. Sexual harassment is defined as:
   A. making a sexual proposition
   B. asking someone for a date
   C. behavior of a sexual nature that's unwanted, unsolicited, and unwelcome
   D. making sexual activity an unofficial job requirement

6. Which action clearly constitutes sexual harassment?
   A. a request for a date
   B. sexual innuendo
   C. persistent requests for dates that are clearly unwelcome
   D. a compliment on your appearance

7. The primary source of sexual harassment is people who:
   A. like to flirt
   B. abuse power
   C. are obsessed by sex
   D. are uncomfortable with new roles for women

8. What most men say they want in the area of sexual harassment is:
   A. for women to quit wearing provocative clothing
   B. for women to be more businesslike
   C. for a woman to speak up directly to the man if they feel that the man is sexually harassing them
   D. for companies to issue clear guidelines

9. If a worker is being sexually harassed, the first step is to:
   A. file a complaint
   B. report it to the boss
   C. let the harasser know, loud and clear, that if the behavior doesn't stop, he or she will be reported
   D. try good humor to improve the relationship

10. A company should resolve sexual harassment complaints by:
   A. keeping the magnitude of such a claim in proportion and not overreacting
   B. appointing a male–female investigative team, preferably of objective outsiders, to carefully investigate and document the claim
   C. protecting people from false accusations
   D. keeping the workforce informed of the progress of the investigation

FINAL SELF-TEST FEEDBACK

Each correct answer is worth 10 points. If you score less than 70 points, you should review the materials and re-take the Final Self-Test.

1. The main issue for career women during child-bearing years is:
   A. No, flexible office space is not mentioned as a factor
   B. Yes, the best answer is, adequate maternity leave, child care, and flexible job arrangements
   C. No, although a factor is adequate and equal pay
   D. No, although a factor is job stability with little or no travel or need to change locale

2. Surveys indicate that the major dilemma men are wrestling with is:

   A. No, although a factor may be getting or keeping a job

   B. No, although a factor is relating well to women

   C. Yes, the best answer is power—the profound difference between personal and collective power

   D. No, although a factor may be expressing feelings

3. Men are more likely than women to experience personal problems from:

   A. No, although one factor is being groomed for violence by society

   B. No, although one factor is experiencing barren father–son relationships

   C. No, although one factor is feeling unable to ask for emotional support

   D. Yes, the best answer is all of the above

4. Men are more likely than women to experience problems from:

   A. No, although a problem may be working for women managers

   B. No, men typically don't take the greater share of household responsibilities

   C. Yes, the best answer is holding the "worst" jobs that are the most dangerous, physically difficult, and "dirty"

   D. No, not all of the above

5. Sexual harassment is defined as:

   A. No, although a problem may stem from making a sexual proposition

   B. No, although a problem could stem from asking someone for a date

   C. Yes, the best answer is behavior of a sexual nature that's unwanted, unsolicited, and unwelcome

   D. No, although a problem may stem from making sexual activity an unofficial job requirement, there is a sex industry where this is accepted

6. Which action clearly constitutes sexual harassment?

   A. No, not merely a request for a date

   B. No, not merely sexual innuendo

   C. Yes, the best answer is persistent requests for dates that are clearly unwelcome

   D. No, not merely a compliment on your appearance

7. The primary source of sexual harassment is people who:
   A. No, although a factor could be liking to flirt
   B. Yes, the best answer is people who abuse power
   C. No, although being obsessed by sex is a distinct problem
   D. No, although discomfort with new roles for women could be a factor

8. What most men say they want in the area of sexual harassment is:
   A. No, although wearing provocative clothing can be problematic
   B. No, although being more businesslike is a factor
   C. Yes, the best answer is for a woman to speak up directly to the man if they feel that the man is sexually harassing them
   D. No, although companies need to issue clear guidelines

9. If a worker is being sexually harassed, the first step is to:
   A. No, although a later step may be to file a complaint
   B. No, although a later step may be to report it to the boss
   C. Yes, the best answer is let the harasser know, loud and clear, that if the behavior doesn't stop, he or she will be reported
   D. No, although a positive step may be to try good humor to improve the relationship

10. A company should resolve sexual harassment complaints by:
    A. No, keeping the magnitude of such a claim in proportion and not overreacting is not a resolution strategy
    B. Yes, the best answer is appointing a male–female investigative team, preferably of objective outsiders, to carefully investigate and document the claim
    C. No, although a factor is protecting people from false accusations
    D. No, keeping the workforce informed is not appropriate for a confidential investigation

THE BOTTOM LINE

Think of this as just the beginning of your exploration into gender similarities and differences. Now that you have the basics, let this be a framework for adding new information—just by noticing and questioning what's presented by the media, by asking people about themselves, by caring and really listening.

Chapter Review

1. Male–female myths and stereotypes include:
   - the typical American family consists of working husband and stay-at-home wife
   - women are either good or bad
   - women are viewed as equal to men by society
   - real men are in control of the situation
   - real men don't cry
   - women are too emotional to be leaders

2. Women and men grow up with different worldviews because of being raised differently and our cultural socialization of girls and boys.

3. Communication styles differ between men and women. Men tend to focus on status and competition, and they report on the facts and want to display how they excel. Women are more concerned with connecting and establishing rapport, cooperating with others, and playing down areas where they excel.

4. Stereotypes affect gender roles and expectations in a variety of ways: men are expected to be aggressive, strong, and independent, while women are viewed as emotional or weaker.

5. Gender roles have evolved and changed due to a shift from a patriarchal system to that of a more equality-based system, primarily as a result of the Civil Rights movement of the 1960s. Changes that accelerated this shift include the women's movement, social change in the 1960s, economic change, recent emphasis on ethical values, management style change, education, and reduction of the pay gap.

6. Cultural barriers to women's career success are self-limiting beliefs, conflicting beliefs, pay inequities, glass ceiling, and inflexible working arrangements.

7. Men respond to women's new roles by:
   - feeling a loss of power
   - feeling pressure to perform and change
   - being more violent
   - coming to grips with a barren father–son relationship
   - asking for emotional support—finally
   - emerging men's movement

8. Men must cope with the following workplace issues:
   - dealing with women managers
   - meeting career demands
   - doing the "worst" or most dangerous jobs
   - holding the "protector" jobs
   - needing career–family balance

9. Sexual harassment is clearly defined by the EEOC. Both men and women need to understand what sexual harassment is, why it occurs, what men and women can do to avoid sexual harassment, and what courses of action are available to those who feel harassed.

10. Strategies to overcoming gender barriers are:
   - value equality in relationships
   - promote gender equality
   - value gender differences
   - communicate across the gender gap
   - support career planning
   - help end pay inequality and the glass ceiling
   - give needed training
   - resolve conflict in career and family demands
   - end gender stereotypes and sexual harassment

6

Understanding the Dominant Culture, Euro-Americans

CHAPTER OBJECTIVES

- Know some stereotypes of Euro-Americans that other groups often hold.
- Understand key past events that led to the current dominant Euro-American culture.
- Recognize how Euro-Americans feel about current multicultural relations.
- Understand typical Euro-American worldviews.
- Identify key Euro-American values.
- Recognize unique ways that Euro-Americans relate to others.

Stockbyte

CHAPTER OVERVIEW

If you are an American citizen and your background is not Euro-American, you must constantly deal with the dominant Euro-American culture, which means you are somewhat bi-cultural. Here is an opportunity to learn more about your "other culture." About 75 percent of the employees in the American workplace are Euro-Americans, which accounts for about three out of every four people you're likely to work with.

We can all be well-served by gaining perspective into how other groups typically view Euro-Americans and what it's like to be a Euro-American— from the stereotypes they encounter to the past events most important to their current situation to the values, customs, and issues most important to them. You can better understand the dominant culture you live in, how the American culture differs from other cultures, and how to work most effectively with Euro-Americans.

HOW DO TYPICAL MYTHS AND STEREOTYPES ABOUT EURO-AMERICANS COMPARE WITH REALITY?

Myths are sayings or stories used to bind together the thoughts of a group and promote coordinated social action. Some myths are based on manipulative, hurtful lies, others on harmless little white lies, and some on powerful truths. Stereotypes are rigid, exaggerated, irrational beliefs, each associated with a mental category, such as a particular group of people. Although stereotypes aren't identical to prejudice, rigid stereotypes about people usually lead to prejudice.

Most of the myths and stereotypes about Euro-Americans and other cultural groups are either false or distorted, partial truths. To bridge the divisive walls these stereotypes hold in place, you must know what they are and other realities that balance or refute them, and move beyond myths to a more realistic view of the Euro-American culture. Following are a couple of examples of the many myths about Euro-Americans.

Myth #1: Euro-Americans Are Privileged, Affluent, and Powerful

On average most Euro-Americans *do* tend to be more privileged, affluent, and powerful than people in other U.S. cultural groups. However, most Euro-Americans don't feel that way. For example, women have traditionally dealt with the sexism inherent in a patriarchal society and have only gradually won some of the rights and privileges that Euro-American men have taken for granted.

Most Euro-American men are less aware of any special privileges or powers they possess than they are of the high expectations family and society place upon them to achieve "success." Most feel pressure to win academic, career, and financial success. Most struggle to compete with other Euro-American men who are also trying to achieve status in these areas. Many Euro-American men feel that in recent years they must also compete with women and minorities who have the advantage of civil rights laws and "preferences."

Myth #2: Euro-Americans Will Understand That My Silence on a Controversial Issue Is an Effort to Avoid Controversy

Women from all cultures and people from Latino and Asian cultures often use silence as a way to keep the peace and preserve harmony. But to virtually all Euro-American men in the work world, especially those who take lead roles, *silence means consent.*

Since they would speak up if they did not agree, especially if the issue were important to them, they assume that others would do the same. These different approaches and interpretations often lead to communication breakdown and misunderstanding. Euro-American men tend to assume that if you want or need something, you'll ask for it. If there's a work problem that's bothering you, you'll let people know. If you're not getting what's coming to you, you'll speak up. Euro-American managers are not likely to play a paternal role to the extent that most other cultures expect. They expect employees to take responsibility and to speak up.

WHAT PAST EVENTS LED TO THE CURRENT EURO-AMERICAN DOMINANT CULTURE?

The American culture was founded by Euro-American men, and their values and customs are still the most dominant. Though it contains many elements of Western culture, meaning European, it has a unique flavor of its own. The pioneering, independent spirit of the founding fathers is an important element, as is the belief in the basic equality of people and their right to be free to pursue the American dream.

The term "American, " as used in this book, refers to those qualities of the U.S. culture generally agreed upon by scholars who look at American values and customs as compared to those of other world cultures. While American culture is based on the values and customs of the dominant group, Euro-Americans, it also includes some aspects of its subcultures, such as African American and Latino American. Although culture changes slowly, the American culture *is* changing to reflect more elements of its subcultures as they become greater in number and larger in size.

Nearly all U.S. corporations and corporate cultures were established by Euro-American men, and they are still 95 percent of the top managers who run the major companies. Therefore, corporate cultures are also a reflection of Euro-American male values. But corporations are changing because the marketplace is now global and the workplace is culturally diverse. Corporate cultures must become open and flexible enough to profit from that diversity. For example, management researchers such as Taylor Cox and Roosevelt Thomas have discovered that corporate cultures are increasingly moving away from the old attitude: "We're just one big happy family," which usually implies a one-way approach that means "new employees must adapt to our corporate culture if they want to stay." They're moving toward a new attitude: "We're learning what it's like to walk in other people's shoes so we can fully appreciate what they need and what they can contribute," which implies a two-way approach. This means "our corporate culture is broad enough and flexible enough to adapt to new employees from a diversity of backgrounds, just as they adapt to us."

HOW DO EURO-AMERICANS FEEL ABOUT MULTICULTURAL RELATIONS IN THE UNITED STATES?

You can work more effectively with Euro-Americans (and, if you are a Euro-American, you can understand your own culture better) if you understand how most Euro-Americans view multicultural relations in the United States. The resulting beliefs, concerns, hopes, and behavioral patterns affect everyday workplace relationships.

Multicultural relationships were the theme of the 1998 National Conference on Whiteness held at the University of Chicago. When discussing this issue and telling their stories, about one-third of the Euro-American participants expressed concerns. But about one-third offered positive guidelines and suggestions for dealing with the concerns, and about one-eighth expressed positive expectations and hopes.

Euro-Americans, like people from other cultures, tend to speak of other "races," rather than other ethnicities or cultures. Most experts say the concept of race is scientifically meaningless because few experts agree on what constitutes a race of people and because intermingling has been so common throughout the world. Still, "race" is seen by most people as the primary basis for our divisive differences.

Underlying Beliefs

Not every Euro-American is willing to acknowledge the notion that there is such a thing as Euro-American or "white" culture, which may stem from at least two beliefs.

Belief #1

Race does not affect my own life in a personal way. Race is something important to people of color, but of no central importance to Euro-Americans.

Yet, the experiences expressed by the participants at the Conference on Whiteness indicated that race, and the fact of being Euro-American, impacted them in a number of different settings, in a multitude of roles, on various occasions. The fact that Euro-Americans do not consciously think of themselves as racial beings is not necessarily a good guide. Clearly, all Americans are affected by the common concept of "race," which experts would refer to as "ethnicity" or "cultural heritage." In fact, there are few other social phenomena that affect us across such a wide range of circumstances.

Belief #2

Being Euro-American does not lead me to have common experiences with other Euro-Americans.

Yet, in listening to people's concerns and hopes, conference participants sensed remarkable familiarity with it all. They seemed to enjoy the sharing that took place, and much of the sharing stemmed from a common understanding of the feelings, issues, and concerns that were expressed. The experience of being Euro-American was articulated by the participants, and they seemed to understand the impact of this shared experience. Euro-American culture, and the Euro-American experience, has a real and significant presence in the American cultural mosaic.

Concerns of Euro-Americans

Many conference participants felt concern about racial distance and polarization. On the positive side, participants who had overcome this distance at some time in their lives reported the experience as very positive, something very valuable to be sought out.

Racism

Racism here refers to stereotyping, prejudice, discrimination, and exclusion from the society. Here are some comment summaries:

1. We live comfortable lives that make us unaware of the hazards people of other subcultures face at the hands of Euro-Americans.
2. Racist acts are second nature for some Euro-Americans who feel they can practice them without paying the price.
3. Outright and blatant discrimination is still practiced by Euro-Americans in a way that is hidden from view in our larger, multiracial society.
4. The group in power, such as Euro-Americans in the United States, uses that power to its advantage, even when on the face of things it proclaims to desire equality.
5. We stereotype people and these stereotypes are often wrong.
6. It is painful to witness discrimination against people from other subcultures and to realize it is Euro-Americans who are doing it.
7. We are sometimes condescending toward people of other subcultures and this prevents us from forming genuine relationships.

Society's Racist Structure

Institutionalized racism creates difficulties, even for those Euro-Americans who want to move beyond racism. Some express a sense of helplessness in trying to create significant change:

1. Racial difference is not a natural concept. Children learn it from adults.
2. Segregation has been present in our lives since we were young.
3. Our society is racially structured, and we are simply pawns in the structure.
4. All groups have racial preferences.
5. Everyone is taught that other cultures are bad.
6. Structural racism is hard to see when you are part of the structure, but its effects are still there.
7. The U.S. government encourages the idea of race as an identifier.
8. In a pluralistic society, it takes a lot of work to consider everyone's feelings and social needs.

9. We sometimes have to choose between our personal desire for closeness to people from other subcultures and the demands of the Euro-
   American culture.

Difficulties in Cross-Cultural Relationships

Some Euro-Americans said that even when they make a concerted effort to
establish cross-cultural relationships, barriers often exist:

1. Being Euro-American creates a barrier to forming genuine relationships with people of color.
2. Difference is relative. When we step outside our Euro-American
   culture, we become "different."
3. When you don't belong to a culture, it can and often will ostracize you.
4. Sometimes, we see color discrimination where it does not exist.
5. Some people of color are furious with us.
6. People of color invoke feelings of fear and aversion in us and it is
   painful to feel these things.

Increased Divisiveness

Many Euro-Americans expressed concern over increased divisiveness:

1. We have lost the sense of opportunity that used to hold people together in the United States.
2. Individualism is fading as a social value, with the politics of
   difference and group difference becoming more important.
3. Being part of the Euro-American culture, and the skills it teaches us, is
   becoming dysfunctional in today's pluralistic society.
4. There is an uncomfortable, and possibly growing, distance between
   Euro-Americans and people from other American subcultural groups.
5. Our society is becoming fragmented.

Not all participants shared each and every concern, but the list reflects
how typical Euro-Americans view their racial experience in the United
States. As such, it provides a description of how and why Euro-Americans
conduct themselves in the way they do.

Positive Expectations and Hopes

Offsetting the concerns are expressions of hope and positive viewpoints
about multicultural relations:

1. Difference makes life interesting.
2. Establishing authentic and trusting relationships across racial
   boundaries is a wonderful experience.

3. Learning about diversity is an essential and positive component of our children's education.

4. Personal relationships can bridge racial and cultural differences.

5. Change can happen quickly and be a positive experience.

6. Being a numerical minority in a pluralistic society does not necessarily mean one will be dominated by others.

7. It is important for us as Euro-Americans to explore our own identity.

8. It feels nice not to be stereotyped as "white" by people of color.

9. We need to see that opportunity in our society applies to people of all races.

Ideas for Dealing with Multicultural Relations

Also offsetting the concerns about multicultural relations that Euro-Americans expressed were suggestions and guidelines for dealing with these concerns.

Moving Beyond Racism

Rising above racism and moving beyond it was a dominant theme:

1. Labels are bad.

2. It is desirable not to be aware of someone's race.

3. We can tell who is Euro-American and who isn't, but we don't think of it like that.

4. Difference does not necessarily mean bad. We are all different and products of a culture.

5. Our concepts as children about racial difference are often misleading.

6. Other types of difference besides race can divide people. Often racial identity is not as important as other identities. Ethnicity is important, too.

7. Euro-American culture has very good and very bad points.

8. Euro-Americans differ among ourselves regarding relationships with people of other subcultures.

9. To really learn about a culture, one must be exposed to it.

10. Personal contact with people of other races is important.

Taking Responsibility

Some Euro-Americans expressed ideas indicating that minorities could take more responsibility:

1. When we send our kids to a school that is predominantly Euro-American, it doesn't necessarily have anything to do with race.

2. People of color use race as an excuse; individuals are made by their own efforts.

3. Being viewed as other than Euro-American can be a positive thing.

4. Sometimes, segregation is positive, as when immigrants band together in communities because they have difficulty negotiating the larger culture.

Many Euro-Americans do in fact informally subscribe to views such as these to guide their own actions and to interpret the actions of others. Because these guidelines are cultural, they are often unquestioned. To many participants, they seemed to simply be statements of what is obviously true.

SELF-TEST #1

Indicate the best answers to the following 10 multiple-choice questions.

1. Most Euro-Americans:
    A. are quite aware of the relative power and privileges they enjoy
    B. feel a relative lack of power and privilege, especially the women
    C. are more aware of cultural success pressures and competition than of power and privilege, especially the men
    D. both b and c

2. Most Euro-American men:
    A. use silence as a method of avoiding controversy
    B. interpret silence on a potentially controversial issue as consent to the prevailing opinion
    C. interpret silence on a potentially controversial issue as possibly a way of avoiding controversy
    D. don't know how to interpret silence

3. The proportion of top management positions held by Euro-American men is:
    A. 35%
    B. 95%
    C. 65%
    D. 55%

4. Euro-Americans who resist the idea that there is a Euro-American culture tend to believe that:
    A. race doesn't affect my own life in a personal way
    B. race is important to people of color
    C. being Euro-American doesn't necessarily mean I have common experiences with other Euro-Americans
    D. all of the above

5. A concern that Euro-Americans express about racism is:

    A. it will lead to racial bloodshed and violence

    B. it is a sin against God

    C. we stereotype people and these stereotypes are often wrong

    D. all of the above

6. A concern Euro-Americans express about society's racist structure is that:

    A. it is falling apart

    B. we're just pawns in society's racial structure

    C. we're one of the few societies that is still racially structured

    D. all of the above

7. A concern Euro-Americans express about the difficulty of cross-cultural relationships is that:

    A. being Euro-American makes it difficult to form such relationships

    B. some people of color are furious with Euro-Americans

    C. people of color invoke feelings of fear and aversion in us, which is painful

    D. all of the above

8. A concern Euro-Americans express about increased divisiveness in the society is that:

    A. we learn the skills to bridge divisiveness but we're not using them

    B. our society is becoming fragmented

    C. we still have a sense of opportunity but it's not holding us together

    D. we're closing the distance between groups but not fast enough

9. A positive view that Euro-Americans express about multiculturalism is that:

    A. segregation has essentially ended

    B. Euro-Americans never engage in workplace discrimination

    C. our society is becoming more unified

    D. difference makes life interesting

10. A way offered by Euro-Americans for moving beyond racism is to be aware that:

    A. difference is not always bad

    B. our concepts as children about racial differences are often misleading

    C. to really learn about a culture, you must be exposed to it

    D. all of the above

SELF-TEST #1 FEEDBACK

Each correct answer is worth 10 points. If you score less than 70 points, you should review the materials and re-take the Self-Test.

1. Most Euro-Americans:
   A. No, in fact most are not aware of the relative power and privileges they enjoy
   B. Yes, although they do feel a relative lack of power and privilege, especially the women
   C. No, although they are more aware of cultural success pressures and competition than of power and privilege, especially the men
   D. Yes, the best answer is both b and c

2. Most Euro-American men:
   A. No, they don't use silence as a method of avoiding controversy
   B. Yes, the best answer is interpret silence on a potentially controversial issue as consent to the prevailing opinion
   C. No, they don't interpret silence on a potentially controversial issue as possibly a way of avoiding controversy
   D. No, they do in fact interpret silence

3. The proportion of top management positions held by Euro-American men is:
   A. No, not 35%
   B. Yes, 95%
   C. No, not 65%
   D. No, not 55%

4. Euro-Americans who resist the idea that there is a Euro-American culture tend to believe that:
   A. No, although this is a factor, race doesn't affect my own life in a personal way
   B. No, although this is a factor, race is important to people of color
   C. No, although this is a factor, being Euro-American doesn't necessarily mean I have common experiences with other Euro-Americans
   D. Yes, all of the above is the best answer

5. A concern that Euro-Americans express about racism is:
   A. No, although this could be a factor, it will lead to racial bloodshed and violence
   B. No, although this could be a factor, it is a sin against God

C. Yes, the best answer is we stereotype people and these stereotypes are often wrong

D. No, not all of the above

6. A concern Euro-Americans express about society's racist structure is that:

A. No, it is falling apart was not a concern that was expressed

B. Yes, the best answer is we're just pawns in society's racial structure

C. No, we're one of the few societies that is still racially structured is not a concern

D. No, not all of the above

7. A concern Euro-Americans express about the difficulty of cross-cultural relationships is that:

A. No, although being Euro-American makes it difficult to form such relationships

B. No, although some people of color are furious with Euro-Americans

C. No, although people of color invoke feelings of fear and aversion in us, which is painful

D. Yes, all of the above is the best answer

8. A concern Euro-Americans express about increased divisiveness in the society is that:

A. No, it wasn't stated that we learn the skills to bridge divisiveness but we're not using them

B. Yes, the best answer is our society is becoming fragmented

C. No, in fact a concern is that we're losing a sense of opportunity

D. No, it wasn't stated that we're closing the distance between groups but not fast enough

9. A positive view that Euro-Americans express about multiculturalism is that:

A. No, not that segregation has essentially ended

B. No, not that Euro-Americans never engage in workplace discrimination

C. No, not that our society is becoming more unified

D. Yes, difference makes life interesting

10. A way offered by Euro-Americans for moving beyond racism is to be aware that:

A. No, although a factor is that difference is not always bad

B. No, although a factor is that our concepts as children about racial differences are often misleading

C. No, although a factor is that to really learn about a culture, you must be exposed to it

D. Yes, all of the above

SNAPSHOT 6.1 The Euro-American culture.

Worldview	Personal Values	Relationships
Conquering nature	Individualism	Friendliness
Progress	Achievement	Generosity
Change	Self-reliance	Many casual friends
Rationalism	Assertiveness	Competition
Scientific method	Work hard–play hard	Cooperative achievement
Facts, practicality	Material success	Fair play
Measuring things	Freedom	Specialized roles
Quantifying things	Self-improvement	Directness
Either–or thinking	Keeping busy	Informality
Change oriented	Staying young	Arms'-length closeness
Future oriented		Step-by-step time

HOW DO EURO-AMERICANS VIEW THE WORLD AND HOW IS THAT DIFFERENT?

The American culture was founded by Euro-Americans, and their values and customs still prevail. Though it contains many elements of Western culture, meaning European, it has a unique flavor of its own. The pioneering, independent spirit of the founding fathers is an important element, as is the belief in the basic equality of people and the their right to be free to pursue the American dream. Important scholars who have contributed to our understanding of the Euro-American culture include Gary Althen, E. T. Hall, Philip R. Harris, Geert Hofstede, Robert L. Kohs, Robert T. Moran, and Edward C. Stewart.

Most Euro-Americans think of themselves as individuals first, the world as basically inanimate, nature as something to be conquered, material success as the major goal, and "doing" as the preferred state. Most value self-improvement and hard work as the way to ensure a better future for themselves and their families. Most Euro-Americans believe in scientific and technological "progress," viewing the world in rational, linear, cause-and-effect terms. People from other cultures usually see Euro-Americans as pragmatic, factual, and future oriented, with a tendency to view things more in either–or terms than the shades between. Snapshot 6.1 gives an overview of the Euro-American culture.

Worldview #1: Controlling Nature

Making progress often requires controlling nature. Most Euro-Americans tend to implicitly assume that the external, non-human world is physical and material, like a complex machine with many parts and therefore does not have a soul or a spirit. Nature, Mother Earth, is not seen as a living entity.

Euro-Americans, probably more than any other group, believe the physical environment is there to be used, even exploited, for human purposes. This contrasts with views common in Asia and among American Indians that stress the unity among all forms of life and inanimate objects. They see people as part of nature and the physical world instead of in opposition to them.

Worldview #2: Making Progress and Welcoming Change

Euro-Americans believe in and value progress—scientific and technological developments that improve our material world. They often use their concept of progress to evaluate others. This concept is unknown by many in the non-Western world and may be rejected by them.

Euro-Americans have traditionally believed that the basic problems of the world are technological and their solution will bring about economic abundance. The final measure of what's good and desirable is how economically feasible or lucrative it is. Progress is usually tied to the human struggle to increase physical comfort, health, material possessions, and standard of living. Also tied to the concept of progress is a feeling of general optimism toward the future, that human efforts can bring about a better future in which there is enough for everyone.

Worldview #3: Using a Rational, Linear, Cause-and-Effect Approach

Most Euro-Americans believe that everything has a cause-and-effect relationship, as in the operation of a machine. They see the world as rational in the sense that they believe the events of the world can be explained and the reasons for particular occurrences can be determined. Effective performance in the real world is based on experience, training, and education, which should be practical.

Euro-Americans believe in the scientific method. This means they focus on facts, figures, and techniques as the means to solve problems that represent obstacles to achieving their goals. Their action orientation leads them to look for a simple cause of an event, so they can plug this cause into their problem-solving process and decide on a course of action. Euro-Americans like to develop alternative courses of action, anticipate their future effects, compare them, and choose the one that seems best for their purpose. They like action plans that are practical, with results that are visible, measurable, and materialistic. Euro-Americans see action (and the world itself) as a chain of events, a connection of causes and effects projecting into the future.

Worldview #4: Getting the Facts, Putting Them to Work

Most Euro-Americans don't pay much attention to theories that don't seem to have a practical application. The role of concepts and ideas is to provide direction for purposeful activity. Theories are judged and tested according to their usefulness in daily life.

Euro-Americans love facts. Their thinking process generally begins with facts and then proceeds to ideas, an inductive process. How good the ideas are depends on how well they work and whether people can bring them into the way they do business. Euro-Americans are somewhat unique in their insistence on practical applications—their continual need to organize their perceptions of the world into a form than enables them to act. They will accept a certain amount of pure science (research for the sake of curiosity), but they expect most research to result in technology or products they can use, something that represents "progress." This operational style of thinking leads to an emphasis on consequences and results.

Euro-Americans especially resist systems of thought that lose sight of the individual. For example, despite many programs of governmental responsibility and care for the individual, Euro-Americans resist unifying them into a system of ideology, some sort of modified socialism. Instead, they cling to the ideal of individual enterprise, a belief that keeps self-identity intact.

Worldview #5: Measuring Things

Euro-Americans prefer qualities that can be measured and like to see the world in dimensions that can be quantified. Even quality and experience can be at least partially quantified, if only as first or last, least or most. Or they can assign them arbitrary values, such as "a scale of 1 to 7." In business, government, and academia, Euro-Americans tend to use statistics to measure success, failure, amount of work, ability, intelligence, and overall job performance.

Worldview #6: Thinking in Either–Or Terms

When Euro-Americans value the scientific method, objectivity versus subjectivity, and measurable outcomes, it allows them to set a numerical cutoff point for whether something is one way or another. This may be one reason Euro-Americans tend to focus on either–or viewpoints rather than many subtle differences. Euro-Americans draw a clear distinction between the subjective or personal and the objective or impersonal.

Euro-Americans often ask such questions as, "Who's your best friend?" or "What's your favorite color?" People outside their culture generally have difficulty answering such questions because the answer depends on knowing additional factors, such as work friends or social friends, color for a room or color for a suit. Euro-Americans often set up unequal dichotomies, with one element valued more than the other; for example, right/wrong, good/evil, work/play, peace/war. These polarities simplify our view of the world, prime us for action, and provide us with our typical method of evaluating by means of comparison.

When it comes to evaluating people, however, Euro-Americans allow more shades of gray. Most are unlikely to give much thought to church views that humans are flawed or evil by nature. They are more likely to see humans as a mixture of good and bad or as creatures of their environment and experience. Most important, they stress their ability to change.

Worldview #7: Using Time to Change the Future

Most Euro-Americans see time as an abstract quality, separate from self. "Time moves fast. You've got to keep up with the times." Time is something we organize, schedule, use, and save. In business time is money, so being on time and using time efficiently are critical.

Euro-Americans are future oriented. They believe they can improve on the present and that action and hard work pays off in creating a better future for themselves. Euro-Americans see any unpleasantness at work, or any stress due to incessant activity, as necessary intermediate steps for change and progress toward the future. In contrast, Latinos, who have a present orientation, focus on immediate events. Chinese, who have a past orientation, focus on traditions.

Self-Analysis 6.1   Your Sense of Time

Purpose: To increase your awareness about how you and others view and use time.

Instructions: *Describe briefly at least one instance when you and someone from a different cultural background experienced conflict, misunderstanding, or problems about time. Use the following list to help you remember your situation:*

- being on time
- meeting deadlines
- feeling hurried, rushed
- using time efficiently
- using time effectively
- being "out of sync"
- feeling impatient over others' slowness

- focusing on past events, tradition
- living for the moment, short-range view
- focusing on the present moment
- focusing on the future, what might happen
- focusing on planning, or long-range view
- other issues about time

WHAT DO EURO-AMERICANS VALUE THE MOST, AND HOW IS THAT DIFFERENT FROM OTHER CULTURES?

Becoming an achieving individual is the name of the game for Euro-Americans. As the most individualistic culture on the planet, Euro-Americans value responsible, autonomous individuals who make their own decisions and go out and achieve in the world. They admire people who work hard, play hard, get rich, and stay young.

Value #1: Becoming an Individual

Euro-Americans love their freedom to be autonomous individuals. Closely related are the values of competition and assertion. They admire people who decide what they want and go for it, who are willing to compete and don't easily give up. They generally don't place as much faith in fate or luck as do people in many other cultures. The meaning of their brand of self-reliance is neither translatable nor self-evident in other cultures.

Value #2: Making Their Own Decisions

Most Euro-Americans encourage their children, from the earliest age, to decide for themselves, to make up their own minds. They encourage them to believe that they're the best judge of what they want and what they should do. Therefore, as adults they're likely to view bankers, teachers, counselors, and other experts as people who can give them advice, not as people who should make decisions for them. Euro-Americans expect to choose their own mates, careers, homes, and to some extent, lifestyles. By contrast, in many other cultures, all or part of these decisions are made by parents.

Euro-Americans believe in democratic processes that are fair, give everyone an equal say, and help groups make action decisions. Most believe in majority rule and that people are capable of helping to make good decisions, although many Euro-American men still accept the chain of command and autocratic decision making in military, government, and business organizations. In contrast, some Asian cultures reach group decisions by feeling around or groping for a voice, preferably that of the chairman, that will express the group's consensus. It's offensive for any one person to urge the group to accept his own opinion about what to do.

Most Euro-Americans believe that personal motivation should come from within. They don't like it when others, such as their managers, impose their own motives on them, especially when the managers issue orders and threats. Euro-Americans value persuasion as the method of coordinating people in organizations. The subtle threat of failure is always in the background, which empowers the manager's persuasive appeals to self-interest and reason. Euro-Americans want to believe that they decide what they must do.

In rank/status cultures, people accept a personal bond between subordinate and superior, which makes the authority figure an acceptable source of motivation. Direct orders, explicit instructions, and demands for personal conformity may be acceptable, and even desirable, in such cultures. To people from such cultures, the Euro-American preference for persuasion may be seen as weakness on a leader's part, and self-determination may be viewed as egotism and a threat to the organization.

Value #3: Competing and Achieving

Euro-Americans tend to think they can achieve just about anything, given enough time, money, and technology. Externalized achievement has traditionally been the dominant motivation of Euro-American men, and they use competition as the primary method for driving themselves and others to achieve. Competition is seen by many as the keystone of American culture.

In many non-Western cultures, affiliation is the primary motivation and way of relating to others. A communal feeling toward each other excludes the incentive to excel over others, either as a member of a group or individually. Euro-American values seem to be evolving, however. For example, some Euro-American men, who formerly felt compelled to be competitive, are becoming more group-oriented and less autonomous in their behavior, as demonstrated in self-managing work teams and other alliances.

Value #4: Working Hard and Playing Hard

Euro-Americans are known to be work oriented and efficient. They act upon persons, things, or situations. Others may see them as living at a fast pace, incessantly active.

Most Euro-Americans fill their waking hours primarily in a *doing* mode, seldom asking if getting things done is worth it. They like the kind of activity that results in accomplishments that are measurable by standards that their culture says are valuable.

Euro-Americans believe hard work is rewarded by success, and failure usually means you didn't know how to do it right, you didn't try hard enough, or you're too lazy to care. In contrast, people in some other cultures fill their waking hours in a *being* mode. Their focus is on valuing the spontaneous expression of themselves as humans or on developing all aspects of the self toward a higher-level, integrated, whole person.

Euro-Americans are somewhat unique in categorizing activities as either work activities or play activities. Work is pursued for a living. You may not necessarily enjoy it, but you must do it and you put it first. In contrast, many non-Westerners rarely allow work to interfere with the amenities of living.

For Euro-Americans, play is relief from the drudgery and monotony of work and is enjoyable in its own right. However, they often pursue play with the same seriousness of purpose as they pursue work. Euro-Americans tend to admire the person who "works hard and plays hard."

Value #5: Gaining Material Success

Most Euro-Americans consider it almost a right to be materially well-off and physically comfortable. People should have shelter, clothing, warmth, and all the other necessities for material comfort. An important part of the good life is each household unit having its own house, car, and other physical possessions. Most Euro-Americans spend great time, effort, and money acquiring such comforts. They expect convenient, rapid transportation, preferably under their control, a variety of clean and healthful foods, and comfortable homes equipped with many labor-saving devices, certainly including central heat and hot water.

The Euro-American stress on material things is related to the achievement value and to the European belief in private property, one that is highly valued and upheld by an entire legal system. It's difficult for many Euro-Americans to imagine, but some cultures don't even have a concept of private property, and some Asian cultures value a person's "state of grace" much more highly than their material wealth.

Value #6: Staying Young

Euro-American culture is a youth culture. It often seems that everyone wants to look and act about 25. In most cultures, such as Asian and Latino, older persons are nearly always catered to, honored, and even revered. In the U.S., they're often ignored, even shunned.

Self-Analysis 6.2　Your Values

Purpose: To learn more about your personal values.

Brainstorming Phase. Focus on these three questions:

1. What are the aspects of my life that I treasure the most? That I wouldn't want to lose? That I would fight to keep?

2. What are those aspects of life that I don't yet have and want most to have? That I would work hard to have?

3. What are my values?

Relax, close your eyes for a few moments, and think about these questions. Remember, the purpose is to learn more about you. Don't evaluate, judge, or analyze what comes up; just accept it.

(continued)

Self-Analysis 6.2	**Your Values** *continued*

Writing Phase. Write a few words about the thoughts and feelings that came up—in whatever sequence you remember them.

Categorizing Phase. Look over what you've written. See if the items fall into any patterns or categories, such as: *family, friends, work, leisure money, power, beauty, truth, intelligence, emotions, and spirituality.* You'll find your own categories, not necessarily these. Play with your list till you see some logical categories; then rearrange it by category, putting the most important categories and values first.

SELF-TEST #2

Indicate the best answers to the following 10 multiple-choice questions.

1. Euro-Americans tend to believe that:
    A. Mother Earth is a living entity
    B. we should stress unity among all forms of live and inanimate objects
    C. making progress often requires controlling nature
    D. the world, including human and non-human aspects, is spiritual

2. Euro-Americans tend to believe that:
    A. real progress comes from scientific and technical developments that improve the material world
    B. the basic problems of the world stem from poor relationships among people
    C. the final measure of what is good is how self-sustaining it is
    D. we should tie progress to the human struggle to increase self-understanding

3. Most Euro-Americans believe that:
    A. everything has a cause-and-effect relationship
    B. the events of the world can be explained
    C. the reasons for particular occurrences can be determined
    D. all of the above

4. The Euro-American thinking process usually:
  A. begins with an idea(s), then proceeds to the supporting facts
  B. values an idea by how complex and consistent it is
  C. focuses on ideas that have practical applications
  D. emphasizes a proper or elegant way to reach an end result

5. A key aspect of American culture is that most Americans tend to:
  A. see many the shades of gray in most situations
  B. view situations in a circular, intuitive way
  C. view situations in a rational, linear, cause–effect way
  D. are fascinated by theories

6. Euro-Americans admire people who:
  A. focus primarily on cooperating
  B. decide what they want and go for it
  C. are lucky in life
  D. know when to cut their losses

7. Traditionally, the primary motivation of Euro-American men has been:
  A. providing for their family
  B. making progress
  C. externalized achievement
  D. teamwork

8. Most Euro-Americans fill their waking hours primarily in the mode of:
  A. being
  B. having
  C. doing
  D. evolving

9. An important part of the typical Euro-American good life is:
  A. having your own home
  B. owning a car
  C. being materially comfortable
  D. all of the above

10. Euro-American culture most glorifies:
  A. youth
  B. experience
  C. wisdom
  D. self-knowledge

SELF-TEST #2 FEEDBACK

Each correct answer is worth 10 points. If you score less than 70 points, you should review the materials and re-take the Self-Test.

1. Euro-Americans tend to believe that:
   A. No, the belief that Mother Earth is a living entity is not prevalent
   B. No, they don't stress unity among all forms of live and inanimate objects
   C. Yes, the best answer is making progress often requires controlling nature
   D. No, the belief that the world is spiritual is not prevalent

2. Euro-Americans tend to believe that:
   A. Yes, the best answer is real progress comes from scientific and technical developments that improve the material world
   B. No, poor relationships among people as a major problem is not a prevalent belief
   C. No, it's not a prevalent belief that the final measure of what is good is how self-sustaining it is
   D. No, it's not a prevalent belief that we should tie progress to the human struggle to increase self-understanding

3. Most Euro-Americans believe that:
   A. No, although they do believe that everything has a cause-and-effect relationship
   B. No, although they do believe that the events of the world can be explained
   C. No, although they do believe that the reasons for particular occurrences can be determined
   D. Yes, the best answer is all of the above

4. The Euro-American thinking process usually:
   A. No, it doesn't usually begin with an idea(s), then proceed to the supporting facts
   B. No, the process normally does not include valuing an idea by how complex and consistent it is
   C. Yes, the best answer is focuses on ideas that have practical applications
   D. No, it usually doesn't emphasize a proper or elegant way to reach an end result

5. A key aspect of American culture is that most Americans tend to:
   A. No, most don't see many the shades of gray in most situations
   B. No, most don't view situations in a circular, intuitive way
   C. Yes, most view situations in a rational, linear, cause–effect way
   D. No, most are not fascinated by theories

6. Euro-Americans admire people who:
   A. No, the best answer is not *focus primarily on cooperating*
   B. Yes, the best answer is *decide what they want and go for it*
   C. No, the best answer is not *are lucky in life*
   D. No, the best answer is not *know when to cut their losses*

7. Traditionally, the primary motivation of Euro-American men has been:
   A. No, though providing for their family is an important motivator
   B. No, though making progress is an important motivator
   C. Yes, the best answer is externalized achievement
   D. No, though teamwork may be an important motivator

8. Most Euro-Americans fill their waking hours primarily in the mode of:
   A. No, not being
   B. No, not having
   C. Yes, the best answer is doing
   D. No, not evolving

9. An important part of the typical Euro-American good life is:
   A. No, although having your own home is important
   B. No, although owning a car is important
   C. No, although being materially comfortable is important
   D. Yes, the best answer is all of the above

10. Euro-American culture most glorifies:
    A. Yes, youth
    B. No, not experience
    C. No, not wisdom
    D. No, not self-knowledge

HOW DO EURO-AMERICANS RELATE TO OTHERS?

Euro-Americans are seen by those in other cultures as friendly and informal, direct and casual. They have many casual friendships and few deeply committed ones. They believe in cooperation and fair play, in specialized roles, and in positive change.

Custom #1: Making Many Casual Friends

Euro-Americans are known to be friendly, informal, and generous. They tend to reject the idea of someone being special or privileged merely because of birth. They are more likely to defer to those who have achieved power and affluence through their own merit. The way they dress and greet each other tends to be informal relative to many cultures. Euro-Americans are known to be generous, willing to come to the aid of people in emergencies, and to embrace a good cause.

To Euro-Americans a "friend" may be a passing acquaintance or a lifetime intimate, but they tend to have many personal relationships that are friendly and informal and to form few deep and lasting friendships. In contrast, people from many other cultures are slow to form friendships, but once committed, they're friends for life. They will do almost anything for a such a friend, such as loan them money or help them move furniture. In these situations Euro-Americans are likely to hire professional help, preferring not to inconvenience friends (or be inconvenienced if the situation were reversed). Euro-Americans' immediate friendliness, forming of instant friendships, and lack of deep commitment are confusing to people from deep-friendship cultures.

Euro-Americans change friends and membership groups more easily than most. Though they tend to spend a great deal of time in social activities, they are likely to avoid personal commitments and intense involvement except with one or two "best friends." Their exchange of invitations and gifts is within a loose, informal framework. The quality of their social interactions tends to stress equality, informality, impermanence, and personal detachment.

Many Euro-Americans need to express friendship and be popular in order to feel self-confident. They often judge their personal and social success by popularity, almost literally by the number of people who like them.

Custom #2: Keeping Arm's Length—Use of Space

Euro-Americans' boundaries tend to be about arm's length. When someone breaks through that boundary, they may feel invaded, and the act often carries sexual or belligerent overtones. The way they use space reflects their desire to have privacy and maintain some distance in their personal lives. Traditionally, the more space and privacy a person has—both in the workplace and at home—the higher their position probably is. Euro-Americans are more willing than others to sacrifice to have more floor space and yard space.

Custom #3: Fitting into Specialized Roles

As a primarily industrial economy, workplace roles have been developed and filled with specialists who deal with specific functions and problems. The organizational hierarchy has been like a machine with interchangeable parts; that is, people with specific skills. Until recently, Euro-Americans did not think of an organization as growing out of the unique qualities that people brought to it and their ability to respond to unique opportunities that unfolded in the environment. Instead, they focused on specialized roles—especially in business, the military, and government, particularly where technical skills and complicated equipment are involved.

Associates from other cultures often find it difficult to understand the Euro-American insistence on separating planning from implementing. That's changing with the movement toward self-directed teams, which merge these two functions.

The same tendency toward specialization of roles often occurs in interpersonal relations. Euro-Americans' friendships are likely to be based on their role activities, such as work, hobbies, sports, children, charities, games, and political or religious interests. They tend to think of others as coworkers, fellow tennis players, club associates, old school chums, neighborhood friends, or PTA parents. This specialization of friends often reflects their reluctance to become deeply involved with more than one or two friends and a wish for privacy. Their separation of occupational and social roles, of work and play, is different from other cultures.

Custom #4: Embracing Equality

An important theme in our relationships is equality. Ideally, just the fact of being human gives each person a certain irreducible value, and interpersonal relations are typically horizontal, conducted between presumed equals. However, big business and big government have traditionally been hierarchical and authoritarian, run by able-bodied, straight, Euro-American men who in practice generally consider themselves the only true equals. When one of them needs to confront another who is a subordinate, he is more likely to establish an atmosphere of equality than are the bosses in rank/status-oriented cultures. However, this value has often not extended to employees who were "too different," such as African Americans or women.

Custom #5: Cooperating and Playing Fair

Although Euro-Americans value competition, they usually compete against a backdrop of cooperation, for competition requires a considerable amount of coordination among individuals and groups. Euro-Americans can do this because they don't commit themselves as wholeheartedly to a group or organization as those from most other cultures. They pursue their own personal goals while cooperating with others who, likewise, pursue their own.

Euro-Americans tend to accept the goals of the group, but if their expectations are unfulfilled, they then feel free to leave and join another group. They can adjust their goals to those of other group members, if necessary, for carrying out joint action. This compromise is practical to Euro-Americans, allowing them to achieve a benefit they couldn't attain on their own. They cooperate in order to get things done, but that doesn't imply that they are giving up their personal goals or principles.

Custom #6: Communicating Informally and Directly

The Euro-American communication style is known for being informal and direct. Most Euro-Americans stress a simple vocabulary, a relative disregard for style, and the use of slang to show they (and the other person) are "one of the gang." As a loose-knit, diverse culture, they must rely more on the specifics of verbal communication, while tight-knit cultures can rely more on vague, nonverbal signals.

The Euro-American's informal, direct approach to interacting with others can seem brusque, rude, or confusing to people of other cultures. Compared to others, Euro-Americans tend to make fewer discriminations among people—quickly moving to a first-name basis with all and relating with

---

Self-Analysis 6.3 | Your Boundaries

Purpose: To increase awareness of how you and others view and use personal space.

Instructions: Describe briefly at least one time when you (or others) experienced conflict, misunderstanding, or problems about personal space, touching, or boundaries. The following situations can jog your memory:

- invasion of privacy—yours or others
- discomfort because of lack of privacy
- invasion of personal body space
- someone in your face
- feeling crowded or claustrophobic
- too much touching
- invasive touching
- too much coldness and distance
- other issues about space, boundaries, or touching

breeziness, humor, and kidding.

While Euro-Americans tend to avoid confrontation, once they decide that a situation with another person must be resolved, they are likely to deal directly with the person. This contrasts with the idea of "saving face" and using a go-between or other indirect approaches that are valued by many other cultures.

FINAL SELF-TEST

Indicate the best answers to the following 5 multiple-choice questions.

1. Most Euro-Americans tend to:
   A. have few personal relationships
   B. make friends for life
   C. do almost anything for a friend
   D. have many personal relationships and few deep, lasting friendships

2. In social interactions, Euro-Americans tend to stress:
   A. status and hierarchy
   B. intimacy
   C. equality and informality
   D. commitment

3. Euro-Americans' personal boundaries tend to:
   A. be small and tight
   B. be about arm's length
   C. be relatively distant
   D. allow much touching

4. Equality in Euro-American organizations has traditionally applied to:
   A. everyone
   B. mainly to men
   C. mainly to Euro-American men
   D. Euro-Americans but not necessarily to other cultural groups

5. The Euro-American communication style is known for being:
   A. focused on style
   B. informal and direct
   C. elegant and diplomatic
   D. vague

FINAL SELF-TEST FEEDBACK

Each correct answer is worth 20 points. If you score less than 80 points, you should review the materials and re-take the Final Self-Test.

1. Most Euro-Americans tend to:
   A. No, most have more than a few personal relationships
   B. No, most make few if any friends for life
   C. No, most tend not to do almost anything for a friend
   D. Yes, most have many personal relationships and few deep, lasting friendships

2. In social interactions, Euro-Americans tend to stress:
   A. No, not status and hierarchy
   B. No, not intimacy
   C. Yes, equality and informality
   D. No, not commitment

3. Euro-Americans' personal boundaries tend to:
   A. No, not be small and tight
   B. Yes, be about arm's length
   C. No, not be relatively distant
   D. No, the best answer is not allow much touching

4. Equality in Euro-American organizations has traditionally applied to:
   A. No, not everyone
   B. No, not mainly to minority men
   C. Yes, mainly to Euro-American men
   D. No, to Euro-American men but not necessarily to Euro-American women or other cultural groups

5. The Euro-American communication style is known for being:
   A. No, not focused on style
   B. Yes, informal and direct
   C. No, not elegant and diplomatic
   D. No, not vague

SKILL BUILDER 6.1   The Case of a Skills Gap at Lights Plus

Note: All people involved in this case are Euro-Americans except Henry.

Phyllis went to a Lights Plus store to buy some track lights she had seen advertised at a special reduced price. **Henry**, an African American salesperson, waited on her. Phyllis explained that the track lights were the only lighting in her home office and she needed lots of light throughout the room. Henry told her the track lights advertised in the sale were very good lights, very popular. He went to the stock room to get the lights and tracks, couldn't find the tracks, and returned to tell Phyllis that they didn't have them in stock.

Instead of giving up, Phyllis insisted on knowing if the lights could be obtained for her, so Henry asked the manager **Mark** about getting the tracks. Mark felt sure there were some tracks in the stock room and quickly found them. A sale was made.

Phyllis called an electrician to install the lights. When he arrived, he pointed out that they gave small spots of very intense light and were not too effective for general lighting. In addition, they were much more expensive than the general-lighting type of track lights that Phyllis needed. She returned them and waited for the general-lighting type to go on sale.

A month or so later, Lights Plus advertised at half price the type of track lights Phyllis needed. She called the store near her to be sure they were still on sale and were in stock. When she walked into the store, Henry greeted her. He showed her the sale track lights, which were packaged in boxes, picked up a couple of boxes, and took them to the cash register. When he entered the transaction, Henry saw that the price displayed on the register was the regular price, not the sale price. Henry said, "Well, these lights are $59.99 a package." Phyllis was exasperated. She said, "Then I don't want them. I don't know why the woman who answered the phone here about an hour ago told me they were still on sale. If she had told me they were now regular price, I wouldn't have made the trip." Henry said nothing and Phyllis left the store, shaking her head.

Driving home, Phyllis recalled her last trip to Lights Plus. Henry had been uninformed about where to find merchandise in the stock room. "Maybe he's uninformed about prices too," she thought. She turned the corner, went back to the store, and asked to speak to Mark the manager. When she explained the price problem, Mark replied, "Oh, yes, that's just one of those computer glitches. Somehow the sale information didn't get into the current computer file. No problem, you can have the track lights at the sale price." When Mark went to pick up the packets, he said, "Now some of these sets are black and some are white, even though the pictures on all the boxes show white lights."

Phyllis thought, "Why didn't Henry tell me that? Without that information, I had a fifty-fifty chance of bringing home lights of the wrong color." (*Note:* The top management of Lights Plus has expressed the company's top-priority objective this way: "Customer satisfaction is the target.")

1. Henry failed to meet the company's target by:
   A. having inadequate information about merchandise in the stock room
   B. having inadequate information about current prices
   C. not properly identifying what each box of merchandise actually contained (color of lights, type of lights, etc.)
   D. all of the above

Feedback

   A. No, though inadequate information about merchandise is part of the problem
   B. No, though inadequate information about prices is part of the problem
   C. No, though improper identification of merchandise is part of the problem
   D. Yes, all of the responses make up the problem

2. Mark was ineffective as Henry's manager because:
   A. he failed to show Henry how to stay on top of the stock available in the stock room and a process for making sure about out-of-stock product before turning away a customer
   B. he failed to train Henry properly about sale prices, computer errors, and a process for checking out price disparities before rejecting a customer's request
   C. he failed to train Henry to properly identify the contents of the boxes
   D. all of the above

Feedback

   A. No, knowing how to manage the inventory is only part of the problem
   B. No, checking sales prices is only part of the problem
   C. No, identifying contents of boxes is only part of the problem
   D. Yes, all of the above make up the problem

In addition, Mark may be assuming that Henry, an African American, has the sort of business savvy that many Euro-American men gain from being a part of the dominant culture. For example, all of his life, Mark has overheard his parents discuss business problems and solutions. As a teenager, he held temporary and part-time jobs dealing with inventory and sales issues, where he tended to identify with supervisors and managers. As a result of his background and experience, Mark automatically takes an assertive, problem-solving approach.

Mark needs to ask probing questions to identify areas where Henry needs training. Then he can begin a training program with the goal of giving Henry full information about the merchandise, company actions, customer service, how to overcome barriers to making sales, including cultural difference barriers, and so forth.

3. Henry should:

    A. quit because he is too uncaring to hold down this type of job

    B. complain to Mark about not giving him adequate information

    C. resolve to sell to every customer that comes through the door, if at all possible, and to overcome any and all barriers to making a sale

    D. ask Mark how to avoid future mistakes

Feedback

    A. No, quitting is a last resort and this response assumes that Henry doesn't care.

    B. No, complaining is usually a counter-productive strategy that focuses on what you don't want. It works better to focus on what you do want, what you are *for* rather than what you are against.

    C. Yes, resolving to overcome all sales barriers implies that Henry takes full responsibility for the results he gets. It means identifying what the barriers are, figuring out what causes them and how to prevent them in the first place, as well as overcoming them. This approach would include asking Mark for help, advice, and training.

    D. No, although this response is on the right track, more is needed.

4. The fact that Henry is a young African American working with nearly all Euro-Americans probably means that:

    A. Henry may be a little intimidated by the customers, his managers, and his coworkers

    B. Henry is less likely to question such company practices as computerized pricing information, picture identifications on merchandise boxes, etc.

    C. Henry is less comfortable than his Euro-American coworkers in questioning customers, responding to them, and relating to them

    D. all of the above

Feedback

A. No, intimidation is only part of the problem

B. No, being less likely to question things is only part of the problem

C. No, being uncomfortable with Euro-Americans is only part of the problem

D. all of these responses may play a role in Henry's performance; diversity training designed especially for his situation could increase his comfort level and effectiveness

SKILL BUILDER 6.2   The Case of New Manager Luis

Luis has been manager of the claims department for three months. He's on his way to the office of his immediate supervisor, **Gale,** for their monthly planning and evaluation session. Walking down the hall, his mind is filled with events of the past few months and what he wants to discuss with Gale.

When Luis applied for the management job, he had five years' experience with National Life Insurance. He had taken the screening exam for the new position and did well on both the written and oral portions. One of Luis' coworkers, **Richard**, also took the test and told Luis that he had done great on it.

Richard had come to National about a year before Luis and had trained Luis in some claims department procedures. Luis learned quickly and they soon had a friendly rivalry going. When their boss Gale was recruited from outside the company, Richard told Luis he heard it was because of pressure to place more women in higher positions. He said the company had recently gone through a government review of its affirmative action program and was found lacking. Richard said, "They brought Gale in mainly because she's a woman." Luis agreed with Richard at the time because he didn't really know the story and he didn't want to argue about it.

Four months ago, Richard told Luis that he really expected to get the claims department manager's job because he had such a good track record with the company and he also had more seniority than the other seven candidates. When Luis got the job, he became Richard's immediate supervisor. Luis felt uncomfortable giving Richard direction. He knew Richard was probably at least as well qualified as he to be boss. He worried about it quite a bit the first month. But he told himself that he must be the most qualified for the job; otherwise, he wouldn't have been selected.

During the second month, Luis noticed that Richard and several other employees seemed reluctant to follow his instructions. Luis attempted to meet them halfway by asking why they weren't doing certain things as he had directed and what they felt should be done. Sometimes, it seemed as if these few employees didn't take him seriously. He could see that efficiency and productivity were beginning to be affected by their resistance and balk-iness. Time and time again Luis told himself that it would take time for his former coworkers to get used to him as their manager and for him to become adjusted to his new role and responsibilities.

Then just last week, Luis overheard a conversation in the lounge. Richard was talking with a coworker and didn't realize Luis was in the next room.

> I don't know about this affirmative action. Why would anyone want to use the past as a reason why they haven't gotten ahead educationally or economically? I think it's time we all stood up for ourselves and accomplish or fail on our own merit, instead of some people falling back on excuses. Why should we American males be discriminated against just because of past history? If people want everyone to be treated equally, then they can't be given an extra advantage at the same time. I know my test scores were higher than some of these people who are being promoted, but they get promoted anyway—just so some job-climbing administrator can brag about his political correctness and make his track record look good. Worst of all, it just amazes me that Luis actually thinks he deserved that promotion.

Luis was stunned at the time. He started thinking about the number of Latino Americans in company management. He could think of only one. Maybe Richard was right. Maybe he really wasn't qualified enough to han-dle the new job.

1. The major problem in this situation is:

   A. Richard's attitude

   B. Luis' lack of confidence, assertiveness, and leadership image

   C. the corporate culture that allows this situation to develop

   D. all of the above

Feedback

   A. No, this is true but incomplete. Richard's attitude is a major problem because he's verbalizing his prejudice and cynicism and is therefore poisoning the environment. This would be a problem regardless of Luis' traits and skills; however, Luis' obvious lack of assertiveness makes him a vulnerable target.

   B. No, this is true but incomplete. Luis' lack of confidence, assertiveness, and leadership image is also a major problem, although Richard's attitude is intensifying the problem.

   C. No, such situations can develop even in corporate cultures that are inclusive, although corporate culture is a long-range, background factor.

D. This is the best response. The first two responses, Richard's attitude and Luis' lack of confidence, are the most immediate causative factors, and corporate culture is a long-range, background factor.

2. Luis should:

A. work on developing a vision of himself as an effective leader

B. discuss the situation with Gale

C. meet with Richard to work on a career development plan

D. all of the above

Feedback

A. Yes, but other action is also needed. Luis immediately needs to begin work on developing a vision of himself as an effective leader so that he can become comfortable in the role and build self-confidence and image, do some selective reading, and attend some seminars that focus on assertiveness and leadership issues. This must be an ongoing, long-term strategy because such change takes time.

B. Yes, discuss the situation with Gale, but other action is also needed.

C. Yes, Luis can work with Richard on a career plan, but only after he has discussed the problem with Gail, gained her support, and discussed a career development plan with her. Then, he should meet with Richard to work on this issue. His goal should be to rise above his own ego concerns, be "big enough" to give Richard a chance to work productively within the department, show support for Richard, and motivate him to excel. One way of motivating him may be to give him some leadership responsibilities within the department—show appreciation for his leadership ability and try to make him an ally. Give the new approach some time to take effect. Later, if Richard continues his poisonous actions, Luis and Gale must take more assertive action.

D. This is the best option because a multi-pronged approach is best in this situation. Luis immediately needs to begin work on developing a vision of himself as an effective leader so that he can become comfortable in the role and build self-confidence and image. He should do some selective reading and attend some seminars that focus on assertiveness and leadership issues. This must be an ongoing, long-term strategy because such change takes time.

Luis needs to discuss the situation with Gale, tell her what he sees as the major problems, offer some solutions, and ask her opinion. Together, they may want to discuss Richard's future with the company and his career development.

Then, he should meet with Richard to work on this issue. His goal should be to rise above his own ego concerns, be "big enough" to give Richard a chance to work productively within the department, show support for Richard, and motivate him to excel. One way of motivating him may be to give him some leadership responsibilities within the department—show appreciation for his leadership ability and try to make him an ally. Give the new approach some time to take effect. Later, if Richard continues his poisonous actions, Luis and Gale must take more assertive action.

3. What should Gale do next?

A. mind her own business

B. speak with Richard about the situation

C. transfer Richard

D. coach Luis in preventing and managing such situations

Feedback

A. No. Gale is responsible for job discrimination and hostile environment situations in her areas of supervision. One way of meeting that responsibility is to show support for all of her employees, to be a resource person when they have problems, and to role model inclusive, respectful behavior.

B. This is the best option, but only as the first step. Gale needs to speak with Richard about the situation. She must show full support for Luis, indicate her confidence in him, his qualifications, and his potential. She can point out the reasons Luis was selected for the position. She should also express appreciation for Richard's abilities. She might mention that Luis has spoken with her about developing a career development plan with Richard. In addition, she should coach Luis in adapting to a management role in a predominantly Euro-American organization.

C. No, not as the next step. However, it is a possibility for Gale to consider. She could work with Luis and Richard on a career development plan that might well include transferring Richard to an area where he could gain valuable experience and skills in preparation for his next promotion.

D. Not the best "next" step. However, once Gale helps Luis work out the "Richard problem," she should help Luis determine some training needs. Luis probably needs help in adapting to a management role in a predominantly Euro-American organization. Gale should be available as a coach and mentor for him. She should show full support for him in all situations, serve as a resource person, make suggestions for how Luis can develop the leadership skills he needs, and make specific suggestions for handling problem situations.

THE BOTTOM LINE

Think of this as just the beginning of your exploration into what it's like to be a Euro-American—and how the dominant American culture differs from other cultures. Now that you have the basics, let this be a framework for adding new information—just by noticing and questioning what's presented by the media and others, by caring and really listening.

Chapter Review

1. Common myths and stereotypes about Euro-Americans are (1) that they feel privileged, affluent, and powerful and (2) that they assume the silence of others on a controversial issue signals a wish to avoid controversy.

2. Euro-American domination is a direct result of this country being founded and built upon the pioneering, independent values of European founding fathers. Nearly all major U.S. corporations were founded by Euro-American men.

3. Euro-Americans think in terms of other races, rather than other cultures and often do not think of themselves as racial beings. This leads to some distancing from other races and cultures.

4. Most Euro-Americans view themselves as individuals first. Most value hard work and self-improvement, believe in scientific and technological progress, and view the world in rational, linear, cause-and-effect terms.

5. Key Euro-American values are being an individual, making decisions, being competitive and achievement oriented, working and playing hard, gaining material success, and staying young.

6. Euro-Americans relate to others by making many casual friends, keeping an arm's-length personal space, fitting into specialized roles, embracing equality, cooperating and playing fair, and communicating informally and directly.

Working With African Americans

7

CHAPTER OBJECTIVES

- Identify the typical African American stereotypes.
- Understand how historical events have influenced African American culture.
- Know key values in the African American community.
- Understand typical African American customs and community life.
- Know the major issues that are important to the African American community.
- Understand barriers to African American career success and how to overcome them.
- Understand how African American employees can contribute to an organization.

PhotoEdit

CHAPTER OVERVIEW

About 12 percent of the people in the American workplace are African Americans, which accounts for about one in eight employees. People who have taken the time and effort to learn about the African American community and its values and customs say they've boosted their ability to work productively with African Americans. Those who belong to the African American culture say studying it has helped them to better understand their own heritage and their strengths.

It's important in today's workplace to develop the level of understanding needed to build good relationships when associates are from another culture—whether you are a new entry-level employee or a top executive. A major key is to learn about an associate's culture and get a feel for his or her background. The more skilled you become at interpreting an individual's actions against the backdrop of his or her culture, the greater success both of you can achieve through working together.

The African American community is made up of many elements, and of course, no one person expresses all of the values and customs discussed here. You may be tempted to use this cultural information to form new rigid categories. To be fair, stay open and flexible as you interact with individual African Americans. Deal with the unique individual, bringing into play your understanding of his or her cultural background.

WHAT ARE THE TYPICAL STEREOTYPES ABOUT AFRICAN AMERICANS?

Most of the stereotypes about African Americans are either false or distorted partial truths. In fact, most stem from the legacy of slavery and segregation that is unique to this American group. In order to justify slavery, a practice that is quite incompatible with the American ideals of human freedom and equality, some Euro-Americans (white persons) created degrading stereotypes of Africans. Such beliefs are passed along from generation to generation and die hard.

Although the proportion of Euro-Americans who hold the more extreme stereotypes is continually declining, responses to a 1992 survey by *U.S. News & World Report* indicate the following beliefs are still held:

1. Are they more violent than whites? Yes, 63 percent.
2. Are they less intelligent? Yes, 53 percent.
3. Are they more likely to prefer to live off welfare? Yes, 78 percent.
4. Do they blame everyone but themselves for their problems? Yes, 57 percent.
5. Do they tend to be resentful troublemakers? Yes, 51 percent.

Bottom line: We have some work to do on these beliefs and attitudes.

Stereotypes are rigid, exaggerated, irrational beliefs, each associated with a mental category, such as a particular group of people. They are often based on cultural myths. Although stereotypes aren't identical to prejudice, rigid stereotypes about people usually lead to prejudice. For example, in the past, perhaps a Euro-American observed an abused African American slave whose rage finally consumed him and who lashed out violently. The Euro-American began saying to others, "African American men are violent." This became a cultural myth and led to a convenient stereotype, a good excuse for keeping African American men under tight rein. Euro-Americans who believed this myth didn't notice that most African American men were not violent, even when degraded and abused. But they noted every time one was violent, and each incident confirmed their belief. This is how stereotyping works.

Myths are stories that a culture uses to express desired values, to bond people in support of these values, and to coordinate social action to maintain the values.

To get to know what it's like to be an African American, you must understand the myths and stereotypes they deal with every time they leave the family circle, or turn on the television, for that matter. To bridge the divisive walls these stereotypes hold in place, you must know what they are, know other realities that balance or refute them, and move beyond myths to a more realistic view of the African American community.

Stereotype #1: African Americans Are More Violent Than Others

A cultural custom that may perpetuate this stereotype is African Americans' preference for using direct confrontation to resolve a conflict. Most Euro-Americans, Asian Americans, and Latino Americans prefer more indirect methods. African American behavior is therefore often seen as hostile and militant, when it's not. This is reinforced by—and reinforces—the stereotype of African Americans as prone to violence.

The reality is that certain behavior that is considered assertive and truthful by African Americans is often interpreted by others as anger or rage about to erupt into violence. What feeds this interpretation is:

- cultural differences about how to express concerns and emotions
- the "violent" stereotype itself; we see what we expect to see and ignore actions that don't fit our stereotypes

While we can prove that African American men have higher criminal arrest and conviction rates, we cannot prove that they are more violent.

Studies indicate that the United States is one of the more violent cultures of the world. More productive than using African Americans as the scapegoats who create violence in society would be addressing violence in the media and society at large.

Stereotype #2: African Americans Are Less Intelligent Than Others

In the workplace and elsewhere, Euro-Americans tend to assume that even highly intelligent African Americans are less competent. Studies by F. A. Blanchard and F. J. Crosby indicate that when it comes to Euro-American men helping each other, the other man's *ability* is the determining factor, not the fact that the man is Euro-American. But when it comes to helping African American men, their *ethnicity*, not their ability, is the major determining factor.

The reality is that school grades and grades on the SAT exam depend more on socioeconomic status than any other factor, including ethnicity according to a metastudy by the American Association of University Women. Children from low-income households, often with no father around, and whose parents have low educational achievement, tend to make lower grades. As socioeconomic status goes up, so do grades—for African Americans, Euro-Americans, boys, girls, and all others.

Many people assume that African Americans value education less than Euro-Americans, since fewer complete high school and college. However, D. J. Solorzano's study indicates that African American high school students and their parents have significantly higher aspirations to achieve a college degree than Euro-Americans at the same socioeconomic level. In both groups, the higher the socioeconomic level, the higher the educational aspirations tend to be. Educational progress is improving, but more work must be done in this area:

- 84 percent completed high school in 2000, compared to 51 percent in 1980
- college enrollment quadrupled, from about 4 percent to 17 percent but was less than the Euro-American rate of 27 percent
- educational attainment is about the same for males and females

Stereotype #3: African Americans Are Lazy and Irresponsible

As a matter of fact, about the same proportion of African Americans as Euro-Americans hold jobs, but African American men received only about 70 percent the pay of Euro-American men in 2003. African American women received 62 percent as much. Median family income was only 64 percent of Euro-American income. In spite of this wage gap, African Americans are industrious and responsible enough to get and keep jobs in downsized mean-and-lean corporations that must be globally competitive and productive. Historically, they have done much of the hard labor that helped establish the U.S. economy. The "lazy" stereotype goes back to the time when most slaves were treated as subhuman children, denied an education, expected to do exactly as the overseer ordered, and offered little or no reward for working harder and smarter. When some didn't act eager and committed, all were branded lazy and irresponsible.

For well-educated African Americans in corporate America, "lazy" and "incompetent" are two of the most frustrating stereotypes. Many who respond to surveys say they're permitted a much narrower range of behavioral styles to achieve their goals than their Euro-American peers. They also become quite frustrated when they perceive they must work twice as hard and must stay in a position longer than necessary—just to prove they're *not* lazy and incompetent and that they *can* handle the next assignment. This stereotype extends to the assumption by Euro-American colleagues that nearly all African Americans are incompetent to handle higher-level responsibilities, as indicated by research studies. Another result: African American professionals are often assumed to be sales clerks, waiters, or other entry-level or menial workers. Social interactions that they enjoy with their colleagues at work may disappear outside the office where coworkers often literally don't recognize them on the street when they're not in "corporate uniform."

Stereotype #4: They Blame Everyone Else for Their Problems

African Americans have been struggling for hundreds of years to rise up from the massive burdens of the past, including 200 years of slavery and another 100 years of legal segregation that included barriers to well-paying corporate or government jobs. They understand that this history is still affecting their chances to build a successful career and life. While virtually all community leaders focus on self-help programs, most believe the government should help the inner-city underclass break out of this prison that was not of their own making. This has led to the stereotype of blaming others and expecting "government handouts."

The reality is that African American progress since the civil rights laws of the 1960s has taken two distinct directions: about one-third have made fairly good progress and are part of the hardworking, tax-paying, responsible middle class. Obviously, these African Americans are not stuck in a victim mentality that blames others for their difficulties. Not all have been so fortunate, however. About one-third are actually worse off, if anything—mired down in inner-city, underclass poverty and crime—and in dire need of help. The other third are hovering somewhere between underclass and middle-class status, most of them struggling to make it on their own. Most community leaders credit the progress that has been made to the people's own bootstrap efforts in combination with civil rights laws and certain successful government programs.

The Growing Middle Class

This one-third has been moving up and out to the suburbs, earning more, sending their children to college, and living better. Findings from the 2000 census:

- 27 percent lived in the suburbs, compared to 13 percent in 1967
- 48 percent owned their homes, compared with 75 percent of Euro-Americans; the proportion has remained fairly stable for the past 20 years
- median home value was $80,600, compared with $123,400 for Euro-Americans

Cultural values and community support played a role in this progress. Studies identify the following qualities typical of middle-class African Americans:

- They have a reverence for learning second only to their reverence for the spiritual.
- Their origins are in the working class, generally in the previous generation—they are first-generation middle class.
- They are more dependent than independent, more employees of others than owners and managers, and have relatively little accumulated wealth—about one-eighth that of Euro-Americans.
- Their progress is a major achievement, usually based upon education, two earners, extended families, religion, and service to others.

The Growing Underclass

Back in the inner city, at the other end of the scale, is another one-third (and growing) who are still trapped in abject poverty. Their profile includes these facts:

- African American median incomes have decreased 10 percent since 1970, reflecting the downward spiral of the underclass. African American families overall make only 64 percent the income that Euro-American families make.
- The poverty rate of 23 percent for all African American families has remained about the same since 1980. This compares to 10 percent for all Euro-American families.
- 57 percent of African Americans live in inner cities, and 40 percent of them are poor (double the 1960 rate), compared to 12 percent of Euro-Americans.
- About 50 percent of all African American children under age 6 live in poverty, most without fathers. Single mothers and older African Americans are more likely to get caught in the poverty trap than are married couples.

Virtually all African American leaders call for African Americans to work hard to improve their lot. Many self-help programs are offered by local churches. Most community leaders believe further help is needed in the form of civil rights laws and the continuation of successful government-supported programs designed to help young women avoid teenage pregnancies, help babies and young children get a good start in life, give teenagers opportunities to participate in positive skill-building activities, and teach people the job skills most needed in the workplace.

Stereotype #5: Many African Americans Are Resentful Troublemakers

This stereotype is related to the violent and blaming stereotypes. It is connected to cultural differences in confronting issues and expressing concerns and to a history of trying to break out of imprisoning discrimination. It is also connected to inner-city underclass crime.

Reality of the Need to Be Assertive

The reality is that most people in the African American community believe in speaking up assertively, especially about perceived injustices. Being genuine, expressing the feelings you are feeling, and directly confronting issues are all highly valued and typical patterns in the African American community. During the days of legal and open discrimination and oppression,

African Americans did not dare express these values outside the community, but younger generations feel it's important to be genuine in all situations. Many feel committed to speaking up in the name of ending unfair discrimination. The point is that expressions interpreted as resentful or troublemaking by persons outside the community may not be meant that way nor seen that way by African Americans—or there may be quite valid reasons for speaking up about unfairness.

Reality of a History of Oppression

This history plays a part in the existence of underclass poverty, family breakdown, single mothers, youth gangs, drugs, and crime. Boys from this environment *are* more likely to become caught up in criminal activity, but it's not just because they're African American. About 25 percent of African American men ages 20 to 25 are in prison, or on probation or parole, and they are dying in disproportionate numbers because of high-risk lifestyles.

Reality of a History of Inequality

A long history of unequal treatment within the legal system is well documented. Discrimination begins with the way many police officers view African American men and extends to the probability that police will arrest them regardless of guilt and will abuse them as prisoners. It includes the higher probability that an African American will be indicted, fail to get a fair trial, be convicted, spend time in prison, and fail to be paroled. The troublemaker stereotype is related to the violent stereotype and becomes self-perpetuating. A Euro-American man who acts just like his African American peer is less likely to be seen as a troublemaker by police and so is less likely to be arrested, abused, and so forth. He retains his "regular guy" image while the African American racks up a criminal record that confirms he is a troublemaker.

Reality of Discrimination

Past and present discrimination *does* have an impact that tends to poison the American society for everyone. The underclass aspects of poverty, hopelessness, drugs, gangs, robbery, violence, crime rates, and prisons affect us all. Many African American leaders say that we as a society *can* afford to pay the price of discrimination by helping the African American underclass get the skills and help they need to break out of poverty. When we refuse, we pay the price of living with high crime rates, and even some rioting, in our cities. We pay far more to keep an African American man in prison than we would to send him to college. Instead of focusing so much on punishing crime, we can save money and decrease crime rates by focusing more on prevention.

Vignette	The Power of the Past

Marie Davis, an officer of the National Association for the Advancement of Colored People (NAACP), tells a story about how past history continues to play out today. Here's a summary of what she said in a televised interview.

There's a perception among white Americans that time has erased slavery's effect. Many people think this was thousands of years ago, but it wasn't really that long ago. My grandfather was born into slavery and freed at the end of the Civil War, when he was still a toddler. Slavery and the prejudice around it caused most white people to accept the stereotype that African Americans are inferior, almost another species.

The prejudice that is the legacy of slavery affects virtually all of us today. For example, my granddaughter recently came to me, crying. Someone had treated her cruelly just because she is black. I never dreamed my granddaughter would be crying like that. Then I cried, too, because I knew what she was going through. I remembered the many times I had cried as a child, cried because I was so hurt.

HOW HAS THE AFRICAN AMERICAN CULTURE EVOLVED?

The African American culture is rooted in enforced slavery. The Civil War ended slavery, but African Americans were still segregated from mainstream society until the Civil Rights era of the 1950s and 1960s. Now, they are moving toward full participation and equality, but historic disadvantage still takes its toll.

Time of Slavery

During and just after America's colonial years, about four million Africans were brought over and made slaves. For 250 years, most Africans in this country were slaves. Slavery had a deep and lasting effect that is clearly present today.

The culture of slavery also affected everyone else in the United States at the time, and most Euro-American's great-grandparents inevitably handed down the interconnecting beliefs about privilege, inequality, and prejudice—by their attitudes and actions, if not by their verbal teachings. Slavery laid the foundation for the prejudice and discrimination that African Americans must cope with today—and for the resulting social problems their leaders are working to overcome.

After Slavery: Free but Segregated

Soon after the Civil War, African Americans' life in the South resembled their cousins' life in the North. The major difference was that segregation was de facto in the North and legal in the South. By the 1890s, laws provided for the "Negro's place" in neighborhoods, parks, schools, hotels, hospitals, restaurants, streetcars, theaters, and hospitals. When laws didn't keep African Americans in their "place," vigilantes did. Every year, hundreds of African Americans who "stepped out of line" in some way were lynched. In 1909, the National Association for the Advancement of Colored People (NAACP) became the first African American organization with the ability to fight for justice in American courts, but its power was very limited.

> In 1896, the Supreme Court said that "separate-but-equal" segregation was constitutional.

Current Culture

A unique legacy of slavery and legal segregation laid the groundwork for these diehard stereotypes. Of all the ethnic groups in the United States, African Americans have traditionally faced the greatest obstacles, which are built on this foundation of entrenched prejudice and discrimination, usually called racism.

Vignette   A Slave Family's Ordeal

Sarah was a young slave woman who worked in the cotton fields on a plantation in Georgia. She was well aware that her masters and any of his plantation bosses could force her to have sex with them. How could she refuse and still survive? She had somehow escaped this fate until recently when Mr. Jones caught her alone in the barn. Soon after, she realized she was pregnant. Her husband Jake knew something was wrong. When Sarah broke down and told him the story, he felt completely humiliated, so powerless in this situation.

Sarah gave birth to a boy, Shane. Everyone noticed what light skin and European-like features he had. Mr. Jones frowned when he heard talk about the baby. The last thing he wanted was his wife noticing a slave child that looked suspiciously like her husband. Soon, Sarah and Shane were taken to the slave market to be sold. She was torn apart from her husband, parents, and all the people she knew. She never saw them again.

In this case, Shane was classified as a Negro, as were all children who were determined to have "even a drop of Negro blood." Before the 1960s, it was illegal for persons from "different races" to marry, yet various types of sexual unions occurred. These rapes and illegal sexual unions explain why, by 1930, anthropologists estimated that 75 percent of African Americans were part Euro-American.

Self-Analysis 7.1 | How It Feels to Be Trapped

Purpose: To find common ground with the people who have the experience of being trapped.

Step 1   You've learned a little about the experience of African slaves in the United States. They constantly lived with at least two major dilemmas: entrapment and degradation. They were trapped in situations that provided no real personal freedom and almost no alternatives. They were told in many ways that they were inferior. Can you think of a situation in which you felt similarly trapped or degraded—physically, emotionally, or psychologically?

Step 2   Go back to that time and place. Relive the situation. What did you feel at the time? What were some of your thoughts?

Step 3   Find common ground with the slaves of the past. Can you imagine what feelings and thoughts you might have had if you were a slave living on a southern plantation around 1800? What comes to mind? Can you imagine how all this might affect the way you would raise your children? How even your grandchildren might be affected?

SELF-TEST #1

Indicate the best answers to the following 10 multiple-choice questions.

1. The proportion of African Americans in the U.S. population is about:
   A. 33% or one in every 3 persons
   B. 12% or one in every 8 persons
   C. 25% or one in every 4 persons
   D. 5% or one in every 20 persons

2. Regarding the five major myths about African Americans, most Euro-Americans today agree with:
   A. only the ones about being violent and being troublemakers
   B. only the ones about living off welfare and blaming others for problems
   C. all of them
   D. only the one about being less intelligent

3. Myths are defined as:

   A. rigid, exaggerated, irrational beliefs about people

   B. prejudiced beliefs about people

   C. stories used to bond people and to coordinate social action

   D. all of the above

4. A cultural custom that may perpetuate the violence myth is:

   A. the tendency to bounce back from hard times

   B. the belief that one must "keep on keeping on"

   C. the use of street language

   D. the tendency to use direct confrontation to resolve a conflict

5. Studies conclude that the best predictor of school grades and SAT scores is:

   A. school district spending per pupil

   B. socioeconomic status of the student's family

   C. ethnicity or race

   D. gender

6. Educational attainment for African Americans from 1980 to 1990:

   A. increased significantly

   B. decreased dramatically

   C. surpassed that of Euro-Americans

   D. was significantly greater for females than for males

7. Since the civil rights laws of the 1960s, African Americans have:

   A. dramatically increased their socioeconomic status

   B. seen increases in both the middle class and the underclass

   C. been relatively satisfied

   D. generally become accepted in the workplace

8. The troublemaker myth is countered by the reality that:

   A. Africans Americans believe in speaking up assertively

   B. there is a history of unequal treatment in the legal system

   C. the burden of past oppression and current discrimination continues to have an impact

   D. all of the above

9. Euro-Americans justified slavery by:

   A. claiming it was essential for survival

   B. blaming English royalty for promoting slavery

   C. denying the humanness of African Americans, viewing them as subhuman

   D. claiming that it was a short-term solution

10. After the Civil War:

    A. segregation laws were passed throughout the South

    B. segregation laws were passed throughout the United States

    C. the Supreme Court ruled against segregation laws

    D. African Americans lived in integrated neighborhoods in northern cities but were segregated in the South

SELF-TEST #1 FEEDBACK

Each correct answer is worth 10 points. If you score less than 70 points, you should review the materials and re-take the Self-Test.

1. The proportion of African Americans in the U.S. population is about:

    A. No, not 33% or one in every 3 persons

    B. Yes, 12% or one in every 8 persons

    C. No, not 25% or one in every 4 persons

    D. No, not 5% or one in every 20 persons

2. Regarding the five major myths about African Americans, most Euro-Americans today agree with:

    A. No, although they do agree with the ones about being violent and being troublemakers

    B. No, although they do agree with the ones about living off welfare and blaming others for problems

    C. Yes, the best answer is all of them

    D. No, not *only the one about being less intelligent*

3. Myths are defined as:

    A. No, rigid, exaggerated, irrational beliefs about people refers to stereotypes

    B. No, prejudiced beliefs about people refers to prejudice

    C. Yes, myths are stories used to bond people and to coordinate social action

    D. No, not all of the above

4. A cultural custom that may perpetuate the violence myth is:

    A. No, the violence myth is not related to the tendency to bounce back from hard times

    B. No, the violence myth is not related to the belief that one must "keep on keeping on"

    C. No, the relationship to the use of street language is minimal

    D. Yes, the best answer is the tendency to use direct confrontation to resolve a conflict. Many people from other cultural backgrounds misinterpret this as a prelude to violence.

5. Studies conclude that the best predictor of school grades and SAT scores is:

    A. No, although an indirect factor could be school district spending per pupil

    B. Yes, socioeconomic status of the student's family

    C. No, ethnicity or race alone is not a predictor

    D. No, gender is not a factor

6. Educational attainment for African Americans from 1980 to 1990:

    A. Yes, it increased significantly

    B. No, it did not decrease dramatically

    C. No, it did not surpass that of Euro-Americans

    D. No, it was not significantly greater for females than for males

7. Since the civil rights laws of the 1960s, African Americans have:

    A. No, all have not dramatically increased their socioeconomic status

    B. Yes, the best answer is *seen increases in both the middle class and the underclass*

    C. No, all have not been relatively satisfied

    D. No, they have made great progress but studies do not indicate the level of acceptance that would indicate relative equality of opportunity

8. The troublemaker myth is countered by the reality that:

    A. No, although Africans Americans believe in speaking up assertively

    B. No, although there is a history of unequal treatment in the legal system

    C. No, although the burden of past oppression and current discrimination continues to have an impact

    D. Yes, all of the above; younger generations of African Americans tend to believe that they must speak out against injustice because of past and current history of unfairness within the dominant culture

9. Euro-Americans justified slavery by:

    A. No, though some may claim that it was essential for survival

    B. No, though some may blame English royalty for promoting slavery

C. Yes, the best answer is denying the humanness of African Americans, viewing them as subhuman; ethical conflicts were avoided by claiming they were more animal than human, that God gave humans dominion over animals

D. No, they don't claim that it was a short-term solution

10. After the Civil War:

A. Yes, segregation laws were passed throughout the South; legal segregation was prevalent in the South, while informal de facto segregation was common in the North

B. No, segregation laws were not passed throughout the United States

C. No, the Supreme Court did not rule against segregation laws until the 1950s

D. No, African Americans did not live in integrated neighborhoods in the North

WHAT ARE THE KEY VALUES OF THE AFRICAN AMERICAN COMMUNITY?

African American scholars have identified at least seven key values that affect how African Americans view themselves, the world, and others. Researchers such as Andrew Billingsley, M. L. Hecht, Thomas Kochman, J. L. White, and James M. Jones, Professor of Social Psychology at University of Delaware, highlight the values of: (1) sharing and interrelating, (2) expressing personal style and uniqueness, (3) being real and genuine, (4) being assertive, (5) expressing feelings, (6) bouncing back, and (7) distrusting the mainstream establishment.

Some of these values are rooted in African tribal values. Others are rooted in the need to bond together and find inner strength and savvy in order to survive the circumstances of slavery and segregation.

Value #1: Sharing and Interrelating

Interconnectedness, interrelatedness, sharing, and interdependence are seen as central and unifying values in the African American community. This is a prominent theme in African American life and language with respect to:

- interactive dynamics between speaker and listener
- the power of words to control

- ways of thinking
- timing
- communication skill

Sharing knowledge and endorsing the group are related to collectivism, which means putting family and community relationships above one's own aspirations. It's acted out in the sharing of self and material possessions within the family. It's also expressed in the call–response pattern found in meetings of church members ("Amen! Praise God!") and other groups ("Right on, Brother!").

Value #2: Expressing Personal Style and Uniqueness

Personal style is important in the way African Americans talk, walk, dress, work—in every aspect of life. This uniqueness in personal style and expression celebrates the individual. But the response of family, friends, and community is crucial to the expression. It's meaningless unless done in sync with others. For example, they may develop their own style of dancing, singing, or strutting by using both some known forms and their own improvisations. But all of this is done with others. Jazz improvisation began with this custom. Musicians play a tune together, but one by one the individual musicians take the spotlight and improvise on the theme in their own way.

In contrast, American individualism refers to a more autonomous expression through personal achievement and self-reliance. It does not rely on the group in the immediate way that African American "personal style" expression does.

Value #3: Being Real and Genuine

At church and at home, African Americans are taught to face up to their circumstances, admit who they really are, and deal with life as it is. Being real and genuine is rooted in a core belief about life: The natural facts, eternal truths, wisdom of the ages, and basic precepts of survival emerge from the experiences of life. Some related common teachings are:

- You can't escape nothing. You've got to pay your dues. If you've been through tragedy, it must be you needed it (for personal growth).
- You cannot lie to life.
- You might as well be who you really are, and tell it like it is.
- You learn the truth through direct experience.

Older people, because of their accumulated experiences, are the reservoirs of wisdom. Realness and genuineness are tied to the values of personal style, assertiveness, and open emotional expression. It means African Americans tend to confront problems they care about in a direct, loud, and passionate way. This is respected when it conveys sincerity and conviction.

Value #4: Being Assertive

African Americans value standing up for personal rights and trying to achieve them without harming others. Assertiveness is a key symbol of standing up for yourself in the face of oppression and taking charge of your own life. Coping with prejudice and discrimination often results in an assertive, determined, confrontational style.

Assertiveness is often expressed in a style that is intense, outspoken, challenging, and forward. It may be done with a loud strong voice, angry verbal arguments, threats, insults, a certain way of dressing, or the use of slang. It can range from calm debates to persuasion to intense expressions of anger.

Actions based on this value often cause misunderstandings outside of the community. Others often misinterpret mere assertiveness as a form of violence, blaming, or troublemaking, linking it to those stereotypes. This assertiveness value is related to genuineness and tellin' it like it is, but others may see it as being over-aggressive, coming on too strong, being too argumentative, or stirring up trouble. The most disturbing interpretation is, "Uh-oh, he's about to get violent."

Value #5: Expressing Feelings

African American style is more self-conspicuous, expressive, expansive, colorful, intense, assertive, aggressive, and focused on the individual than the style of most other cultures. They use more:

- expressive communications patterns
- direct questions
- public debate and argument
- active nonverbal expression
- emotional intensity
- self-presentations through boasting and bragging

They tend to negotiate more loudly and intensely than others. When African Americans engage in public debate of any kind, their style is often high-key. They see their style as a natural and sincere expression of their thoughts and feelings and accept others' passionate style in the spirit in which it's intended: honest engagement, participation, and expression that helps people know each other and ultimately contributes to unity. In general, African American culture allows members great freedom to express their feelings.

Value #6: Bouncing Back

Resilience and revitalization are admired and have been a key to survival. Older members are respected because they have:

- been through the experiences that can only come with age
- been "down the line," seen the comings and goings of life
- survived the cycles of oppression, struggle, survival, backlash, and renewed struggle
- stood the test of time and adversity, paid their dues, and transcended tragedy
- most, important, learned to "keep on keepin' on"

A lively sense of humor and spiritual beliefs support the bouncing back value.

Value #7: Distrusting the Establishment

History has taught African Americans to distrust the establishment. The trust gap shows up in work relationships when African Americans use pro-

---

Vignette   Seeing Anew Through Informed Eyes

People who have studied the African American culture learn to look for accurate interpretations of behavior. Bill, who completed a diversity course, tells about his experience.

I overheard an African American having a telephone conversation the other day. He got so loud and vehement that I became very uncomfortable, even though I wasn't involved. Then, I remembered what I had learned about the African American culture. I looked and listened more closely. I saw that he was smiling part of the time and his body was fairly relaxed.

Then, I shifted my perception, opening up to the possibility that he wasn't really angry and about to explode. I began to hear a very different conversation, one in which the guy was just being real and genuine, asserting his thoughts and feelings, and tellin' it like it is.

tective hesitation before they speak up or take action around Euro-Americans. They take time to think about how their words or actions might reinforce negative stereotypes or how they might make themselves vulnerable to betrayal or attack. Where they have a choice, they may avoid working with Euro-Americans. Trust can be built, but it tends to be a relatively slow and difficult process. One action perceived as betrayal can break the delicate new structure.

WHAT CUSTOMS ARE ASSOCIATED WITH THE AFRICAN AMERICAN COMMUNITY?

The core values of the African American community are reflected in typical customs in three major life areas: community life, family life, and personal relationships.

Life Area #1: Customs in Community Life

Some important aspects of community life that reflect the core values are church customs, the use of a dialect often called "Black English," and differences in how time is viewed.

Spiritual and Church Customs

The church took on a major role in advocating social change throughout the twentieth century, with ministers becoming leaders in the Civil Rights movement. The church still plays a central role in virtually every aspect of African American life, including major efforts to help the underclass break out of the shackles that keep them in poverty. Most offer an array of self-help programs.

Sense of Time

Members of most African tribes view time as circular with a focus on the present. They generally have no way of expressing a distant future, which can affect their ability to excel in long-range planning. Some of this time concept has survived in the African American community. Therefore, some African Americans must struggle to adapt to a corporate focus on such planning.

Africans also emphasize whether something is done only at the present moment or whether it's done habitually—an either–or viewpoint. This contrasts with the Western view of time as linear, with an emphasis on the point on the time line that an event occurs—in the past, present, or future—among infinite numbers of potential points in time.

Life Area #2: Customs in Family Life

The sharing value is expressed in the practice of seeing relatives and close friends as an extended family, while the distrust factor results in "tough" child-rearing practices.

Extended Families

Among African Americans, the term *parents* often refers to natural parents, grandparents, and others who assume parental roles and responsibilities from time to time. Relationships with key people who are not blood relatives are considered essential to the maintenance of the family. This custom is rooted both in the African American tribal heritage and in the need to withstand the stress spawned by the slavery system and the survival struggles that are still prevalent.

Child-Rearing Practices

The strict, no-nonsense discipline used by many African American parents, sometimes seen as harsh or rigid to some Euro-Americans, is actually functional and appropriate discipline by caring parents. They see it as preparation for survival in a hostile environment, one that is prejudiced and discriminatory against them.

Life Area #3: Customs in Personal Relationships

The sharing value means that most African Americans place especially high value on trusting and helping one another. Most have one style for relating to acquaintances and a somewhat different style for relating to friends, and they may appear indifferent or uninvolved in their interactions with persons outside the community.

Relationship Style with Acquaintainces

African Americans are guided in their communication with other African American acquaintances, such as coworkers and casual friends, by the following four types of guidelines.

Follow role prescriptions. African Americans generally pay more attention to this than Euro-Americans. Still, they place even more emphasis on individual roles that express each person's style than on conventional roles. This reflects their value for expressing personal uniqueness.

Be polite. Politeness is viewed as more an individual than societal trait, and deciding your own rules for politeness is more important to African Americans than it is to other American subcultures.

Watch your words. African Americans tend to be much more cautious about what they say to people outside the community.

Support "brothers and sisters." African Americans especially value conversations within the community that are supportive, relevant, and assertive, reflecting the cultural values of sharing and being positive.

Relationship Style with Friends

African Americans are likely to develop closer, more intimate friendships than Euro-Americans. They're likely to be more intimate in discussions of school, work, religion, interests, hobbies, and physical condition. On the other hand, Euro-Americans are likely to be more revealing and intimate in discussions of love, dating, sex, and feelings about these issues. African American stress on intimacy may fall into these four types of action.

Acknowledge the individual. Allow others to express themselves through assertiveness and individual style and accomplishment. Appreciate their uniqueness and their individual expressions of who they are.

Develop intimacy. The value of sharing is achieved through talking about family and other personal topics. It includes these kinds of actions:

- giving and receiving friendly advice, leading to positive feelings
- taking specific actions to establish trust as the most crucial element of relationships
- expressing sensitivity, support, affirmation, honesty, and brotherhood or sisterhood
- accepting criticisms and requests without compromising the friendship

Be supportive. Do such things as:

- offer solutions to a problem or advice on personal issues
- seek mutual understanding
- express individuality
- affirm the other person or the culture
- establish trust and intimacy

Appreciate the culture.   Focus on the similarities in our beliefs, attitudes, and interests. Express pride in our common roots and the cultural background itself.

Male-Female Relationships

African American culture presumes that all women have a general sexual interest in men and are sexually assertive, so they aren't considered less respectable or more available when they express these traits. African American men are more direct in their expression of sexual interest, and the women aren't insulted by this—they generally feel confident about how to reject or accept such overtures. The men are normally not offended by a rejection if it's done in good humor—on the other hand, they don't like being ignored or rejected in a degrading way.

Life Area #5: The New Urban Village—Integrating African Values

A growing movement is afoot in the African American community, a movement that emphasizes African heritage and values and integrates them with American values and the American dream. According to this view, Eurocentric and Afrocentric values differ as shown in Snapshot 7.1.

American Dream

Regarding the Eurocentric ultimate goal, many African Americans say the ultimate illusion of the American dream is that anyone who is focused, educated, and persistent can fight his or her way to the top and enjoy the distinction of being number one. If being number one means others are number two, and so forth, then obviously everyone cannot make it.

The Urban Village

This concept is a recent African American approach. It's grounded in the Afrocentric view, but also recognizes that the Eurocentric view sets the rules of the American marketplace. It incorporates the concept of Afrocentric rites of passage, especially important for inner-city youth, as well as the principles of Kwanzaa. A key principle of the urban village is: *It takes a village to raise a child.*

The keys to success include networking, mentoring, and cooperative economics. The motto is economic empowerment. Virtually every African American church and community organization now operates some sort of economic program, from economic literacy and job training classes to community loan funds. Weekend mentoring programs focus on exposing urban youth to business leaders and role models.

SNAPSHOT 7.1   Comparison of Afrocentric and Eurocentric viewpoints.

Eurocentric Viewpoint	Afrocentric Viewpoint
Survival of the fittest is central theme, implying that those who have power are the fittest. Competition is a major theme in interactions with other humans and nature. Humans devise the battlefields where life is played out. Those who accumulate the most of what costs the most are the winners, the best. War is the ultimate form of competition: Cold War, Star Wars, war on crime, war on drugs. ↓ Ultimate goal is to be number one, the symbol of achievement and worth.	Humans are one with nature. All entities experience cyclical, periodic, and inevitable changes. In humans, these changes are seen as life crises, which are disruptive but can be eased by group rituals of the passage from one life phase to the next. The death–rebirth cycle reflects the law of regeneration and applies to all of nature: systems become spent and must be regenerated. When one life phase ends, a new one begins. Rites of passage reflect nature's cycle: separation from the old, transition to the new, and integration of old and new.

Kwanzaa

This is a way of life that honors the African heritage with the purpose of encouraging a greater sense of unity, identity, and purpose among African Americans. The seven Kwanzaa principles focus on unity, self-determination, collective work and responsibility, cooperative economics, purpose, creativity, and faith. Many of its symbols and terms come from African tradition, but it's the creation of African Americans that goes back to 1966. The Kwanzaa annual celebration takes place around the Christmas holidays.

Kwanzaa and the urban village model are approaches that recognize the realities of African American life in the American society. They are seen by many African Americans as positive, empowering, practical approaches that are grounded in the interdependence and spirituality of an Afrocentric worldview.

WHAT MAJOR ISSUES ARE IMPORTANT TO AFRICAN AMERICANS?

Here is a brief summary of issues that are important to African Americans:

1. The stereotypes—violent, criminal, less intelligent, lazy, irresponsible, incompetent, blame-shifting, and resentful troublemakers.

2. Learning barriers—rooted in beliefs about inferior intelligence and resulting in lower expectations, poor schools, lower socioeconomic status, and other educational problems

3. The lack of a level playing field in all life areas—poverty traps, poor schools, greater difficulty getting loans for houses and businesses, barriers to getting and keeping good jobs, the pay gap regardless of occupation, and inadequate political power.

4. Suspicions that most are underclass criminal types—the reality and paradox of an upwardly mobile middle class, but also a downwardly mobile underclass—and the desperate straits of young men caught up in gangs, drugs, and crime.

5. Inequality in the legal system, from police harassment and brutality to greater probability of arrest, indictment, and conviction.

6. The necessity of constantly dealing with the power and privilege of the Euro-American majority and being pegged at the lowest rung of the societal ladder.

7. The need to act almost white in order to be successful in corporate America; the related need for welcoming, inclusive corporate cultures that respect all persons' ethnicity, value their differences, and appreciate their contributions.

8. The glass ceiling to better jobs in corporate America.

SELF-TEST #2

Indicate the best answers to the following 10 multiple-choice questions.

1. Sharing and interrelating are prominent in African American life with respect to:
   A. individualism
   B. self-reliance
   C. ways of thinking
   D. personal achievement

2. Expressing personal style and uniqueness is important in the way African Americans:
   A. walk
   B. talk
   C. dress
   D. all of the above

3. Being real and genuine is rooted in this core belief:
   A. you can't trust the establishment
   B. you got to keep on keeping on
   C. boasting and bragging are not the same thing
   D. wisdom and basic precepts of survival emerge from the experiences of life

4. Being assertive is a key symbol of:
   A. standing up for yourself
   B. controlling feelings
   C. avoiding conflict
   D. controlling others

5. The African American community handles the expression of feelings by:
   A. expecting members to control themselves
   B. confining such expression to appropriate times and places
   C. allowing members great freedom of expression
   D. often preferring indirect expression

6. The bouncing-back value primarily refers to:
   A. inspiration from the young people who typically bounce back from failure
   B. coming back and getting even for injustices
   C. surviving physical illness
   D. respect for older members who have survived through many experiences

7. African American families tend to:
   A. use the term *parents* to include grandparents and other close relatives
   B. include key people who are not blood relatives
   C. protect children from life's difficulties
   D. both a and b

8. A traditional African view of time includes:
   A. no way of expressing a distant future
   B. an either–or viewpoint of whether something is done now or is done habitually
   C. a lack of emphasis on things done at various points in time
   D. all of the above

9. African American style in relating to acquaintances is to:
   A. acknowledge the individual and develop intimacy
   B. appreciate the culture and be supportive
   C. follow role prescriptions, be polite, and watch your words
   D. develop intimacy and be supportive

10. A key aspect of male–female relationships is:

   A. show sexual interest indirectly

   B. both women and men are sexually assertive

   C. women are easily offended when men make direct sexual overtures

   D. men are easily offended when women reject their overtures

SELF-TEST #2 FEEDBACK

Each correct answer is worth 10 points. If you score less than 70 points, you should review the materials and re-take the Self-Test.

1. Sharing and interrelating are prominent in African American life with respect to:

   A. No, not to individualism

   B. No, not to self-reliance

   C. Yes, to ways of thinking; sharing and interrelating are primarily world viewpoints, ways of thinking about the world

   D. No, not personal achievement

2. Expressing personal style and uniqueness is important in the way African Americans:

   A. No, although a factor is the walk

   B. No, although a factor is the talk

   C. No, although a factor is dress

   D. Yes, all of the above; in fact, all aspects of being a unique individual are included in this value

3. Being real and genuine is rooted in this core belief:

   A. No, not in you can't trust the establishment

   B. No, not in you got to keep on keeping on

   C. No, not in boasting and bragging are not the same thing

   D. Yes, in wisdom and basic precepts of survival emerge from the experiences of life. What happens in daily life, through the years, tells you what is real. The wisdom of older members of the culture, who have been "down the line" is treasured because they understand, more than others, what is real.

4. Being assertive is a key symbol of:

   A. Yes, standing up for yourself

   B. No, not controlling feelings

   C. No, not avoiding conflict

   D. No, not controlling others

5. The African American community handles the expression of feelings by:
   A. No, not by expecting members to control themselves
   B. No, not by confining such expression to appropriate times and places
   C. Yes, by allowing members great freedom of expression
   D. No, not by preferring indirect expression

6. The bouncing-back value primarily refers to:
   A. No, although a factor could be inspiration from the young people who typically bounce back from failure
   B. No, not coming back and getting even for injustices
   C. No, although a factor could be surviving physical illness
   D. Yes, respect for older members who have survived through many experiences. This value does not exclude a or b, but refers primarily to response d.

7. African American families tend to:
   A. No, although they do use the term *parents* to include grandparents and other close relatives
   B. No, although they do include key people who are not blood relatives
   C. No, they do not tend to protect children from life's difficulties; in fact, they tend to prepare and expose children to the inevitable difficulties
   D. Yes, both a and b

8. A traditional African view of time includes:
   A. No, although a factor is no way of expressing a distant future
   B. No, although a factor is an either–or viewpoint of whether something is done now or is done habitually
   C. No, although a factor is a lack of emphasis on things done at various points in time
   D. Yes, all of the above. Remember, this is African, not necessarily African American, but there is some carry-forward of this view in the current culture.

9. African American style in relating to acquaintances is to:
   A. No, a style with close friends is to acknowledge the individual and develop intimacy
   B. No, a style with close friends is to appreciate the culture and be supportive
   C. Yes, follow role prescriptions, be polite, and watch your words. Acquaintances receive a more distant, formal treatment than close friends.
   D. No, a style with close friends is to develop intimacy and be supportive

10. A key aspect of male–female relationships is:
    A. No, sexual interest is shown directly
    B. Yes, both women and men are sexually assertive. They tend to show interest directly and are not easily offended if overtures and rejections are made with good humor.
    C. No, women are not easily offended when men make direct sexual overtures
    D. No, men are not easily offended when women reject their overtures

---

HOW CAN THE BARRIERS TO CAREER SUCCESS OF AFRICAN AMERICANS BE BROKEN?

You can play a role in helping African American associates overcome the "less-intelligent" stereotype that leads to lower expectations for their skill development, promotability, and corporate success. You can also play a role in helping them break through the glass ceiling to better jobs. And, by understanding the typical career phases African Americans experience, you can learn how to support them in overcoming typical personal barriers and corporate-culture barriers at each phase.

Barrier #1: Breaking Out of Lower Expectations of Success

A real barrier for many African Americans is the stereotype that they are less intelligent. Many have internalized this belief. All must deal with Euro-Americans in the workplace who hold this stereotype and therefore expect African Americans to be less competent learners and achievers.

You've learned that the higher the socioeconomic status of a family, the higher the grades and SAT scores of their children. The children do well in school and are therefore likely to get good jobs and earn good incomes when they grow up, which in turn increases the likelihood that *their* children will do well in school. Some predominantly African American schools have identified differences in the failure and success cycles. They've adopted success cycle teaching and learning strategies to help children boost their academic achievement.

Some corporations have adopted these same strategies to help all employees, including African Americans, break out of failure cycles and establish success cycles.

What You Expect Is What You Get

Failure and success cycles are affected by what people expect. Here's what expectancy theory is all about: You communicate in words and actions your beliefs and expectations about what a worker can achieve. If that worker values your opinion, then your expectations have a powerful impact on that person's skill development and performance. If you believe the coworker will do well, she's more likely to believe she'll do well, she's more likely to actually do well, and she's more likely to credit her success to her own ability. Belief leads to performance.

> *Once an African American family is able to break the cycle of poverty and get good jobs, the cycle tends to stay broken for that family.*

If a worker thinks you're an important person, that you have knowledge or you can make a difference, then what you expect can affect the following aspects of her performance:

- how fully she believes she can succeed
- how hard she tries
- how intensely she concentrates
- how willing she is to take reasonable risks, which is a key factor in developing self-confidence and new skills
- how she interprets her success or failure

Failure Cycle

Here's how the failure cycle works: When you believe a worker has inferior abilities and therefore you have lower expectations for him than for others, you set up a failure cycle as follows:

- you assume that he is intellectually inferior, which leads to
- his internalized belief that he is intellectually inferior, which leads to
- low self-confidence about succeeding at intellectual tasks, which leads to
- poor performance on intellectual tasks, which leads to
- avoidance of intellectual tasks

We can therefore conclude that avoidance of intellectual challenge is affected by fears and self-doubt, which are rooted in a history of strong negative stereotypes that Euro-Americans hold about African Americans' intellectual capabilities.

When a worker expects to fail, or assumes he can't succeed, or believes "I don't have what it takes," here's what's likely to occur:

- He takes a dim view of trying again.
- He loses his motivation and often gives up trying to learn.

- He blames the failure on his own lack of ability (or aptitude and potential) rather than on inadequate or erroneous effort, which is correctable.
- By this process he, in effect, internalizes the low opinion originally held by you (or others).

What makes African Americans unique in this regard is that they are singled out for the stigma of genetic intellectual inferiority. This negative stereotype suggests to African Americans that they should understand any failure in intellectual activity as confirmation of genetic inferiority. No wonder many African Americans shy away from any situation where the rumor of inferiority might be proved true.

Success Cycle

African Americans tend to experience greater success when they engage in sports, socializing, and entertaining others because of assumptions and stereotypes that they are "innately" gifted in these areas. Many of them have established success cycles in these areas. But suppose you are an important person in an African American worker's life. Here's how you can set up a success cycle:

- you assume that she can master a job task, which leads to
- her internalized belief that she can master the job task, which leads to
- self-confidence in her ability to master the job task, which leads to
- willingness to put forth effort on the job task, which leads to
- development of job skills

If she has a failure during this process, her self-confidence allows her to see it as merely an error, not a sign of incompetence. Failure is just an opportunity to find out what doesn't work and correct it, a lesson for how to succeed next time.

Your positive beliefs and resulting expectations for her success help her build self-confidence. She becomes inspired and willing to put forth the effort necessary to achieve specific job goals, which leads to learning, achievement, and growth in that job area. This achievement becomes the foundation for increased self-confidence in the next cycle. The success cycle is a process in which success increases self-confidence and effort, leading to even more success, over and over in the upward spiral. It's circular and feeds back on itself, moving upward in a geometrically expanding spiral, as shown in Snapshot 7.2.

What You Can Do

Here's how you can encourage a success cycle during the learning phases.

SNAPSHOT 7.2   Skill development cycle.

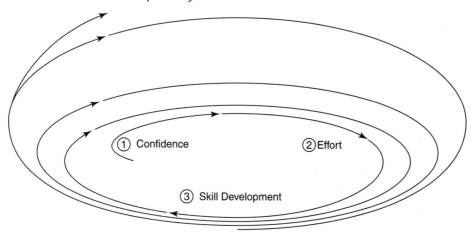

During the confidence phase.   Begin with your own stereotyped beliefs, assumptions, and expectations. Get them straight. When you're sure you have a "you can" attitude, you'll know your verbal and nonverbal messages are likely to convey positive expectations.

During the effort phase.   Take a positive attitude toward performance evaluation. Encourage African Americans to attribute their successes to ability, boosting their confidence level. Help them to see their failures as either a lack of effort or some correctable error—as a learning tool for creating success the next time around. The key question is, how can I do it differently next time?

During the skill development phase.   Help African American employees assume responsibility for their own performance and development, and let them know you are there as a resource person. Pay special attention to training and development, bringing in appropriate new opportunities as skills are built. Keep the cycle going.

Barrier #2: Breaking Through the Glass Ceiling

Corporate America cannot yet claim a diverse workplace that looks like America as a whole. African Americans have moved into better-paying occupations, but most still hit a glass ceiling at middle-management levels or even below, according to government reports.

Barriers to Better Paying Occupations

Looking at the American workforce as a whole, only about 5 percent of *all* managers and professional persons are African American, though they are 12 percent of the population. This includes government jobs, where they have made the greatest progress, so corporate rates are even lower. Still, this is an overall increase of 52 percent since 1978.

The unemployment rate for African American men aged 20 to 24 remained higher than 20 percent well into the 1990s, more than double the rates for Euro-American men. The most common occupation for African American men is laborer and for women, clerical. Since the 1960s, women have made better progress than men, most moving from jobs as agricultural or domestic worker to office worker. However, African American women still tend to be:

- placed into training programs for traditionally female occupations
- discouraged from attempting innovative careers
- dependent upon the public sector for employment
- kept out of better private-sector jobs by rigid ethnic barriers

External and Internal Attitudes

In American society, traditional prejudice and discrimination toward diverse groups results in a package of feelings and experiences that most members of these groups bring to the workplace. As a leader, you need to be aware of these factors that affect African Americans in a wide range of ways. Some have managed to ignore or rise above most of them. Others may have a problem in one area and none in the others. Knowing what to look for can help you give the right kind of support.

Whether your role is that of manager, team leader, or responsible coworker, you can identify ways to support African Americans leaving stereotypes behind and focusing on developing themselves for the next job promotion. The focus may be on increasing their flexibility, networking ability, bottom-line influence, computer literacy, highlighting their own strengths, and other areas relevant to their career plan.

The barriers that most African Americans face in the workplace consist of a mixture of the burdens society has imposed upon them and how that has affected them personally.

Barrier #3: Breaking Through Blocks at Each Career Phase

You can help African Americans break through career blocks by understanding the career phases typical for African Americans and by giving

GLASS CEILINGS AND OTHER BARRIERS

Most African Americans come to the workplace with some combination of the following factors:

- a history of oppression and exclusion from the mainstream activities of society
- a sense that they're seen as different (in a negative way) from Euro-Americans
- being positioned in a one-down status
- being barred or discouraged from seeking a better position in society—or in life
- lack of equal opportunities
- as a result: lower self-concept, self-esteem, and self-confidence

These problems, and sometimes their solution attempts, have led to other problems as mentioned in *Wall Street Journal* surveys of African Americans who have chosen to leave their corporations:

- hitting the glass ceiling and lacking opportunity and upward mobility
- feeling pressured to "act white" and to repress their ethnic identity in order to fit in, make others feel comfortable, and succeed
- feeling misplaced in a corporate culture where work life and social life focus only on Euro-American customs
- having to prove themselves, over and over again, due to being African American
- dealing with the assumption, and resulting stigma, that they are an "affirmative action hire"
- coping with ethnic stereotypes

To succeed in most corporate cultures, African Americans must learn to:

- pay as much attention to monitoring and developing their career strategies as they do to achieving specific job goals
- market themselves within the company and outside of it
- network and establish relationships with other people in other divisions
- tap into the grapevine and keep up with what's going on

support at each phase. African Americans who enter the corporate world typically move through several phases that might be described as:

- *Entry-level* phase—dealing with organizational and personal prejudice
- *Adjustment and frustration* phase—dealing with anger and frustration
- *Career development* phase—developing skills in conflict management and management of prejudice
- *Mastery* phase—refining protective hesitation and integrating core skills

Entry-Level and Adjustment Phases

Managing attitudes.   Many African American applicants come to the organization with a positive but naive attitude. They usually encounter personal as well as organizational prejudice and may become angry, hostile, and culturally paranoid. If they decide to stay, they then adjust and plan their growth rather than allow anger and resentment to stifle it. They find ways to recapture their earlier positive attitude, so that negative attitudes cease to be a barrier to learning. Successful African American employees somehow retain a positive attitude even in the midst of prejudiced behaviors.

Gaining confidence.   In the early phases, most African Americans have great difficulty seeing themselves in a leadership position because they've been taught that Euro-American men lead, African Americans follow. They often apologize in various ways for taking leadership or initiative or for being put in even a temporary leadership position. They may have difficulty directing Euro-American males and therefore not be as self-confident as the norm because of their discomfort with empowerment. Before they become comfortable with having and using power, their walk may be less assured, their voice tone may lack authority, and their attitude may be more *May I?* than *This is what we can do.* Keep in mind that, typically, African Americans are required to demonstrate competence at the next level before they are promoted, whereas Euro-American males are typically promoted on the basis of their potential. Ask yourself periodically:

- Am I doing my share to see that people are treated equally? That everyone gets a fair chance at plum assignments and promotions?

Coping with stereotypes.   Even when African Americans achieve the desired results, they typically must devote extra energy to ensure that the results are properly seen by the right people. This is because decision makers often harbor negative stereotypes that prevent them from seeing such achievements:

- Are you open to seeing everyone's achievements and potential?
- Are you helping others to see clearly?

Career Development Phase

Dealing with trust issues.   Overcoming African American mistrust of the input from Euro-Americans is still an issue for most African American employees, even at the career development stage. They may establish a one-to-one relationship with their manager, but they rarely expand this to a generalized attitude toward all Euro-Americans. During this phase, African American employees usually keep their misgivings to themselves, choosing instead to behave in a manner of trust. They need to identify and access one or more mentors.

Gaining support.   These employees must develop and use a network of supporters, whether the members are prejudiced or not. A commitment to succeed becomes the prime goal of successful employees. By now they should understand that waiting to be adopted by a Euro-American mentor is risky, so they may need to take the initiative to locate potential people in the organization and find a mentor:

- Are you willing to be a supporter or mentor?
- Are you encouraging others to support African American colleagues?

In this phase, two of the most important job skills to be acquired are *conflict management* and the *management of prejudice*.

Managing conflict.   If African Americans can't deal with conflict constructively, they're likely to be blamed as a *cause* of any conflict they become embroiled in. African Americans tend as a group to be more open and straightforward in their interactions than do Euro-Americans. They typically want to confront conflict directly and solve the problem quickly. In many organizations, however, the norm is conflict avoidance. If so, the African American's style will be seen as inappropriate. African Americans are more likely to confront the other person as soon as they're aware of a conflict situation. If that's inappropriate, they'll do it later in private. Euro-Americans in many corporate cultures will discuss the situation with the other person's boss and may talk about it with others, before they'll openly confront the person involved in the conflict:

- Are you willing to accept an open, direct style of conflict resolution?

Managing prejudice.   Most African American employees already have a range of skills for counteracting and neutralizing Euro-Americans' demeaning, prejudicial actions. For example, *protective hesitation* is a common African American strategy for dealing with prejudice and the hostile situations it engenders. It's based on the value of distrust of the establishment. The strategy consists of deliberately hesitating before interacting or preparing to interact with Euro-Americans, in order to think about how to protect oneself from possible psychological assault or to avoid reinforcing negative stereotypes about African Americans. Such preventive hesitation involves using caution and preplanning. This behavior has been handed down from parents to children through generations and so comes naturally to many African Americans by the time they're adults. It can be especially helpful at the career development phase when the employee is being assessed for promotion potential:

- Are you willing to understand protective hesitation and to discover the underlying dynamics of prejudice and defense?

The Mastery Phase: Mutual Support

One of the key insights successful African Americans say they used in the mastery phase is that making mistakes or failing is not an option for African American managers. When they fail, they fail for the entire group of African American employees. Most have made protective hesitation a way of life in the corporation. Key to their style is preplanning, careful thought, and caution in relying on Euro-Americans as resources. Through trial and error, they take their rage and use its energy to help them achieve productive results:

- Are you willing to build trusting relationships by consistently being honest, direct, and supportive?

HOW CAN I HELP AFRICAN AMERICANS CONTRIBUTE TO AN ORGANIZATION?

As a leader, you need to recognize the strengths that each of your team members brings to the organization and to build on those strengths. African Americans bring many assets to the workplace that can be used in numerous ways. They can contribute to team processes, to the development of networks and business relationships that are especially valuable for the organization, and to connections with the African American marketplace.

Planning, Creating, and Problem Solving

Work teams must deal with fast-paced change—by recognizing niches, developing profitable products and services, moving in on the right opportunities at the right time, solving problems, and optimizing total quality. The best work teams develop a high level of skill in generating ideas, planning, and problem solving—and they do this through synergy, creativity, and innovation as well as by discipline and application.

You can help team leaders and members recognize the value of African American strengths, such as *personal style, holistic worldview, inferential reasoning, and flexible approximation.* These traits can add to the team's strengths. Some of these traits may seem foreign to those accustomed to typical business traits and approaches.

- You can help your team realize that a different approach can sometimes score winning points, that "differentness" can be an asset.

Building Relationships

Relationships are the name of the game in the marketplace. Business is built upon networks of relationships among team members, customers, suppliers, other departments, the community, professional organizations, regulating agencies, and others. African Americans have a special advantage when they apply their tendencies toward: a people focus, sharing, nonverbal communication skills, and expression of feelings.

For example, in team relationships, African American members can set a tone that could help the team avoid game playing and hidden agendas through focusing on the values of directness, emotional expressiveness, and sense of justice. To be most effective, expression of these values may need to be stepped down to an intensity that other team members can accept.

- You can help African Americans members develop appropriate expressions of their strengths.
- You can also provide guidance about expressing the justice and distrust values in ways that avoid the stereotype of the resentful African American or the troublemaker.

Connecting with the African American Marketplace

African Americans obviously have an inside edge in understanding other African Americans, the community, and the marketplace. They can contribute great strength to the organization in gaining African American market share. These customers and businesspersons like to do business with companies that "look like America" and therefore include African Americans. South Africa and other African nations also represent growth market opportunities for many organizations, and African American team members provide an obvious advantage in those markets.

> *African Americans now represent over $630 billion a year in spending power, and the market is growing.*

- You can recognize these connections and the related opportunities to use African American employees' understanding of their own culture and related cultures.

■ You can make others aware of these connections and opportunities and use your influence to help African Americans make valuable contributions to the success of your team and your organization.

FINAL SELF-TEST

Indicate the best answers to the following 6 multiple-choice questions.

1. A key African American strength is:
   A. a focus on material success
   B. a focus on specific times, numbers, and spaces
   C. a holistic worldview
   D. preference for order and tradition

2. The trend of African American managers and professionals leaving corporate jobs is caused by:
   A. the glass ceiling
   B. pressure to modify their ethnic identity
   C. coping with stereotypes
   D. all of the above

3. The feelings and experiences that many African Americans and other minorities may bring to the workplace include:
   A. self-reliance
   B. independence
   C. low self-concept, low self-esteem, and low self-confidence
   D. confidence in their promotability

4. A barrier faced by most minorities, especially African Americans, is:
   A. a history of oppression
   B. exclusion from the mainstream activities of society
   C. feelings of being inferior to those in a dominant position
   D. all of the above

5. The most significant barrier facing the upward mobility of African Americans and other minorities in today's corporations is:
   A. the glass ceiling
   B. discriminatory policies
   C. closed recruiting practices
   D. language differences

6. Which is NOT a step in the Success Cycle?

   A. the manager's assumption that the employee can master a job task

   B. the employee's internalized belief that she or he can master the job task

   C. the employee's self-confidence in his or her ability to master the job task

   D. the employee's focus on physical tasks and avoidance of intellectual tasks

FINAL SELF-TEST FEEDBACK

Each correct answer is worth 15 points. If you score less than 70 points, you should review the materials and re-take the Final Self-Test.

1. A key African American strength is:

   A. No, not a focus on material success

   B. No, not a focus on specific times, numbers, and spaces

   C. Yes, a holistic worldview

   D. No, not preference for order and tradition

2. The trend of African American managers and professionals leaving corporate jobs is caused by:

   A. No, although a factor is the glass ceiling

   B. No, although a factor is pressure to modify their ethnic identity

   C. No, although a factor is coping with stereotypes

   D. Yes, all of the above. Those that have been surveyed indicate that all three situations are factors in their decision to leave.

3. The feelings and experiences that many African Americans and other minorities may bring to the workplace include:

   A. No, self-reliance is not predominant

   B. No, independence is not predominant

   C. Yes, low self-concept, low self-esteem, and low self-confidence. The impact of many experiences of denigration, stereotyping, prejudice, and discrimination in the dominant culture often leads to these consequences.

   D. No, confidence in their promotability is not dominant

4. A barrier faced by most minorities, especially African Americans, is:
   A. No, although a factor is a history of oppression
   B. No, although a factor is exclusion from the mainstream activities of society
   C. No, although a factor is feelings of being inferior to those in a dominant position
   D. Yes, all of the above are significant factors

5. The most significant barrier facing the upward mobility of African Americans and other minorities in today's corporations is:
   A. Yes, the glass ceiling is one of the results of discriminatory policies, among other causes
   B. No, although a factor is discriminatory policies
   C. No, although a factor is closed recruiting practices
   D. No, not language differences

6. Which is NOT a step in the Success Cycle?
   A. No, in fact the manager's assumption that the employee can master a job task is the first step
   B. No, in fact the employee's internalized belief that she or he can master the job task is the second step
   C. No, in fact the employee's self-confidence in her or his ability to master the job task is the third step
   D. Yes, the employee's focus on physical tasks and avoidance of intellectual tasks is not part of the Success Cycle, but it is part of the Failure Cycle

SKILL BUILDER 7.1
The Case of Jason, African American Manager

Jason has applied for an assistant manager's position at Drysdale Corporation. He's looking for opportunities to learn and grow in his career and wants to leave his current job because such opportunities are lacking. His ultimate career goal is to become CEO of a large corporation. With his degree in business administration and plans to complete an MBA, he thinks he has a chance—if he can find the right firm—even though he's an African American. When Jason is escorted around the Drysdale offices, he sees no African Americans, a few Asian Americans, and one Latino American.

Nearly everyone is Euro-American, and they mostly seem too busy to pay much attention to Jason or spend time with him. But Jason really believes in the Drysdale Corporation and decides to accept their job offer.

Soon after he begins work, he notices that ethnic jokes and comments are common at Drysdale. Jason doesn't look like a typical African American because his mother is Euro-American. He speaks up several times, saying he doesn't appreciate jokes and comments that belittle people from any ethnic group. Most of the comments stop, but so does the already-sparse friendliness of Jason's coworkers. While the environment is not particularly warm at Drysdale, Jason still believes he can achieve career success here because he loves the work itself.

Jason knows he's a rapid learner and a responsible person, one who works effectively and efficiently. His performance evaluations during the next year and a half are all excellent and his manager **Ken** seems to be encouraging. In fact, Jason believes he is one of the most productive workers in the company. He meets his time targets and maintains high work quality. But Jason is getting restless. His work is becoming routine to him and therefore boring. He has asked Ken several times about a promotion and expanded job responsibilities. Ken has been vague, telling Jason to "hang in there and I'll keep an eye out for job opportunities for you." In the meantime, several management positions have opened up at Drysdale and been filled by others.

1. The key issue in this case is probably:

   A. Jason is expecting too much too soon.

   B. Jason does not yet have the experience and skills he needs for promotion.

   C. Jason is experiencing ethnic discrimination and has hit the "glass ceiling."

   D. The company has not yet found a good job fit at the next level for Jason.

Feedback

   A. No, others with similar experience and seniority are being promoted.

   B. No, his colleagues are being promoted and his performance evaluations are excellent.

   C. This is the best answer because his qualifications are good but the environment is not particularly warm or friendly.

   D. No, his skills and performance should be just as apt and transferable as those of his colleagues who have been promoted.

2. Jason's best response at this point in time is probably to:

A. Get an agreement from Ken on exactly what he must do to merit promotion (specific goals and standards) and expect to get it if he achieves as agreed.

B. Go to Ken's manager to ask why he hasn't received the promotion he believes he has earned.

C. File a discrimination complaint with the Equal Employment Opportunity Commission.

D. Resign.

Feedback

A. Yes, this is the best action at this point.

B. This is the second step Jason should take if he can't get satisfaction from Ken.

C. Definitely not at this point and probably never unless he wants to stall his career progress for years. The EEOC expects employees to seek all reasonable remedies through the company before filing a complaint. Employers take a dim view of employees who go outside the company to file legal complaints.

D. Definitely not at this point. Give this company a chance first. The next company may be just as bad or worse. Always have a firm job offer lined up before you resign and try to leave on good terms. On the other hand, always be looking around and creating possible job options elsewhere.

SKILL BUILDER 7.2
The Case of Karla, African American Salesperson

Karla is a salesperson at Ellison's Furniture, the only African American on the small sales force of 20 persons. She has been very successful selling furniture, makes a good salary plus commission, and during the year she has been at Ellison's, has made top salesperson of the month three times. Karla enjoys her work but feels isolated from most of her coworkers. Most of them are Euro-American men, and five are Euro-American women. The manager *Daniel* is Euro-American and has been very supportive of Karla's training, development, and sales work. He often praises her work and encourages her to "keep it up."

Rachel is the only salesperson who has seemed willing to spend much time with Karla during coffee breaks or at lunch. While Karla doesn't think of Rachel as a close personal friend, she does view her as more than just a business colleague. She's also a friend.

From time to time, Karla has overheard comments of her coworkers about the good times they've had together at various parties and outings that they plan. She can't help thinking about the fact that she is never included. Last week as Karla approached the employees' lounge, she heard someone saying, " . . . at Rachel's party last Saturday . . . " Karla stopped dead in her tracks. She felt as if someone had punched her in the stomach. What a blow to discover that even her friend, her only "real work friend," had thrown a party and excluded her.

Daniel has noticed that during the past week Karla has seemed quieter and more withdrawn than usual. He is concerned because he believes that Karla's success as a salesperson is largely due to her outgoing, cheerful personality. When he gets a chance to talk privately with Karla, he says, "Is everything okay, Karla? You've been awfully quiet the past few days."

1. **Karla's best response at this point is probably to:**
   A. Tell everything to Daniel, then continue to do excellent work, being friendly and good-natured with everyone.
   B. Confront Rachel with her betrayal.
   C. Resign.
   D. Deny there's a problem in response to Daniel, then continue to do excellent work, being friendly and good-natured with everyone.

Feedback

A. Telling everything to Daniel, while doing good work, is her best response, at least as the first step. Daniel has been supportive and may be able to improve the situation. Doing excellent work and being friendly is always a productive response, though other measures are often needed. It's always wise to generate other job options for many reasons. In this case, Rachel needs other options for locating a fair and equitable job situation.

B. No, confronting Rachel is not best. Rachel is under no obligation to socialize with Karla. Friendships and personal "chemistry" cannot be forced.

C. Definitely don't resign, at least not before she has a new job lined up. However, she should look around, make contacts, put out feelers, and create a demand for her services elsewhere.

D. No, denying the problem means passing up Daniel's offer of support. Of course, she should continue to do excellent work and be friendly.

2. Daniel's best response at this point is probably to:

A. Plan some office social events that include everyone.

B. Institute a team approach to selling.

C. Hold some training seminars that focus on diversity, inclusiveness, and similar issues.

D. All of the above.

Feedback

A. No, social events would be good, but other measures can also be taken. At these events Daniel can be especially friendly to Karla, bringing her into conversations, asking her to assist, etc. He can role model the kind of inclusive, positive attitudes and behaviors he would like everyone to adopt.

B. No, a team approach is excellent, but other measures can also be taken. The type of contact that changes prejudice is the type where members are dependent upon each other to achieve meaningful, important goals. Teamwork situations often break down the walls that separate people.

C. No, training seminars would be good, but other measures can also be used.

D. Yes, this is the best option because a multi-pronged approach works best in these situations. Of course, Daniel may face some constraints—budgetary, top management acceptance, employee acceptance—but the more workable strategies he can implement, the better his chances of bringing about positive change.

THE BOTTOM LINE

Now you have more information about the stereotypes and myths African Americans face. You have a basis for noticing and questioning what the media presents and what people say. You have a better sense of how to ask African Americans about themselves. Soon, you'll be as capable of building relationships with African Americans as you are with people from your own ethnic group.

Chapter Review

1. Typical African-American stereotypes are the following:
   - more violent
   - less intelligent

- lazy and irresponsible
- blame others for their problems
- resentful troublemakers

2. The African American culture is rooted in enforced slavery that technically ended with the Civil War. However, segregation—whether legal or de facto—continued to segregate African Americans from mainstream America until the Civil Rights era of the 1950s and 1960s and still impacts today's society.

3. Key values in the African American community include sharing and interrelating; expressing personal style and uniqueness; being real, genuine, and assertive; expressing feelings; bouncing back; and not trusting the establishment.

4. Key customs of the African American community include:
   - expecting the church to play a vital role in virtually every aspect of community life
   - viewing time as circular with a focus on the present and on whether things are done now or habitually, rather than as a time-line with infinite points into the future
   - relying on extended family relationships
   - using a distinctly different relationship style with close friends than with acquaintances, but consistently supporting other African Americans
   - expressing sexual interest directly and handling sexuality comfortably

5. The issues most important to African Americans are stereotypes, barriers to learning, lack of a "level playing field," suspicions that most are criminals, inequality in the legal system, the need to deal with the power and privilege of Euro-Americans, the need to act white in order to succeed, and the glass ceiling.

6. We can help African Americans meet the following challenges:
   - overcoming lower expectations of success by breaking out of failure cycles into success cycles
   - breaking through the glass ceiling
   - breaking through blocks at each career phase (adjustment, career development, and mastery phases)

7. African Americans bring many assets to the workplace and can contribute to team processes of planning, creating, and problem solving; building relationships, and connecting with the African American marketplace.

Working With Arab Americans

8

CHAPTER OBJECTIVES

- Identify typical stereotypes and myths about Arab Americans.
- Understand how myths and stereotypes have evolved from past events.
- Identify current Arab American demographic profiles.
- Describe Arab American values and customs.
- Understand the issues that are important to the Arab American community.
- Identify the key leadership challenges and opportunities for working effectively with Arab Americans.

CHAPTER OVERVIEW

About 1 percent of people in the American workplace are Arab Americans, estimated at about 3 million people. Most Arab Americans were born in the United States, and an even larger majority have U.S. citizenship. Most trace their ancestry to Arabic-speaking places in southwestern Asia and northern Africa, a region known as the Middle East. Not all people in this region are Arabs. The differences that seem to separate Arab Americans from other Americans can be much smaller than the variations that at times differentiate them from one another. It takes time to learn about their culture and the issues that concern them, but it's essential and rewarding for us to do that. Misunderstanding ultimately hurts each one of us.

What's it like to be an Arab American? Too often, they are defined in simplistic terms. Although the Arab culture is one of the oldest on Earth, it is misunderstood in many parts of the United States. There are no easy, one-size-fits-all answers. Language, culture, and religion are distinct qualities that act in different ways to connect Arabs and to distinguish them from one another.

You're about to get a little taste of what it's like to be an Arab American in the American society and how this experience can affect interactions in the workplace.

HOW DO TYPICAL MYTHS AND STEREOTYPES ABOUT ARAB AMERICANS COMPARE WITH CURRENT REALITY?

Stereotype #1: The Nomadic Desert-Tribe Arab

Let's start with this oldest stereotype that the media has portrayed: Arab sheiks in the desert with their harems and camels. It was not difficult for this cultural bias to deepen in direct proportion to U.S. interests in the Middle East.

> Since the terrorist attack on the World Trade Center of September 11, 2001, dark myths and stereotypes about Arabs have spilled over onto Arab Americans.

In fact, most Arab families live in urban areas, but portrayals of Arabs as desert dwellers have distorted the picture. Bedouins, nomadic people depicted in movies, make up only about 2 percent of Arab people. Many Arabs live in metropolitan areas. For example, one of the largest cities in the world is Cairo, with a population of more than 6 million.

While most Arab countries are more hot and dry than cold and wet, they do have a range of climates. You will find coastal areas, river delta regions, plateaus, and mountains, including some that get snow.

Stereotype #2: The Oil-Rich Sheik

The oil-rich sheik is a newer stereotype that has permeated advertising, television, and movies. The implication for Arab Americans is that they have rich relatives somewhere in the Middle East. Actually, these moguls are few and far between, and the rest of the Arab population tends to be in the poverty-stricken category. How many Arab Americans are from oil-rich countries? Relatively few. The area around the Persian Gulf is one of several oil-producing areas in the world, but not all Arab countries produce oil, and very few Arabs are rich from oil. Arab Americans are teachers, lawyers, grocers, executives, and students. If you think about them only in terms of stereotypes, other facets of their experience are ignored and your perception of them is one-dimensional.

Stereotype #3: The Arab Terrorist

This is the most damaging stereotype for Arab Americans, carrying the implication that they're likely to have terrorist connections. Media practices help sustain this fallacy. The broader Arab American community is usually invisible in the news—except when there are highly volatile political events. Then, the most visible Arab Americans and their institutions can be vulnerable to scapegoating.

One prominent example is the 1995 Oklahoma City bombing tragedy in which initial suspicions of a Middle-Eastern link prompted incidents of anti-Arab backlash. Scapegoating is a human failure of understanding and wisdom. Americans resent being made scapegoats by Muslim political extremists who blame all of the world's ills on Western decadence. Moving beyond stereotypes requires that we all recognize this tendency to scapegoat and avoid it.

A person from any ethnic group is just as likely to have connections with terrorists as an Arab American is. Many types of people have committed acts of terror. However, news accounts seem to more often stress Arab terrorists than they do other terrorists. A tiny handful of terrorists can have, and have had, a devastating impact on the world, as in the recent September 11 attacks. Yet, so far no Arab Americans fall into the terrorist category.

What is a terrorist? Is he someone who will murder persons based only on their national or religious affiliation? Consider the Americans who murdered strangers they thought looked like Arabs. At least two such murders occurred soon after the September 11 attacks. Such "terrorist" acts included the murder of a store owner who was actually from India and wore the turban and beard of the Sikh religion. He had donated $75 to a Costco fund for 9–11 victims only a few hours before his death, according to Costco's *Inside* magazine. Such attacks were extremely rare, however. Most Americans responded to 9–11 with maturity and wisdom and don't wish to be painted with the same brush as these rare terrorists in their midst.

Stereotype #4: The Violent Muslim Fundamentalist

To begin with, most Arab Americans are Christian, not Muslim, according to the Arab American Institute. Also, there are at least two major types of Muslims. Even among those two sects, Muslims come in many shades and stripes, just as Christians do.

In recent years, certain Muslim individuals and groups have declared *jihad*, or holy war, on Americans and American interests. The term *Islamic fundamentalist* is often used in the media to refer to these people who use Islam to justify political actions. This usage has blurred the distinction between religion and politics. The term *fundamentalist*, whether applied to Muslims or Christians, is a largely American term that indicates strict adherence to a traditional code of belief and behavior.

Throughout history, political groups and leaders have used religion to justify many political actions, including violence. This is an old, all-too-common story. However, even among Muslims who are traditional and conservative, very few condone terrorist acts. Fairness and accuracy mean attributing political actions to the group, government, or party responsible and not to a religion that has about 1.2 billion followers around the world. The Muslim holy book, the Quran, teaches nonviolence.

Stereotype #5: The Subservient Arab Woman

This stereotype stems from the image of Arab Americans as strict Muslims. While most Arab women live in Islamic households, less than one-fourth of Arab Americans do. They live in Christian households. By American standards, Arab women do lack personal freedom—from a little to a lot, but that refers primarily to Muslim women. Even then, the degree of freedom varies widely from country to country.

Stereotype #6: The Dark, Swarthy (Dangerous?) Arab Man

The media often seems to prefer images of people who look different or exotic. In trying for a more interesting image, they may emphasize the difference between Arab Americans and non-Arab Americans. Most Arab Americans do not wear traditional clothing. They dress like Americans generally dress.

The media tends to ignore Arab Americans except when there is a national or international crisis and they want to get the Arab American "take" on it. This keeps Arab Americans out of sight except when they are associated with trouble. The solution would be to cover Arab Americans consistently and continuously. This would result in a fuller and deeper knowledge of this community.

Arabs may have light skin and blue eyes or olive-to-dark skin and brown eyes. Hair textures differ. The United States has, at different times, classified Arab immigrants as African, Asian, European, white, or as belonging to a separate group. Most Arab Americans identify more closely with nationality than with ethnic group.

Arab Americans came to the United States for the freedom and equal opportunity that the country symbolizes. And although the first wave of immigrants did confront the ethnocentricity, ignorance, and anti-foreign sentiments of the pre-war period, they were rarely singled out for abuse or exclusion. This changed with the development of the Arab–Israeli conflict, which created a highly-charged political arena in which the United States became a strategic player and a strong supporter of the state of Israel. Arab Americans began to experience significant stereotyping, harassment, defamation, and exclusion brought on by the widespread perception of Arabs as immigrants from hostile enemy lands.

HOW HAVE THESE MYTHS AND STEREOTYPES EVOLVED?

Let's begin with the first wave of Arab Americans who immigrated to the United States. About half of today's Arab Americans descended from the first wave of immigrants around the turn of the century, and they faced only the typical stereotypes and prejudice that most newcomers must work through. The second wave has come since World War II. They've had a tougher time because of increasing tensions in the Middle East revolving around U.S. policy on two issues: (1) oil resources and (2) the state of Israel.

First Wave

The first wave of Arab persons arrived in the United States between 1875 and 1920. Most were from Lebanon, Syria, and Palestine and about 90 percent were Christian. Most were fleeing the changing economic and political conditions in their home countries. The first wave consisted primarily of farmers or village artisans who were relatively poor with little or no education. They came to seek opportunity, intending to return home when they amassed enough money. Most settled in Arab communities and learned enough English to get by. Many eventually brought their families over and became permanent residents.

The earliest Arab American communities were built around a network of peddlers and their suppliers. Many of the suppliers became the first community leaders and acted as representatives to the outside world. What also seems to have set the Arab American experience apart was the relative degree of affluence that they quickly achieved. In the early 1900s—when miners, factory workers, and farm laborers earned around $600 per year—Arab American pack peddlers were earning about $1,000. Another strength that set them apart was the relative degree of ease with which they assimilated into the mainstream.

Syrians, both Muslim and Druze, made up much of the remaining 10 percent of the first wave. This group, which came at the end of the peddling era in the 1920s and during the rise of the mass retail consumer market, flocked to the industrial cities of the heartland, like Toledo, Ohio, and Detroit-Dearborn, Michigan.

Like most immigrant groups, Arab Americans had to struggle with negative stereotyping, ethnic slurs, prejudice, and discrimination. They faced poor working conditions, long hours, low wages, and an antagonistic society. They struggled with identity, culture, and marginality, forming ethnic communities that helped them establish their identity.

Second Wave

Beginning in the late 1940s, the second wave of Arab immigrants came from a wide variety of countries, including those listed in Snapshot 8.1.

Most wanted to escape the civil wars, famines, and hardships that followed World War II. They were primarily educated, bilingual, politicized, and nationalistic, having come from Arab nations that had gained their independence from European colonial nations immediately after the war.

SNAPSHOT 8.1   Second wave countries of origin.

Algeria	Lebanon	Saudi Arabia
Bahrain	Libya	Somalia
Djibouti	Mauritania	Sudan
Egypt	Morocco	Syria
Iraq	Oman	Tunisia
Jordan	Palestine	United Arab Emirates
Kuwait	Qatar	Yemen

They identified themselves as Arabs and planned to settle permanently in the United States. Many were students, and there were many more Muslims in this group than in the first wave.

Both waves were pushed out of their homeland by harsh political and economic conditions. They were pulled to the United States by work opportunities due to industrialization. They came to work primarily in factories, the travel industry, and as tradespersons.

Since the 1970s, in both popular culture and government policy, anti-Arab stereotypes have placed a stigma on Arab ethnicity in America. In response, Arab American activists became determined to document and publicize the Arab American experience as a political imperative, a defensive tool against ignorance and hostility.

Terms to Use for Arab Americans

Here are some terms recommended by the Arab American Institute:

- *Arab American.* Do not hyphenate when referring to a person.
- *Arab-American issues.* Hyphenate when using Arab-American as an adjective.
- *Arab or Arab country.* Arab is used as a noun for a person and as an adjective.
- *She speaks Arabic.* Arabic is the name of the language and is not usually used as an adjective.
- *Saudi Arabian citizen, Arabian Peninsula, Arabian horse.* Arabian is an adjective that usually refers to Saudi Arabia.
- *Irani American, Egyptian American, etc.* When ethnicity or nationality are relevant, it is precise and accurate to specify the country of origin. Other terms are "of Iraqi heritage" or "of Jordanian descent," but only if ethnicity is relevant. Arab Americans come from many places, so use the relevant perspective.

■ *The Islam religion. Muslim worshippers.* Mohammedanism and Mohammedan are incorrect usages. Islam is the religion. Muslims are the members.

WHAT DO WE KNOW ABOUT ARAB AMERICANS TODAY?

Prior to 1980, the U.S. Census Bureau did not gather information on Arab Americans as a group. Although Arab Americans are still not designated as a distinct category, the Bureau has been collecting information on them. Although some Arab Americans feel a stronger identity with other minorities (people of color) than with Euro-Americans, the Bureau still officially classifies them as part of the majority "white" group.

On average, Arab Americans are younger, better educated, and more affluent than most Americans. Arab Americans are among the fastest growing ethnic groups in major metropolitan areas. First, let's look at some well-known Arab Americans and some interesting information about Arab Americans as a group.

WELL-KNOWN ARAB AMERICANS

Some well-known Arab Americans are:

■ **Najeeb Halaby,** former head of the Federal Aeronautics Authority, was CEO of Pan-American Airlines.

■ **Queen Noor** of Jordan, daughter of Najeeb Halaby, who married King Hussein and became the first Arab American to be queen of a foreign country.

■ **Paul Anka,** Canadian-born Arab American and a famous singer and songwriter.

■ **Danny Thomas,** the late comedian and actor, who founded St. Jude's Children's Research Hospital.

■ **Marlo Thomas,** feminist actress, daughter of Danny Thomas, wife of TV talk show host Phil Donahue. Marlo was the first actress ever to play a single, independent young woman living apart from her parents in the TV series "That Girl."

■ **Kristy McNichol,** actress once picked by *People* magazine as one of the "50 most beautiful people in the U.S."

WELL-KNOWN ARAB AMERICANS   *continued*

- **Dr. Michael DeBakey,** the Houston surgeon who invented the heart pump and went on to become chancellor of Baylor University's College of Medicine.
- **Bobby Rahal**, Indy 500 winner.
- **Doug Fluti,** Heisman Trophy-winner who threw the "miracle touchdown" pass for Boston College; the first American college quarterback to pass for 10,000 yards.
- **Casey Kasem and Don Bustany**, creators of radio's American Top 40.
- **Jacques Nasser**, president and chief executive officer of Ford Motor Co.
- **Helen Thomas,** former dean of the White House press corps.

Non-Arab Middle Easterners

Many people who are perceived to be Arab Americans are not actually of Arab origin, but are of Middle East origin. The Arab group is the largest in the Middle East in terms of population and land holdings, but there are a number of non-Arab groups. From the Arab region are Assyrians, Berbers from Morocco, Chaldeans, and Kurds, who speak languages rooted in pre-Arabic times.

Assyrians are Semites, closer in culture to the Jews than to the Arabs. They practice a unique early form of Christianity.

Chaldeans are also Semite people, their religion is Catholic, and they speak the Chaldean language. While they foster a separate identity, they also have an Iraqi nationality and some shared concerns with Arabs. They are the largest of these types of groups in the United States, with some large communities in Michigan, California, and Arizona, and the largest is in Detroit.

The Kurds are a large, unique minority who speak a very ancient language that is not part of the Arab language group. They have no national homeland and live in areas of Turkey, Iraq, Iran, and Syria. Some Kurds are Sunni Muslims, others are Shiite Muslims, and still others are Yazdis who follow an ancient religion similar to Zoroastrianism.

Iran is not an Arab country. It is in the Middle East, between Iraq and India, and it is an Islamic country, so many of its issues are similar. Iran is descended from the Persian empire and has a different language and cultural history than the Arab countries. The dominant language in Iran is Farsi, although Arabic and other languages are spoken there as well. *Persian* is sometimes used to describe either the language or the ethnicity, but the terms *Farsi* and *Iranian* are not interchangeable.

SNAPSHOT 8.2   Arab American countries of origin.

Lebanon	45%	Jordan	4%
Syria	14%	Iraq	2%
Egypt	11%	Other	4%
Palestine	9%		

Population

Estimates of Arab Americans living in the United States are about 3 million, or about 1 percent of the U.S. population. The number of Arab Americans is the subject of some debate. Estimates vary because the U.S. Census Bureau does not use an Arab American classification and because people identify themselves in various ways. Some Arab Americans identify themselves as Middle Eastern, for example. Recent immigrants from many countries are reluctant to give personal and confidential information to the government, and an increasing number of people have more than one ethnicity.

Countries of Origin

Contrary to popular assumptions or stereotypes, a sizable majority of Arab Americans are native-born, and nearly 82 percent are citizens. While Arab Americans come from all of the Middle Eastern countries, the majority trace their roots to six nations (as shown in Snapshot 8.2) according to John Zogby.

Lebanese

Over half of Arab Americans are Christians who trace their heritage to Lebanon, which was part of Greater Syria in those "first-wave" days, and they were known as Syrians then. Most of them came in the first wave and settled primarily in New York and New England. Since 1965, nearly 100,000 new immigrants have come from Lebanon, many settling in Michigan, California, Texas, and Ohio as well as in the older Lebanese communities.

Syrians

Arab Americans from Syria make up 14 percent of the population. Also predominantly Christian, as part of the first wave, Syrians and Lebanese forged the Arab American identity and founded such institutions as the Southern Federation of Syrian and Lebanese American Clubs and the renowned fundraising arm of St. Jude Children's Research Hospital, ALSAC (Associated Lebanese and Syrian American Charities). Despite this history of blurred identities between Lebanese and Syrian origins, the population of Syrian Americans equals or surpasses that of Lebanese Americans in eastern Pennsylvania, Rhode Island, and New Jersey.

Egyptians

Egyptians are 11 percent of the Arab American population. Many came to the United States in the 1950s as students, professionals, and skilled workers. Most wanted to escape the chaos of Egypt's struggle for independence from European colonialism. The Arab–Israeli war of 1967 provided another push. Egyptian Americans, both Muslim and Coptic Christian, are known for their high educational and occupational levels. At least 60 percent hold a bachelor's degree or higher, compared with 20 percent of the U.S. population as a whole. Most are business or professional persons—in medicine, research, education, technical, and other professions.

Palestinians and Jordanians

Arab Americans from Palestine, 9 percent of the total, have been predominantly Christian immigrants from cities or from towns and villages of the West Bank. A refugee program in the mid–1950s provided visas for thousands of Palestinians displaced in the Arab–Israeli war of 1948. Since the 1960s, an estimated 65,000 Palestinians, including those carrying Jordanian passports, have been admitted to the United States, most of them Christian. And while most Americans probably think of Palestinian residents as Muslims, a minority of Palestinians are Christian. The total number of immigrants who came with Jordanian passports make up about 4 percent of the Arab American population.

Iraqis

Immigrants from Iraq make up about 2 percent of Arab Americans. The majority are Christians who identify themselves as Chaldean or Assyrian. Iraqis, like Egyptians, are educated and well represented in the professional and business sectors of the U.S. economy. Since the Persian Gulf War of 1990, thousands of refugees have been resettled in the United States, and thousands more immigrants have fled the deteriorating economic and health conditions in their homeland.

Where Arab Americans Are Located

Arab Americans live in all 50 states, but about a third are concentrated in California, Michigan, and New York. Another third are in these seven states: Illinois, Maryland, Massachusetts, New Jersey, Ohio, Texas, and Virginia. About half of Arab Americans live in 20 metropolitan areas. The top six are Los Angeles, Detroit-Dearborn, New York, northeastern New Jersey, Chicago, and Washington, D.C.

As is the case with most immigrant groups, Arab immigrants have had a tendency to settle in U.S. cities rather than in the countryside. About 90 percent of Arab Americans are urban dwellers, compared to about 75 percent of Americans overall. Of even greater significance, about 97 percent of Arab immigrants settle in urban areas, compared with the 87 percent of U.S.-born Arab Americans who are urbanites.

Major settlements of Arab Americans are found in the:

- northeast—where Arab Americans are more likely to be found
- midwest—in Detroit-Dearborn, Cleveland, Chicago, Toledo
- south—with large, influential Southern Federation of Syria-Lebanon Clubs
- west—in growing southern California and San Francisco Bay Area communities

Those in the Northeast are more likely to be U.S.-born, while in the West they are much more likely to be immigrants.

By far the most concentrated areas of Arab American settlements are in the distinctly Arabic neighborhoods in the city of Dearborn. Michigan's vibrant expanse of ethnic, civic, and religious institutions have made it the new cultural and political magnet for the Arab American community nationwide. Unlike anywhere else in the country, Arab Americans make up 20 percent of Dearborn's population and more than 40 percent of the students enrolled in public schools.

Age Patterns

The newer wave of immigrants is younger, more likely to be foreign born and less likely to be assimilated with respect to marriage and language. New immigrants obviously are more likely to speak their first language and to cling to the traditions of the old country, including marrying within their ethnic community and having larger families than typical Americans.

They contribute to a younger Arab American population where most are from 20 to 44 years old. Not only are Arab Americans as a group younger than the U.S. population generally, they also are younger than most other ethnic groups. While nearly half are younger than 25, only 6 percent are over 65. The median age of Arab immigrants is 23, while that of U.S.-born Arab Americans is 29.

The proportion of Arab Americans who attend college is higher than the national average.

Educational Level

Arab Americans are, on average, better educated than non-Arab Americans. Compared to the norm, about twice as many Arab Americans, in percentage terms, earn degrees beyond the bachelor's degree. Key determining factors are country of origin, length of time in the United States, and gender.

Arab Americans place great value on education, and many of the second-wave immigrants came here already educated or for the specific purpose of obtaining higher education. A greater percentage of U.S.-born Arab Americans have high school diplomas, compared to immigrants, while the latter are more likely to have college degrees:

- 82 percent of Arab Americans have high school diplomas
- 36 percent have a bachelor's degree or higher
- 15 percent have graduate degrees

Occupations

Certain images or pictures come to mind when people think of the Arab immigrants to the United States: a man driving a taxi, a housewife with a head scarf rounding up several children, the man behind the counter at the local convenience store. Arab Americans who came to this country in order to establish themselves in business and retail have not disappeared. Arab Americans continue to demonstrate an almost unparalleled need for independence and freedom, as their disproportionate presence in the retail and professional trades shows. Otherwise, Arab Americans' occupational patterns generally mirror the national pattern of proportion of people who are working or who are unemployed and the types of jobs they hold.

Arab Americans work in all occupations. Collectively, they are more likely to be self-employed, to be entrepreneurs, or to work in sales. About 60 percent of working Arab Americans are executives, professionals, or office and sales staff. At the local level, Arab Americans are most likely to be executives in Washington, D.C. and Los Angeles, salespeople in Cleveland and Anaheim, and manufacturing workers in Detroit. As with all people, employment choices may be influenced by nationality, religion, education, socioeconomic status, and gender.

Bottom Line: Arab Americans are more likely to be self-employed, less likely to work for local government, and much more likely to hold managerial and professional specialty occupations than the average American.

Income

Arab Americans overall have the highest mean income of any U.S. group. But this doesn't tell the whole story. Older U.S.-born Arab Americans tend to be significantly more affluent than the overall American population, while younger immigrants show much less affluence. Many Arab immigrants' earnings put them below the poverty line. About 20 percent of Arab immigrant households have an income of $5,000 or less. Since a greater percentage of Arab American households are headed by someone foreign-born than among the other groups, the median income has been pulled down. Here are some specific figures:

- 1990 median income: $39,580
- 66 percent are employed
- 77 percent work in the private sector
- 12 percent are government employees
- 11 percent live below the poverty level

Non-citizens are much more likely to be below the poverty level than naturalized citizens, and the time spent in America for Arab Americans of both groups certainly appears to reduce the percentages of those below the poverty level.

Individually, Arab Americans are at every economic strata of American life. Nationally, Arab American households have a higher than average median income. Like occupational patterns, this varies by location.

Family Size

Arab American families are, on average, larger than non-Arab American families and smaller than families in Arab countries. Traditionally, more children meant more pride and economic contributors for the family. The cost of having large families in the United States, however, and an adaptation to American customs seems to encourage smaller families.

SELF-TEST

Indicate the best answers to the following 10 multiple-choice questions.

1. Typical stereotypes that Arab Americans must deal with include:
    A. lazy
    B. slow learners
    C. overly passive and polite
    D. violent fundamentalist
2. The religion of most Arab Americans is:
    A. Christian
    B. Baptist
    C. Muslim
    D. Fundamentalist

3. The most common occupation of Arab American men is:

    A. taxi driver

    B. convenience store clerk

    C. self-employed entrepreneur

    D. computer programmer

4. The average educational level of Arab Americans is:

    A. 82% have high school diplomas

    B. 36% have a bachelor's degree or higher

    C. 15% have graduate degrees

    D. all of the above

5. Most Arab Americans trace their heritage to:

    A. Syria

    B. Egypt

    C. Lebanon

    D. Palestine

6. The first wave of Arab American immigrants came to the United States between:

    A. 1940–1970

    B. 1875–1920

    C. 1775–1820

    D. 1800–1820

7. The proportion of Arab Americans in the American population is thought to be about:

    A. 10%

    B. 20%

    C. 5%

    D. 1%

8. The 1990 median income of Arab Americans is:

    A. the highest of any U.S. group

    B. the lowest of any U.S. group

    C. about the same as the U.S. average

    D. significantly less than that of Euro-Americans

9. What percentage of Arab Americans is employed?

    A. 45%

    B. 66%

    C. 95%

    D. 39%

10. The Arab American population is:

A. younger than the U.S. population generally

B. older than the U.S. population generally

C. mostly from 44 to 66 years old

D. mostly from 15 to 25 years old

SELF-TEST FEEDBACK

Each correct answer is worth 10 points. If you score less than 70 points, you should review the materials and re-take the Self-Test.

1. Typical stereotypes that Asian Americans must deal with include:

A. No, not lazy

B. No, not slow learners

C. No, not overly passive and polite

D. Yes, violent fundamentalist

2. The religion of most Arab Americans is:

A. Yes, Christian

B. No, not Baptist

C. No, not Muslim although this is the second largest group

D. No, not Fundamentalist, which is not considered a religion

3. The most common occupation of Arab American men is:

A. No, not taxi driver, which is a stereotype

B. No, not convenience store clerk, which is a stereotype

C. Yes, self-employed entrepreneur

D. No, not computer programmer

4. The average educational level of Arab Americans is:

A. No, although it is true that 82% have high school diplomas

B. No, although it is true that 36% have a bachelor's degree or higher

C. No, although it is true that 15% have graduate degrees

D. Yes, all of the above

5. Most Arab Americans trace their heritage to:

A. No, although many have ancestors from Syria

B. No, not Egypt

C. Yes, Lebanon

D. No, not Palestine

6. The first wave of Arab American immigrants came to the United States between:
   A. No, 1940–1970 would represent the second wave
   B. Yes, 1875–1920
   C. No, not 1775–1820
   D. No, not 1800–1820

7. The proportion of Arab Americans in the American population is thought to be about:
   A. No, not 10%
   B. No, not 20%
   C. No, not 5%
   D. Yes, about 1%

8. The 1990 median income of Arab Americans is:
   A. Yes, the highest of any U.S. group
   B. No, not the lowest of any U.S. group
   C. No, not about the same as the U.S. average
   D. No, not significantly less than that of Euro-Americans

9. What percentage of Arab Americans is employed?
   A. No, not 45%
   B. Yes, 66%
   C. No, not 95%
   D. No, not 39%

10. The Arab American population is:
    A. Yes, younger than the U.S. population generally
    B. No, not older than the U.S. population generally
    C. No, not mostly from 44 to 66 years old
    D. No, not mostly from 15 to 25 years old

WHAT ARE TYPICAL VALUES AND CUSTOMS OF MIDDLE EASTERN CULTURES?

Some common threads of Middle Eastern cultures include the language, certain worldviews, family values, and customs—with the Arabic language considered the most consistent unifying factor. These common threads have been taken from the works of such Arab American scholars as Baha Abu-Laban, Barbara Aswad, Barbara Bilgé, Joanna Kadi, Alixa Naff, Mohammed Sawaie,

Michael W. Suleiman, Faith T. Zeady, and John Zogby. We will frequently speak here of Middle Eastern cultures as they exist in those countries. Arab Americans vary in their adoption of the cultural values and customs. Most are affected to some extent, recent immigrants the most, and successive generations less and less.

Each choice to become "more American" can require some giving up of their cultural heritage, and therefore can create inner conflict; for example:

- Changing their names to common American names enhances acceptance in the mainstream culture but takes away some of their unique identity.
- Using English almost exclusively creates an erosion of their Arabic language skills.
- Becoming American means giving up certain advantages of communal life in their homeland, such as the close proximity of family members in the same neighborhood, economic support from close-knit extended families, and a collective identity.

Language

The Arabic language is one of the great unifying and distinguishing characteristics of the Arab people. However, second- and third-generation Arab Americans may not speak it at all. Those who do speak it usually know that there are at least four major Arabic dialects, and they can identify a speaker's region of origin by his or her accent.

> Modern Standard Arabic (MSA) is a pan-Arabic language used in formal letters, books, and newspapers. It's also spoken at Middle East peace conferences and on television news.

Arabic is one of several languages written from right to left instead of left to right, as English is written. Instead of Latin characters, Arabic is written in the 28-character Arabic alphabet. Arabic letters are connected like script, and fine writing is an art form.

The four main language groups in the Middle East are Arabic, Hebrew, Persian (Farsi), and Turkish. Arabic and Hebrew are Semitic languages, Farsi is of Indo-European origin, and Turkish originated in Korea. Other languages are Kurdish, which comes from an ancient form of Farsi, and Berber.

It is much more common for Arab Americans to speak more than one language than it is for most Americans. People in many countries place more emphasis on learning languages than Americans do, so many immigrants come to the United States speaking two or three languages. Most Arab countries emphasize the importance of knowing a foreign language, and they are very familiar with Western media.

While over 90 percent of Arab Americans speak English fluently, nearly half speak a language other than English at home, and about one-third speak only English at home.

In recent years, there has been a resurgence in the study of Arabic in universities, as well as in community schools or classes. As greater numbers of Muslims entered during the second wave, the importance of Arabic to the practice of Islam has helped promote the proliferation of classes. These first-generation Muslims are motivated by religious concerns. At the other end of the spectrum, fourth- and fifth-generation Arab Americans have developed a deeper interest in Arabic culture because of a growing concern about the crisis situation in the Middle East. The uniqueness of the political situation in the Arab World has stimulated their interest.

Worldviews and Religions

Arab American identity tends to be a compromise between two cultures, which may conflict at times. Traditional values may include:

- identity of the honor of family/clan/society with virginal morality of females, leading to a clear double standard for males and females
- reverence for past traditions
- conformity and stability
- high esteem for elders due to their life experience and wisdom

While Arabs in urban areas, especially younger ones, may not hold as tightly to these traditional Middle Eastern cultural values, they are influenced by them. These values may conflict with an American worldview that is likely to value:

- equality of females with males, leading to an acceptance of greater autonomy and freedom for females than in the past
- more focus on the future than on past traditions
- more focus on change and innovation than on holding to tradition
- relatively greater admiration for youthful looks and ways than for elders' wisdom

Worldviews, of course, are based on beliefs and values, which usually stem from adherence to, or resistance to, certain religious beliefs. In the Middle Eastern countries, Arabs are connected by culture, especially by language, and although most Arabs are Muslim, Islam is not the uniting factor. Therefore, you must distinguish religion from culture if you want to understand your Arab American colleagues. Arabs belong to many other religions, including Christianity and Judaism. In fact, 77 percent of

Arab Americans are Christian and only 23 percent are Muslim. Here is the breakdown:

Muslim	**23%**
Christian:	**77%**
Catholic	42%
Orthodox	23%
Protestant	12%

Christians

Although Arab Americans are frequently stereotyped as Muslims, over three-fourths are Christian, having descended from the first wave of Christian immigrants. This fact made it relatively easy for them to fit into American society. It made it easier for them to intermarry with Euro-American Christians, further facilitating their cultural integration. Many Arab American Christians have kept their Orthodox and Eastern Rite church affiliations (Greek Catholic, Maronite, Coptic). This helped them retain their ethnic identity, and their religious practices are not that different from those of the mainstream Euro-American culture, and so have not interfered with their acceptance.

Muslims

It is more difficult for Muslims to fit into U.S. society because of significant differences in religious beliefs that affect social practices. Although Muslims make up less than one-fourth of the Arab American population, Arab American communities in some regions may be predominantly Muslim. In fact, since the 1950s, Arab American Muslims represent the fastest growing segment of the Arab American community. They have many religious traditions and practices that may compete with prevailing American behavior and culture.

Traditional Muslims place importance on women's modesty and reject interfaith marriage. They express disapproval of American standards of dating and the growing belief in equal rights for males and females. Religious practices that direct personal behavior may make Muslims more visible than most religious minorities and often vulnerable to bigotry. Examples include men's beards and turbans and women's head coverings, as well as practices that require accommodation in such places as work, school, and the military.

Integration of Church and State

Fundamentalist Muslims may experience some difficulty between the Koran's instructions to "fight against the rule of the infidel to bring about Allah's dominion on earth" and the American government's foundation in separation of church and state. Americans live under human democratic law rather than under "God's law" as Muslim fundamentalists interpret it. "God's law" enforced by government is called the *Shari'a*. Actually, the American principle of "separation of church and state" can be irritating to fundamentalists of any religion. On the other hand, American Muslims may interpret this Koranic instruction as a command to live an *inner* life according to God's law, as do many fundamentalist Americans of the Christian and other faiths. This interpretation seems to work also for the millions of Muslims who live in other countries where human laws take precedence over the *Shari'a*.

Muslims Worldwide

In the Middle East, although most Arab countries are predominantly Muslim, only about 12 percent of Muslims worldwide are Arabs. There are more Muslims in Indonesia, for example, than in all Arab countries combined. Large populations of Muslims also live in India, Iran, Malaysia, Pakistan, Turkey, and several Russian republics. Still, Islam has a strong Arab flavor since the religion's holiest places are in the Middle East, and the Quran (also Koran), their holy book, was originally written in Arabic.

Muslim Belief

Muslims believe the Quran contains the word of God as revealed to the prophet Muhammad in the eighth century. The Quran has many passages that are similar to those in the Bible, which Muslims also regard as a holy book. That means Muslims have much in common with Christians and Jews. For example, they believe in one God and in the patriarchs and prophets of the Old Testament. They also believe that Jesus was one of the prophets, but was not the same as God.

Muslims refer to God as Allah. After Mecca, the other holiest cities are Medina in Saudi Arabia and Jerusalem in Israel. An imam, sometimes called

THE FIVE PILLARS OF ISLAM

The five pillars of Islam refer to sacred obligations:

1. adherence to the belief "there is no god but God, and Muhammad is his prophet"
2. prayer five times a day
3. sharing of alms with the poor
4. fasting from sunrise to sunset during the holy month of Ramadan
5. pilgrimage to the holy city of Mecca (in Saudi Arabia) once during a lifetime for those who are able financially and physically

> The most important Muslim observance each year is Ramadan.

a sheik, is a leader of prayer at a mosque. He gives sermons on Friday, the holiest day of the typical Islamic week. Islam does not have the same kind of hierarchy as some other religions. There is no top official or ruling board for Islam. Muslim mosques and associations are independent, and Muslims are not required to be members of a mosque.

The two main branches of Islam are called Sunni and Shi'a. Most Muslims worldwide and in the United States are Sunni, though Shi'as dominate in some countries such as Iran, Iraq, Bahrain, and Lebanon.

The African American religious group called Nation of Islam is closely related to Islam, but it evolved in the twentieth century and has some unique practices. On the other hand, most African American Muslims are not part of the Nation of Islam.

Religious Education

When immigrant Arab American parents describe how they raise their children in an Arab fashion, they use religion as the underlying theme. Religion serves several purposes:

- It helps parents maintain social rules that may otherwise disappear outside their native country and instill expected behaviors.
- It provides the children with a sense of identity.
- It provides a moral code for children growing up in the United States.
- It reinforces their own fear of God, which they want to pass on to the children.

Concern for retaining customs among their mostly U.S.-born children has prompted Arab American Muslims in large communities to open private Islamic schools.

Family Values and Customs

Generally, family is more important than the individual and more influential than nationality. People draw much of their identity from their role in the family. Historically, this has fostered immigration in which members of an extended family or clan help one another immigrate. Many Arab Americans maintain ties with relatives in their home countries.

Arab families are traditionally patriarchal and extended. Name and inheritance pass from father to sons. Family name is established and maintained through the actions of every family member. Actions of females must be guarded in order to protect the family name. Gender and religion are the primary aspects of Arab identity. Adolescents tend to talk mainly about gender, while their parents are more likely to identify themselves with religion.

Religion represents the system of meaning that the parents rely on to justify the behaviors they expect from their children and to demonstrate the significance of their cultural identity, according to Arab expert M.W. Suleiman.

The extended family may include parents, children, grandparents, uncles, aunts, and cousins living in one household. They provide financial, social, and emotional support for one another.

Gender Differences

In traditional households, boys and girls are raised with different standards and expectations.

Manly honor.   Gender roles vary greatly by country of origin, whether the family came from a rural or urban area, and how long they have been in the United States. The principle of "manly honor" motivates most Arabs as well as other people of the Middle East and those of Muslim countries. The roots of women's repression in these regions lie in authoritarian tribal practices and the overarching concern with protecting the "honor" of the patriarchal name and the identity of the clan or tribe.

Girls' sexual morality.   Accordingly, in Arab Muslim households, boys and girls are raised in dramatically different ways. Girls are taught that the American girl is perceived as immoral, while the Arab girl is respected. Great pressure is placed on girls to be "moral." The actions of girls is restricted and limited at home. They are closely monitored. There are dramatically different sexual standards for girls and boys, men and women.

Arab boys acquire more material objects than girls and have more freedom. They are expected to take increasing responsibility to uphold the family name by watching over their sisters' actions. If he hears rumors about his sister's behavior, he is expected to take immediate action to regulate her behavior. When other males are present, he feels even greater pressure to intervene.

Typical marriages.   Arab Americans are more likely to live in households where both partners are of Arab background. In fact, about 29 percent live in households headed by two Arabs.

Arab Americans typically get married at a younger age than non-Arab Americans, although this is changing. As women follow careers, they are not expected to marry so young. Since most Arab Americans were born in the United States, they frequently marry people from other cultures. In the home countries, typical marriages may be arranged by parents. The woman's family may demand and receive a large dowry (money or other assets) from the man's family. Arab women might marry older men who can provide greater financial security. Recent immigrants may adhere to these customs and even arrange a marriage with someone from the country of origin. For most Arab

Americans, however, couples meet and ask their families' approval before getting engaged, or make their own decision and then tell their families.

Arab American men are more likely than women to be single, while women are more likely to be married. U.S.-born Arab American women are twice as likely to be single as Arab-born women, though at 18 percent, single-women immigrants are perhaps higher than might be expected. Not surprisingly, women are more likely than men to be widowed.

Muslim Social Customs

Muslims have a number of social customs that differ from those of other cultures, involving physical proximity, shaking hands, and wearing certain garments.

Using physical space.   Arab cultures are known as preferring the closest physical proximity to one another of any major culture. When they are interacting, they tend to sit or stand so close that they can actually feel and smell the other's breath. They also tend to engage in more touching than other cultures.

Handshaking.   Americans typically offer to shake hands in greeting or when being introduced to someone. When meeting Arab Americans, if you believe they might be Muslim, it's best to wait until they extend their hand before you extend your own. There are a couple of religious reasons for this. First, traditional Muslim men observe "manly honor" by not invading a woman's space. He will not touch her or make direct eye contact if she is not a family member. This is a sign of respect and a part of his "gender separation duties." The other reason has to do with remaining untouched around prayer time.

Body covering.   Some Muslim women wear garments that cover their faces or heads, and in countries ruled by Muslim authorities, this may be required and strictly enforced by law. The practice is rooted in Islamic teachings about women's modesty. Covering is not universally observed by Muslim women and varies by region and class. Some church officials have declared that women's entire bodies and faces must be covered. This covering is called a burka in Afghanistan. Others require a long garment, a head covering and a veil that covers all of the face except the eyes. Still other rulings allow the face to show, so a long garment and a scarf will do.

The head scarf might be called a hijab or chador, and the long garment an abayah, jilbab, chador, or burka. Practices vary. In Iraq and Saudi Arabia, for example, a woman may wear a long garment and a cloak that covers her head, while underneath is a traditional dress, casual clothes, or a business suit. The cover garment comes off when she moves from public to private space.

Black garments usually signify mourning, which may last from a few days to many years, depending on religious custom.

Food. Middle-Eastern food is considered very tasty by most connoisseurs. It is varied, but has some staples. Wheat is used in bread, pastries, salads, and main dishes. Rice is often cooked with vegetables, lamb, chicken, or beef. Couscous, a rice-like grain, is often served alongside a meat dish. Lamb and mutton are more common than other meats. Arab recipes often call for beans and vegetables, including eggplant, zucchini, cauliflower, spinach, onions, parsley, and chickpeas. Middle Eastern vegetarian food is among the world's most delicious.

WHAT ISSUES ARE CURRENTLY MOST IMPORTANT TO ARAB AMERICANS?

Arab Americans are especially interested in Middle Eastern events because many of them have relatives there as well as cultural or religious commonalities with people who live there. Some issues that significantly affect the Arab American community are the Israel–Palestine conflict, U.S. oil policy in the Middle East, Muslim condemnation of American personal morality, fair treatment of Arab Americans, and Arab American representation in the U.S. political system.

Issue #1: Israel–Palestine Conflict

In addition to conflicts between Arab countries and Israel, there is also conflict between and within Arab countries. These conflicts are rooted in some of the world's oldest religions, ethnic differences, and boundaries drawn during twentieth century colonialism. One reason many Arab American families immigrated was to escape the very conflicts that continue today. Most have a keen interest in news from the Middle East—and Mideast issues can unify the Arab American vote.

By far the most crucial Middle East conflict is the struggle over territory and rights between Israel and Palestine. The most unifying viewpoint in the Arab world seems to be that the United States has acted with extreme favoritism toward Israel and with great disregard for the plight of Palestinian residents and refugees. Further igniting the smoldering resentment over this perceived unfair favoritism is the belief that the United States has the power and influence to end this conflict. General opinion is that the U.S. government lacks the will and determination to effect a fair and just resolution of this ongoing crisis. This is the smoldering fire of resentment that occasionally ignites into demonstrations and acts against American interests.

Issue #2: U.S. Mideast Oil Policy

The fact that the United States has become more and more dependent on oil and gasoline to fuel its huge energy consumption has led to continuing conflicts in the Middle East oil-producing region. These range from the 1970s gasoline shortage and Iranian hostage situation to the 1990 Gulf War with Iraq to current struggles. The Gulf War was especially devastating in the minds of many Arabs, and its bad taste lingers on. The United States is often perceived as a big bully, throwing its weight around in order to take care of its own insatiable appetites. Also, many Arabs resent feeling power-less and left behind in the burgeoning global economy, which adds a little fuel to the smoldering fire.

Issue #3: American-Arab Culture Clash

Adding a little more fuel may be the culture clash rooted primarily in dif-ferences between certain Islamic and American cultural values. Arab Amer-icans are obviously concerned about these fundamental differences between East and West.

Islamic Culture

Islamic cultures are generally governed by the rule of a king, religious leader, or strongman. Governmental and economic institutions are run by men, and family and community see their honor as dependent on the honor of the women.

Government.   Arab nations virtually never have democratic governments. They are either monarchies, plutocracies, or theocracies, and in all instances the laws tend to uphold certain restrictions of the Muslim faith. Because of its non-democratic political systems, the socioeconomic structure of most Arab nations is pyramidal. At the top is a tiny, very wealthy elite, supported by a small middle class and a huge lower class. The powerlessness felt by poverty-stricken masses, who nevertheless have access to television programs that showcase Western affluence, adds fuel to the fire of resentment.

Women's honor.   The Islamic-related laws of these countries usually in-clude sexual freedom for men who may have multiple wives and mistresses. They legalize the sexual repression of women who may be cruelly punished for any deviation from premarital virginity and post-marital monogamy. Women are expected to stay covered, silent, submissive, and obedient.

Restrictions on personal freedom and growth can include laws that re-quire all types of body coverings, from partial to complete. Some laws re-quire the husband's permission for doing almost anything. Others forbid driving and even going to school. American entertainment is seen as rife with immoral pornography, a license for women to do as they please. There is little room here for a diversity of beliefs. In fact, diversity is seen as a dire threat. Many Arab Americans were happy to leave this rigidity behind.

The Muslim practice of requiring women to be covered draws our attention to the object of concern, the woman and her power to harm the community's honor. This concern has become epidemic in recent years.

In non-Arab countries, such as Afghanistan, we saw the Taliban government virtually imprisoning women in a form of house arrest. Pakistan significantly constricts women's freedom, and Indonesia, Malaysia, Turkey, and Iran grant them somewhat greater freedoms. Iran is an Islamic state that under the Khomeini government severely restricted women's rights. Now, it is slowly moving toward some forms of democracy that in turn allow women more freedom. The rulers of Saudi Arabia and the United Arab Emirates place much greater restrictions on women than do the governments of Algeria, Egypt, Jordan, and Syria.

In each case, these restrictions are related to the degree of separation of church and state—more separation means more freedom.

Islam as religion or as culture.   Certainly, not all Muslims agree that the subordination of women is a necessary part of the religion. Some historians, such as Ahmed, say that early Islam actually opened up possibilities for gender egalitarianism, but the male-centered teachings won out over the ethical teachings of Islam. This led to many laws and practices that restricted women, but not men. Some historians, such as Soraya Altorki, therefore make a distinction between Islam as religion and Islam as culture. They say the religion actually places women and men as equals, in contrast to the cultural level of social relations, which does not. Neither does the Quran require veiling and seclusion. These experts are concerned that some Islamic groups are returning to these strict practices, claiming that such traditions represent a more "pure and true" Islam.

American Culture

Americans value democracy based on separation of church and state, a system that allows for a diversity of religions and belief systems.

The middle class and freedom.   Democracy has led to a socioeconomic structure that is more diamond-shaped. A tiny, wealthy elite is at the top, supported by a huge middle class that is relatively affluent, and a small lower class, 10 to 15 percent, that lives in relative poverty.

Individual freedom that does not violate others' rights is given top priority. Diversity is valued. Whether it's diverse individuals, cultures, beliefs, abilities, or lifestyles—diversity is seen as a source of creativity and power.

Women and the feminine.   Monogamy is the only legal form of marriage, so divorce and remarriage is the American way of having more than one spouse in a lifetime. Although the United States has its own history of denial of women's rights, most Americans now see the repressive treatment of women as an immoral violation of basic human rights.

A growing core of advanced thinkers, as outlined by Riane Eisler, senses the need for individuals to embrace the traditional feminine strengths—of connection with people as equals, compassion, caring, and nurturing. These are needed to balance the masculine strengths—of achievement and competition for status. They believe we desperately need this renewed balance of "the feminine" in order to avoid the violence, wars, and Earth damage that threaten our very survival. Emotional intelligence and intuitive intelligence are needed to balance our heavy rational intelligence. As individual leaders gain this balance, so will our nations and our world.

A comparison of Islamic and American cultures is shown in Snapshot 8.3.

Generation Gap

Second-generation Arab Americans may be unaware of traditional customs that are based in tribal-like identities. They were born in the United States, so their identities are not as intertwined with religious, gender, ethnic, and class origin as the identity of their immigrant parents. The parents may want to postpone identity loss and curb the children's assimilation into the larger American culture. They may pressure daughters to marry within the ethnic group. Sons may not be as pressured as daughters because they can carry forward the family name even when they do marry outside the ethnic group.

Issue #4: Discriminatory Profiling

Because of these East–West conflicts, the fair treatment of Arab Americans has emerged as a concern. Long before any U.S. terrorist attacks, the Arab as villain was a favorite scapegoat of popular American culture. This set the stage for acts of discrimination and bigotry that have affected Arab Americans at home and resulted in a range of reactions.

Political activism.   Arab Americans of the second wave came from independent nation states and arrived in America with an Arab political consciousness unknown to earlier immigrants. Because they were highly aware of a region in conflict, they sought to establish an Arab American political community.

The Israeli defeat of the Arab nations in 1967, the continuing occupation of Arab lands by Israel, the oil boycott of the 1970s, and the negative stereotyping of Arabs in the American media—all have focused attention on

SNAPSHOT 8.3   A comparison of Islamic and American cultures.

Islamic Culture	American Culture
Political System	
• Monarchy, plutocracy, theocracy with laws often based on Islamic practices	• Democracy based on separation of church and state
Socioeconomic Structure	
• Pyramidal with huge poverty class	• Diamond with huge middle class
Typical Laws That Affect Human Rights	
• Polygamy for men; monogamy for women	• Monogamy
• Sexual affairs legal for men, illegal for women	• Individual rights and freedom given top priority as long as actions don't violate rights of others
• Laws can require women to cover body, get permission from husband for many life activities, and may prohibit activities ranging from driving to working to getting an education	• Movement toward equal rights and opportunities for men and women
	• Movement toward balancing masculine strengths with feminine strengths
Typical Values	
• Women's modesty as source of family, community honor	• Women's roles changing, becoming more diverse
• Reverence for traditions of past	• Moving beyond tradition, future-focus
• Conformity and stability	• Change and innovation
• High esteem for elders	• Youth and a young orientation
Views on Diversity of Beliefs and Lifestyles	
• Diversity seen as dire threat to the culture and the world	• Diversity valued as source of creativity and power

the central role that the U.S. government and media play in the Middle East crisis. It is these second-wave immigrants whose political consciousness and public pride played a key part in mobilizing the Arab American community and refocusing its energies on political and social issues.

U.S. government policy.   Stereotypes seeped into public policy. Beginning in the 1970s, a number of government investigations, executive orders, and legislative provisions aimed at combating terrorism violated the rights of some Arab Americans. An activist response emerged as Arab American intellectuals, students, and professionals coalesced to counter the bias they saw in American policy and culture. Organizations to educate and advocate the Arab American point of view laid the groundwork for the first publicly engaged movement to represent the needs and issues of Arab Americans and create a national sense of community and common purpose.

Arab American organizations.   The second wave of immigrants inspired the establishment of the national Arab American organizations, which have served as an emerging political movement and have also created a cultural bond across the immigrant generations. Organizations founded in the 1980s to respond to these political, civic, and cultural challenges include the National Association of Arab Americans, the Association of Arab-American University Graduates, the American-Arab Anti-Discrimination Committee, and the Arab American Institute

Recent anti-terrorism policies of airline-passenger profiling and the use of secret evidence by immigration judges have disproportionately affected Arabs and Muslims and have raised concerns about selective prosecution. Arab Americans ask only for fairness and justice. As a group, they are at least as anxious as others about terrorist acts.

Issue #5: Representation in U.S. Politics

Arab Americans tend to be politically active. For decades, they have voted, run for office, and been elected. In 1998, for example, 12 Arab Americans campaigned for the U.S. Congress in 10 states. Prominent Arab American politicians have included:

George Mitchell, U.S. Senate Majority (Democratic) Leader
    Spencer Abraham, Energy Secretary
        Donna Shalala, Secretary of Health and Human
           Services

John Sununu, New Hampshire governor and White
    House Chief of Staff

Ralph Nader, presidential candidate in the 2000
    election

> *Exit polls indicate that in 1996 most Arab Americans voted Democratic (54 percent), while 38 percent voted Republican and 8 percent voted Independent, according to John Zogby, founder of the Arab American Institute.*

Fully 86 percent of Arab American adults were registered voters during the 2000 campaign, the first in which both major presidential candidates addressed Arab Americans as a group.

The Arab American Institute is one of several that lobby on behalf of issues that concern Arab Americans. It supports presidential and congressional candidates who are receptive to Arab American concerns. Another active organization is the American Arab Anti-Discrimination Committee, a civil rights group.

HOW CAN I HELP THE ORGANIZATION MEET THE NEEDS AND WANTS OF ARAB AMERICANS?

Arab Americans have great contributions to offer work teams and organizations. Helping them meet the challenges that face them and rise to emerging opportunities will have high payoffs for you as a workplace leader. Here are some major ways you can help:

- Don't assume they are Arab or Middle East experts.
- Protect them from typical stereotyping.
- Get to know them as individuals.
- Recognize their personal strengths and potential.
- Capitalize on their networking skills.

If you have asked the right questions, you are unlikely to make the mistake of thinking your Arab American colleague is an expert about a language she doesn't speak, a country he never visited, or a religion she has never studied.

Give Protection from Stereotyping

You know the current issues and the tendency of some people to stereotype and scapegoat Arab Americans. As a workplace leader, you can offer protection by being sensitive to Arab Americans' viewpoints and experiences, by speaking up during tense situations, and by serving as a role model in your respect for Arab Americans. Find a way to get information about Arab Americans to your colleagues. Even better, campaign for one or more formal diversity training sessions.

Get to Know Them as Individuals

The Arab American community is diverse itself. So always use the information in this chapter as background information that can help you to ask the right questions and never use it to make assumptions about an Arab American colleague. Ask about key variables, tactfully at the right time and place; for example:

- What is your cultural heritage?
- How long has your family lived in the United States?

- Tell me about your family.
- What is your religious affiliation?
- Do you speak more than one language?
- What are your career goals? Your goals for this job? Your aspirations with this company?

Recognize Their Personal Strengths and Potential

You've learned that Arab Americans as a group have a history of being independent, achieving, well-educated, hard working, and productive. As you get to know individual colleagues, determine if they fit this profile, other strengths they may have, and areas of potential that may be developed. Explore together the ways their strengths can be used to achieve career goals that also help your team and your organization thrive and succeed.

Capitalize on Their Networking Skills

Arab Americans are known as masters of the network approach to doing business. Get to know those who work on your team. If they have these skills, explore ways to use this ability and the contacts it generates. As part of this approach, look for opportunities to integrate the contacts this colleague may have in the Arab American community as well as opportunities for trade with Arab countries in the global marketplace.

FINAL SELF-TEST
Indicate the best answers to the following 10 multiple-choice questions.

1. The most unifying factor in Arab culture is:
    A. the Islamic religion
    B. the Arabic language
    C. manly honor
    D. family values

2. When immigrant Arab American parents raise their children, they focus on:
    A. social customs
    B. the morality of the girls
    C. the manliness of the boys
    D. religion to help them maintain social rules and expected behavior

3. Boys and girls in most Arab American Islamic families are:
    A. expected to apply the same social rules and behaviors
    B. taught that American girls are typically immoral

    C. given approximately the same amount of material objects

    D. given about the same degree of freedom

4. A major difference between Islamic and American cultures involves:

    A. how people view diversity (of beliefs and lifestyles)

    B. the desire for an affluent lifestyle

    C. the role of international institutions

    D. all of the above

5. Arab American participation in politics today tends to be:

    A. rather passive

    B. inactive as less than half register to vote

    C. quite active

    D. fragmented

6. The structure of the typical Arab family is:

    A. patriarchal and extended

    B. tribal

    C. matriarchal

    D. lateral

7. One of the most important Arab American issues is:

    A. unemployment

    B. language barrier

    C. Israel–Palestine conflict

    D. educational inequity

8. To help Arab American employees contribute to the workplace:

    A. ask them to apply their expertise about Arab issues

    B. rely on them as an in-house expert on Middle East matters

    C. don't assume they're Arab or Middle East experts

    D. ask their advice about Islamic religious practices

9. A skill that many Arab Americans are known to possess is:

    A. automotive

    B. computer

    C. clerical

    D. networking

10. Some Muslims avoid shaking hands because:

    A. this is not a customary greeting in their culture

    B. they are not allowed to touch Christians

    C. they avoid cross-gender contact other than with close relatives

    D. they are basically a non-touching society

FINAL SELF-TEST FEEDBACK

Each correct answer is worth 10 points. If you score less than 70 points, you should review the materials and re-take Final Self-Test.

1. The most unifying factor in Arab culture is:
   A. No, although the Islamic religion is important
   B. Yes, the Arabic language
   C. No, although manly honor is important
   D. No, although family values are important

2. When immigrant Arab American parents raise their children, they focus on:
   A. No, although social customs are important
   B. No, although the morality of the girls is very important
   C. No, although the manliness of the boys is important
   D. Yes, the best answer is religion to help them maintain social rules and expected behavior

3. Boys and girls in most Arab American Islamic families are:
   A. No, they actually have different social rules and behaviors
   B. Yes, the best answer is they're taught that American girls are typically immoral
   C. No, they are not given approximately the same amount of material objects
   D. No, they are not given about the same degree of freedom

4. A major difference between Islamic and American cultures involves:
   A. Yes, the best answer is how people view diversity (of beliefs and lifestyles)
   B. No, both have a desire for an affluent lifestyle
   C. No, not the role of international institutions
   D. No, not all of the above

5. Arab American participation in politics today tends to be:
   A. No, not rather passive
   B. No, not inactive as less than half register to vote
   C. Yes, quite active
   D. No, not fragmented

6. The structure of the typical Arab family is:
   A. Yes, patriarchal and extended
   B. No, although Arab cultures generally are described as tribal

C. No, not matriarchal

D. No, not lateral

7. One of the most important Arab American issues is:

A. No, unemployment is not an issue

B. No, the language barrier is not an issue

C. Yes, the Israel–Palestine conflict

D. No, educational inequity is not an issue

8. To help Arab American employees contribute to the workplace:

A. No, don't assume they have expertise about Arab issues

B. No, don't assume they are experts on Middle East matters

C. Yes, the best answer is, don't assume they're Arab or Middle East experts

D. No, don't assume they are experts on Islamic religious practices

9. A skill that many Arab Americans are known to possess is:

A. No, not automotive

B. No, not computer

C. No, not clerical

D. Yes, many are skilled at networking

10. Some Muslims avoid shaking hands because:

A. No, in fact this is a customary greeting in their culture

B. No, in fact there are no general bans about touching Christians

C. Yes, they avoid cross-gender contact other than with close relatives

D. No, in fact they are basically a high-touch society

SKILL BUILDER 8.1
The Case of Mona: Suspicions, Suspicions

Mona was raised in the Muslim faith in Lebanon and became an American citizen several years after she married **Hank, an American Catholic**. During the early years of their marriage, Hank's job with the U.S. State Department sent them to several Middle Eastern countries. Mona was proud of representing American interests in this part of the world. Hank, who spoke Arabic fluently, considered Mona a great asset in his work because of her familiarity with the cultures he worked with.

Now Mona and Hank have two school-aged children, Hank's assignment is in Washington D.C. Wanting to get out of the house, earn some money, and still be available when her children need her, Mona takes a job in the fine jewelry department of Windsor, a large upscale department store chain featuring clothing and accessories. This job fits Mona's needs. Windsor is located in the mall near her home, the job pays well, and store management has agreed to give her a 35-hour a week schedule that's compatible with her children's school schedules.

Mona has had the job about a year now. A few months ago, one of her coworkers, **Vickie**, was promoted to manager of fine jewelry. Since then, Mona has found the job environment increasingly unpleasant. This is because Vickie, a Euro-American, is continually making critical remarks about minority customers who come into the store and often seems suspicious of them. Mona notices that she treats minority customers and employees differently than Euro-Americans.

For example, when a Filipino American customer said he would pay cash for a $500 watch, Vickie pushed the security alarm, which causes a security person to telephone her. She reported the customer as suspicious because he was carrying a large amount of cash. Yet within a week, a Euro-American woman came in and paid cash for a $1,000 item and Vickie did not report her.

Another example: Vickie told Mona and **Ashton**, an African American coworker, to leave their purses in their employee lockers and carry their personal items to the worksite in clear plastic bags. This is normally required to prevent employee shoplifting. After Ashton quit, Vickie hired a Euro-American woman to replace her. Every day she carries her purse to the worksite. No plastic bags for her.

Sultan, a Pakistani coworker, quits next. Of the three minorities in the department, only Mona is left. In fact, the department now consists of only Vickie, Mona, and **Pat**, the new Euro-American employee.

Mona talks with Hank about Vickie's attitude, saying, "She says things to me that are insulting in a subtle way. She seems to think that I'm so passive that I'll never talk back. She treated Ashton the same way. Come to think of it, she tried to treat Sultan that way too, but he fought back, and she treated him better after that."

After September 11, 2001, Mona notices that Vickie's attitude toward minorities becomes even more suspicious, especially toward Arabs and Arab Americans. A day or two after the attack, Vickie actually says to Mona, "You know, it would be better to prohibit Arab persons from living here in the United States. After all, any one of them could become a terrorist-in-waiting." Mona objects, saying that many Arab Americans are children. Vickie replies, "Even the children are terrorists-in-waiting as far as I'm concerned." Mona is appalled. To make matters worse, Vickie repeats this type of comment a couple more times in front of other employees.

In early October, Windsor managers hold a Thursday meeting to discuss the drop in sales, part of the general economic slump since 9–11. They decide they must lay off some peripheral personnel, such as some cashiers, but no salespeople yet. However, at this meeting Vickie volunteers to lay off

Mona. Her **manager Jeffrey** doesn't comment. The next day, Friday, Mona feels Vickie's animosity under her sharp comments and actions. On Saturday, Vickie tells Mona she will be laid off, saying, "You're only a part-time person and sales are off." She implies that Mona's sales are dropping and that customers have complained about her. This is not Mona's experience and it's the first time Vickie has made these accusations.

Mona goes to **Jan, the Human Resources officer**, to complain about Vickie's discriminatory treatment of her and other minorities. Jan tells Mona there's nothing she can do because Vickie is the authority in this situation. On Monday, Mona receives a letter telling her she is laid off. She goes to Human Resources and asks for a copy of her file. They put her off, saying they'll send it to her later. When she receives it, there's nothing in it but her original hiring papers.

1. What should Mona do?

   A. Keep following up with Human Resources until she gets results.

   B. Go to Jeffrey, Vickie's manager, briefly outline the history of Vickie's attitudes and actions, and ask for fair treatment.

   C. Immediately go to the EEOC.

Feedback

   A. No, Human Resources is not cooperating with Mona, and it is probably true that they have no authority to take action in this situation.

   B. Yes, Mona should go to Vickie's manager, Jeffrey. He does have the authority to override Vickie's decision, demote her, promote or transfer Mona, or take other appropriate action. Mona should give Jeffrey the whole story about Vickie's suspicious attitudes and discriminatory actions. She should stick with the facts, be objective and professional, and avoid personal opinions or emotions.

   C. No, filing an EEOC complaint must be a last resort, after Mona has done all she can to resolve the problem with her employer. If the employer will not resolve the problem, then the employee has the option of filing an EEOC complaint. If their ruling is not favorable to Mona, she must decide whether to pay a lawyer to file a civil lawsuit.

2. What action should HR officer Jan take?

   A. Request a meeting with Mona, Vickie, and her manager Jeffrey to establish the facts in the case and then take the appropriate action.

   B. Back up Vickie's decisions, as she is the manager.

   C. Investigate the situation so they can prepare a good defense to the EEOC complaint.

Feedback

A. Yes, when Mona complained to Human Resources officer Jan, she should have asked for a meeting with Mona, Vickie, and Jeffrey to discuss the discriminatory and hostile treatment of Mona. They might want to contact Ashton and Sultan to determine their reasons for leaving. The likely outcome would be that Vickie would be removed as manager with the clear understanding that managing diversity is an essential managerial skill.

B. No, this action is passive and short-sighted and can cost the company in the long run if they have to prepare to defend themselves before the EEOC and perhaps later in court.

C. No, if there is a possibility that the complaining employee has a good case, then it is poor policy to prepare to defend an EEOC complaint. This establishes poor employee relations and wastes valuable time, energy, and therefore money.

What happened

In the next few weeks, Mona called Human Resources four times, trying to get her job back, but was unsuccessful.

Vickie hired two people to work in the fine jewelry department. Shortly after that, Windsor removed Vickie as manager, and she returned to being a floor salesperson.

Mona, getting no results from Windsor, contacted the Justice Department. She was advised to file a claim with the EEOC, which she did. She also hired a lawyer to help her with the case and is asking for back pay and a small amount for punitive damages. Windsor offered her a job, but after all the trauma, Mona no longer wishes to work for them.

Mona now works two jobs, one in the morning while the children are in school, and another in the evening, when her husband is home to care for them.

SKILL BUILDER 8.2   The Case of Omar: Accusations

Omar Abu Jassar was born in Amman, Jordan. His father had lived and worked in the United States, where he met Omar's mother, a Euro-American. They went to live in Jordan, so Omar is legally a citizen of both Jordan and the United States. Omar went to school and married in Jordan. Then, in 1990 when he was 23 years old, Omar and his wife came to the United States. He settled in Alameda in the Bay Area of California. Over time, he and his wife had two children and his mother came to live with them. Omar held several jobs and eventually graduated from the electronics program of a trade school.

In February 2001, Omar went to work as an engineering technician for Celerity Systems, a high-tech defense contractor, in Cupertino, California. For the first seven months, Omar's work experience was pleasant and productive. He got along well with **Jim, his manager**, and with the other 55 employees at the Celerity facility. He and Jim had weekly status meetings to update each other on projects and tasks and coordinate Omar's work. Jim never indicated that Omar had any problems. Jim has always held these meetings with each of the technicians who report to him. Omar's experience with these meetings was that they were practical ways of communicating.

In June, Omar got approval to take four days of personal leave to move his family from Alameda to Stockton, where housing was significantly cheaper and the commute to Cupertino was faster. Also, Omar could carpool with his boss Jim, who lived nearby.

Omar was happy in his job and all seemed well until the day after the September 11 attack on the World Trade Center. On that day, **Beverly, a Latino American lesbian**, started talking about the attack with four or five coworkers, including Omar. She said, "Those G _ _d_ _ _ Arabs, we ought to get rid of all of them. The d_ _ _ Muslims, get them out of here. We should go over and nuke them all." No one objected to Beverly's comments. All of a sudden, Omar sensed a wave of hostility, as if he were in danger, perhaps even physical danger. Right then, he decided to lie low, keep quiet, and try to fade into the background.

About a week after Beverly's outburst, Jim called Omar to his office and told him he would have to lay him off. He mentioned budgetary problems, as well as certain "performance and attendance problems." He said, "Omar, when we've checked your desk several times, you weren't there. Also, lately you have not always been working a full eight-hour day. Apparently my weekly coaching sessions with you have not solved your performance problems."

Omar is amazed by all this. To begin with, Jim had suddenly converted the routine weekly status meetings to coaching sessions. Omar also found it incredible that Jim would expect him to be at his desk all the time. As he said to his wife, "My job requires that I interact with people in the lab, with other team leaders, and so forth. If Jim found that I was away from my desk, why didn't he just page me? He could have found me in seconds that way." Finally, Omar couldn't believe that Jim would accuse him of not working an 8-hour day since they carpooled together. In fact, Omar had accrued 72 hours of paid time off because he had not taken all of his sick and personal leave days.

1. What should Omar do next?

A. Have a meeting with Jim, point out the inconsistencies in his performance appraisal, and ask for reconsideration.

B. Ask for a joint meeting with Jim's manager and the H.R. Department and present his side of the situation.

C. File a complaint with the EEOC.

Feedback

A. Yes, having a meeting with Jim is the best answer because it is the first step—what Omar should do next. He should present his case to Jim and point out the inconsistencies in Jim's assessment of his performance.

B. No, asking for a joint meeting is not the best next step. However, if Omar and Jim cannot resolve the problem, then Omar's next step is to appeal to Jim's manager and to the H.R. Department.

C. No, filing an EEOC complaint is not the best next step. However, if Omar takes the other two steps and still does not get fair results, he then has the option of filing a complaint with the EEOC and with the California Department of Fair Housing and Employment.

2. What should Celerity management do next?

A. Issue a tolerance, non-hate company policy and review all personnel actions involving Arab Americans.

B. Back up Jim and other managers in their personnel decisions.

C. Investigate the backgrounds of all Arab American employees.

Feedback

A. Yes, this is the best response. Celerity should issue a tolerance, non-hate policy directive immediately upon realizing that throughout the United States there was tension, backlash, and the danger of harassment or even violence in the workplace. They should send the memo to all employees and follow up with a training session on Arab Americans led by a diversity consultant.

They should review thoroughly any proposals by managers to lay off or otherwise dismiss, demote, or disadvantage Arab Americans. Now is the time for patience and fairness. It is important to remember that no Arab American has been involved in a terrorist act. The people actually involved are not American citizens. And even Arabs who are not American citizens, but who are here with valid papers to work or go to school, deserve fair treatment.

B. No, this is not a good response unless a thorough investigation reveals that accusations against Omar are true.

C. No, to single out Arab Americans for such treatment, without due cause, is illegal and unconstitutional.

The key issues in this case are stereotyping, prejudice, and discrimination. By calling the dismissal a lay-off instead of a firing, the company denies Omar the right to collect unemployment insurance between jobs, which would increase their insurance premiums.

What actually happened

Omar filed a complaint with the EEOC and state Fair Housing and Employment. But the company made a good case for themselves, and both agencies found the company "not guilty" of unfair dismissal. So far as the hostile environment issue, the company said that Beverly was not directing her harangue at Omar. They claimed that shortly after September 11, they sent out a memo, a policy directive, telling employees to stay calm and to avoid racial stereotyping. Omar never received such a memo. So far as performance issues, it was Omar's word against Jim's. Omar had been with the company less than nine months, which wasn't enough time in service to accumulate a strong documented track record of good performance. This fact probably worked against his case.

THE BOTTOM LINE

Now you have more information about the stereotypes and myths Arab Americans face. You have a basis for noticing and questioning what the media presents and what people say. You can help to clarify to others some of the facts about people from this group. Showing this kind of support can help to build powerful relationships with Arab Americans.

Chapter Review

1. Typical myths and stereotypes about Arab Americans include the nomadic desert-tribe type, the oil-rich sheik, the Arab with terrorist connections, the violent Muslim fundamentalist, the subservient Arab woman, and the dark swarthy dangerous Arab man.

2. Arab Americans immigrated to the United States in two waves. Most in the first wave (1875–1920) were Christians from Lebanon. Many in the second wave (after WWII) were better-educated Muslims, who are affected by the increasing conflicts over U.S. policy in the Middle East.

3. On average, Arab Americans are younger, better educated, and more affluent than most Americans. They are more likely to be managers, professionals, self-employed.

4. Arab American valuses and customs include:
   - the Arabic language is the predominant unifying element.
   - more than three-fourths of them declare their faith as Christianity, not Islam.
   - Arab honor of men, the family, and society relies heavily on the sexual morality of the women in the family.
   - boys and girls are raised with different standards, especially in Muslim families.

5. Issues currently important to Arab Americans are the Israeli–Palestinian conflict, U.S. Mideast oil policy, American–Arab culture clash, discriminatory profiling, and representation in U.S. politics.

6. Key leadership challenges and opportunities for working with Arab Americans are:
   - protecting them from stereotyping
   - getting to know them as individuals
   - recognizing personal strengths and potential
   - capitalizing on networking skills

Working With Latino Americans

9

CHAPTER OBJECTIVES

- Identify typical myths about Latino Americans.
- Recognize current Latino American demographic profiles.
- Understand key Latino American worldviews.
- Identify Latino American values regarding personal relationships.
- Define ways an organization can meet the needs and wants of Latino Americans.
- Know how Latino Americans contribute to an organization.

PhotoEdit

CHAPTER OVERVIEW

About 12 percent of the employees in the workplace are Latino Americans—about one in every eight people you'll meet. Latino American communities include people from many countries. Although most of their values and customs are woven from common Latino threads, each country also has its own unique design. For example, you'll find distinct cultural differences among Latino Americans from Mexico compared to those from Puerto Rico or Cuba or other origins. And of course no one person expresses all the values and customs discussed here. This information can give you a deeper, broader understanding of Latino Americans you may meet. On the other hand, remember the necessity of dealing with each person as a unique individual from a particular cultural background.

WHAT ARE SOME COMMON MYTHS ABOUT LATINO AMERICANS?

Certain myths, based on stereotypes about Latino American traits and abilities, tend to support barriers to career success. These myths are either false or consist of distortions and partial truths. You need to understand what they are and the realities that contradict them.

Myth #1: Latino American Workers Are Qualified Only for Menial Jobs

Related myths are: *They can't speak English well, they have only the most menial-level skills, they're not productive, they have a "mañana" attitude.*

Reality #1.   Latino Americans are a diverse group. Many of them have been in the United States for generations and are highly educated. Some groups, such as Cuban Americans, have business qualifications comparable to Euro-Americans. Recent immigrants frequently have language, education, and skill barriers to qualifying for better jobs. Some companies operating in urban areas with large Latino immigrant populations have found that providing remedial education and job training results in a pool of skilled, loyal workers.

Reality #2.   Studies indicate that most Latino Americans identify with the American dream of getting ahead, which means they're willing to learn the skills and approaches it takes—including how to be productive and meet time requirements. Also, when Latino Americans feel they are part of an in-group, they tend to be extremely loyal. The "mañana" ("tomorrow") stereotype is a misunderstanding of their concept of time. "Tomorrow" does not mean that they procrastinate. To the contrary, most have a strong "get it done" work ethic.

Myth #2: Latino Americans Are too Emotional and Excitable to Be Leaders

This myth is a typical example of mistaking a person's style, based on cultural customs, with that person's substance of job achievement and potential.

Reality #1.   Latino Americans generally hold views about expressing emotions that are different from Euro-Americans' views. More on this later.

Reality #2.   The resulting behavior is a difference in style, not substance. The dozens of Latino nations throughout the world function quite effectively with Latino leaders. Style need not inhibit Latino Americans' ability to lead as long as Euro-Americans learn to understand various leadership styles. Also, after Latino Americans have been in an American corporate culture for a while, they naturally tend to modify their style a little.

Myth #3: Latino Americans Are too Passive, Polite, and Lacking in Conviction to Be Good Leaders in the Workplace

Here is another example of mistaking style for substance.

Reality #1.   This myth looks only at surface behavior that reflects key cultural values and fails to take into consideration the values themselves and the contribution they can make to an effective leadership approach. Again, the myth focuses on style, not substance.

Reality #2. Euro-Americans and others can learn what these behaviors really mean and how they can enhance team relationships and other workplace situations. For example, the values of harmony and positive interpersonal relationships that are so important to Latinos have always been important in the workplace and are increasingly crucial to business success.

Reality #3. Latino Americans do learn to adapt to American corporate cultures and how to be appropriately assertive in that arena. Euro-American and other leaders can help them adapt.

Myth #4: Latino American Men Are Macho and the Women Easily Intimidated

Although Latinos generally are viewed as passive and polite, the men are often stereotyped as being macho with their women—and with each other in bars and similar settings. They're said to have a quick smile and quick knife and love to fight. The *machismo* stereotype is that the male is strong, in control, and provides for his family, while the woman is submissive and lacking in power and influence.

Reality #1. This stereotype has not been fully researched, and some studies indicate that male dominance in marital decision making is not the rule among Latino American couples. What research does indicate is that the machismo style is changing along with changing economic realities and new job opportunities for Latino American women.

Reality #2. Most modern cultures are based on some form of patriarchy. Latino cultures have their own brand. The "quick knife" stereotype is mainly a phenomenon of youth gangs, and most every U.S. cultural group has some youth gangs. In all cases, they're a small minority of the total population and have little or nothing to do with employee relationships.

Reality #3. Latino Americans, especially the largest group, Mexican Americans, tend to be one of the most cooperative, accepting groups in the United States, and getting along is one of their highest values. This is true for both the men and the women.

WHO ARE THE LATINO AMERICANS?

Some of the most interesting aspects of the Latino American population are:

- It is diverse, with people from many parts of the world.

- It is young and fast-growing, with many recent immigrants and some citizens who resided in the American West before Euro-American settlers came.
- It is concentrated in a few states, and mostly in cities.
- Educational levels and language barriers vary by subgroup.
- Job discrimination, lower income, and relative poverty are issues.

A Diverse Population of Many Subgroups

You already know that about 12 percent of all Americans are Latino Americans. However, they are most likely to think of themselves as Mexican American or Cuban American or some other name that indicates their country of origin. Latino American groups in 2000 included:

Mexican American	58%
Puerto Rican American	10%
Cuban American	4%
Central American	5%
South American	4%
Other Latino American	19%

Latino Americans include about a million descendants of Spanish and Spanish American settlers. Many of them have ancestors who lived in the West before it became part of the United States. As a group, they don't have the same profile or issues as the other subgroups because they were never immigrants to the United States.

Fast-Growing and Young: Babies and Immigration

The Latino American population grew by 57 percent between 1970 and 1990, over seven times as fast as the rest of the nation, according to the U.S. Census Bureau. It grew again by 58 percent from 1990 to 2000—four times greater than the growth of the U.S. population, which increased by only 13 percent. This rapid growth is expected to continue because of immigration and the Latino American group's relative youth and higher birth rate:

- About 35 percent are under age 18, compared to 26 percent of the U.S. population.
- Their median age is 26, compared to 35 for the entire U.S. population.
- They produce nearly twice as many children as Euro-Americans, 3.3 compared to 1.8.

SNAPSHOT 9.1   Where Latino Americans live.

Region	Proportion of Latino Americans Who Live Here	Proportion of Population Who Are Latino Americans
West	43%	25%
South	33%	12%
Midwest	9%	11%
Northeast	15%	2%

Concentrated in a Few States, and in Cities

How likely you are to work with a Latino American depends on where you live. Latino Americans are most likely to live in the West, followed by the South, as shown in Snapshot 9.1.

Latino immigrants tend to settle in the state where they first enter. Therefore, most Mexican Americans (55 percent) live in the West, especially in California and Texas, but nearly a third (32 percent) live in the South. Most Puerto Rican Americans (61 percent) live in New York, and most Cuban Americans (74 percent) live in the South, especially in Florida.

The tradition of most Latino immigrants has been that of rural peasant, mostly from Mexico. But by 1980, because of their migration to work in U.S. cities, most became urban dwellers. In America's 10 largest cities, an average of one in every four people is of Latino origin: about 60 percent in Miami and San Antonio, 46 percent in Los Angeles, and 27 percent in New York.

Wide-Ranging Educational Levels and Language Barriers

Language ability is related to educational level, which varies by subgroup. English language skills vary. Latino Americans are evenly divided between those who are fluent in English and those who aren't. All speak Spanish. About half still speak Spanish at home, although 75 percent also use English. Educational levels are relatively low for the Latino American population as a whole, as follows:

- 57 percent hold high school diplomas, compared to 88 percent of Euro-Americans
- 27 percent have less than a ninth-grade education, compared to 4 percent of Euro-Americans

- 11 percent hold university degrees, compared to 28 percent of Euro-Americans

The least educated are those from Mexico, Central America, Dominica, and Puerto Rico. The best educated are Spanish Americans and South Americans, whose levels are almost as high as the national average, closely followed by Cuban Americans.

Education is highly valued by all Latino American groups, even though they have the lowest educational level of any U.S. group. Studies indicate that more Latino American high school students want a college degree than do Euro-American students at the same socioeconomic level. And Latino American parents' aspirations for their children's education is just as high as Euro-American parents'.

Job Discrimination, Lower Income, and Relative Poverty

Latino Americans are twice as likely as Euro-Americans to work as minimally skilled or skilled laborers. Conversely, Euro-Americans are twice as likely to hold managerial or professional positions. Here are some facts from the Census Bureau about Latino American workers:

- 20 percent work in service occupations, compared to 12 percent of Euro-Americans
- 22 percent work as laborers and operators, compared to 12 percent of Euro-Americans
- 14 percent work in managerial or professional occupations, compared to 33 percent of Euro-Americans
- management jobs in U.S. companies of more than 100 employees: Latino Americans hold less than 1 percent, though they are 12 percent of the U.S. workforce
- Average household income in 2000 was $33,000, compared to $46,300 for Euro-Americans—a pay gap of $13,300 or 28 percent.
- 23 percent live in poverty, compared with 8 percent of Euro-Americans
- 75 percent of Latino American families fall in the middle- to upper-income category

Causes of poverty include fewer job opportunities for the less skilled and educated—and lower wages for those who do have jobs. Single mothers have high poverty rates, and 30 percent of Latino American families are headed by single mothers, compared to 20 percent of Euro-American families. The earnings ratio of Latino Americans to Euro-Americans has been in a decline for several years, with the pay gap increasing by one-half percent per year.

SELF-TEST #1

Indicate the best answers to the following 10 multiple-choice questions.

1. Latino Americans in the workplace tend to be:
   A. qualified for laborer jobs
   B. willing to learn the skills and approaches needed for success
   C. focused on mañana
   D. unable to achieve high levels of productivity

2. Latino Americans tend to view emotions:
   A. as feelings to be acted out, no matter where or when
   B. differently than Euro-Americans
   C. as dangerous, to be repressed
   D. with great humor

3. The Euro-American attitude that Latino Americans are too polite and passive to be good leaders:
   A. overlooks the group orientation such behaviors reflect, and its advantages
   B. is a myth that looks only at style, not substance
   C. omits the willingness to learn and adapt
   D. all of the above

4. The machismo image mainly refers to Latino American men who:
   A. look down on women in the workplace
   B. must be boss in the workplace
   C. within their families are strong and in control
   D. all of the above

5. Most Latino Americans, or their ancestors, came from:
   A. South America
   B. Mexico
   C. Puerto Rico
   D. Cuba

6. The largest Latino American population resides in the:
   A. West
   B. South
   C. Midwest
   D. Northeast

7. Growth rate of the Latino American population in the past 20 years has been:
   A. Less than that of the U.S. population in general
   B. About half that of the U.S. population

C. Nearly 20 times that of the U.S. population

D. From 4 to 7 times greater than that of the U.S. population

8. The Latino American growth rate is expected to continue because of:

A. the group's relative youth

B. higher birth rate

C. illegal immigration

D. both A and B

9. Latino Americans live primarily in:

A. the West and Midwest

B. the West and South

C. the West and Northeast

D. the South and Midwest

10. The overall education level of Latino Americans is relatively:

A. high, with 88 percent holding high school diplomas

B. low, with 57 percent holding high school diplomas

C. average, with 75 percent holding high school diplomas

D. average, with only 4 percent having less than a ninth-grade education

SELF-TEST #1 FEEDBACK

Each correct answer is worth 10 points. If you score less than 70 points, you should review the materials and re-take the Self-Test.

1. Latino Americans in the workplace tend to be:

A. No, although they may be qualified for laborer jobs

B. Yes, willing to learn the skills and approaches needed for success

C. No, they are not focused on mañana

D. No, in fact they are able to achieve high levels of productivity

2. Latino Americans tend to view emotions:

A. No, although feelings are to be expressed, they are not to be acted out, no matter where or when

B. Yes, differently than Euro-Americans

C. No, not as dangerous, to be repressed

D. No, not with great humor

3. The Euro-American attitude that Latino Americans are too polite and passive to be good leaders:

A. No, although it does overlook the group orientation such behaviors reflect, and its advantages

B. No, although it is a myth that looks only at style, not substance

C. No, although it does omit the willingness to learn and adapt

D. Yes, all of the above

4. The machismo image mainly refers to Latino American men who:

A. No, it's not about looking down on women in the workplace

B. No, it's not about being boss in the workplace

C. Yes, it's primarily about being strong and in control within their families

D. No, not all of the above

5. Most Latino Americans, or their ancestors, came from:

A. No, although many come from the various countries of South America

B. Yes, Mexico

C. No, although a large group is from Puerto Rico

D. No, although a large group is from Cuba

6. The largest Latino American population resides in the:

A. Yes, the West

B. No, although many do reside in the South

C. No, not the Midwest

D. No, not the Northeast

7. Growth rate of the Latino American population in the past 20 years has been:

A. No, not less than that of the U.S. population in general

B. No, not about half that of the U.S. population

C. No, not nearly 20 times that of the U.S. population

D. Yes, from 4 to 7 times greater than that of the U.S. population

8. The Latino American growth rate is expected to continue because of:

A. No, not only because of the group's relative youth

B. No, not only because of higher birth rate

C. No, not because of illegal immigration

D. Yes, both a and b, because of the group's relative youth and higher birth rate

9. Latino Americans live primarily in:

A. Not, not the west and midwest

B. Yes, the west and south—where there are common borders with Mexico

C. No, not the west and northeast

D. No, not the south and Midwest

10. The overall education level of Latino Americans is relatively:
    A. No, not high, with 88 percent holding high school diplomas
    B. Yes, low, with 57 percent holding high school diplomas
    C. No, not average, with 75 percent holding high school diplomas
    D. No, not average, with only 4 percent having less than a ninth-grade education—actually, 28 percent are in this category

WHAT ARE THE KEY LATINO AMERICAN WORLDVIEWS?

You'll better understand Latino personal values if you first understand their basic worldview—how they see reality. Basic to what Latino countries have in common is the influence of Spanish culture, which includes an aristocratic hierarchy based on a powerful patron who protects his subjects. They in turn serve him and owe him their loyalty. Therefore, the societies that developed in the Latino countries normally consisted of a small, privileged group of the served and a mass of underprivileged servers. Researchers such as Geert Hofstede, Peter J. Duignan, Lewis H. Gann, Philip R. Harris, and Robert T. Moran have identified some typical Latino American worldviews:

1. Closeness to the spirit world
2. A sense of destiny or fatalism
3. Acceptance of hierarchy and status
4. Emotional expression and the passion factor
5. Use of space as up-close and personal
6. Future time as unknowable
7. The American dream

Worldview Value #1: Closeness to the Spirit World

Latino spiritual beliefs are closely tied to the Catholic Church, a belief in fate, and a unique attitude toward the relationship between life and death. The spirit world lives alongside Latino Americans, particularly Mexican Americans, in their everyday lives. They perceive less distinction between the living and the dead than do most Euro-Americans. They believe the dead are just beyond the veil of physical reality and there's nothing to fear from these spirits of relatives and friends.

They incorporate symbols of the afterlife and death—such as ghosts, skeletons, and skulls—into their holidays. They wear the symbols as costumes, similar to some of our Halloween costumes, and use them as themes in toys, confections, songs, and dances. Latino Americans tend to think of death as "passing on" and treat it as an old friend or special person. They frequently joke about death and include the theme in their play. This theme is related to their fatalistic sense of life and death and draws on some aspects of a worldview that originated in their ancient Indian past.

The Mexican American relationship with death and the dead may be better understood by studying how they observe the Day of the Dead, part of a three-day celebration in early November. First, along with other Americans, they observe Halloween. The next day is known as All Saints Day, and they observe religious rites. The third day is the Day of the Dead, the most important of the three days. Rituals may include altars set up in churches, homes, and shop windows; an all-day picnic in the cemetery; a candlelit procession in costume; and an all-night vigil in the cemetery. Many Latino Americans believe that the spirits of family and friends who have passed on are present at these events and that their spirits in fact move in and out of the physical world all the time.

The Roman Catholic Church remains one of Latin America's major cultural institutions and has played a large role in shaping the various cultures of all Latin nations. Priests tend to be more involved in the family lives of Catholic churchgoers than are church leaders in other denominations. Most professing Christians in Latin America are Catholics, as are about 80 percent of Latino Americans. Their religious commitment varies widely, from indifferent to highly committed. Most are nonpracticing.

Erosion of beliefs and practices increases with second-generation Latino Americans. In recent years an increasing number are joining Protestant churches, primarily those of an evangelical, fundamentalist nature.

Worldview Value #2: A Sense of Destiny or Fatalism

Latinos are less likely than Euro-Americans to believe they're in control of their own destiny. This dependence on fate or destiny stems from ancient American Indian mysticism combined with a Latino interpretation of Roman Catholic Church teachings.

Many believe that outside forces govern their lives, for life follows a preordained course and human action is determined by the will of God. Those who hold this belief are therefore willing to resign themselves to the "inevitable," bow to fate, and take what comes. This is in direct contrast to the typically Euro-American belief that "God helps those who help themselves," or that people create their own reality. Fatalism can result in an attitude that Americans often interpret as passivity, procrastination, or laziness and that they attribute to a *mañana* tendency (tomorrow's good enough for me). After all, if it's God's will, if it's written in the stars, why fight it? This belief is tied to the acceptance of unequal status discussed next.

Worldview Value #3: Acceptance of Hierarchy and Status

Hierarchy and status is a strong element in virtually all Latino countries. People are born into a tiny upper class or a huge lower class. The middle class in most Latin countries is small but growing. Traditionally, the masses live in destitute poverty and the elite live with great wealth. The upper classes are more formal and elaborate than in the United States. The work you do is directly related to your social class; therefore, to do any manual labor, even helping out as a house guest or pitching in to help an office worker, would be undignified and inappropriate.

In recent years, nearly all of the political unrest, upheaval, and terrorism in Latino countries has centered on attempts to break down the hierarchy. Opposing groups try to break the hold of the rich aristocracy and multinational corporations on the wealth of the land.

The hierarchy–status worldview includes accepting one's place, showing respect for social status, accepting the powerful superior and power distance, and trusting the government.

Accepting One's Place

Latino Americans tend to accept their social status, even when it's extremely inferior to that of the ruling class. They tend to value the stability that comes with everyone knowing their place and staying in it, living up to societal expectations. Social climbing is frowned upon, and people who are seen as "trying to get ahead" are not admired. Such attempts, if successful, are seen as disturbing and disruptive, threatening the relative social position of many people. Climbing also appears as crass materialism and greed to many, and it shows disdain for sensitive human relationships.

Showing Respect, or Respeto

People show respect for someone of superior status by their tone of voice and manner. The traditional belief is that the reason people are poor or rich, have power or don't, is because of God's will. A patron is a man of power or wealth who receives loyalty from people of lesser status. He may be the boss, a politician, a landowner, or a businessman. The patron makes the decisions, and others don't question him. Whereas Americans attempt to minimize differences between persons due to status, age, sex, and so on, Latinos tend to stress them.

Accepting the Powerful Superior

Those in positions of authority maintain their leadership by their ability to dole out resources to their followers and to help and protect them when they need it. The relationship is reminiscent of a parent–child relationship.

Authority figures tend to set clear standards and boundaries for compliance with their policies and rules.

Patriarchal values may explain why in recent surveys Latino Americans tended to express less tolerance for gays and lesbians than do Euro-Americans.[1] On the other hand, Latinos tend to be more tolerant regarding skin color. Social class is not tied to skin color in Latin American countries as it has been historically in the United States.

Accepting Power Distance

Where Euro-Americans attempt to minimize differences between persons due to status, age, or gender (sometimes called "power distance"), Latino Americans tend to stress these differences. Latinos tend to show greater deference and respect toward certain respected or powerful groups of people, such as the rich, the educated, and older people, and toward certain professions, such as doctors, priests, and teachers. They place a higher value on conformity and obedience, and they support autocratic and authoritarian attitudes from those in charge of organizations or institutions. People generally fear disagreeing with those in power. The less powerful try to meet all the expectations of the powerful.

Trusting the Government

The acceptance of social status, so traditional in Mexico and most other Latino cultures, is reflected in most Latino Americans' view of government's role. In a recent survey, most Latino Americans agreed with most Euro-Americans that individuals are responsible for providing for their own needs.[2] However, nearly twice as many Latino Americans as Euro-Americans felt the government should provide jobs, and significantly fewer Latino Americans expressed distrust of government.

Worldview Value #4: Emotional Expression—the Passion Factor

Latino Americans highly value their emotions. Their culture encourages them to fully experience their feelings and places fewer restrictions than does Euro-American culture on expressing feelings—especially the ones that reflect caring and passion for life.

Several studies seem to confirm that this passionate tendency still exists in Latino Americans.[3] For example, studies indicate that Latino Ameri-

---

[1] Reported by Sylvana Paternostro in her book *In the Land of God and Man* (New York: Dutton, 1999).
[2] 2000 *National Hispanic Survey*, The Latino Coalition, www.TheLatinoCoalition.com.
[3] Studies reported by Gregory Rodriguez in his book *From Newcomers to New Americans* (Washington, D.C.: National Immigration Forum, 1999), www.immigrationforum.org.

cans who respond to surveys are more likely to choose the extreme response categories (strongly agree, strongly disagree) than the middle categories, more so than Euro-Americans. Overall, the less time Latino Americans have spent in the United States, the more they prefer to make extreme choices. They see the middle categories (somewhat agree) as a way of hiding a person's real feelings. The research results also imply that that the longer Latino Americans live in the United States, the more they tend to modify the way they express emotion.

Worldview Value #5: Space—Up Close and Personal

In general Latino Americans like to be physically closer to others than do Euro-Americans, and so they stand closer together when they converse. This preference is related to their close, mutually dependent relationships and their frequent expression of warm feelings. They are a contact culture that feels comfortable when physically close to others. Therefore, when they brush close to another, moving into what Americans would consider personal body space, they find no reason to say, "excuse me," as most Americans would. Latino Americans are also more likely to touch each other during a conversation.

Differences in personal space affect the emotional reactions of people in interactions. Latino Americans may seem too pushy as they close in on Euro-Americans, who in turn may seem cold and distant as they back away.

Worldview Value #6: Time—Who Knows What the Future Holds?

In Latin countries it's not unusual for a business person to promise to give you a product or service by the deadline date you want even though they're unlikely to be able to meet the deadline. The main reason for agreeing is to make you happy in the moment. The backup reasoning is that the future is very uncertain, and some miracle may occur that will enable them to meet the deadline.

> Mañana (literally, "tomorrow") doesn't refer to procrastination or laziness, but to the concept that the future is indefinite.

Therefore, they know they can make you happy now, and they might be able to make you happy then. Latino Americans typically focus more on the present moment than do Euro-Americans. Latino Americans spend less time thinking about the future and planning for it, partly because they see the future as too uncertain to do much planning. This view is related to their sense of fate. The typical Euro-American approach is to start with now and project thoughts into the future. The past is past; it doesn't need to get in the way. Latino-Americans are more concerned with tradition and more willing to continue with things as they have traditionally been. An example is the willingness of the poor masses in Latin American countries to accept their lot in life, although this view has been changing somewhat in recent years.

Meeting deadlines and being on time for work and business appointments is generally the same for Latino Americans as for Euro-Americans. The main difference in attitudes toward promptness is in social situations, where it is typically less important for Latino Americans. The focus there is on relating to people in the moment, so the passage of time is not in immediate awareness.

The bottom line: Euro-Americans are considered to be generally future oriented because they stress planning for the future, being able to delay gratification, being on time, and making efficient use of time. Present-oriented Latino Americans put less emphasis on these traits and tend to have a more flexible attitude toward time. They feel they are on time even if they arrive 15 or 20 minutes after the appointed time. They place greater value on the quality of interpersonal relationships than on the length of time in which they take place. They may consider highly efficient or time conscious people as impolite or insulting.

Worldview Value #7: The American Dream

Most Latino Americans buy into many aspects of the American Dream. They also express a deep desire to pass on to their children their cultural and religious traditions, especially the Spanish language and commitment to the family. First-generation Latino Americans are naturally less Americanized or acculturated than those of the second- and third-generation, for obvious reasons, but certain aspects of the Latino culture tend to be important across generations. This leads to a merging of the Latino and American cultures.

The Acculturation Process

Immigrants go through a stage of crisis or conflict due to culture shock, followed by finding a way to adapt to American culture, such as

1. *assimilating* completely the American culture
2. *integrating* the American and Latino cultures
3. *rejecting* American cultural patterns

The ability to speak English has become a reliable measure for evaluating how successfully a Latino American has acculturated. Strategies include:

- *assimilating* English, speaking it almost exclusively
- *integrating* the old and the new by becoming bilingual
- *rejecting* the new and continuing to speak Spanish almost exclusively

The higher the education level, the more successful the acculturation tends to be. Acculturation is important because it affects Latino Americans' mental health status, levels of social support, political and social attitudes, crime rate, and workplace skills. Integration generally works better than assimilation or rejection.

Integration: A Blend of Values

Although Latino alienation, anger, and rage exist, most Latino Americans identify themselves with the United States. Only about a third of them identify themselves as Mexicans, Cubans, or Latinos first and Americans second. Most see their heritage as more European than Indian, just as Euro-Americans do. This raises the question: Are most Latinos predominantly Spanish, Indian, or a unique blend? Anthropologists seem to agree that approximately 95 percent are at least part Indian, but the Spanish cultural influence is strong. The cultural mixture of Indian and European elements that occurred in Latin American countries has further blended with Euro-American influences in the United States to produce a value system within Latino American communities that is itself a blend.

The American Dream

Despite the prejudice and discrimination that have resulted in segregation and lower socioeconomic status than the mainstream, most Latino Americans believe they're better off in the United States than they would be in their country of origin. On the whole they tend to be law-abiding citizens. They love their Latino heritage but identify primarily with Euro-Americans and value the American Dream. Most parents work hard to send their children to school. They want them to learn a profession and become solid citizens.

WHAT ARE LATINO AMERICAN VALUES REGARDING PERSONAL RELATIONSHIPS?

Latino Americans place the highest priority on relationships, especially these six types of relationship values:

1. *Familismo*: family relationships come first
2. *Simpatico*: getting along is crucial
3. *Personalismo*: relating in a personal way
4. *Amor Propio*: Reluctance to self-disclose, protecting honor
5. *Machismo* and gender roles
6. *Communication patterns*: often indirect, always sensitive

Relationship Value #1: *Familismo*

The Latino culture is collective, so family obligations rate higher than individual aspirations. Family and group closeness is their most important priority. Family comes first, and extended family next. There's a much stronger sense of mutual dependence and undying loyalty than among most Euro-Americans, including greater respect for older members. And extended families are more common.

Family First

The family is the center of personal existence, more so than for most U.S. families. Latino Americans' identities are closely tied to that of their family and its members. The tight bonds of love and loyalty may exclude outsiders to a greater degree. Families are inward-focused and members rely on these relationships for their emotional security. Parents exercise strong authority throughout their lives. Within the family, members tend to be quite open, honest, and communicative. But family business is considered private and to discuss it with outsiders would be a betrayal.

Extended Family

The family may include many more members than most Euro-American families: grandparents and great-grandparents stay close and aunts, uncles, and cousins may be almost as close; even some close friends may be included.

Mutual Dependence

Latino Americans typically have high levels of mutual personal dependence that includes these factors:

- relying on relatives for help and support
- feeling obligated to provide material and emotional support to relatives
- being highly sensitive to family relationships
- constantly checking with relatives about the way they see various behaviors and attitudes
- being influenced by relatives' perceptions and feelings
- feeling what family members feel—mutual empathy
- conforming to relatives' beliefs and wishes
- sacrificing for the welfare of the family or in-group members
- trusting the members of the in-group

It's expected that members will ask others for any assistance they need and that they'll give it when asked. While Euro-Americans expect to repay favors quickly, Latino Americans are comfortable with being indebted to those in their in-group. For them, if you were to repay a friend's favor too quickly, they might see it as almost an insult, as though you think your friend's help was grudging or done out of an expectation of gain.

This value helps to protect each person against physical and emotional stress by providing natural support systems. As a result, Latino Americans place the highest value on building interpersonal relationships in in-groups that are nurturing, loving, intimate, and respectful. While Euro-Americans value such relationships, they also value more confrontational and segmented relationships as an aid to independent growth.

Undying Loyalty

Latino Americans have incredibly strong ties and loyalties to family and friends. If an employee is asked to transfer to another location, many people in an extended family may be involved in the decision. If an employee loses his job or is transferred, the whole family may quit. If one is mistreated on the job, fellow employees who are also relatives will react as if they were personally being mistreated. As a result, disputes can have a more complex quality than Euro-Americans are accustomed to. The net effect may be for Latino Americans to hold back their true thoughts and feelings until they can stand it no longer. Then, they may strike out in ways they later regret. Therefore, they may go to great lengths to avoid disputes or use a third party to intercede or to mediate a dispute.

Relationship Value #2: *Simpatico*—Getting Along

Getting along with others is extremely important to Latino Americans. They tend to acquiesce to the wishes of others and to agree with them in order to maintain *simpatico*, a Latin form of harmonious relationship. Most try to do what's expected by family and society and to be courteous.

Agreeing and Acquiescing

Latino American acquiescence refers to agreeing with others regardless of personal opinions and feelings. It may include providing the "correct" answer as they perceive it, independent of their actual experiences. This is a rather extreme type of response frequently used by Latino Americans, especially by the less educated immigrants, men and women alike.

Getting Along

Closely related to acquiescence is the tendency to respond in socially desirable ways in order to be simpatico. The Latino cultural value of *simpatico* encourages these responses in order to promote smooth, pleasant social relations. *Simpatico* persons are:

- polite and respectful
- don't express criticism, confrontation, or assertiveness

- show a certain level of conformity and empathy for the feelings of other people
- try to behave with dignity and respect toward others
- value working toward harmony in interpersonal relations

Latino Americans therefore are more likely to give socially desirable responses and to perceive assertive or aggressive behaviors differently than Euro-Americans do. They tend to avoid at all costs having face-to-face confrontations or unpleasantness with business associates, coworkers, or friends.

Doing What's Expected

The willingness to conform to others' expectations is highly valued in Latino cultures, but so is the willingness to rebel at those rare times when too much has been too much for too long. Latino Americans conform because they want to please and support important others and because they want others to think well of them and accept them. In this close-knit culture, a frequent concern is "What will they say?" A potential problem for people from other cultures is figuring out what Latino Americans are really thinking and feeling before resentment builds to the breaking point and the relationship is severed.

Being Polite

Latino Americans place greater importance upon courtesy than do Euro-Americans and tend to offer profuse thanks, praise, and apologies. Elaborate courtesies are common and constant among the upper and middle classes. Lower-class people may reserve such treatment for special occasions and for "superiors" and strangers.

Relationship Value #3: *Personalismo*—Relating in a Personal Way

To relate well to people from a Latino culture usually means relating everything to them on a personal level. Instead of talking in generalities, you would talk in terms of:

- how situations relate to them personally
- their families
- their town
- most of all, their personal pride

Especially for the male, the more the communication is personalized, the more successful it tends to be. In fact, Latino Americans tend to trust only those with whom they have a personal relationship, for only those persons can appreciate their soul, or inner self, and therefore only those persons can be trusted. It's difficult or impossible, therefore, to do business with a Latino without establishing a personal relationship.

When doing business in Latino countries, Euro-Americans find they must spend more time building rapport than usual before they can move to discussing the business at hand. Small talk before and after discussing business is extremely important for building empathetic relationships. This tendency has some carryover, of course, to Latino Americans who immigrate to the United States.

Relationship Value #4: Reluctance to Self-Disclose

The value of *personalismo* does not mean that Latino Americans will say what they're really thinking and feeling to people outside their ingroup. The values of *simpatico* and power distance often mean they are less likely than Euro-Americans to self-disclose. When people reveal personal information, they become vulnerable to how the listener will use that information, and their *amor proprio*, or personal honor, could be damaged. Males are even less likely to self-disclose than females, especially with someone they are likely to interact with in the future or in culturally unfamiliar situations. When Latino American males do self-disclose, it's usually with Latino American females, who pose the least threat of responding with scorn, rejection, or other blows to self-respect.

Relationship Value #5: *Machismo* and Gender Roles

Most agree that sex roles are more strictly defined in Latin cultures than in the United States. Men's higher status is more noticeable, they're allowed more sexual freedom, and there are greater differences in men's work and women's work. Men are more dominant, and there are greater differences in men's and women's socially acceptable activities, attributes, and roles. The degree and importance of these values vary from one Latin culture to another.

Machismo

The machismo pattern of behavior represents male power and an attitude toward the world, especially toward women. While Latino men have a poetic, romantic side, the machismo aspect is aggressive and sometimes insensitive. This image consists of virility, courage, competitiveness, a readiness to fight, and a determination to conquer. Men are expected to be assertive, to be leaders, to be in control, and to earn the respect of other men by their masculinity. Machismo is basically about men impressing each other. In business, this means that a man should be forceful, confident, unafraid, and take the lead.

At home, it means men are less likely to participate in household and child care responsibilities. Insofar as their social standing will allow, they avoid any manual or menial work, which is considered degrading for men of the middle or upper classes.

A man is supposed to protect and defend the honor of the women in his family, but women in other families are fair game for sexual advances. This obviously leads to a conflict of values and some tense situations. The dark, extreme side of machismo involves wife-beating, excessive gambling, fighting, heavy drinking, and a tendency to have children with other women.

Both boys and girls are socialized to admire a less-dark machismo image, and Latino husbands virtually always "wear the pants" in interactions with the outside world. However, if the wife is a strong Latino woman, she may actually control the home, children, and husband.

Women's Lot

Women are restricted by traditional views about their sexuality, assertiveness, and work roles. "Madonna or whore, no in-between, that's how we're seen," say liberated Latino women. The Madonna, or good woman, marries as a virgin and martyrs herself to her family. She accepts men as the dominant ones and experiences her lot as saintly suffering. Most mothers hold great power with their children, and even adult sons hold them in great esteem.

The bad woman is an essential figure if men are to make their sexual conquests outside marriage, but afterward she may be seen as little more than an unpaid prostitute. This viewpoint is held to some extent in most cultures and tends to be especially strong and have a special religious flavor in the Latin cultures.

Women are expected to be reserved and modest with men outside the family. Assertive women are generally disliked, often more by other traditional women than by men.

More Latino Americans than Euro-Americans believe that mothers should not have outside jobs. A little more than half say they don't think married women with children should have the opportunity to pursue their own careers, even if they're able to look after their home and family while doing so. On the other hand, women who work nearly always have a greater say in family decisions than those who don't. Women in Latino countries are blossoming into careers today, similar to the way U.S. women did in the 1970s and 1980s.

Relationship Value #6: Communication Patterns

Latino Americans often speak indirectly out of concern for others' feelings and consideration for others' sensitivity to criticism. They may use speech to impress, follow some unique nonverbal patterns, and have clear expectations about how to say hello and good-bye.

Speaking indirectly. Latino Americans are frequently indirect in their communication with strangers and outsiders. It may appear evasive, but it's intended to be courteous. It may be difficult to determine exactly what they are thinking and feeling. They may use a go-between in order to communicate unpleasant messages or make requests.

High concern for feelings. Latino Americans may tell you what you want to hear, regardless of the "truth," out of great concern for your feelings. This reflects their belief that their own opinion doesn't matter as much as respecting your feelings and giving you the response you'd like to have. This conflicts with the American value of "telling it like it is."

High sensitivity to criticism. How Latino Americans take criticism is closely tied to the relative status of the people involved. Usually, if criticism comes from a higher-status person, it's accepted sheepishly; if it comes from an equal, it may be treated with humor; and if it comes from a lower-status person, it may not be tolerated since this would signal weakness and invite more criticism and even derision.

Using speech to impress. The better educated tend to display their vocabulary and style in order to impress, and any Latino American may use it to tease equals and intimates. Men may use this type of speech to size up each other and to establish dominance or leadership in relationships.

Nonverbal signals. As in all cultures, most nonverbal messages are not sent consciously. Here are some typical messages:

- Around higher-status persons, the posture shows deference: head and shoulders slightly lowered, hands behind the back or out of sight.
- Using your forefinger to call someone is very rude and may be an obscene gesture.
- Pointing at people is rude and may be associated with the evil eye.
- Gesturing with your hand, palm upturned toward a person, is okay.
- Touching your elbow with your palm means you think someone is a tightwad, so you'll probably want to avoid this.

Saying hello and good-bye. If several people are in a group when you arrive, you're expected to go around and greet everyone, shaking hands, or if you know them well enough, embracing them. The "Hi, everyone" greeting would be considered rude. Likewise, upon leaving, you're expected to say good-bye to each person individually. A general "See you later" or equivalent is also considered too breezy or abrupt.

SELF-TEST

Indicate the best answers to the following 10 multiple-choice questions.

1. The Latino American sense of status and hierarchy is:
   A. found in few countries of the world
   B. the way the average Latino American retains self-empowerment
   C. of Spanish origin—a powerful patron who rules over and protects his subjects
   D. mostly confined to Latino American religious communities

2. Latino employees are more likely than Euro-Americans to:
   A. feel close to their manager
   B. feel alienated from their manager
   C. show greater deference and respect to their manager
   D. report work problems to their manager

3. Latino Americans are more likely than Euro-Americans to:
   A. hide their feelings
   B. act out angry feelings
   C. share feelings only with close family members
   D. value, experience, and express their feelings

4. In general, Latino Americans tend to:
   A. be physically more distant than Euro-Americans
   B. be physically closer to others than Euro-Americans
   C. set personal boundaries at arm's length
   D. set physical boundaries similar to those of Euro-Americans

5. "Mañana" refers to the concept:
   A. that the future is indefinite
   B. of laziness
   C. of procrastination
   D. that tradition (yesterday) is most important

6. The Latino American concept of time focuses mainly on the:
   A. past
   B. present
   C. future
   D. unknown aspects of past, present, and future

7. In Latino cultures, family is:
   A. the center of personal existence
   B. the source of personal individualism

C. almost as important as amor proprio

D. open to outsiders as well as insiders

8. "Simpatico" refers to:

A. undying loyalty

B. protecting one's honor

C. maintaining harmonious relationships by acquiescing and agreeing

D. not revealing personal information

9. "Personalismo" refers to:

A. getting along

B. being polite

C. agreeing and acquiescing

D. talking in terms of the other person's situation, personal pride, family, town.

10. The typical Latino American communication pattern is to:

A. speak directly of concerns

B. go directly to the person you have a problem with

C. make requests directly

D. speak indirectly out of concern for others' feelings

SELF-TEST FEEDBACK

Each correct answer is worth 10 points. If you score less than 70 points, you should review the materials and re-take the Self-Test.

1. The Latino American sense of status and hierarchy is:

A. No, in fact it's found in many countries of the world

B. No, it's not related to self-empowerment of the mass of people

C. Yes, it's of Spanish origin—a powerful patron who rules over and protects his subjects

D. No, in fact it's found in many of the world's communities

2. Latino employees are more likely than Euro-Americans to:

A. No, they're not more likely to feel close to their manager

B. No, they're not more likely to feel alienated from their manager

C. Yes, they're more likely to show greater deference and respect to their manager

D. No, they're not more likely to report work problems to their manager

3. Latino Americans are more likely than Euro-Americans to:
   A. No, they're not more likely to hide their feelings
   B. No, they're not more likely to act out angry feelings
   C. No, they're not more likely to share feelings only with close family members
   D. Yes, they are more likely to value, experience, and express their feelings

4. In general, Latino Americans tend to:
   A. No, not more distant physically than Euro-Americans
   B. Yes, physically closer to others than Euro-Americans
   C. No, they don't set personal boundaries at arm's length
   D. No, they don't set physical boundaries similar to those of Euro-Americans

5. "Mañana" refers to the concept:
   A. Yes, that the future is indefinite
   B. No, it's not about laziness
   C. No, it's not about procrastination
   D. No, it's not about tradition (yesterday) is most important

6. The Latino American concept of time focuses mainly on the:
   A. No, not the past
   B. Yes, the present
   C. No, not the future
   D. No, not the unknown aspects of past, present, and future

7. In Latino cultures, family is:
   A. Yes, the center of personal existence
   B. No, it's not related to personal individualism
   C. No, it's not almost as important as amor proprio
   D. No, it's not open to outsiders as well as insiders

8. "Simpatico" refers to:
   A. No, it's not about undying loyalty
   B. No, it's not about protecting one's honor
   C. Yes, maintaining harmonious relationships by acquiescing and agreeing
   D. No, it's not about withholding personal information

9. "Personalismo" refers to:
   A. No, it's not primarily about getting along
   B. No, it's not primarily about being polite
   C. No, it's not primarily about agreeing and acquiescing
   D. Yes, talking in terms of the other person's situation, personal pride, family, town

10. The typical Latino American communication pattern is to:
    A. No, they often don't speak directly of concerns
    B. No, they usually don't go directly to the person they have a problem with
    C. No, they often don't make requests directly
    D. Yes, they typically speak indirectly out of concern for others' feelings

HOW CAN ORGANIZATIONS MEET THE NEEDS OF LATINO AMERICANS?

Here are some ways you can help your organization attract and retain talented Latino American employees:

1. Provide the flexibility they need to meet their family obligations.
2. Help them understand the organizational necessity for accurate information and goal achievement.
3. Assist them in turning conflict avoidance into greater sensitivity in conflict resolution.
4. Help them overcome promotion anxiety.

Need #1: Meeting Family Obligations

Work is important to most Latino Americans. They want the American dream, but family comes first. Therefore, when it comes to the following kinds of issues, the Latino American is more likely than the Euro-American worker to put family concerns before work concerns:

- job relocation that requires the family to move
- overtime work that conflicts with family obligations
- the need to be absent in order to deal with family problems, illnesses, or emergencies

Coworkers and managers must put this in perspective in order to understand the true dynamics of the situation.

Latino American workers will generally consult with the family when deciding to take a job, to seek or accept advancement, and whether to leave a job. For you to understand and work with Latino American employees, you must know about and understand their family concerns that impact work decisions and performance.

In Latino cultures, people are hired and promoted based primarily on family and personal ties. Latino American employees may expect the company to give their relatives and close friends preferential treatment. Managers may need to explain differences in company policy and in U.S. corporate cultures.

Need #2: Understanding Organizational Needs for Information and Goals

Latino cultures tend to value accurate data less highly than the American business culture. Most Latino businesspersons see nothing unusual or harmful in withholding information in order to gain or maintain power. While goals are important, the process of achieving the goals and the symbolic messages implied by various aspects of the process may be more important. In contrast, the success of U.S. corporations often hinges on effective and efficient goal achievement, doing what works, and getting accurate data and passing it on to those who need it to do the best job. These values are so pivotal that Latino American employees may benefit from special training sessions on these topics.

Need #3: Learning to Turn Conflict Avoidance into Resolution with Sensitivity

The Latino value of simpatico compels most Latino Americans to avoid interpersonal conflict on the job. They try to emphasize positive behaviors in agreeable situations and de-emphasize negative behaviors in conflictive circumstances. This affects methods of conflict resolution and needs to be addressed in work team situations. Latino American employees need to understand why conflict is being addressed openly instead of ignored. They need to be reassured about the organization's need for openness, the expectation of openness, and why it is valued. Also, the team needs to respect Latino American members' sensitivities and find ways of resolving conflict that all can accept comfortably. Latino American workers may lead others in finding ways to combine openness with sensitivity and compassion.

Need #4: How to Deal Constructively with Promotion Anxiety

Career development has some unique aspects for Latino American employees. For one thing, the employees, especially the men, may see more risk than Euro-Americans in applying for a promotion. If they don't get it, they not only experience a loss, but their self-respect will suffer. Also, they may believe they'll be seen as competitive and too ambitious by their peers.

Latino Americans tend to view competition as disruptive, leading to imbalance and disharmony. To overcome such barriers, leaders can begin working on career development with employees from the beginning. At periodic one-on-one meetings, career goals and ways of meeting them can be discussed. In this way, each step of development and advancement comes about naturally and the threats are diluted.

HOW CAN I HELP LATINO AMERICANS CONTRIBUTE TO AN ORGANIZATION?

Latino American employees have the potential to become highly contributing members of the organizational team, and the Latino American marketplace offers lucrative opportunities as well. Here are a few suggestions:

1. Help them use Latino American employees' love of group affiliation to enhance work teams.
2. Be sensitive to their sense of honor and good name.
3. Appeal to their idealist side in creating visions, goals, and standards.
4. Relate to them in ways that show respect for Latino American values and issues.
5. Value their understanding and connections with Latino communities.

Opportunity #1: Help Them to Enhance Work Team Relationships

Since personal relationships are what Latino Americans value the most, they can make major contributions to productive team projects.

Highlight the Group Value

The tradition of small group loyalty among Latino Americans offers a valuable opportunity for leaders to promote group values:

- Latino Americans place a very high value on belonging to a group and on cooperation and harmony within the group. Once they feel they are an accepted part of a work team, they are very comfortable functioning in this structure.
- For best results, Latino Americans need to feel personally close to the people in the group; otherwise, their first loyalty will lie elsewhere.
- Once they're committed to the team, motivational appeals and rewards geared to the team and the employees' contributions to the team can be the most powerful.
- Latino Americans tend to feel extreme loyalty to their in-groups. On the other hand, they may have difficulty adapting to an impersonal culture and to large groups in which personal recognition rarely occurs.

Remember, Latino Americans tend to give greater importance to relationships than to tasks. Keep these points in mind:

- Ask yourself, on a regular basis, how you can make the relationship value an asset.
- Ask how you can create opportunities for them to work on tasks with others or to share projects.
- When delegating, coaching, and giving feedback, speak to them in terms of relationships where possible.

Promote Assertive Expression

Latino Americans' reluctance to self-disclose can pose a problem for optimal team functioning. Members often must know what's going on inside each others' heads in order to solve problems and keep operations flowing smoothly. When the corporate culture respects and values Latino Americans, their culture, history, and beliefs, then they are more likely to reveal their thinking and feelings to other team members.

Encourage Decision Making

In Latino cultures, those in authority make the decisions, and subordinates don't pass judgment on leaders' ideas or question their decisions, as this would imply a lack of confidence in their judgment. Sometimes U.S. managers think they've communicated to Latino American workers that they can make certain decisions, only to find that the decisions are simply not made. U.S. managers may need to explain in detail the decision-making process. They may need to reassure employees about when they can make certain decisions, when the team expects them to participate in making decisions, and when managers expect their input, feedback, or questioning of ideas and decisions.

Opportunity #2: Be Sensitive to Honor and Good Name

Coworkers and managers who offer feedback, evaluations, comments, or criticisms of Latino Americans' work would do well to understand and remember the importance of personal dignity, honor, and good name. If this is violated, the employee may feel compelled to leave. It may be futile to try to separate the person from the work or the end result. Latino Americans are likely to take criticism personally no matter how objective you try to be. Therefore, try these tips:

- make the feedback personal but supportive and offered with great understanding and empathy
- always give such feedback in private

- always offer it in a supportive, warm, concerned way
- always treat them as adults

Opportunity #3: Appeal to the Idealist Side with Visions and Goals

The idealist aspect of Latino culture can be an advantage when it motivates Latino American employees to support the organizational vision and mission and to achieve the goals and standards set by the group or the company. Their idealism can inspire and energize other employees. On the other hand, the trickster aspect may impel them to test the boundaries to see how strict the work team or the managers will be about holding them to performance standards.

Opportunity #4: Show Respect for their Values and Issues

Values around hierarchy and status, *personalismo* and *simpatico*, are important in work relationships. Also, women managers need to understand effective ways of interacting with Latino American men.

The Manager and Respeto *Status*

Respect for status and authority runs deep in Latin cultures, but respect for the person, regardless of position, runs even deeper. Latino American employees generally expect that the boss will be demanding. They often expect the boss to tell them what to do and exercise fairly close direction until it's done. On the other hand, they can be led to use their own initiative if the leader makes it clear what types of initiative are expected and that this does not conflict with the leader's authority. The combination of challenge and support can help them be productive and feel comfortable on the job. Such an approach is likely to establish an effective working relationship and engage the Latino American's sense of strong loyalty.

Relationships with Personalismo

When a manager is generally warm, friendly, and encouraging with a Latino American employee, that deeper personal respect tends to develop. Otherwise, such employees may assume the manager is displeased with them. On the flip side, when the manager allows the employee to express his or her personality and share personal concerns, a greater rapport develops.

Since almost all relationships are more personalized in Latin America than in the United States, Euro-American leaders may have difficulty understanding the implications of simpatico. In American business cultures, people tend to value the separation of business matters from personal relationships and concerns. However, it's quite possible to balance the Latino Americans' need for their leaders to show personal understanding and warmth and the Euro-American leaders' need for some professional distance. The reverse is also true. Euro-American employees can understand that the Latino American manager's concern for their personal and family matters is not intended as a prying or controlling ploy. It's the leader's way of showing proper concern for each person.

Relationships and Simpatico

A certain charm is seen as crucial for dealing effectively with others and such *simpatico* is a quality that increases one's status. In fact, it's the surest form of acceptance in Latino culture. On the other hand, rudeness or insensitivity in a leader is shocking to Latino Americans. To them, courtesy is synonymous with education, and they would wonder how such a rude person could ever be given a responsible position. Latino Americans greatly admire leaders who can get the job done while exercising smooth social skills that boost the employees' self-esteem and honor.

The Woman Manager of Latino American Men

While machismo is often a misunderstood stereotype and is changing, it is still a factor to consider. Latino American men may have more difficulty than Euro-American men in dealing with a female manager. They are likely to react negatively to being corrected or criticized, especially where other men can hear, since this would be seen as a major attack on their honor. The more assertively the woman comes on, the more difficult it is for the employee. Therefore, women managers need to be especially sensitive to these feelings and to search for positive, tactful ways to achieve their purposes.

Occasionally, a Latino American employee will make sexual overtures. It's important for the manager to keep in mind the implications of the Latino good woman–bad woman concept. She can nip such advances in the bud with clear I-messages, such as "I never get romantic with another employee; it wouldn't be fair to the others." She can then continue to be warm and friendly, making sure she is also businesslike and professional, sending the clear nonverbal message, "I like you and respect you and I will not have a romantic or sexual relationship with you."

Opportunity #5: Value Latino Connections and Understanding

With about 75 percent of Latino American families in the middle- to upper-income brackets, Latino American spending power in 1999 was nearly $400 billion and growing. The U.S. media have responded dramatically to this market. New Spanish-speaking television and radio stations are popping up, especially throughout the Southwest. Many established magazine publishers such as *Newsweek, People, Cosmopolitan,* and *Popular Mechanics* have launched Spanish versions. And the National Association of Hispanic Publishers estimated that there were over 1,000 Latino American newspapers in 1997.

The U.S. Latino American market is huge. Fiesta Foods of Texas is a classic success story based on meeting the needs and wants of this demographic group. Other companies have capitalized on the "roots phenomenon"; that is, people like to buy goods and services that reflect their distinctive cultural heritage. There are many lucrative marketing niches to fill here.

Even greater are the markets in all the other Latino countries. NAFTA and other trade agreements are opening up greater-than-ever trade opportunities with those nations. Latino Americans obviously understand Latino cultures better than anyone, and they're more likely than others to have key connections in Latino communities. They can be of invaluable help in dealing with those markets, customers, suppliers, and other associates. Corporate representatives who can speak the language and know the customs offer the company a valuable competitive edge.

FINAL SELF-TEST

Indicate the best answers to the following 6 multiple-choice questions.

1. Most Latino Americans identify themselves primarily with:
   A. Mexico
   B. family and friends in their home country
   C. the United States
   D. their Spanish heritage

2. Before accepting a new job, most Latino Americans will:
   A. check out possibilities with other firms
   B. consult with the family
   C. need to know if it is upwardly mobile or not
   D. all of the above

3. In dealing with conflict resolution, Latino Americans often need:
   A. to be reassured about the organization's need for openness
   B. to understand why conflict is being addressed instead of ignored
   C. respect for their simpatico sensitivities
   D. all of the above

4. Traditional Latino Americans tend to place higher importance on:

   A. tasks

   B. goals

   C. relationships

   D. opportunities

5. Traditional Latino American employees are likely to expect that the boss will:

   A. expect them to take initiative

   B. leave certain decisions to them

   C. pitch in and help out with the work sometimes

   D. be demanding, tell them what to do, and give close direction

6. Traditional Latino American employees expect the boss to:

   A. take a personal interest in them

   B. be distant and professional at all times

   C. be a little brusque because of his status difference

   D. keep business and personal matters distinctly separate

FINAL SELF-TEST FEEDBACK

Each correct answer is worth 15 points. If you score less than 70 points, you should review the materials and re-take the Final Self-Test.

1. Most Latino Americans identify themselves primarily with:

   A. No, although most came from Mexico

   B. No, although most stay in touch with family and friends in their home country

   C. Yes, the United States and the American dream

   D. No, although they cherish their Spanish heritage

2. Before accepting a new job, most Latino Americans will:

   A. No, most probably won't check out possibilities with other firms

   B. Yes, most will consult with the family

   C. No, most won't need to know if it is upwardly mobile or not

   D. No, not all of the above

3. In dealing with conflict resolution, Latino Americans often need:

   A. No, although they do need to be reassured about the organization's need for openness

   B. No, although they do need to understand why conflict is being addressed instead of ignored

    C. No, although they do need to respect for their simpatico
       sensitivities

    D. Yes, all of the above

4. Traditional Latino Americans tend to place higher importance on:

    A. No, although tasks are important

    B. No, though they can understand and achieve goals

    C. Yes, relationships

    D. No, although most welcome opportunities

5. Traditional Latino American employees are likely to expect that the
   boss will:

    A. No, not expect them to take initiative

    B. No, not leave certain decisions to them

    C. No, not pitch in and help out with the work sometimes

    D. Yes, be demanding, tell them what to do, and give close direction

6. Traditional Latino American employees expect the boss to:

    A. Yes, take a personal interest in them

    B. No, not be distant and professional at all times

    C. No, not be a little brusque because of his status difference

    D. No, not keep business and personal matters distinctly separate

SKILL BUILDER 9.1   The Case of Evelyn Sanchez, Supervisor

Evelyn Sanchez is a Customer Services Supervisor for Buckman's, a large
mail-order house. Her duties include making sure that work is distributed
and completed under strict deadlines, approving certain transactions, and
reviewing employees' work. She is required to set quarterly goals for herself
and train employees to cross-sell to customers in ways that meet their needs.

    Evelyn's team includes 10 employees of diverse backgrounds, including
African American, Euro-American, Latino American, and Asian American.
Most of the employees are bilingual. **Rosita**, a Latina American, is hired as
a new member of Evelyn's team. One day when Evelyn stops by to check on
how Rosita is doing, they lapse into speaking their native Spanish. **Ophelia**,
an African American team member, is working nearby. She feels uncomfortable because she doesn't know what the two are saying. It's no big thing,
and she tries to forget her discomfort. However, Evelyn comes by almost
every day and has a brief conversation in Spanish with Rosita. Finally,
Ophelia mentions her discomfort to Evelyn. She says, "I feel really left out
when you two speak on and on in Spanish—and it keeps happening. I wish

we could all speak the same language around here." Evelyn replies, "Lighten up, Ophelia, we're not talking about you nor are we sharing secrets. We're just chatting, and it's good for our heart and soul to be able to converse in our beautiful *Español* now and then." Ophelia becomes more disturbed each day as Evelyn and Rosita have their little Spanish conversations. She decides to complain to **Gene**, the general manager.

1. The key issue here is:
   A. over-sensitivity in the workplace
   B. the use of language in the workplace
   C. envy and suspicion in the workplace
   D. exclusion in the workplace

Feedback

   A. No, while sensitivity is an issue, over-sensitivity probably is not. Most people like to understand what's going on around them, especially when the boss is involved.
   B. Yes, this is the key issue. Most bilingual employees expect that English will be the official language of the workplace and other public places in the United States. In most workplaces, therefore, employees should speak English. It's natural for others to feel left out when they're within hearing distance of a conversation and can't understand what's being said. The tendency is to feel a little suspicious that they're being talked about or that secrets are being shared. On the other hand, most people believe it is unfair and extreme to punish coworkers for occasionally lapsing into their native language.
   C. No, while envy and suspicion play a role, the key issue is the use of language.
   D. No, while feelings of exclusion play a role, the key issue is the use of language.

2. Evelyn should:
   A. continue to speak Spanish when that feels natural
   B. talk with Ophelia about her over-sensitivity
   C. confine her conversations in Spanish to private situations
   D. refuse to speak Spanish on the job and instruct others to speak English only

Feedback

   A. Not a good idea.
   B. Not a good idea.

C. Yes, this is the best approach. Ophelia has made it clear that such conversations bother her. Evelyn, as supervisor, has a responsibility to role model appropriate, sensitive, inclusive behavior that promotes team harmony. This would mean confining her conversations in Spanish to private situations outside the hearing of Ophelia and other non-Spanish-speaking employees.

D. No, there is probably no need to go to this extreme. It does make sense to talk to employees about the need to act in ways that include all and to role model that behavior by speaking English only in job-centered situations and in other situations at work when persons who don't speak Spanish are within hearing.

3. Gene should:

A. counsel with Ophelia about being more tolerant

B. counsel with Evelyn about role modeling inclusive behaviors

C. counsel with Ophelia about minding her own business

D. all of the above

Feedback

A. No, tolerance is not the key issue.

B. Yes, this is the best option. Evelyn as supervisor is responsible for role modeling inclusive behavior. It should not be difficult for Evelyn to remember to speak English when she is around others who do not speak Spanish.

C. Not the key issue, as a supervisor is responsible for role modeling inclusive behavior.

D. No, one of the other responses is the best one.

SKILL BUILDER 9.2   The Case of Gino George, Sales Rep

Gino George is a sales rep for Delcor, a telecommunications company. Five years ago, he completed a degree in business administration and went to work in the finance department of Delcor as a junior accountant. He was the only Latino American in his department, and he got along well with his coworkers. He earned good performance reviews and merit increases, and two years ago, he applied for and got the sales rep job.

Gino likes being in sales. He especially likes getting a commission on every sale he makes. Because he's a good salesperson, his salary is significantly higher than it was as an accountant. Gino is proud of the fact that he can help his Euro-American coworkers when they must deal with Spanish-speaking clients. In fact, Spanish-speaking clients have learned to ask for Gino, making him a valuable asset to Delcor. On the other hand, being the only Latino American makes Gino feel somewhat isolated. For example, coworkers frequently "forget" to inform him of meetings or invite him to group events. Few of them talk with him about anything outside of business matters.

Recently, Gino was going over some files in the office. A couple of other sales reps entered the adjacent cubicle, and Gino overheard their conversation. Jeff said, "I heard that Dave's raising our sales quotas for the spring quarter. Business is always slow in the spring. How are we going to sell more than last year? If we don't meet that quota, we won't get our bonus." Ralph replied, "I think it's Gino's fault. He just gives Dave ideas. If he weren't such an eager beaver, Dave wouldn't start thinking that the rest of us should do better." "Yeah," said Jeff, "Any ideas on how we can send Gino back to the accounting department? Let him count beans!"

Gino is very upset by the news that his coworkers view his achievements so negatively. He hates being viewed as a trouble maker and difficult person. He decides to pull back on his sales efforts and to be satisfied with barely meeting his quotas.

Today, Dave receives the news that he's being promoted and that he should recommend a replacement to take over his job. As Dave goes through the performance evaluations of all his team members, he narrows the choice down to Gino and Jeff:

- Jeff has a high school diploma, experience as a salesperson with one other company, and has been with Delcor for three years as a sales rep. He gets along well with coworkers and is well accepted as "one of the gang."

- Gino is better qualified, with his bachelor's degree that includes technical expertise in the telecommunications field. He has been building a better track record as a sales rep than Jeff has, but the coworkers don't seem to be as receptive to him as they are to Jeff.

Dave calls Gino and Jeff into his office. He tells them that they're both in the running for the job and sets up times to interview each of them separately. Gino is concerned. He really wants the promotion, but he's worried about being accepted in the managerial role. On the other hand, if Jeff gets the job, he'll probably offer Gino little or no support and encouragement. He'll probably make it tough for Gino.

1. The key issues in this situation are:

    A. blatant ethnic prejudice and discrimination on the part of colleagues

    B. subtle ethnic prejudice and discrimination on the part of colleagues

    C. placing the need to be liked above the need for job achievement

D. the corporate culture

E. both B and C

Feedback

A. Not the best answer. Some of the employees are blatant about disliking a colleague that excels to the point of "making them look bad" in comparison. They don't include Gino as a close friend or social friend, but the reason is not clear. Therefore most observers would say this may be subtle discrimination, but it certainly is not blatant.

B. No, his colleagues do not include Gino as a close friend or social friend, but the reason is not clear. Most observers would say this may be subtle discrimination, but other factors are important, too.

C. No, although too much emphasis on the need to be liked is a key issue, and it's one Gino can do something about. He is apparently placing his need to be "simpatico"—to get along and not cause trouble—above his need to do well in his job.

D. No, while the corporate culture is always a factor, the information given in this case does not point toward clear corporate culture factors.

E. The best answer is both subtle discrimination and need to be liked.

2. Dave should:

A. recognize the subtle discrimination and Gino's simpatico need

B. work with Gino on his need for simpatico versus need for job achievement

C. work with the entire group on issues around competition, achievement, team harmony, and inclusiveness

D. all of the above

Feedback

A. No, recognizing discrimination is good, but more is needed.

B. No, working with Gino on job achievement is good, but more is needed.

C. No, working with the group is good, but more is needed.

D. Yes, all three strategies are necessary. Dave needs to recognize what may be going on here and work with Gino on this issue. The other sales reps may be exercising subtle prejudice and discrimination by excluding Gino. Certainly, Gino seems to have effective social skills in dealing with customers, making it seem unlikely that his difficulties with coworkers stem from poor social skills. Dave should consider working with the entire group, as well as privately with Gino, providing appropriate training and a show of support for Gino. While Gino deserves the promotion, repair work needs to be done before he takes over the position.

THE BOTTOM LINE

Think of this as just the beginning of your exploration into what it's like to be an Latino American. Now that you have the basics, let this be a framework for adding new information—just by noticing and questioning what's presented by the media, by asking Latino Americans about themselves, by caring and really listening.

You'll become more and more at ease with Latino American associates, and they'll become more comfortable with you. Soon, you'll be as capable of building relationships with Latino Americans as you are with people from your own ethnic group.

Chapter Review

1. Common myths about Latino Americans are that they are only qualified for menial jobs, too emotional and excitable to be leaders, too passive and polite to be good leaders in the workplace, and that Latino men are macho and Latino women are easily intimidated.

2. Latino Americans are a diverse culture with diverse origins. Latino Americans come from Mexico, Puerto Rico, Cuba, Central America, South America, etc. The Latino American culture grew by 57% between 1970 and 1990, seven times faster than the rest of the nation, and they are most likely to live in the western or southern United States. Educational levels are among the lowest in the nation, and Latino Americans are twice as likely as Euro-Americans to work as minimally skilled or skilled laborers.

3. The typical Latino American worldview includes the following:

   ■ Closeness to the spirit world
   ■ A sense of destiny or fatalism
   ■ Acceptance of hierarchy and status
   ■ Emotional expression and the passion factor
   ■ Use of space as up-close and personal

- Future time as unknowable
- The American Dream

4. Latino Americans place the highest priority on personal relationships—especially the following:
   - *familismo:* family comes first
   - *simpatico:* getting along is crucial
   - *personalismo:* relating in a personal way
   - *amor propio:* reluctance to self-disclose, protecting honor
   - *machismo:* gender roles
   - indirect, sensitive communication patterns

5. Organizations can meet the needs of Latino Americans by providing flexibility in meeting family obligations, helping them understand the organizational need for accurate information and achieving goals, assisting them in turning conflict avoidance into conflict resolution, and helping them overcome promotion anxiety.

6. Latino Americans can contribute to the organization by using their love of group affiliation to enhance work teams; appealing to their sense of honor and good name; tapping their idealism to help create visions, goals, and standards; respecting Latino values and issues; and capitalizing on their understanding and connections with Latino communities.

10

Working With Asian Americans

CHAPTER OBJECTIVES

- Identify typical myths about Asian Americans.
- Understand how the current situation has evolved from past history.
- Identify current Asian American demographic profiles.
- Describe Asian American core values.
- Understand the issues that are most important to the Asian American community.
- Understand how organizations can meet the needs of Asian American employees.
- Describe how Asian Americans can contribute to your team and your organization.

CHAPTER OVERVIEW

You're likely to have many Asian American colleagues if you live on the East or West Coast or certain urban areas of the country. Only 4 percent of Americans are Asian Americans, but they're clustered in certain cities and regions. People who take the time and effort to learn about Asian Americans and their values and issues, can boost their ability to work productively with these coworkers.

Asian Americans are likely to think of themselves in terms of the country where they or their ancestors were born. They see themselves as Chinese Americans, Filipino Americans, Japanese Americans, and so forth. The Asian American community is quite diverse. However, there are some distinct common threads in their cultural fabric. Learning about Asian Americans can help you:

- understand their perspective or situations.
- understand the meaning of their actions.
- ask questions that will help you get to know them better.
- avoid forming rigid ideas and stereotypes.
- be open and flexible as you interact with individual Asian Americans.

WHAT ARE SOME MYTHS ABOUT ASIAN AMERICANS?

Most of the myths are either false or distorted, partial truths.

Myth #1: Asian Americans Are too Passive and Polite to Be Good Managers

This is a career-bashing stereotype with hardly a kernel of truth. One implication is that they're polite and therefore lack the conviction and backbone to stand up to the heat a supervisor must take. Another implication is that they're compliant, therefore passive, which means they don't have the ambition it takes to move up the competitive corporate ladder. The behavior of Asian Americans is often misread by people who don't understand their cultural values and training. There are many ways to be productive and effective. Look at the substance of their performance, not just their work style.

In their own countries, Asians are obviously the business and political leaders. In the United States, Asian American small business owners have established an impressive success record, overcoming great odds. Even women who work on assembly lines can be surprisingly assertive and persistent beneath their "face" of compliance and cooperation according to recent studies.

Myth #2: Asian Americans Are Unemotional and Inscrutable

Euro-Americans often complain that they can't tell what Asian Americans are thinking or feeling, so they're labeled as unemotional and inscrutable. In fact, Asian Americans experience the same emotions as other people. Their cultural values call for self-discipline in expressing emotions and for indirectness in communicating.

Myth #3: Asian Americans Tend to Retain Their Foreign Ways so It's Difficult for Them to Fit in

Asian Americans have traditionally coped with the exotic, perpetual foreigner stereotype because Euro-Americans have seen them as:

- immigrants who represent a small segment of the American population
- people of color who bear distinct physical differences
- people from a culture and lifestyle that is just too different for comfort
- people who can never be completely absorbed into American society and politics

Discriminatory laws and practices have reinforced this separateness. In fact, one-fourth to one-half of the members of most Asian American groups were born in this country. Many are even third- or fourth-generation Americans. Further, they can be understood fairly well by anyone who is willing to spend a little time and effort learning about them. Asian cultures can offer much ancient wisdom to those who are open to different ways of viewing situations. Incorporating different ideas can lead to the discovery of new business opportunities and problem solutions.

Myth #4: Asian Americans Have Learned How to Make It in American Society By Working Hard and Being Thrifty

This model minority myth is true, as far as it goes. On the up side, it makes Asian Americans more acceptable in business and society in general. But it ignores the complexities and difficulties of their situation. The downside is:

- The "hard worker" image sets up unrealistic expectations that they'll gladly make major sacrifices for their work, work for less than Euro-Americans, work harder, and work longer hours.
- It's easy to assume that such a model minority group has no pressing social or political issues that we must address.
- It causes undue resentment from other minorities.

The reality is that Asian Americans pay a high price for "making it." As a family unit, they work harder and longer for less pay than Euro-Americans and they get less help from society.

Myth #5: Asian Americans Can't Seem to Master English Grammar and Pronunciation—They Have Communication Problems

Asian languages are about as different from English as a language can be. Therefore, becoming fluent and proficient is a long, arduous process for Asian Americans. Most work diligently and continually to improve their communication skills. In general, they believe in mastering English, and nearly all believe that English should be the only official U.S. language. The reality is that virtually all Asian Americans who were born in the United States are fluent in English and in fact may not be fluent in their ancestral Asian language.

Myth #6: Asian Americans Are Good in Technical Occupations, But They Don't Have Creative or Leadership Potential

This stereotype is a faulty distortion that creates a huge barrier to career mobility. It's related to the idea that Asian Americans are technical coolies, computer nerds, or memorization whizzes, great at crunching numbers but short on people skills and creativity. It stems from the tendency of immigrant students with some language deficiencies to focus on what they *can*

do well, which often includes mastering quantitative tasks and usually includes diligently studying, practicing, and memorizing. As a group, Asian Americans do score better than any other group on math tests. But as a matter of fact, Asian American students demonstrate a broad range of aptitudes and talents. Those who were born in the United States do not have the language problem and are likely to gravitate to a wider range of career areas.

Myth #7: Asian Americans Know about All Things Asian

Some Euro-American businesspersons tend to look upon their company's "token" Asian Americans as the resident experts on all things Asian American—and Asian, for that matter. This assumes they know everything about the country their parents or grandparents immigrated from, its culture, adaptation of its people to the American culture, and which local restaurants are the best source of its cuisine. For some Asian Americans, this stereotype has become a pet peeve. The reality is that many of them were born in the United States, are more American than Asian, and may be no more of an expert on "things Asian" than the average American.

WHAT PAST EVENTS LED TO THESE MYTHS?

Americans have always valued the ideals of equal opportunity and fairness, but reality has not always matched that ideal. From the beginning, Asian immigrants have faced many obstacles to acceptance in America. Recent generations are, however, more Americanized and face fewer barriers to success.

The Chinese: Gold, Railroads, and Exclusion

The first group of Asian Americans were men from China who came during the 1850s California gold rush. They came hoping to find some gold, return to China, and finance better lives for their families. Few found gold. Most found work building railroads, waterways, and similar projects. There was overt prejudice against them from the beginning. The 1882 Chinese Exclusion Act was the first law that prohibited the entry of immigrants on the basis of nationality. However, during the early 1900s, entry laws were loosened. Asians, including their families, came—Japanese as well as Chinese. At this time, various laws segregated them:

- The western states passed Alien Land Acts that barred them from owning land because they were "aliens ineligible to citizenship."
- They were legally classified as "nonwhite" for many purposes, catching them in the segregation net cast around African Americans.
- Restrictive covenants were written into many deeds making it illegal to sell the property to a "nonwhite."
- State laws prohibited intermarriage.

- School segregation was practiced in districts that had significant numbers of Asians, such as in San Francisco.
- Public theaters, pools, and beaches were often off-limits to them.

The Japanese: Migration, War, and Concentration Camps

The Japanese painfully discovered that their achievements in America did not lead to acceptance when—during World War II—they were placed in concentration camps. Congressmen feared that Japanese Americans might provide information that would help the Japanese navy launch an attack on the West Coast. No case of such spy activity was ever filed. The prisoners lost virtually all of their assets except those they could carry with them. Their greatest economic loss was the income they weren't allowed to earn during their internment. The camps were surrounded by barbed wire and were patrolled by armed soldiers who shot and killed several of the Japanese they were guarding. This wartime exile and incarceration was and still is the central event of Japanese American history, making their history unique among Asian Americans. In 1988, the U.S. government formally apologized to these families and began paying reparations.

Civil Rights Laws of the 1960s

Most of the discriminatory laws were in force until the 1960s. The new Civil Rights laws had a great impact on Asian American's options. Housing segregation was still a reality and most private clubs were closed to them. But higher education opened up, and streams of second-generation students poured in, most choosing "safe" majors in the professions, such as accounting, education, dentistry, or pharmacy. Employment patterns tend to be less discriminatory in professions where credentials open doors—and private practice can be lucrative, especially within one's minority community.

Generation Gaps

To understand the experience of various generations of Chinese and Japanese Americans, you must understand the cultural differences between the generations.

First generation.   The first generation includes those who immigrated from China or Japan in the early years of this century. They tended to be relatively isolated in their ethnic communities and retained their old cultural ways.

Second generation.   The second generation includes those born in the 1940s to 1960s. They're more Americanized but are still strongly affected by their Asian cultural heritage. They began to find a voice of their own and

become distinct from their parents' generation. Now mature and aging adults, they're primarily a low-profile group.

Third and fourth generations. These generations include those born during or after the 1970s. While increasingly molded by the American culture, they still retain certain aspects of their Asian community's worldview and values. Many have never faced overt discrimination, and a few have never had close ethnic ties or friendships with other Asian American families. Most are definitely more American than Asian. They go to the university and are eager for good jobs, especially in the professions such as medicine, engineering, and law. They're entering occupations and fields once considered closed to them, such as advertising, the performing arts, journalism, and broadcasting.

WHO ARE THE ASIAN AMERICANS?

The seven major groups of Asian Americans have many common cultural threads. Many of their values and customs are similar. However, each group came to the United States under somewhat different circumstances and therefore have faced different situations. Here are the countries of origin of that 4 percent of the U.S. population in 2000:

1. China   24%
2. Philippines   18%
3. India   16%
4. Vietnam   11%
5. Korea   11%
6. Japan   8%
7. Other country of origin   12%

Asian Americans doubled in number between 1980 and 1990, due primarily to immigration, and increased again by 63 percent between 1990 and 2000.

Where and How They Live

The following facts provide a general demographic picture of where Asian Americans live and how they live:

- **Over half live in the West**. In fact, 54 percent do.
- **Many are foreign born**. About 66 percent are foreign born. Southeast Asian Americans have the highest percentage and Japanese Americans the lowest.
- **Some are recent immigrants**. Thirty-eight percent entered the United States during the 1980s, mostly refugees. Most live in the West, especially in California.

- **They live longer**. The life expectancy of Chinese Americans and Japanese Americans is 80, compared to 76 for Euro-Americans, perhaps because of diet differences.

- **They have less crime**. FBI reports indicate that arrest rates of Asian Americans for serious crimes between 1980 and 1985 were well below their proportion in the population. Since the 1930s, Asian Americans in California have had lower rates of crime and delinquency than the general population.

- **They're relatively young**. Thirty is the median age, compared with the national median of 33.

- **Most groups have larger families**. Asian American families average 3.8 persons, compared to 3.2 for all U.S. families.

- **Most speak another language**. Sixty-five percent speak another language at home, 56 percent don't speak English well, and 35 percent are isolated from mainstream society because of the language barrier.

Education and Work Achievements

The following gives a general picture of the educational achievement, work experiences, and income levels of Asian Americans:

- **They have more high school graduates than average Americans**—87 percent, compared to 81 percent nationally. Averages range from 88 percent for Japanese Americans to 31 percent for Hmong.

- **They have more college degrees**—47 percent, compared with 27 percent for all Americans.

- **Asian Indian Americans are the best educated**. Asian Americans from India, or of Indian ancestry, are the most highly educated group in the United States. Over 65 percent of the men and half of the women have degrees, compared to 27 percent for all Americans. Nearly all speak English, and few have language barriers, which is related to India's history as a British colony. More than 72 percent of them have jobs, compared with 65 percent of all Americans. Nearly half of all foreign-born Asian Indian workers are managers and professionals. This is twice the proportion for all Americans, which is 24 percent. They have the highest per capita income, $18,000, after Japanese Americans. Many are part of an Indian "brain drain" that occurred during the 1980s and was caused when India trained more professionals than its businesses could profitably employ.

- **Asian Americans have more workers than any group**—67 percent, compared with 65 percent nationally. Groups with an employment rate higher than 70 percent are the Filipino Americans, Asian Indian

Americans, and Thai Americans. Twenty percent of Asian American families contain three or more workers, compared with 13 percent nationally.

- **More hold more high-status jobs than average**—31 percent are managers and professionals, compared to 26 percent nationally, due primarily to higher education levels and the tendency to start their own business or practice.

- **Asian Americans' pay doesn't match educational level**. Median income per person in 1997 was $18,226, compared to $20,425 for Euro-Americans. While median income *per family* looked good in 2000 at $51,200, Asian American families had 3.2 persons. Euro-American family income was $44,400, but there were only 2.5 persons per household. That means two things: 1) Asian American income must provide for more family members, and 2) more persons in their families go out to work than in Euro-American families.

- **Poverty rate is average**. The Asian American poverty rate is 11 percent, compared to 12 percent nationally. Southeast Asian poverty rates range from 35 to 64 percent, with Chinese American and Korean American rates at 14 percent and rates for Filipino Americans, Japanese Americans, and Asian Indian Americans under 10 percent.

- **Japanese Americans are the most affluent**. By 1990, Japanese Americans were the most successful of any Asian American group by most standards. Their educational attainment runs a close second to the top U.S. achievers, Asian Indian Americans. They have the highest per capita income of any Asian American group at $19,400, well above the national median of $14,100. The poverty rate of 7 percent is near the lowest.

- **Hmong hill tribes from Laos have the greatest challenges**. As an aftermath of the Vietnam War, the United States has accepted many war refugees from Vietnam, Cambodia, and Laos. About 60,000 belonged to the Hmong hill tribes of Laos, who subsisted as semi-nomadic farmers who carved fields from the jungle, farmed them for a while, then moved on to repeat the process elsewhere.

  They have a strong family and clan system, and families are traditionally large, so they average 6.6 children, the highest birth rate of any U.S. group. They had no experience with written language until 1960 when missionaries came to Laos, so most speak little or no English and have the lowest educational achievement of any U.S. group. Adapting to a high-tech workplace that's based upon quite sophisticated uses of written information is a major challenge. Only 29 percent of Hmong Americans had jobs in 1990, their average income was $2,600, and most depended on public assistance to survive. They have dramatically improved their lot in recent years!

SELF-TEST #1

Indicate the best answers to the following 10 multiple-choice questions.

1. Typical stereotypes that Asian Americans must deal with include:

   A. lazy

   B. slow learners

   C. overly passive and polite

   D. overly emotional

2. The "foreign, exotic" stereotype refers to Euro-American viewpoints that Asian Americans are:

   A. immigrants who represent a small segment of the American population

   B. people who can't be completely assimilated

   C. from cultures that are just too different for comfort

   D. all of the above

3. The first laws that served to segregate Asians in the United States were:

   A. restrictive covenants written into many deeds making it illegal to ever sell the land to a nonwhite

   B. legal classification of Asian immigrants as "nonwhite"

   C. miscegenation laws prohibiting intermarriage among the "races"

   D. Chinese Exclusion Act

4. The central event in Japanese American history was:

   A. Civil Rights laws of the 1960s

   B. 1988 U.S. law to pay reparations to wronged Japanese Americans

   C. placement of Japanese Americans in U.S. concentration camps during WWII

   D. Alien Land Acts during the early 1900s

5. The best way to describe the prevalent Asian American assimilation pattern is:

   A. they retain their cultural values and practices

   B. like father, like son, like grandson

   C. speaking the native Asian language is a primary value

   D. second- and third-generation members are increasingly Americanized

6. Most Asian Americans or their ancestors have immigrated from:

   A. Japan

   B. China

   C. Philippines

   D. Korea

7. Most Asian Americans:
   A. are foreign born
   B. speak a foreign language
   C. live in the West
   D. all of the above

8. Statistics on Asian Indian Americans' education reveal that:
   A. they have the highest educational levels after Japanese Americans
   B. they have the highest educational levels of all U.S. groups
   C. more of the women have degrees than the men
   D. they are highly educated but must overcome the language barrier

9. On average, an Asian American is more likely than the average American to:
   A. have a college degree
   B. hold a high-status job
   C. live in poverty
   D. all of the above

10. Southeast Asian Americans, especially those from the hills of Laos:
    A. adapt fairly well to the freedom of the U.S. culture
    B. have language barriers that are fairly easy to overcome
    C. have the highest birth rate of any U.S. group
    D. all of the above

SELF-TEST #1 FEEDBACK

Each correct answer is worth 10 points. If you score less than 70 points, you should review the materials and re-take the Self-Test.

1. Typical stereotypes that Asian Americans must deal with include:
   A. No, not lazy
   B. No, not slow learners
   C. Yes, overly passive and polite
   D. No, not overly emotional

2. The "foreign, exotic" stereotype refers to Euro-American viewpoints that Asian Americans are:
   A. No, although there is a stereotype that they're immigrants who represent a small segment of the American population
   B. No, although there is a stereotype that they're people who can't be completely assimilated

    C. No, although there is a stereotype that they're from cultures that are just too different for comfort

    D. Yes, the best answer is all of the above

3. The first laws that served to segregate Asians in the United States were:

    A. No, although there were restrictive covenants written into many deeds making it illegal to ever sell the land to a nonwhite

    B. No, although there was legal classification of Asian immigrants as "nonwhite"

    C. No, although there were miscegenation laws prohibiting intermarriage among the "races"

    D. Yes, the Chinese Exclusion Act

4. The central event in Japanese American history was:

    A. No, not the Civil Rights laws of the 1960s

    B. No, not the 1988 U.S. law to pay reparations to wronged Japanese Americans

    C. Yes, the best answer is placement of Japanese Americans in U.S. concentration camps during WWII

    D. No, not the Alien Land Acts during the early 1900s

5. The best way to describe the prevalent Asian American assimilation pattern is:

    A. No, although they retain some cultural values and practices

    B. No, although there are some similar values from father to son to grandson

    C. No, speaking the native Asian language has not been a primary value

    D. Yes, second- and third-generation members are increasingly Americanized

6. Most Asian Americans or their ancestors have immigrated from:

    A. No, not Japan

    B. Yes, China

    C. No, not the Philippines, although this is the second largest group

    D. No, not Korea

7. Most Asian Americans:

    A. No, although it's true that most are foreign born

    B. No, although it's true that most speak a foreign language

    C. No, although it's true that most live in the West

    D. Yes, all of the above

8. Statistics on Asian Indian Americans' education reveal that:

    A. No, they don't have the highest educational levels after Japanese Americans

    B. Yes, they have the highest educational levels of all U.S. groups

    C. No, it's not true that more women have degrees than the men

    D. No, because most speak English

9. On average, an Asian American is more likely than the average American to:

    A. No, although they are more likely to have a college degree

    B. No, although they are more likely to hold a high-status job

    C. No, although they are more likely to live in poverty

    D. Yes, all of the above

10. Southeast Asian Americans, especially those from the hills of Laos:

    A. No, they do not adapt fairly well to the freedom of the U.S. culture

    B. No, their language barriers are not easy to overcome

    C. Yes, they have the highest birth rate of any U.S. group

    D. No, not all of the above

WHAT ARE THE CORE VALUES COMMON TO ASIAN AMERICAN CULTURES?

Chinese, Japanese, and Koreans are physically and culturally very similar, with many of their cultural similarities stemming from Confucianism. The beliefs of other major Asian religions, such as Buddhism and Hinduism, tend to foster similar values. While Asian cultures are quite complex and diverse, there are definitely some common threads that will help guide you in building relationships.

The Vietnamese culture has been strongly influenced by the Chinese culture. India has its own culture, with major influences from the Hindu religion and the British culture, while the Philippine culture has been influenced by the Spanish culture and Catholicism. Even so, both India and the Philippines reflect many common Asian values and cultural patterns.

The best uses of this information about Asian American cultural patterns are:

- to help you understand how they might view situations or what their actions might mean
- to figure out what questions you might ask in getting to know them better
- to avoid forming rigid ideas and new stereotypes based on this information
- to be open and flexible as you interact with individual Asian Americans

Asian American values and issues have been identified by such researchers as Richard W. Brislin, Esther Ngan-Ling Chow, Karen Hossfeld, Harry Kitano, Pyong Gap Min, Rochelle Sharpe, Ronald Takaki, Tomoko Yoshida, William Wei, and M. B. Zinn. Core values include:

- putting group concerns before individual desires
- promoting group harmony
- accepting status differences—the hierarchy
- revering education
- communicating indirectly and vaguely
- the Filipino culture—a Latino flavor
- the Korean culture—some unique viewpoints

Value #1: Putting Group Concerns Before Individual Desires

All Asian cultures are collective, depending a great deal upon each other within close-knit families, extended families, and community groups. Members are expected to honor the group by:

- seeing the group as the most important part of society
- focusing on a group of people who are working toward a goal as more important than focusing on each one as individuals
- valuing group recognition and group reward above individual reward
- emphasizing a sense of belonging to the group and security within the group
- extending tight, strong family ties to other relatives and close friends
- placing central emphasis on a strong network of social relationships
- making public service a moral responsibility
- viewing personal saving and resource conservation as more important than consumption
- placing fairness with the group and community above gaining wealth

Value #2: Promoting Group Harmony

Putting the group first naturally leads to the value of putting group harmony first. Customary ways of achieving this goal include the following beliefs and actions.

Disciplined Emotional Expression

Most Asians are taught that harsh words, scolding, temper flares, and similar emotional expressions will cause the other person to lose face and also to lose respect for the speaker. For example, to show your anger is seen as:

- the same as admitting loss of control
- a lapse in training and self-discipline
- a loss of face for you

As a result, in face-to-face relations, Asian Americans tend to maintain the amenities and cordialities, no matter how they are feeling. All of this is true *unless* things have gone too far—and it's almost impossible for people outside the culture to estimate when things are about to go too far.

Avoidance of Open Conflict

This includes avoiding personal confrontations, as well as not saying no, not giving others unpleasant messages, or doing this in a very indirect way.

Modesty

Everyone, especially females, is expected to show modesty by:

- avoiding statements that can be perceived as boasting or self-congratulatory, as in an overuse of the words "I," "me," and "mine"
- being reticent to talk about themselves or their own accomplishments
- not drawing attention to themselves
- responding to compliments by belittling their abilities

Self-Effacement

It's often appropriate for persons to act as if they are of lower status in order to show selfless humility and give honor to others. Highly respected people often assume an attitude of self-effacement in social and business contacts. Putting yourself forward is usually viewed as proud arrogance and invites scorn. To make a joke at someone else's expense and to cause embarrassment is highly resented in business. Also, "good" businesspersons place a higher value on allowing others in the group or community to save face, and therefore preserve harmony, than on achieving higher sales and profits.

Maturity: Focusing on Others, Conforming, Giving

The individual is expected to be extremely sensitivity to others' feelings and wishes, giving second place to his or her own feelings and wishes. When persons are flexible, defer to others, or comply with the wishes of others in order to maintain harmony, they show maturity and self-discipline.

Asian cultures expect people to conform to the wishes of those of higher status. This maintains harmony even when there is internal conflict between what persons want and what they think they should do. The key thing for you to remember: When an Asian American gives in to another person, it's not necessarily a passive or weak gesture, but is often a sign of tolerance, self-control, flexibility, and maturity.

Mature persons are sensitive to the need to give to others who have given to them, to pay back devotion, generosity, and favors

Value #3: Accepting Status Differences: The Hierarchy

Protocol, rank, and status are important parts of all Asian cultures, ranging from the extremes of the Hindu caste system to the Confucian system, which states:

- Everyone is expected to honor certain binding obligations to immediate family, relatives, clan, province, and state.
- Society should be structured to minimize deviations from these obligations.
- Women are subordinate to men, sons to fathers, younger brothers to older brothers, wives to husbands, and everyone to the state.
- Elders are especially respected, even revered, pampered, and appeased. Their every wish and desire is catered to whenever possible. Every home, no matter how poor, provides the best room for the honored grandparent.

Across all religions and cultures, the Asian belief in hierarchy includes:

- Valuing a sense of order, propriety, and appropriate behavior between persons of varying status.
- Basing status on occupational position, education, wealth, and family background.

Typical Customs or Behaviors

The customs that reflect the status value include:

- When you meet someone, quickly establish whether that person has higher status than you. If so, show proper deference.
- Address people by their title and first name in all but informal or family situations.
- Respect seniority and the elderly.
- Prefer sons to daughters. Daughters go to their husband's family and so you lose the value they could bring you. As your children are growing up, you must protect your daughters and can give your sons more social freedom.
- Parents must arrange marriages for their children, aiming for partners with the highest status possible.

Respect for the Manager's Status

In the United States, it's appropriate at certain times for managers to roll up their sleeves and work alongside people to get things done. Pitching in when there's an emergency is a sign you're a good sport, one of the guys. Many Asian Americans, especially the immigrants, would interpret it this way:

- This is an insult to me as a worker.
- You're implying that I can't get the work done the way I should.
- Such work is below your station as a manager.
- I can't have the same respect for you now.
- If you do this again, or do it insensitively, I'll really lose face. I may have to resign.

Value #4: Revering Education

Education is revered in Asian cultures, especially where there's a strong Confucian influence. Being educated is a high moral virtue and is a rigid prerequisite for moving up from lower to higher political and social standing. Scholars are given the greatest respect, have the highest rank, and are often among the most powerful and wealthy in society. Asian Americans therefore:

- value education as a moral virtue
- value position in society and see education as the best way to achieve a good position and some financial security
- consider education an investment in family status

Value #5: Communicating Vaguely, Indirectly, Silently

Asian Americans may sometimes seem vague, indirect, or strangely silent.

Being Vague

In close-knit cultures, such as Japan, where everyone grew up in the same society, people can speak a sort of "shorthand" and be understood. In fact, being direct and making specific references may be seen as insulting. Being vague, indirect, or ambiguous is valued. As a result, people will often leave their sentences unfinished so listeners may mentally form the conclusion for themselves. After all, they know what the speaker is getting at— to "go on and on" might insult the listeners' intelligence. When these tendencies carry over into the U.S. workplace, coworkers can become quite confused.

Being Indirect

You've learned that being indirect is an Asian way of avoiding open conflict and preserving harmony. Pay special attention to situations in which an Asian American associate may need to say no, confront an issue, or deliver some other unpleasant message. Remember that even when that person is trying to be direct in the Asian way, you may still consider it indirect. And their indirect message may be so subtle that you don't get it.

Saying No

To say no is an insult, could damage feelings and disrupt harmony, and is therefore bad manners. Asian Americans may say *yes*, meaning "I heard you," and then go about doing the opposite with little sense of breaking an agreement. When an Asian American man, for example, disagrees with you, says no, or conveys unwelcome information, he may do it so indirectly and subtly that you won't know it's been done. Later, if his actions reflect a lack of agreement, you may conclude that he not only was unemotional and in-scrutable, but perhaps evasive, sneaky, dishonest, or even corrupt. Probably, he was merely being polite.

- You can help by understanding these vague or indirect communication patterns and asking your Asian American associates to fill in the blanks.

Not Interrupting

If you were listening to a friend and didn't understand something she said, would you wait, expressionless, until she had finished a long explanation, expecting her to take responsibility for your understanding? Probably not. But if all of the people you know believe that's the way to listen, then such behavior would be normal. For many Asian Americans, not interrupting is basic courtesy that is essential for conversations to proceed.

- You can help by encouraging Asian American associates to interrupt you in order to ask questions if they don't understand you.

Keeping Longer Silences

When you finish speaking, how do you react when your listener is silent for a minute or more? Most Americans view such long silences as extremely un-comfortable and feel compelled to fill them in with comments or questions. For many Asian Americans, a few moments of quiet contemplation after lis-tening may be essential, and your comments are distracting.

- You can help by becoming comfortable with such silences and refraining from filling such moments with talk.

Other Behavioral Customs

A few other customs you may need to understand include:

- It's okay to call for someone to come to you by holding out your arm with your palm *down*, using a scratching movement. To turn your palm *up* and use the fingers to motion, which is typical in the United States, is considered rude.

- Meals are often more ritualistic, communal, and time consuming than in the United States. The talk is considered more important than the food.

- Colors and numbers often have different meanings than they have in the United States.

The Filipino Culture: A Latino Flavor

This is primarily an Asian culture with a strong Latino flavor. Many Filipinos have Spanish surnames and most are Catholic because the Spanish ruled the Philippines for 300 years. American rule for 50 years established English as a major language. Since their independence in 1950, a unique Filipino culture has been developing. In addition to the typical Asian values, these Latino-type values are also important:

- the importance of saving face, avoiding shame, and maintaining face, honor, and self-esteem all have a special Latino flavor
- personalistic view of the universe and fatalistic view of the future
- very flexible sense of time in social situations, which may begin an hour or more after the appointed time

The Korean Culture: Some Unique Viewpoints

Korean Americans hold most of the same values as other Asian Americans. Two distinct concepts in the Korean culture that you should know about are *kibun* and nonpersons.

Kibun: Inner feelings, Mood

The closest English translation of *kibun* may be "mood." When your *kibun* is good, you function smoothly and easily and feel great. If your *kibun* is upset or bad, you may bring transactions to an abrupt stop and feel depressed, awful. Part of the intention of businesspeople is to enhance the *kibun* of all parties. To damage the *kibun* could end the relationship and even create enemies. Class or status is involved, with those of lower status doing more nurturing of the *kibun* of the higher.

Nonpersons

Koreans who fail to follow the basic rules of social interaction are viewed as nonpersons. Koreans show very little concern for nonpersons' feelings, their comfort, or whether they live or die. Nonpersons are simply not worthy of much consideration. Korean Americans obviously must modify this attitude in order to function effectively in a diverse society; however, some variation of it probably survives and affects relationships, especially among first-generation immigrants.

WHAT ARE THE KEY ISSUES THAT ARE IMPORTANT TO ASIAN AMERICANS?

Key issues that are important to Asian Americans include

1. the model minority stereotype, which is a mixed blessing
2. male–female dynamics and differences
3. educational issues

Issue #1: Model Minority—A Mixed Blessing

In the 1960s, reporters began writing about the high education attainment, high median family income, low crime rates, and absence of juvenile delinquency and mental health problems among Asian Americans. Proponents of this model minority stereotype often ask, "Why can't African Americans succeed like this? (and not bother us)." This stereotype has been a mixed blessing for Asian Americans; it carries with it advantages and disadvantages.

Model Minority Advantages

The main advantage to Asian Americans of the model minority stereotype is that it showcases their cultural strengths, especially strengths connected with their success in running small family businesses.

The model minority image eventually increased job opportunities for Asian Americans. Business managers say they favor hiring Asian Americans because they:

- work hard and are productive
- invest in higher education, even at the cost of financial hardship
- are willing to work unusually long hours
- maintain a frugal lifestyle
- persevere in their goals and their work projects
- identify with the American dream of hard work leading to a better life

- save small amounts of money until they can invest in a small business
- use frugal strategies to keep their businesses going

Small Business Ownership: Strategies and Challenges

A key aspect of the model minority image is Asian Americans' ability to start and hang onto small family businesses. Community credit associations and small family enterprises have traditionally been common in Asian countries. Immigrants who can't find work may use these strategies:

- Join mutual aid associations in the ethnic community that provide needed financing and support, and members agree not to compete. Associations may loan capital, fix business locations and prices, locate employees, and help members in distress.
- Start businesses that are nonthreatening to the Euro-American majority because they're small and they specialize in limited areas.
- Work long hours for a certain minimum income.
- Give jobs first to family, then to extended family, neighborhood, and ethnic group members, in that order.
- Give employees as much job security as possible, with layoffs a last resort.
- Provide job flexibility to free employees to go to school or work at second jobs.
- Make the primary goal a long-range one: to sustain the business over the long term.

  Factors that limit growth and expansion include:

- owners' inadequate English skills
- dependence on ethnic customers whose per capita wealth is lower
- reluctance to go outside the Asian American community to get money that would be needed for business expansion

Advantages of Small Business Ownership

Small business owners have contributed greatly to the image of Asian Americans as the model minority. Families who have managed to build and hold onto at least a minimal level of business success have achieved the following advantages:

- **Protection from discrimination**. For most of this century about half the Asian American male population worked for such small businesses, effectively shielding themselves from the open labor market with its discriminatory practices.

- **Higher educational attainment**. Owners were able to accumulate money to send their children to college. Between 1940 and 1960, there was a dramatic increase in the percentage of Asian Americans who completed high school and went to college.
- **More opportunities**. Small business success and higher educational attainment enhanced Euro-Americans' perception of Asian Americans as productive workers.

Model Minority Costs: Disadvantages

Several disadvantages offset the Asian American success story

- They get less return on their educational investment than do Euro-Americans. Even though about twice as many have degrees, they average only 70 percent of Euro-American men's income.
- They are disadvantaged in getting the better-paying jobs.
- Most have a lower living standard than their income implies because 90 percent live in high-cost areas such as San Francisco.
- More of the family members work than in Euro-American families and they work more hours on average.
- Underemployment is more common. Rather than be unemployed, most will accept low-paying, part-time or seasonal jobs.
- It overlooks the fact that some recent immigrants, such as Hmong Americans, have major problems.

Issue #2: Male–Female Dynamics and Differences

Most Asian cultures are extremely patriarchal, and women are significantly more subjugated in these cultures than in the American culture.

Family Culture Clash

Culture clash often affects husband–wife dynamics, especially in families that have immigrated since the 1960s. That's when women's pay and work status began improving and traditional male jobs in manufacturing plants began deteriorating. Problems often arise over these events:

- The wife finds a better-paying job than the husband, upsetting the male status in a hierarchical family structure.
- The wife must learn to be assertive, decisive, and efficient on the job, which conflicts with her role as a shy, patient, and resilient wife and mother.
- Children at school learn they must speak up, express opinions, and ask why in order to succeed, but are expected to keep quiet and do as they're told at home.

- Girls must also speak up at school, but at home they're supposed to be even more reserved and compliant than boys.

Stereotypes of Asian Women Workers

Women who don't have the educational credentials to land better-paying jobs often take manufacturing assembly-line jobs. They typically encounter myths, stereotypes, and other barriers to promotion, such as:

- Immigrant women are more likely to be content with such jobs. (In fact, most want to advance.)
- They're unqualified for better-paying jobs. (In fact, they're trainable.)
- They have a man who earns more than they do. (In fact, about 80 percent are the main income earners in their families.)
- Their patience and superior coordination better suits them to assembly line production involving tiny, intricate circuitry.
- Their small size makes it easier for them to sit quietly for long periods, doing small detail work.
- Their strong task orientation, high achievement motivation, and hard work qualify them as reliable production workers.
- They're childlike, obedient, and submissive, good qualities for assembly-line work but not for managerial roles.
- Most U.S. citizens would not be content for long with such boring, low-paying jobs, but Asian American women are.

Reality: Beneath the Passive Surface, Active Achievement

Most Asian American women on assembly lines are actually active, goal-oriented doers according to studies by Elaine Chow and Karen Hossfeld. They're disadvantaged in at least three aspects of the social structure—that is, being an ethnic minority, a woman, and within a lower socioeconomic class.

The problems they experience with their supervisors (nearly all Euro-American) stem primarily from the following:

- supervisors' perception of their inabilities
- disrespect for Asian women
- unreasonable work assignments
- unfair performance evaluation
- accusation of job errors
- inappropriate decisions regarding promotion
- intolerance of language accents
- apparent discrimination

How do Asian American women handle the problems resulting from these stereotypes? Here are some facts from the survey:

- About half have no difficulty challenging their supervisor about problems.
- Well over half have difficulty expressing anger and demanding their fair share from supervisors.
- Those of higher occupational status have more to lose and more difficulty demanding their fair share.
- Almost all attempt to establish congenial working relationships with people at all levels of the organization.
- Two-thirds have little difficulty in protesting unfair treatment by their Euro-American *coworkers* (as distinguished from their supervisors).
- Most had more difficulty protesting to Euro-American women than to the men, since they tend to consider the women as natural allies and hesitate to break that feeling of camaraderie.
- Only 6 percent said they choose to say nothing offensive to coworkers or to ignore incidents they think are unfair.

Typical styles for dealing with workplace situations are indirectness, congeniality, assertion, and confrontation. The style a woman uses depends primarily on how extreme or important the work problem is to her.

Adapting or being indirect seems to fit the passive stereotype. Silence is sometimes a temporary reaction in the process of coping. It may be part of a defensive stand in which they protect themselves from the hurt by pushing their tolerance to the limit. Variations of the approach include avoiding problem situations as much as possible, doing little about them, or hoping a problem will go away. They might write to a supervisor, talk to a supervisor about an offensive coworker, or make an impersonal telephone call to a coworker, all in the hope of finding a solution to the problem. Most don't carry this style to the extreme of quitting, which they would see as defeatist. A frequent pattern is to begin by adapting and later to shift to a more active strategy.

Being congenial is a style used sometimes to show a willingness to cooperate in solving workplace problems. It involves personal consideration, friendliness, and candidness to achieve some kind of equity with coworkers. Women using this style may emphasize commonalties, such as being women or being Asian Americans, in order to establish rapport, dispel issues of inequity, and neutralize feelings of injustice. They are more apt to use this style with Euro-American women than with men.

Asserting themselves is a direct style for claiming certain work rights and independence. It includes negotiating their time, effort, intellect, commitment, and personal involvement with other workers. About half the women use this style, and they're more likely to do so when they deal with

Euro-American male workers than with females. It includes expressing their viewpoints and judgment of a situation, demanding explanations from offensive workers, and focusing their efforts on problem solving. This approach is active, goal-oriented, and a way of taking charge of their own lives. Women using this approach expect to negotiate a solution to a problem. For example, they may want some agreement about work hours that don't interfere with their family obligations.

Confronting the person involved in the situation is a somewhat aggressive style of fighting prejudice and discrimination at work. The women directly protest against those coworkers they view as insensitive and threatening to their survival. They fight back in the face of apparently overwhelming odds in order to protect their work rights and to show they won't compromise themselves to what they see as others' unreasonable demands. Some even go as far as quitting their job rather than be pushed around, the ultimate form of resistance. They see it as affirming self-respect and human dignity, even above job security.

Issue #3: Educational Issues

Educational issues include getting into top universities and establishing Asian American studies programs.

Getting into Top Universities

Asian American high school graduates tend to have unusually high academic achievement and a disproportionate number qualify for admittance to top universities. Some university officials have acknowledged that their affirmative action policies and practices may have had an unintentional adverse impact on these Asian Americans. During the 1980s, the admission *rate* of Asian American applicants to universities was lower than that for any other ethnic group.

Asian Americans organized to ensure that their educational rights are not violated, because access to quality higher education, perhaps more than any other issue, is something they feel very strongly about. Many Asians immigrate to the United States precisely to allow their children to receive such an education. While most see the value and necessity for affirmative action, in order to level the playing field for all ethnic groups, the community is somewhat divided on affirmative action in university admissions.

Establishing Asian American Studies Programs

Many Asian American university students are asking for a more "relevant" education, meaning a multiethnic curriculum that includes the history of discrimination in the United States and an accurate portrayal of the contributions and struggles of people of color. This interest reflects a new cultural awakening among Asian American students, along with a rising political consciousness. Instead of choosing between their Asian heritage and the American culture, some young Asian Americans are forging a new culture of their own, one that goes beyond a simple blending of East and West. This culture directly reflects the historical experience and current life circumstances of Asians in America. In university courses about Asian Americans, they may get a glimpse of this emerging culture and even be encouraged to help create it.

SELF-TEST #2

Indicate the best answers to the following 10 multiple-choice questions.

1. Putting group concerns before individual desires is based primarily on:
    A. admitting loss of control
    B. being modest
    C. seeing the group as the most important part of society
    D. communicating directly

2. Promoting group harmony is achieved primarily by:
    A. disciplining one's expressions of emotion
    B. avoiding open conflicts with people
    C. showing modesty and self-effacement
    D. all of the above

3. Asians express modesty primarily by:
    A. valuing group recognition
    B. responding to compliments by belittling one's own abilities
    C. trying to be fair
    D. accepting status differences

4. To show anger in Asian cultures is seen as:
    A. self-effacing
    B. saving face
    C. a loss of face for the person expressing anger
    D. conforming to group standards

5. "Good" businesspersons are likely to:
    A. place a high value on allowing others to save face
    B. preserve harmony
    C. care more about group harmony than higher sales and profits
    D. all of the above

6. To most Asian Americans, silence while another is speaking, and for a few moments after another has spoken, probably means the listener:

A. is uncomfortable with what was said

B. doesn't understand what was said

C. is contemplating what was said

D. is shocked by what was said

7. The model minority stereotype refers to the fact that Asian Americans:

A. are willing to work for less than most Euro-Americans

B. as a group have greater financial success and fewer social problems than some other minority groups

C. have a lower cost of living than most groups

D. get maximum return on their education

8. A key "model minority advantage" that Asian Americans have enjoyed is the image of:

A. visibility as foreigners

B. technical coolie

C. political activism

D. hard work and productivity

9. Asian American small businesses have been successful primarily because:

A. their small scale and specialization in limited areas have meant they were nonthreatening to the Euro-American business community

B. of short-range goals

C. of an ability to get large infusions of cash

D. of hiring Euro-Americans in Euro-American neighborhoods

10. Many Asian Americans are concerned about getting into top universities because of:

A. their English language deficiencies

B. many of them have straight-A high school records, making the Asian American group of qualified candidates overly large for affirmative action purposes

C. prejudice against Asian Americans

D. all of the above

SELF-TEST #2 FEEDBACK

Each correct answer is worth 10 points. If you score less than 70 points, you should review the materials and re-take the Self-Test.

1. Putting group concerns before individual desires is based primarily on:

   A. No, it's not based on admitting loss of control

   B. No, it's not based on being modest

   C. Yes, seeing the group as the most important part of society

   D. No, it's not based on communicating directly

2. Promoting group harmony is achieved primarily by:

   A. No, although an important factor is disciplining one's expressions of emotion

   B. No, although an important factor is avoiding open conflicts with people

   C. No, although an important factor is showing modesty and self-effacement

   D. Yes, all of the above

3. Asians express modesty primarily by:

   A. No, not by valuing group recognition

   B. Yes, by responding to compliments by belittling one's own abilities

   C. No, not by trying to be fair

   D. No, although a related factor could be accepting status differences

4. To show anger in Asian cultures is seen as:

   A. No, showing anger is not seen as self-effacing

   B. No, showing anger is not seen as a way of saving face

   C. Yes, a loss of face for the person expressing anger

   D. No, showing anger does not conform to group standards

5. "Good" businesspersons are likely to:

   A. No, although they do place a high value on allowing others to save face

   B. No, although they do preserve harmony

   C. No, although they do care more about group harmony than higher sales and profits

   D. Yes, all of the above

6. To most Asian Americans, silence while another is speaking, and for a few moments after another has spoken, probably means the listener:

   A. No, it doesn't mean the listener is uncomfortable with what was said

   B. No, it doesn't mean the listener doesn't understand what was said

   C. Yes, it probably means the listener is contemplating what was said

   D. No, it doesn't mean the listener is shocked by what was said

7. The model minority stereotype refers to the fact that Asian Americans:

   A. No, although most are willing to work for less than most Euro-Americans

   B. Yes, the best answer is as a group they have greater financial success and fewer social problems than some other minority groups

   C. No, they don't have a lower cost of living than most groups because they tend to live in high-cost-of-living areas, but they do have more persons per household, which reduces cost of living

   D. No, in fact they don't get maximum return on their education

8. A key "model minority advantage" that Asian Americans have enjoyed is the image of:

   A. No, visibility as foreigners is not an advantage

   B. No, technical coolie is a stereotype, not an advantage

   C. No, they are not known for political activism

   D. Yes, hard work and productivity

9. Asian American small businesses have been successful primarily because:

   A. Yes, their small scale and specialization in limited areas have meant they were nonthreatening to the Euro-American business community

   B. No, they don't focus on short-range goals

   C. No, they aren't known for an ability to get large infusions of cash

   D. No, in fact they tend to hire Asian Americans in Asian American neighborhoods

10. Many Asian Americans are concerned about getting into top universities because of:

   A. No, the concern is not English language deficiencies

   B. Yes, too many qualified Asian American candidates for affirmative action purposes

   C. No, the concern is not prejudice against Asian Americans

   D. No, not all of the above

HOW CAN THE ORGANIZATION MEET THE NEEDS OF ASIAN AMERICANS?

As a leader you have many opportunities and challenges in working effectively with Asian Americans, in supporting their ability to contribute to work teams, and in building mutual respect and trust. Three major ways you can help meet their needs are:

1. Provide support in overcoming barriers.
2. Avoid typical assumptions and stereotypes.
3. Help people get to know Asian American coworkers.

Need #1: Provide Support in Overcoming Barriers

Some typical barriers to job success faced by Asian Americans include:

- being typecast as technologists (technical coolies) and therefore not being considered for higher-level positions
- being discriminated against because Euro-Americans are uncomfortable with their cultural style, which is considered too "foreign and strange"
- communicating and verbalizing problems, especially crucial with first-generation immigrants
- being misunderstood because of their values and behaviors, such as humbleness and passiveness; such behavior is not necessarily an indicator that they are not qualified for leadership roles

Need #2: Avoid Typical Assumptions and Stereotypes

You've learned about the most typical myths, stereotypes, and assumptions that can hamper good working relationships. Here are a few reminders.

Remember, They're Americans, Not Foreigners

Non-Asian Americans have a tendency to look upon Asian Americans as foreigners because of their Asian appearance. Most Asian-appearing workers you'll encounter will be Asian Americans. They're Americanized in varying degrees and possess varying language skill levels. Keep in mind that they aren't foreigners.

Determine Generational Status

There tend to be significant differences between first-generation immigrants and second-, third-, and fourth-generation Americans. By open, direct, but tactful conversations, you can share information about your background and learn about each associate's background. Be sure that your tone or manner is not in any way condescending or patronizing.

Getting information can help you to understand the associates' values, viewpoints, and actions. Keep in mind that information you've absorbed about such groups as third-generation Japanese Americans or recently arrived Hmong Americans can only provide general guidelines. Keep an open mind, get to know each individual, and avoid the tendency to use such information to form rigid stereotypes about these people.

Ascertain Citizenship Status

For workers who are not American citizens or permanent residents, find out about their status, which can help you better understand their background. For example, some initially come as foreign students, then get work visas. Their values and actions therefore tend to stem from Asian values and practices, and they are less Americanized.

Companies must sign papers for Asians to keep their work visas, which frequently makes such workers feel dependent on the company. Such workers may be more submissive, obedient, and compliant, a situation some companies prefer and capitalize upon. Take the lead in respecting such workers.

Don't Make Assumptions about Language Ability

Some leaders assume Asian Americans are fluent in an Asian language and have problems with English. When Euro-Americans make such comments as "You speak very good English" or "Where did you learn to speak English so well?" Asian Americans who were born and raised in the United States may be understandably taken aback. It's one more reminder that even though they consider themselves as American as anyone, others tend to see them as foreigners.

Asian Americans are often embarrassed or frustrated when others expect them to be bilingual. For example, a worker who is third-generation Chinese may speak little or no Chinese. Let multiple language skills emerge and be used as an asset after you establish the facts.

Most important, when discussing an Asian American employee's skills, qualifications, and career goals, you can help to identify any communication skills or problems that he or she has and try to get remedial training.

Don't Assume They're Cultural Ambassadors

Don't try to make an Asian American worker your token Asian expert. Asian Americans appreciate people who don't assume they're experts in their ancestors' culture, just as they appreciate those who don't assume they're bilingual. For example, Japanese Americans who were born and raised in the United States are not necessarily experts in Japanese cuisine, culture, or politics. They do not necessarily agree with economic or political developments in Japan. Again, it's better to ask about special bicultural expertise than to make assumptions.

Avoid Such Terms as "Oriental"

For many Asian Americans the term Oriental, meaning Easterner, conjures up old Hollywood stereotypes (e.g., Charlie Chan and Tokyo Rose) depicting mysterious, unknowable, exotic Asians. It brings up unpleasant memories for many. Also, some consider it Eurocentric, since it describes Asia as east of Europe. A case could be made that it's west of the Americas, and that the Americas are the East to Asians.

People with Spanish Surnames May Be Filipinos

Many types of people may have Spanish-sounding names. For example, many Filipinos took Spanish surnames during the era of Spanish colonialism. They are not Latinos, although their values and practices probably reflect a Spanish influence.

Constantly Question Your Assumptions about Behaviors

Always question your assumptions about why an Asian American acts a certain way. For example, in the American business culture, "silence is consent," and if someone doesn't speak up about a decision being made during a meeting, we assume he or she has no objections. But in Asian cultures, "silence is golden" and "maintaining harmony is virtuous." Check your assumptions and then ask. Above all, look beyond surface behaviors and get to know Asian American team members personally in order to help them develop their talents and make appropriate career plans.

Need #3: Help People Get to Know Asian American Coworkers

You can take a leadership role and influence others in the workplace by providing information about Asian American myths and realities, their cultural patterns and strengths, and guidelines for building productive relationships with them. Occasionally, review the Asian American values and practices you have just learned. Do further research on your own.

You can help others get to know Asian American associates by including them on team projects. This can provide for in-depth contact with other employees and increased comfort levels.

HOW CAN ASIAN AMERICANS CONTRIBUTE TO THE ORGANIZATION?

You can learn to recognize Asian Americans' potential contributions and respond by:

- building on typical Asian American traits
- recognizing Asian American values as strengths
- applying some leadership strategies
- helping Asian Americans make marketplace connections

Opportunity #1: Build on Typical Asian American Traits

Some Asian American characteristics that are important in business include:

- They're interested in long-range benefits.
- Once they decide upon who and what is the best choice, they are steadfast.
- They stick to their word.
- They're punctual.

    What can you do to build on these traits?

- You can identify situations in which these traits are an especially good fit.
- You can point out the good fit to Asian American associates and to others.
- You can help them verbalize to team members the value of developing these practices.

Opportunity #2: Recognize Asian American Values as Strengths

Nearly all values and behavior patterns represent a two-sided coin in the workplace. One side is the advantages these can bring to the career achievement and organizational contribution of the employee. The other side is the barriers they could erect. You can learn to recognize the cultural and individual values and behaviors of team members. You can figure out ways to enhance them and bring them into the work situation in constructive ways. Here are some ideas.

Work with the Value of Strong Obligation to Family

In most American corporate cultures, workaholics are rewarded and people who do not consistently put the company first are viewed as lacking commitment. While most Asian Americans place high value on hard work and perseverance, when family members need them, family obligations must come first.

- You can understand and respect Asian American priorities regarding family and work. By doing so, you're likely to win the respect and loyalty of these employees.

Respect Their Values Regarding Hard Work and Cooperation

Some managers take advantage of the Asian American tendency to value hard work and cooperation by piling on the work. Asian Americans are patient, but not stupid. Eventually, such exploitation will backfire.

Most Asian Americans emphasize trust and mutual connections, a major aspect of building cooperative business relationships.

- You can help them put their value for trust and mutual connections to good use for the team, the organization, and for their own careers.

Understand Their Values of Modesty and Humility

By American corporate culture standards, many Asian Americans may appear to be too passive and too lacking in self-confidence and ambition to be given tough assignments that call for traditional leadership skills. In Asia, such qualities are seen as positive, and the American standards are likely to be seen as egocentric and arrogant, as pushing or imposing oneself on others. First- and second-generation Asian Americans tend to value modesty and humility more highly than later generations.

Properly used, such values can be quite appropriate for facilitative team leaders. Further, such values do not mean that the worker lacks self-confidence, ambition, or assertiveness, qualities that vary among Asian Americans, just as they do among Euro-Americans. Asian Americans merely tend to express them in a more low-key, indirect manner. Similarly, we usually reward employees who tactfully question the status quo, speak up, take initiative, or find a better way of doing things. Asian Americans do not necessarily behave in this manner.

- You can help find ways to reward and motivate Asian American employees who are not as verbal or assertive as Euro-American employees.
- You can help show them when and how to be assertive.

Understand the Values of Indirectness and Respect

Instead of assuming that that they are devious, uncommunicative, or dishonest, get to know them as individuals so you can reach a deeper understanding of the values of indirectness and respect in their communication patterns. Another aspect of respect involves the use of space and touching. Asian cultures like more space between persons when communicating and less touching than is typical in the United States.

- Upon meeting, a slight bow or brief handshake is appropriate.
- Follow their lead about how far apart to stand or sit from each other.

Understand Their Expression of Emotion

You have learned that Asian Americans are less likely to express emotions than are people from other cultures. To maintain harmony, they avoid openly expressing such emotions as anger, resentment, and jealousy. In addition, they may hide their emotions when they sense they're in a "hostile foreign environment" that causes them to feel vulnerable, intimidated, or threatened. People from all cultures are likely to show less emotion, as a protective device, when they feel like a foreigner or minority.

- You can see them first as Americans and as a part of the group you're working with.
- You can help them explore and express feelings that need to come out and be dealt with in order to build honest, trusting work relationships.

Opportunity #3: Apply Leadership Strategies

Here are some strategies that may be especially appropriate for Asian American workers.

Explain Deviations from Traditional Boss–Worker Practices

Asian cultures tend to be more hierarchical and status-oriented than current American corporate cultures. Most corporations have moved beyond the old authoritarian boss–obedient employee model that still fits the pattern of many Asian cultures.

If you're a supervisor, have a conversation with Asian American employees in which you share your ideas of the leader–worker relationship. Once you understand their expectations, you can help them understand your own deviations from that expectation.

- If they expect the boss to make all decisions, you can explain why workers in this company participate in decision making.
- If they would be personally humiliated if you pitched in to help complete a task, you can explain how this is viewed in the corporate culture and what it means.

Use the Team Approach

One way to bridge the gap between Euro-American emphasis on individual initiative and Asian American emphasis on obedience to authority is to structure tasks to be performed by teams. Gradually introduce independent decision making by doing it as a group. Working in teams can also help Asian Americans and coworkers get to know each other at deeper levels, which breaks down walls of prejudice. It can also take advantage of Asian Americans' group-oriented values and skills.

- You can suggest opportunities for working together in teams.
- You can encourage Asian Americans to contribute their group-oriented values and traits to help the team become more close-knit and productive.

Help Bring Problems to the Surface

Harmony and compliance are two Asian American values that have upsides and downsides. A downside can be an unwillingness to confront relationship problems. Most Asian Americans are taught that in troublesome situations, they should act as though nothing has happened. If they acknowledge a relationship problem, then they must take action and the action may be extremely serious. As a result, they tend to be long-suffering and patient, but resentment may build. In team situations, it's usually important to bring problems and troublesome feelings to the surface and deal with them—if they're important enough to an individual to eventually create communication and relationship barriers.

- You can work with Asian Americans in developing such team-related skills.

Provide Assertiveness Training

You have learned that even minimally educated Asian American women can be assertive on the job when they believe it's necessary or desirable. But because Asian cultures focus on humbleness and subordinating personal desires for group interests, Asian American employees often need some training about the role of assertiveness in the American workplace. For more than 20 years, Euro-American women have benefited from such training. Asian American employees also respond well to assertiveness training and can reap similar benefits.

- Help provide assertiveness training by your own examples and explanations.
- Encourage your organization to provide formal training sessions.
- Encourage Asian American associates to attend such training. If the situation is touchy, you may want to go yourself and ask them to come with you.

Build Trust

Our history of prejudice and discrimination may have created some trust barriers in inter-cultural relationships. When Asian Americans perceive that a Euro-American is trying to "buddy up" to them, they may respond internally with some distrust and suspicion. If you're a Euro-American, you must find ways to overcome this barrier.

- Begin by raising your awareness of the ways in which messages can be misunderstood or misinterpreted and give special attention to clear communication.
- Then, be very consistent in your messages and positions, and always follow through on agreements. Trust is built through the experience of another person as honest, fair, consistent, and reliable. Letting someone down, even once, can shatter newly built trust.

Express Sincere Personal Concern

Cooperative relationships are normally personal ones. Get to know Asian American workers as people in order to understand their goals and needs, which are usually tied to family status and needs. In this way, you show that you understand the value of cooperation and want to establish a cooperative relationship.

- Establish personal relationships with Asian American associates.
- Find out what's most important to them and make their priorities a major part of your discussions and of the relationship.

Communicate Clearly and Check for Understanding

Cultural differences often cause misperceptions and misunderstandings. Therefore, you must find ways to send clear, unmixed messages that involve requests, assignments, expectations, or explanations. Then, you must check for understanding in ways that uncover misperceptions.

- If in doubt, be very specific and factual in making requests and giving instructions. Don't say, "You might want to think about doing xyz." Ask, "Can you do xyz before you leave today? How does that fit your schedule?"
- Check for understanding. Don't ask questions that can be answered yes or no; for example, "Is that clear?" Ask questions that clearly establish whether the person understands, such as "How do you plan to go about doing that?"

Choose Motivators and Rewards According to Employees' Values

Rewards, such as individual recognition, may not be as effective for motivating Asian American employees as they are with Euro-Americans. The same is true for perks and benefits.

- You can talk with Asian Americans about their values, goals, and expectations.
- Together, you can develop rewards that they value and that serve as effective motivators for them.

Opportunity #4: Help Asian Americans Make Marketplace Connections

Many companies are realizing the potential of the growing Asian American market, and nearly all U.S. companies are doing more and more business with Asian countries in the global marketplace. Asian American employees tend to have a special touch with such clients and also are an invaluable resource in developing strategies and action plans for doing business in such markets.

Help Them Connect with the Asian American Marketplace

Asian Americans have greater consuming power than their share of the total population. Companies such as Coca-Cola and AT&T have established Asian American marketing departments and have tried to reach Asian American communities with donations and advertisements. Companies are targeting the rapidly increasing Asian American clientele. They are putting more Asian American models in their television commercials and advertisements. Some are looking to Asian American culture—art, music, dance, clothing designs, movies, and food—for inspiration and to make connections with the Asian American markets.

- You may be able to help your organization recognize and use Asian American employees as a valuable resource and connection in such efforts.

Help Them Connect with Asian Countries

Virtually all economists expect Asian countries to play a more important role as American economic partners in the twenty-first century. Some locations that are emerging as economic tigers are Singapore, Taiwan, Hong Kong, and South Korea. New trade relations with China are opening up a market of over a billion people.

- You may be able to help your organization see that Asian American employees can provide insights into these global markets, insights that can serve as valuable links.

Final Self-Test

Match each of the statements with the Asian American group it best describes.

a. Chinese American   d. Japanese Americans

b. Filipino American   e. Korean Americans

c. Southeast Asian hill tribes   f. Asian Indian Americans

_____ 1. have the highest educational levels of any U.S. group

_____ 2. the largest Asian American group

_____ 3. have a strong Spanish influence in their culture

_____ 4. most are war refugees

_____ 5. helped build the railroad that opened the West

_____ 6. have a personalistic worldview and fatalistic view of the future

_____ 7. most speak little or no English and have little formal education

_____ 8. were imprisoned in U.S. "concentration camps"

_____ 9. consider their mood or inner feeling to be of key importance

_____ 10. are the most successful of any Asian American group by most measures

Final Self-Test Feedback

Correct responses to the 10 matching questions are worth 10 points each. If you score less than 70 points, you should review the materials and re-take the Final Self-Test.

a. Chinese American   d. Japanese Americans

b. Filipino American   e. Korean Americans

c. Southeast Asian hill tribes   f. Asian Indian Americans

___f___ 1. have the highest educational levels of any U.S. group

___a___ 2. the largest Asian American group

___b___ 3. have a strong Spanish influence in their culture

___c___ 4. most are war refugees

___a___ 5. helped build the railroad that opened the West

___b___ 6. have a personalistic worldview and fatalistic view of the future

___c___ 7. most speak little or no English and have little formal education

___d___ 8. were imprisoned in U.S. "concentration camps"

___e___ 9. consider their mood or inner feeling to be of key importance

___d___ 10. are the most successful of any Asian American group by most measures

SKILL BUILDER 10.1   The Case of Office Whiz Connie

Connie has been working for six years for Crystal Fizz, a manufacturer of drink mixes. She is one of six employees in the plant office, the youngest at age 27, and the only Asian American. Connie has learned how to do most all of the major functions in the office and likes her job. However, she's become disillusioned with the work environment. If it weren't for the good pay and benefits, she'd be gone. In fact, she's thinking about looking for a job elsewhere.

A year ago, **Bob**, the owner and manager, hired **Jim,** who performs duties similar to the ones Connie does. Soon, Jim was making comments that disturbed Connie, such as "I can't understand what you're saying half the time" and "Why don't you do things the American way—whatever the American way is?" Connie's response has been to ignore and avoid Jim as much as possible. However, Bob soon was consulting Jim about various company decisions. Bob sometimes takes Jim with him to important business meetings. Connie is never included in this way, and she recently discovered that Jim makes about 10 percent more than she.

Company employees get four weeks of vacation. Before Jim came, Connie never took all four weeks at one time because of office demands. It was typical for her to come into the office even when she could have taken some time off simply because there was much important work to be done. Now she finds she doesn't care about that anymore. She came back from a four-week vacation last month, and she plans to take all of the time off she has coming to her. She feels that she is being treated unfairly and has no real chance of advancement.

1. The major problem is:
  A. unequal opportunity
  B. Connie's lack of assertiveness
  C. hostile working environment
  D. all of the above

Feedback

  A. No, unequal opportunity is a problem, but that's not all.
  B. No, lack of assertiveness is a problem, but that's not all.
  C. No, hostile working environment is a problem, but that's not all.
  D. Yes, this is the best option. The main problem is Bob's differential treatment of Connie and Jim, stemming from what appears to be unconscious bias and subtle discrimination. He is giving Jim more opportunity for advancement by including him in important meetings and decisions. Bob is also paying Jim more for work that

is similar to Connie's, even though Connie, with her longer time in service, should be getting more than Jim. Jim's bias is not so subtle, and he is creating a hostile environment for Connie. Bob, as the employer, is ultimately responsible for the work environment.

2. Connie should:

A. be patient

B. determine exactly what she wants, then be assertive in confronting the problems

C. resign

D. show them both how their actions are illegal

Feedback

A. No, she's been patient long enough. It's getting her nowhere.

B. Yes. With **Jim**, she should be more assertive and tell him when his comments are hurtful and demeaning. With **Bob**, she should ask for a meeting. Some purposes and potential outcomes of this meeting could be to:

- make Bob aware of Jim's behavior toward her
- point out the ways in which she interprets Bob's behavior as preferential toward Jim
- explain to Bob that the hostile environment and discriminatory treatment have discouraged and de-motivated her
- remind Bob of her dedication, high performance, and loyalty over the years
- share with Bob her career goals, long range and short range
- reach an agreement with Bob about her future with the company
- get a raise that is commensurate with her service and performance

C. No, don't resign before trying to solve the problem.

D. No, focusing only on legality is not enough. A better strategy is first to be positive and point out the advantages to Bob and the company if he shifts to fair and equal treatment toward her.

3. In response to the meeting with Connie, Bob should:

A. calm Connie and pay more attention to her in the future

B. speak with Jim about his poor attitude and actions toward Connie

C. be open to hearing Connie's view of the situation

D. tell Connie she may be happier with another firm

Feedback

A. No, calming Connie and paying more attention is good, but more is needed.

B. No, speaking with Jim is good, but more is needed. For example, Bob needs to change his own beliefs and attitudes and become a role model of appropriate behavior toward Asian American women.

C. Yes, Bob first needs to listen to Connie. Then, if necessary for convincing himself, he can review her performance and her value to the company. He must realize that if he wants to retain her services, he must change his beliefs, attitudes, and actions toward her and other Asian American women. He is also responsible for setting an inclusive, supportive tone in the workplace, acting as a role model and seeing that Jim shows respect for Connie.

D. No, telling Connie to accept things as they are or find another job would cause Bob to lose a very valuable employee.

SKILL BUILDER 10.2   The Case of Doug Fong, Manager

Doug Fong is a restaurant manager for Jollytime, a chain of over 250 fast-food restaurants. Each restaurant has a day manager and a night manager. One of its strategies for quality control is to send "mystery shoppers" to every restaurant at least twice a month. These undercover employees check on the quality of the food, the cleanliness of the restaurant, and the quickness of the service. Restaurants are categorized as low-level, medium-level, or high-level based on the following criteria: gross sales, annual profit, percentage of increase in sales and in annual profit, and scores assigned by mystery shoppers.

Doug Fong is a first-generation Asian American who has been with Jollytime for 10 years and is respected by the other managers. He's a hard worker, often working 12-hour days. Seven years ago, he was promoted to manager of a low-level restaurant in a neighborhood that is primarily Euro-American, but also somewhat multicultural. After two years, he was transferred to a medium-level restaurant in Huntville, an African American neighborhood. Restaurant profits increased the next two years, and regional managers were pleased with Doug's ability to handle the challenging Huntville location. They transferred him to Sunset in a multicultural but heavily Euro-American area. Doug told a colleague, "I'm sad to leave Huntville because I've built a trusting relationship with my employees and my customers. There were a few troublemakers around, but I really didn't have any problems."

Doug's been at Sunset for three years. The restaurant was ranked third, then sixth, and then second on the top-50 list of all Jollytime restaurants.

Profits increased each year, and mystery shopper ratings have been out-standing. Doug has done well in managing a diverse group of employees. They speak well of him. For example, Kevin, a Euro-American food server, says, "Doug is a great manager; he treats everyone fairly." And Ruben, a Latino American cook says, "I've worked with Doug for nearly three years and he knows how to motivate people."

Doug wants to move up to district manager. He has only a high school diploma, but he's a rapid, eager learner. For example, he's learned to do all the accounting for his restaurant, and the auditors have always approved his work. A district manager is responsible for 10 to 12 restaurants, overseeing their cur-rent operations and improvement plans. The job requires good communica-tion skills and a knowledge of accounting principles, including budgeting.

Doug has never asked for a promotion. He has operated on the belief that his hard work and excellence speak for themselves and that he'll be offered a promotion when the time is right. In the past two years, two dis-trict manager positions opened up, and the managers who were leaving picked their successors. All of the district managers that Doug has met are Euro-American men with college degrees.

Jim Davis was one of the outgoing district managers. His job had been to oversee restaurants in Oakland, which is predominantly African American. Doug decided to overcome his reticence and speak to Jim about the possibil-ity of taking his place. Jim told Doug, "You're an extremely well-qualified man-ager—no doubt about that. But maybe the Oakland area is not the best place for you." Jim obviously doubted that Doug was assertive enough to handle the employees there. He said, "Let's wait for an opening in an area that's more multicultural. That would be a better fit." A few weeks later **Jordan Jones**, a Euro-American, was named new district manager for the Oakland area.

Now, a year later, the buzz is that Jones has failed miserably in oversee-ing the Oakland restaurant managers and he'll be replaced soon. **Jack Barnes**, the division manager will name the replacement.

1. The key issue in this case is:
   A. Doug lacks assertiveness in campaigning for a promotion
   B. management holds stereotypes about Asian American assertiveness
   C. Doug is not really qualified for the promotion
   D. both a and b

Feedback

   A. No, though Doug lacks assertiveness, that's not the entire key issue.
   B. No, though stereotypes are a problem, they are not the entire key issue.
   C. No, Doug seems to be qualified.

D. Yes, the key issue is two-fold—lack of assertiveness and managerial stereotypes. Management has overlooked the fact that Doug has a successful track record in dealing with African American clients and employees. While Doug may lack assertiveness in some areas, it has not affected his ability to manage, even in potentially difficult African American situations. However, Doug's lack of assertiveness in dealing with management is probably reinforcing the stereotype they hold.

2. If you were Doug Fong, what would you do?

A. be patient

B. reassess his viewpoint and behavior regarding the promotion

C. ask for a meeting with Jack

D. both b and c

Feedback

A. No, he's been patient for too long.

B. No, though reassessing is good, it's not enough.

C. No, though asking for a meeting is good, it's not enough.

D. Yes, Doug needs to reassess and adopt some new self-empowering beliefs and attitudes about how to wage a promotion campaign. He should prepare and practice a presentation that stresses his track record and highlights specific achievements and details to back up his claims. He should then request a meeting with Jack.

3. What should Jack Barnes do?

A. tell Doug he'll think about it

B. give Doug the promotion

C. tell Doug he's not qualified yet

D. transfer Doug to another restaurant

Feedback

A. No, although Jack may want to step back and reassess his beliefs and attitudes about Doug and other Asian American employees, as well as review the record, he must make a decision soon.

B. Yes, he should give Doug the promotion. The facts point to the probability that Doug is highly qualified and motivated and that he will do a good job.

C. No, don't put him off. Doug has been very patient. If he is bypassed again, he may either become de-motivated or decide to leave.

D. No, the facts do not indicate that transferring Doug is desirable or necessary.

THE BOTTOM LINE

Think of this as just the beginning of your exploration into what it's like to be an Asian American. Now that you have the basics, let this be a framework for adding new information—just by noticing and questioning what's presented by the media, by asking Asian Americans about themselves, by caring and really listening.

Keep learning about the stereotypes, myths, prejudice, and discrimination Asian Americans deal with constantly. Ask what it's like to live in their community—what are the values, customs, and issues most important to them. You'll become more and more at ease with Asian American associates, and they'll become more comfortable with you. Answers to your questions will begin to fall into place and you'll be as capable of building relationships with Asian Americans as you are with people from your own ethnic group.

Chapter Review

1. Typical myths and stereotypes about Asian Americans are the following:
   - too passive and polite to be good managers
   - unemotional and inscrutable
   - retain their foreign ways so they don't fit in
   - have made it in America because they work hard and are thrifty
   - can't master English and have communication problems
   - excel in technical occupations, but aren't creative and don't have leadership potential
   - know about all things Asian

2. Today's stereotyping of Asian Americans is rooted in discrimination that started with the Chinese who began immigating during the 1850s. The overt prejudice against them resulted in the 1882 Chinese Exclusion Act. Other laws were passed to segregate Asian Americans. During WWII, Japanese Americans were placed in concentration camps to prohibit spy activity.

3. Asian Americans are from China, the Phillipines, Southeast Asia, Japan, India, and Korea—just to name a few. Over half of all Asian Americans live in the West. They tend to live longer than Euro-Americans, they have lower crime and delinquency rates than the rest of the population, and more have high school diplomas and college degrees than the rest of the population.

4. Core values common to Asian Americans are the following:
   - put group concerns before individual values
   - promote group harmony
   - accept status differences
   - revere education
   - communicate vaguely, indirectly, and silently

5. Key issues important to most Asian Americans are the model minority stereotype, male–female dynamics and differences, and educational issues.

6. Organizations can meet the needs of Asian Americans by providing support in overcoming barriers, avoiding typical assumptions and stereotypes, and getting to know Asian American coworkers.

7. Asian Americans can contribute to the organization by building on typical Asian American traits, recognizing Asian American values and strengths, applying leadership strategies, and making marketplace connections.

Index